Horsman, Reginald.
Josiah Nott of
Mobile

NOV 1 8 '92	DATE DUE		

Southern Biography Series
William J. Cooper, Jr., Editor

JOSIAH NOTT OF MOBILE

JOSIAH NOTT

OF MOBILE

Southerner, Physician, and Racial Theorist

Reginald Horsman

Louisiana State University Press
Baton Rouge and London

Copyright © 1987 by Louisiana State University Press
Manufactured in the United States of America

Designer: Diane B. Didier
Typeface: Galliard
Typesetter: G&S Typesetters, Inc.
Printer: Thomson-Shore, Inc.
Binder: John H. Dekker & Sons, Inc.
10 9 8 7 6 5 4 3 2 1

Library of Congress Cataloging in Publication Data

Horsman, Reginald.
  Josiah Nott of Mobile.

  (Southern biography series)
  Bibliography: p.
  Includes index.
  1. Nott, Josiah Clark, 1804–1873.   2. Southern
States—Biography.   3. Physicians—United States—
Biography.   4. Racism—United States—History—
19th Century.   5. Black race.   I. Title.   II. Series.
CT275.N77H67   1987   572'.092'4 [B]   86-27784
ISBN 0-8071-1366-2

Published with the assistance of a grant from the
National Endowment for the Humanities

Frontispiece courtesy of Library of Congress

CONTENTS

ILLUSTRATIONS

ACKNOWLEDGMENTS

I wish to thank the College of Letters and Science of the University of Wisconsin-Milwaukee and the American Philosophical Society for helping to support the research that led to this book.

ABBREVIATIONS

ANSP   Academy of Natural Sciences of Philadelphia
CPP   College of Physicians of Philadelphia
HSP   Historical Society of Pennsylvania, Philadelphia
LC   Library of Congress
NA   National Archives
RG   Record Group
SCL   South Caroliniana Library, University of South Carolina, Columbia
SHC   Southern Historical Collection, University of North Carolina Library, Chapel Hill

JOSIAH NOTT OF MOBILE

PROLOGUE

In December, 1865, southern physician and racial theorist Josiah C. Nott wrote to his friend Ephraim Squier that he was thinking of moving from Yankee-occupied Mobile to New York. Because the population of New York was "without political principles, without morals, without religion, & without negroes," he wrote, it would suit him remarkably well.[1] Nott certainly had principles and morals, but he had devoted much of his life to an ardent defense of the proposition that blacks were inherently inferior to whites, to attacks on the scientific validity of the account of the origin of human beings given in Genesis, and to a passionate belief in the justice of the South maintaining its own way of life, including slavery. In his day, Nott was a major ethnologist with an international reputation. In the 1840s and 1850s he was a correspondent, visitor, and often friend of many of the most prominent northern and European scientists interested in racial questions. On receiving a false report of his death in 1868 the *Anthropological Review* of London published an appreciation stating that the man who had been "the most unflinching advocate of truths, however unpalatable themselves, which anthropology has had in the United States, is now departed from amongst us." To do proper duty to his subject, the writer stated, "to illustrate both the extent of the work he performed and the additions he made to anthropological science, would be practically to write a history of transatlantic anthropology, from the death of Dr. Samuel George Morton to a very recent period."[2]

1. Nott to Squier, December 5, 1865, Ephraim G. Squier Papers, LC. This is also the letter referred to and quoted elsewhere in the prologue.
2. *Anthropological Review* (London), VI (1868), lxxix–lxxxiii.

Although Nott was best known internationally as an ethnologist, in the South his reputation in this field only added to his distinction as a surgeon and general physician. He was one of the two or three best-known surgeons in the South, and he frequently wrote on surgery, yellow fever, and general medical matters. Throughout his life he maintained an extensive medical practice, and it was a matter of pride to him that the Mobile clergymen who hated his views on religion had no hesitation in making use of his medical services.

As an ethnologist Nott made powerful and ardent enemies, but his many friends loved him. His Mobile colleague Dr. William H. Anderson said that Nott "was the charm of every circle that he entered."[3] A physician who came to know him during his few years in New York after the Civil War later wrote a brief memorial "as a small tribute of admiration and affection to a man who in the writer's estimation fulfilled as completely as any one he ever met, the place which belongs to the highest type of physician, surgeon and man."[4] This was the man who in his December, 1865, letter to Squier wrote that "I have long since regarded the human race as a failure, & thought that they ought to be wiped out & made fossil remains of, for benefit of another breed of Naturalists." The death of seven of his eight children and the defeat of the South had left Nott bitter but not crushed. The United States government, he believed, was pursuing policies in the South after the Civil War that would make life unbearable for later generations. But let it pass, he told Squier—"Posterity has never done anything for me."

His letter to Squier rushed wildly on, laying out his disappointments, his hurts, his hatreds. Nott's medical college in Mobile, for which before the war he had raised large sums of money from the Alabama legislature and private donors, and for which he had toured Europe to spend more than $10,000 on medical specimens for its museum, had now been taken over by the Freedmen's Bureau for a Negro school. "I confess it does not increase my love for the Government," he wrote, "when I pass by every day or two & see two or three hundred negroes racing through it and tearing everything to pieces—The Chemical Laboratory is occupied by negro Cobblers."

Nott viewed himself more than anything else as an ardent pursuer of

3. William H. Anderson, *Biographical Sketch of Dr. J. C. Nott* (Mobile, 1877), 9.
4. William M. Polk, "Josiah C. Nott," *American Journal of Obstetrics*, LXVI (1913), 958.

scientific truth among the thickets raised by those he viewed as pigheaded and old-fashioned clergymen. Most of his writing on ethnology attempted to prove that there was not one but many races and that blacks were inherently inferior to whites. He believed passionately in the southern cause, brought up his sons to die for the Confederacy, and thought that the future of republican democracy was as much tied up in the southern ability to retain its institutions as scientific truth was tied up in proving that Genesis was not a true account of the origin of human races. Nott was an impassioned racist who firmly believed in the integrity of what he was doing, and he both influenced and was influenced by some of the best minds of his time throughout the United States and Europe. To the end of his life, when all he had defended had collapsed, he still believed that he had devoted himself to the passionate pursuit of scientific truth.

Chapter 1
FORMATIVE YEARS

Josiah C. Nott had strange roots for a militant southern physician who spent much of his life baiting the clergy, attacking the scientific validity of the Bible, and ardently defending racial inequality. On his father's side, he was linked to the heart of clerical New England, on his mother's to the Scotch-Irish South Carolina frontier. The first American Nott had settled in Wethersfield, Connecticut, by 1640. This John Nott established a long and prolific line of intelligent and opinionated Yankees and Yorkers. The first American Notts were solidly prosperous landowners, but John's grandson Abraham, who graduated from Yale College in 1720, was for more than thirty years the minister of the Second Congregational Church in Saybrook, Connecticut. Two of his sons produced distinguished but very different lines.

The main northern branch, that of Stephen Nott, bore ministers, teachers, and abolitionists. Stephen's son Eliphalet was president of Union College for more than sixty years and influenced college education throughout America. Another of Stephen's sons, Samuel, was a famous Connecticut minister and teacher; Samuel's son of the same name was in the first group of American missionaries who went to India in 1812, and later he joined the fight against slavery. Eliphalet's grandson Charles Cooper Nott was a good friend of Abraham Lincoln, became a colonel in the northern army in the Civil War, and for forty years served on the United States Court of Claims. He wrote extensively and was later described as "a man of great energy, definite convictions and strong interests." The characterization could fit most of the Notts.[1]

1. For the Notts see Nathaniel Goodwin, *Genealogical Notes* (1856; rpr. Baltimore, 1969), 165–68; Henry R. Stiles, *The History of Ancient Wethersfield, Connecticut* (New York, 1904),

The thin southern branch of the family was descended from Abraham's son Josiah. Most of Josiah's children followed a traditional pattern—his son Clark was town clerk of Saybrook—but his son Abraham eventually struck out on his own. He went to Yale to prepare for the ministry, but on his graduation in 1787, deciding that he had no call and worried about his health, he sailed to a different world in the distant state of Georgia. Sparsely populated Georgia was still mostly Indian country in the 1780s, and even Savannah was fortified against Indian attack. Abraham Nott became a tutor on a plantation on the Sapelo River. His employer was the father of a future Georgia governor—the rabidly outspoken George M. Troup. In the following year Abraham decided to prepare for a new career in a more developed state. He moved to Camden, South Carolina, and began to study law in the office of Yale graduate Daniel Brown. Abraham was admitted to the South Carolina bar in 1791 and in the following decades rose rapidly in the legal profession in his adopted state. The seeds of intelligence and energy that his sons inherited from their northern ancestors were to be nurtured in the very different soil of South Carolina.[2]

In the 1790s South Carolina was a state of sharp contrasts. Power was held predominantly by the low-country, coastal aristocracy, whose wealth stemmed from large-scale plantation slavery. In winter their presence helped make Charleston a lively and cosmopolitan city. This coastal region had the largest proportion of slaves in America, and in the early years of the nineteenth century the numbers of slaves increased dramatically as South Carolina temporarily reopened the foreign slave trade. Although the main lines of coastal development were already well established, the rest of South Carolina was in a state of transition in the fifty years after the Revolution. The middle region of the state, an area of pine trees and sand hills, began to develop rapidly only after 1800, and the piedmont area, above the fall line, although entered by pioneers shortly

521–22; Codman Hislop, *Eliphalet Nott* (Middleton, Conn., 1971), 4–9; Franklin B. Dexter, *Biographical Sketches of the Graduates of Yale College* (6 vols.; New York, 1885–1912), I, 230, III, 154–59; *Vital Records of Saybrook, 1647–1834* (Hartford, 1952), 100–101; *Catalogue of the Officers and Graduates of Yale University in New Haven, Connecticut, 1701–1924* (New Haven, 1924). The quotation is from the *National Cyclopaedia of American Biography*, XXVIII (New York, 1940), 11. Various individuals of the Nott line are also included in other standard American biographical dictionaries.

2. For Abraham Nott's career to 1791 see the *Dictionary of American Biography;* John B. O'Neall, *Biographical Sketches of the Bench and Bar of South Carolina* (2 vols.; Charleston, 1859) I, 121; James D. Bailey, *History of Grindal Shoals and Some Early Adjacent Families* (Gaffney, S.C., 1927), 70; Dexter, *Biographical Sketches of the Graduates of Yale*, III, 565–67.

after the middle of the eighteenth century, was only just beginning to pass out of a raw, frontier condition.[3]

As a young lawyer from the North, Abraham Nott decided to try his chances far up-country among the Scotch-Irish Presbyterians in the Union District; in 1792 this district had a total population of some seventy-seven hundred, including more than twelve hundred slaves. Here at Union Court House, much closer to the North Carolina backcountry than to Charleston, Abraham laid the basis of his family fortunes. Opening a law office in the private house in which he boarded, Nott quickly gained an excellent reputation throughout the district.[4] The many Scotch-Irish Presbyterians who had moved south along the mountain valleys to settle in the backcountry of South Carolina found much to like and trust in the learned and witty New Englander. Politician William L. Smith, who visited Union in the spring of 1793, found that Abraham Nott was already "a kind of oracle" to the people, and Smith was delighted that Nott was prepared to defend the principles of Alexander Hamilton in an area that distrusted Hamilton.[5] Those who later knew Nott as a lawyer and judge testified to the acuteness of his mind and the power of his intellect, but it was also said that he was a man of "very prepossessing manners and genial temperament," who was "gifted with a rich vein of humor and a remarkable readiness at repartee."[6] These qualities were to be inherited by his children.

With his law practice a success, Abraham Nott in August, 1794, married Angelica Mitchell, a woman of little fortune but rare spirit, who helped to give their children some of the combativeness that infuriated their enemies. Angelica Mitchell's parents had come into this frontier region from Granville County, North Carolina, in the mid-1760s, after the South Carolina–Cherokee war. Permanent settlement had begun along the Broad, Sandy, Tyger, and Pacolet rivers of South Carolina in the 1750s. Most of the pioneers were not from South Carolina but from the back-

3. See William W. Freehling, *Prelude to Civil War: The Nullification Controversy in South Carolina, 1816–1836* (1966; rpr. New York, 1968), 7–24; Richard J. Hooker (ed.), *The Carolina Backcountry on the Eve of the Revolution: The Journal and Other Writings of Charles Woodmason, Anglican Itinerant* (Chapel Hill, 1953), xxi–xxiv; Robert L. Meriwether, *The Expansion of South Carolina, 1729–1765* (1940; rpr. Philadelphia, 1974), 113–15.

4. Bailey, *History of Grindal Shoals*, 27; John Drayton, *A View of South-Carolina* (Charleston, 1802), 104.

5. The quotation is from George C. Rogers, *Evolution of a Federalist: William Loughton Smith of Charleston (1758–1812)* (Columbia, 1962), 245.

6. Columbia *Telescope*, July 2, 1830; Bailey, *History of Grindal Shoals*, 71 (quotation).

country of states farther north. Scotch-Irish and Germans followed the valleys south from Pennsylvania, Virginia, and North Carolina.[7]

Angelica Mitchell was born in December, 1771, on Sandy River. Her mother apparently died soon after her birth, and before the Revolution her father, Joab, plunged westward into the wilderness to the new Watauga settlements of North Carolina. He never returned to his family. He had owned land in North Carolina but was unable to sign his name. Left without parents, Angelica depended on her mother's family. They had made a greater mark in the world than her Mitchell connections. Her mother, Mary Henderson, came from a family that had moved from Hanover County, Virginia, to Granville County, North Carolina, just before the middle of the eighteenth century. One of Angelica's uncles, General William Henderson, had been a leader of the South Carolina settlements in the Pacolet River region, and he served with distinction in the Revolution. Another uncle, Richard Henderson, achieved fame as a promoter of Kentucky settlement. It was with one of William Henderson's sisters, Mrs. Adam (Ann) Potter, that Angelica found a home on the eve of the Revolution. In that conflict Angelica's relatives were ardent rebels and were prominent in the internecine struggles of up-country South Carolina.[8]

Angelica Mitchell's childhood was tumultuous, for revolutionary fighting swirled around her childhood home on the Pacolet River. After Charleston was taken by the British in May, 1780, Tory troops swept through the up-country destroying cornfields, seizing or killing cattle, stripping the houses of their provisions and the inhabitants of their possessions. Angelica Mitchell's home was twice raided by Tory forces. More than fifty years later Angelica still had vivid recollections of this time. She remembered that the family generally lived "without bread, meat or salt,

7. For the South Carolina backcountry see Meriwether, *Expansion of South Carolina,* 156–66, 257–60; *A History of Union County, South Carolina* (Greenville, S.C. 1977), 1; George Howe, *History of the Presbyterian Church in South Carolina* (2 vols.; Columbia, 1870–83), I, 295–96, 332, 421–22.

8. See the Draper Manuscripts, 23VV268–71, State Historical Society of Wisconsin, Madison; Zae H. Gwynn, *Court Minutes of Granville County, North Carolina, 1746–1820* (Rocky Mount, N.C., 1977), 43, 60; Zae H. Gwynn, *Abstracts of the Early Deeds of Granville County, North Carolina, 1746–1765* (Rocky Mount, N.C., 1974), 66–67, 81, 121–22, 126–27, 134, 206, 247–48, 262; Worth S. Ray, *Colonial Granville County and Its People* (Baltimore, 1965), 221–23, 227–30; James G. M. Ramsey, *The Annals of Tennessee to the End of the Eighteenth Century* (1853; rpr. Kingsport, Tenn., 1926), 134–38; Bailey, *History of Grindal Shoals,* 24–26, 50–52, 83–85.

on roasting ears. When we killed a beef, a pint of salt with hickory ashes preserved it. We went without shoes, & sewed woolen rags around our feet." Early one morning, when they went to milk the cows, they heard the noise of the battle of Cowpens—"a noise like the burning of a cane break." All morning they sat on a fence and listened. The trials of her childhood clearly strengthened rather than shattered Angelica and left her with a rugged resilience, a characteristic she shared with her son Josiah.[9]

Along with resilience, Angelica Mitchell was highly intelligent. She was to prove an able match for Abraham Nott. One lawyer who knew her well said she "was a most extraordinary woman, endowed with great intelligence, industry, benevolence, and firmness." A local historian who knew her and who also gained his impressions from a variety of local residents said she was "one of the most intellectual and best informed women of her day." His praise went far beyond the usual nineteenth-century laudation of wifely virtue and simple goodness: "She was a woman of rare endowments. She had a fine mind, far more than ordinary culture, a kindly and pleasant disposition, united to great energy of character, and a fortitude that seemed never to give way under the severest trials. In my life, I have never known her superior, and no one who could compare to her in all qualities that go to form the highest character of woman." Even on her tombstone (she died at the age of seventy-seven) it was written that she was highly intelligent and well-read and that as "a companion to be delighted in, her conversation was rich, sparkling and racy."[10] An unusual epitaph to be found in a mid-nineteenth century graveyard, it was probably composed by one of her independent-minded sons.

In the years following his marriage, Abraham Nott's career flourished. The Union District was still a backwater in South Carolina, but it was emerging from the crude frontier state. Nott bought the property on the south side of the Pacolet River, just above Grindal Shoals, that had been owned by his wife's uncle Adam Potter and on which his wife had spent much of her childhood. There he began to build up a prosperous plantation that was to remain as a family home until well into the nineteenth

9. Reminiscences of Angelica Mitchell, in Draper MSS, 23VV268–71; Elizabeth F. Ellet, *The Women of the American Revolution* (3 vols.; 2d ed.; New York, 1848–50), I, 284–96. For the war in South Carolina and the battle of Cowpens, see Jerome J. Nadelhaft, *The Disorders of War: The Revolution in South Carolina* (Orono, Me., 1981); Henry Lumpkin, *From Savannah to Yorktown: The American Revolution in the South* (Columbia, 1981).

10. O'Neall, *Bench and Bar of South Carolina,* I, 123; Bailey, *History of Grindal Shoals,* II, 72.

century. In the first decades of the century, as the up-country was gradually linked to the central parts of the state, Nott's plantation began to
flourish. Although he owned only seven slaves in 1800, by the time of his
death in 1830 he had more than fifty. He grew corn, oats, rye, and wheat
and raised cattle, sheep, and hogs. For about ten years the Pacolet plantation was the year-round home for the Nott family; later they usually visited it in the summer.[11]

In the late 1790s Abraham Nott's fame as a lawyer began to spread outside his immediate district, and for a time he entered politics. In the
course of the 1790s Nott became a member of the flourishing South Carolina Federalist party, and in 1798 he was elected to Congress as a representative from the up-country. He was described by another South Carolina
politician as "a young lawyer from N. England of good principles."[12]
Nott had the reputation of being an independent thinker in political
matters, and he was less ardently partisan than some other South Carolina Federalists, as demonstrated by his opposition to the renewal of the
Sedition Act in 1799. Nott served only two years in Congress. His support of the Federalist party at the time when it was about to be overwhelmed in the South made any longer involvement in national politics
difficult, and along with other southern Federalists he alienated the elec-
torate by his support of Aaron Burr against Thomas Jefferson in the tied
presidential election of 1800. When he ran for a judgeship in 1801, he was
easily defeated. Back on his plantation in 1802 he complained to one of his
political friends that he was "shut up in a remote corner of the earth," but
in reality Union was now much less remote than it had been twenty years
before, and Nott's reputation as a lawyer was beginning to spread around
the state. He was now able to contemplate transferring his main legal
practice to the state capital, Columbia.[13]

11. Union District, South Carolina, Census of 1800, in Record Group 29, Records of the
Bureau of the Census, NA; Union County, South Carolina, Census of 1830, in RG 29, NA;
appraisal of Abraham Nott's personal estate, July 27, 1830, in Estate Papers, Union County,
Box 18, Package 16, South Carolina Department of Archives, Columbia (microfilm); Bailey,
History of Grindal Shoals, 71.

12. The quotation is in Rogers, *Evolution of a Federalist*, 342. See also James H. Broussard,
The Southern Federalists, 1800–1816 (Baton Rouge, 1978), 14, 235; Marvin R. Zahniser, *Charles
Cotesworth Pinckney: Founding Father* (Chapel Hill, 1967), 204–205; Lisle A. Rose, *Prologue
to Democracy: The Federalists in the South, 1788–1800* (Lexington, Ky., 1968), 179–85.

13. Rogers, *Evolution of a Federalist*, 352–54; Broussard, *Southern Federalists*, 36–37, 240;
David Hackett Fischer, *The Revolution of American Conservatism: The Federalist Party in the
Era of Jeffersonian Democracy* (New York, 1965), 405; quotation from Nott to John Rutledge,
February 20, 1802, in John Rutledge Papers, SHC.

To make this change, Nott took a young partner to maintain his office at the Union Court House. David Johnson, a future governor of South Carolina, had come to study law with Nott in 1799. After Johnson was called to the bar in December, 1803, Nott invited him into partnership and moved most of his own work to Columbia. He kept his plantation on the Pacolet but also took up residence in the state capital. There, on March 31, 1804, Josiah Clark Nott was born. He was named for his Connecticut grandfather, Josiah Nott, and for Josiah's wife, whose maiden name was Clark; the name Clark had also been given to one of Abraham's brothers. At the time of Josiah's birth the Notts already had three children—William Blackstone, Henry Junius, and Selina. Another son had died in the previous year, and in the following years Angelica was to give birth to three more boys and two more girls.[14]

Columbia had been founded after the Revolution on the sand hills of the central part of the state, alongside the Congaree River. The legislature began meeting there in 1790, and the surrounding region attracted settlers from all parts of the state. Low-country planters and up-country settlers mingled in the region and helped create a far more homogeneous South Carolina. The most successful of the up-country pioneers were now to establish great plantations in the newly settled areas. Wade Hampton I, whose parents had been killed by Indians early in the Revolution, came out of the backcountry to become one of the richest planters in America, with a large plantation near Columbia and huge estates in Louisiana. He knew members of the various branches of Angelica Nott's family, and for a time in the Revolution he had lived at the house of one of her aunts. The Hampton connection was a help to the Notts in Columbia. Abraham Nott became Hampton's legal agent, and their children were to move in the same social circles.[15]

At the beginning of the nineteenth century, Columbia was a small country town with more than a hundred houses, mostly built of wood, laid out in a regular pattern. It was a quiet town except when the legis-

14. O'Neall, *Bench and Bar of South Carolina,* I, 278–79; Bailey, *History of Grindal Shoals,* 60. For the Nott family, see the works cited in note 1 above and discussion later in the book. For the death of Abraham Nott's son, see Nott to John Rutledge, June 16, 1803, in Rutledge Papers.

15. For early Columbia, see Helen K. Hennig (ed.), *Columbia: Capital City of South Carolina, 1786–1836* (Columbia, 1936), 6–69. For Wade Hampton see Charles E. Cauthen (ed.), *Family Letters of the Three Wade Hamptons, 1782–1901* (Columbia, 1953), 7, 13; Bailey, *History of Grindal Shoals,* 46–49; "Diary of Edward Hooker, 1805–1808," American Historical Association, *Annual Report,* 1896, I (Washington, D.C., 1897), 846.

lature was in session. When New Englander Edward Hooker rode up to it for the first time in November, 1805, he described it as "a neat handsome little town on an elevated tract of ground, commanding on the west and south a view of 8 or 10 miles, and shrouded on the east and north by immense forests of pine." Some of the streets were lined with Pride of India trees, but there was little grass—the dry, sandy soil was often bare. The town had more to offer than most of its size because of its position as the center of state government and because it was the site of South Carolina College (later the University of South Carolina).[16]

Abraham Nott's career flourished after his move to Columbia. He was soon able to leave his Union District practice to David Johnson, and by 1810 his reputation was such that the Republican-controlled South Carolina legislature appointed him as a judge. In the following years, as an important judge and an up-country plantation owner, Nott became a respected member of the South Carolina establishment. In 1824, when the South Carolina Court of Appeals was organized, Nott became its president. In 1833, a few years after Abraham's death, one of his sons was described by a prominent South Carolinian as a member of "one of the most respectable families in our State."[17]

Josiah Nott's childhood was spent in Columbia and on the Pacolet River plantation. Although his father was from New England and his mother had spent her youth on the up-country frontier, he felt perfectly at home among the best families of South Carolina. Later, when he was in his forties, he said of South Carolina Senators John C. Calhoun and Pierce Butler that "I have been intimate with them from Childhood & they are old Cronies of my father."[18] Although Nott inherited an academic and scholarly bent, he identified with the southern aristocracy and ultimately used his intellect to defend a militant southern position. Near the end of his life, it was said that "he unites the sentiments and manners of a southern gentleman with the acquirements of the *savant*."[19] The hab-

16. F. A. Michaux, *Travels to the West of the Alleghany Mountains* London, 1805), in Thomas D. Clark (ed.), *South Carolina: The Grand Tour, 1780–1865* (Columbia, 1973), 39; "Diary of Edward Hooker," 845, 852–56.

17. O'Neall, *Bench and Bar of South Carolina*, I, 121–22; Hennig (ed.), *Columbia*, 162, 167; David J. McCord to David B. Warden, April 21, 1833, in David Baillie Warden Papers, Maryland Historical Society, Baltimore.

18. Nott to Ephraim G. Squier, February 14, 1849, in Squier Papers, LC. For the plantation, see Bailey, *History of Grindal Shoals*, 71; comment of Josiah C. Nott, in *New Orleans Medical and Surgical Journal*, IV (1848), 588.

19. Willis Brewer, *Alabama: Her History, Resources, War Record, and Public Men: From 1540 to 1872* (Montgomery, 1872), 408.

its, merits, and prejudices of a southern gentleman he imbibed from his life as a boy and youth in South Carolina; his fervor as a *savant* was stimulated both by a family that loved the intellect and by his later experience at South Carolina College; his racial ideas, repugnant to a later generation, were shaped by the impact of European and American thought in the peculiar circumstances of the South in the years before the Civil War.

Josiah's formal early education was obtained at the Columbia Male Academy. This academy, which received support from the state, had opened in 1798 as a grammar school teaching Latin and Greek. By 1816 its classical scholars also received instruction in reading, writing, arithmetic, English grammar, and geography. It was first headed by Abraham Blanding, Massachusetts-born and a graduate of Brown University. He was assisted by Columbia's first Presbyterian preacher, David Dunlap. One of Josiah's older brothers went from the academy to South Carolina College in 1810, and it was the accepted school for the sons of the Columbia gentry, including Wade Hampton II. Judge Nott interested himself in the academy and helped develop the idea of a lottery to establish a female counterpart.[20]

Whatever the impact of Josiah Nott's early education in stimulating the interests already begun at home, there is no doubt that the direction of Nott's ideas was given a definite shape by his experiences at South Carolina College. This was a state school that had opened its doors to students at the beginning of 1805. It began with a strong emphasis on classics but in the next two decades broadened its curriculum into the sciences. It had marked success and was soon attracting students from all over the state; as early as 1808 the college had more than one hundred students in attendance.[21]

From the time of the college's foundation Judge Abraham Nott was closely linked to its progress, and as a member of the Board of Trustees he was usually on the committees supervising and directing the details of college building and operations.[22] By the time his son Josiah went there in

20. Hennig (ed.), *Columbia*, 101–102; Edwin J. Scott, *Random Recollections of a Long Life, 1806 to 1876* (Columbia, 1884), 60; Robert Mills, *Statistics of South Carolina* (Charleston, 1826), 702–704; Nell S. Graydon, *Tales of Columbia* (Columbia, 1965), 31–32, 35; Edwin A. Alderman and Joel C. Harris (eds.), *Library of Southern Literature*, IX (Atlanta, 1909), 3797; typed material re Josiah C. Nott in the University of South Carolina Archives, Columbia.

21. Daniel W. Hollis, *University of South Carolina*, I, *South Carolina College* (Columbia, 1951), 30–74.

22. *Ibid.*, 69–71; John M. Bryan, *An Architectural History of the South Carolina College, 1801–1855* (Columbia, 1976), 48, 145, 148.

the early 1820s the college had undergone a dramatic change by the appointment of Thomas Cooper to the position of president. Cooper placed the college in the van of advanced thinking in the United States. His ideas fascinated the young Josiah Nott. Some of them he was to repeat for the rest of his life.

Under its first president, Jonathan Maxcy, a Yale graduate, the college had begun to show signs of floundering. A visitor in 1819 commented that the students "are very disorderly, frequently disturbing congregations on the Sunday, because the Doctor is too idle to preach, and thereby keep them together." He described seeing "these learned young gentlemen stretched on a table, with their learned legs carelessly hanging out of their chamber windows, which seemed nearly all broken. Want of discipline is here too palpable, but there is no lack of whiskey." [23] With the coming of Cooper the college was not to lack energy, but there was more to worry about than too much whiskey and a lack of preaching.

Thomas Cooper was a remarkable choice for South Carolina College. Over the previous thirty years he had gained a reputation on two continents for brilliance, freethinking, and anticlericalism. Cooper, who was born in England in 1759, attended Oxford without taking a degree. He wanted to be a physician and attended some medical courses in London, but his father objected. He then read law, moved to Manchester, became increasingly interested in chemistry and ultimately geology, and entered industry. When he began to write, he quickly gained a reputation as a radical, arguing for human equality and the right of revolution, attacking the slave trade, seeking parliamentary reform, and supporting the French Revolution. Cooper was a materialist and expressed disbelief in an immortal soul, but he claimed that this belief was compatible with Christianity. Above all else, Cooper emphasized the importance of freedom of expression and a relentless search for truth. [24]

Cooper's activities, particularly a journey to France to express solidarity with the French revolutionaries, did not endear him to the British authorities, and like other English radicals he decided to seek a haven in the United States. By 1794 he was settled on the upper Susquehanna in Pennsylvania. He practiced law, prescribed as an amateur physician, and again began publicly to express disagreement with authority. In 1800

23. William Faux, *Memorable Days in America: Being a Journal of a Tour to the United States* (1823; rpr. New York, 1969), 53–54.
24. The standard source for Cooper, and my source for this and the following paragraph, is Dumas Malone, *The Public Life of Thomas Cooper, 1783–1839* (1926; rpr. Columbia, 1961), 4–174.

he was tried for seditious libel and given a six-month jail sentence. The downfall of the Federalists and the coming of Jefferson to power created a more favorable climate of opinion for Cooper, and for a time he served as a Pennsylvania judge.

In 1811 Cooper began his career as a college teacher, first as professor of chemistry at Carlisle College and later in the chair of applied chemistry and minerology at the University of Pennsylvania. Jefferson admired Cooper and was anxious to appoint him to a professorship in his new University of Virginia. The appointment was arranged in 1819, but during a delay while building was completed Cooper came under considerable attack from Virginia clergymen. His attacks on orthodox religion were well known, and he had been particularly scathing toward the Presbyterian clergy. While waiting for the Virginia situation to be resolved, Cooper applied for a one-year appointment as professor of chemistry at South Carolina College. He went there in January, 1820. In the spring the trustees offered him a permanent position, making him professor of geology and minerology as well as professor of chemistry. When in May, 1820, Professor Maxcy died, Cooper was appointed to the position of president.[25]

The speed with which the college trustees accepted the brilliant but controversial Cooper testified to the tolerance of many South Carolinians on religious and educational matters. That Cooper was able to keep his position for fourteen years, in spite of increasingly vigorous attacks, also testified to the speed with which he adopted extreme southern positions on states' rights and slavery. He combined these strong southern views on politics and race with continued opposition to organized religion. He was a man who was either loved or hated. One South Carolinian later commented that Cooper was "replete with all sorts of knowledge, a living encyclopedia . . . good-tempered, joyous, and of a kindly disposition." But it was also said that while he was president of South Carolina College, "infidelity and irreligion took possession of the seat and center of knowledge."[26] His peculiar combination of views proved particularly agreeable to Josiah Nott. The passionate defense of slavery, the emphasis on states' rights, and the disbelief in the authority of the Bible on scientific matters all characterized the thought of the mature Nott.

Cooper at first tried to act with moderation, but because of his views

25. *Ibid.*, 211–53; Hollis, *University of South Carolina*, I, 76–77.

26. W. C. Preston, *South Carolinian*, May 17, 1855, in Evert A. Duyckinck and George L. Duyckinck, *Cyclopaedia of American Literature* (2 vols; New York, 1855), II, 250. The remark on infidelity and irreligion is quoted in Clement Eaton, *The Freedom of Thought Struggle in the Old South* (New York, 1964), 305.

on the geological history of the earth and his opinion of the harmful role of the clergy it was only a matter of time before he encountered religious opposition within the state. In 1820 and the decades before the Civil War, the orthodox believed in the literal truth of the account of creation given in Genesis. Even the most respectable geologists had to exercise great caution when they suggested that the world was much older than the less than six thousand years that was accepted by the clergy. But Cooper was never cautious for long. He went far beyond most scientists in challenging religion in general and the scientific authority of the Bible in particular. The famous physician J. Marion Sims, who began to attend South Carolina College in 1830, commented much later in his life that Cooper "was a pronounced infidel, and every year lectured on the 'Authenticity of the Pentateuch' to the senior class, generally six or eight weeks before their graduation." A longtime resident of Columbia had the same opinion—Cooper, he said, "was generally regarded as an infidel, though he professed to be a Unitarian." [27]

Josiah Nott's years at South Carolina College in the early 1820s were stormy ones for both the college and the state of South Carolina. The intellectual climate of the college improved markedly for the better after Cooper's arrival in 1820. He toughened admission standards, strengthened the course of studies, and reduced the number of students. Usually there were fewer than one hundred students on campus each year. Cooper won their ardent support, and they became his strongest defenders in the various attacks on him. They argued that he did nothing to influence their religious principles. But in the fall of 1822, when Nott entered the college as a sophomore, the first of a series of attacks was launched on Cooper and his influence. Complaints to the legislature, inspired by the up-country Presbyterian clergy, led the South Carolina House of Representatives to appoint a committee of inquiry. The committee cleared him, but in January, 1823, Cooper lashed back, arguing that the prosperity of the institution was threatened by "the systematic hostility of the clergy generally, to any seminary of education which is not under their government and control." This unwise rejoinder stirred the fires anew, and throughout 1823 the war of words raged, with Cooper attacking the Presbyterians in the state while arguing that he only sought the truth. [28] His

27. J. Marion Sims, *The Story of My Life* (1884; rpr. New York, 1968), 82; Scott, *Random Recollections,* 68 (second "infidel" quotation); Malone, *Public Life of Cooper,* 254; Hollis, *University of South Carolina,* I, 98–100.

28. Hollis, *University of South Carolina,* I, 80–93, 108; Malone, *Public Life of Cooper,*

arguments and his baiting of the clergy were to be echoed by Nott in the 1840s and 1850s.

The young Josiah Nott had ample opportunities to learn of the Presbyterian faith at first hand. His mother came from a Scotch-Irish family, was connected to the church all her life, and was much admired by the Presbyterian clergymen with whom she came into contact. His father's religious experience was more complex. His clerical heritage in New England and his training for the ministry at Yale had not led him to become a clergyman. Feeling no calling, he had chosen the law. Yet, in South Carolina, he was closely connected with the Presbyterian church. In 1812 he was one of the leaders in the move to build a Presbyterian church in Columbia. It was dedicated in 1814, and when in 1818 a new minister was needed, Abraham Nott helped choose him. Abraham was never an elder of the church, but near the end of his life he did serve for a year as president of the corporation.[29] One gains the impression that Abraham Nott supported religion as part of the established order but that his intellectual bent denied him full religious ardor. At least two of his sons—Henry and Josiah—were to move from his formal acceptance to skepticism. In both cases it seems likely that Thomas Cooper helped to crystallize their ideas. Henry graduated before Cooper came to the college but took up a professorship there in 1825.

Although the degree to which Nott shared Cooper's religious views was to make him a somewhat unusual southerner in the mid-nineteenth century, he was far more typical of the South in his sharing of Cooper's views on states' rights, slavery, and blacks. The 1820s were decisive years in the shaping of a South Carolina sectionalist position. Anxiety felt by South Carolinians because of the high density of slaves in their coastal regions was accentuated by a federal government that seemed increasingly willing to assume powers that might be used contrary to the interests of the state. The movement for a protective tariff was intensely disliked by a state that saw its interests intimately connected with trade to Europe, but more threatening was the gradual shift of northern and European opinion to an antislavery position. Most South Carolinians found

259–77, 266 (quotation). The outline of Nott's college career can be followed in the University of South Carolina Archives. He was a member of the Euphradian Society, one of the two debating societies, but was often absent from its meetings (Euphradian Society Records, University of South Carolina Archives). It was usual at this time to enter the college as a sophomore.

29. Howe, *History of the Presbyterian Church in South Carolina*, I, 257, 259, II, 661; First Presbyterian Church of Columbia Papers, SCL.

it impossible to conceive of a state in which a large number of free blacks would live closely with whites.[30]

Nott's college years saw a crystallization of South Carolina's fears on the problems of slavery. In the early summer of 1822, the state was shocked by the revelation that Denmark Vesey, a free black in Charleston, had been planning a slave uprising. The betrayal of the plot led to the hanging of more than thirty blacks and the banishing of another thirty. The fears that were stimulated by Denmark Vesey were constantly reexcited in the next nine years by both rumors and actual uprisings and finally in 1831 by the serious Nat Turner outbreak in Virginia. After 1822 South Carolinians never again rested easy on the subject of slavery. In December of that year, the legislature passed an act requiring that free colored seamen were to be jailed when their ships were in port in the state.[31]

As president of South Carolina College, Cooper was as eager to join the political arguments about the tariff and slavery as he was to raise religious questions about the Bible and the authenticity of Genesis. His outspokenness on political matters offended many South Carolina Unionists but helped him regain much of the support his religious opinions had cost him. Cooper took a strong states' rights stance and in 1824 wrote a pamphlet attacking the tariff. Not only did he defend slavery but he became one of the first intellectuals in the South to maintain that the Negro race was inherently inferior to the white. He made this allegation in a Columbia newspaper as early as 1823 and in the following years argued that the Negroes were an inferior variety of the human species.[32] In later years his pupil Josiah Nott was to take this argument further and argue that an inferior Negro race constituted a separate species with a separate origin. Both Cooper and Nott were proof that liberal thinking on scientific and religious matters could be combined with extreme racism.

At South Carolina College, Josiah Nott was brought into intimate contact with more controversial ideas than he would have found at any other college in the United States. With Cooper at its head, the college became a hotbed of religious unorthodoxy and states' rights fervor. Clearly, many young men went through the college untouched by their experience and

30. See the discussion in Freehling, *Prelude*, 49–133.

31. *Ibid.*, 53–64, 112–15; John Lofton, *Insurrection in South Carolina: The Turbulent World of Denmark Vesey* (Yellow Springs, Ohio, 1964), 182–239; Marina Wikramanayake, *The World in Shadow: The Free Black in Antebellum South Carolina* (Columbia, 1973), 146–64.

32. Malone, *Public Life of Cooper*, 281–89.

simply accepted the more usual religious assumptions in South Carolina in the 1820s. But Nott came from a family in which the intellect was always finely honed and brilliant and unusual conversation was the norm. To the typical background of a young South Carolinian of the 1820s Nott added a fascination with unorthodox ideas. For the rest of his life he always maintained that the pursuit of scientific truth was his ultimate and undeviating goal, even when he became the most fervent of southern apologists for the permanent subordination of the black race. And it was science, not law or politics, that attracted him when he graduated from South Carolina College in 1824. He decided to become a physician. This was a career Nott's brother William was already following and one which Thomas Cooper had wanted but had been denied. Of the six Nott boys only one—Henry Junius—was to enter his father's profession, and he quickly deserted the law for a career as a college teacher and writer. The other five Nott boys—William, Josiah, James, Rufus, and Gustavus Adolphus—all became physicians, and one of their sisters—Sophonista—married one. Although five physicians in one family was unusual, physician sons were common among the South Carolina gentry. Medicine attracted some of the brightest and best-connected young men of South Carolina.[33]

In the first decades of the nineteenth century, medical education was usually at best a combination of apprenticeship and brief formal work in medical school; many physicians still practiced without a degree. An apprentice entered the office of a practicing physician, read medical works under his direction, observed and ultimately helped in giving treatment, and went with the doctor on visits to his patients. The most prosperous and dedicated students broadened their training by attending one of the best American medical schools and by traveling to the main European medical centers—in these years usually Paris, Edinburgh, London, or Dublin. To obtain a formal medical degree in the United States, students were expected to combine some apprenticeship with attendance at two terms of lectures; each term was four months in length. Terms usually ran

33. Nott's fellow graduates in 1824 are listed in Maximilian La Borde, *History of the South Carolina College* (2d ed.; Charleston, 1874), 535. The Nott brothers all attended South Carolina College, and there is information on them in the University of South Carolina Archives as well as scattered information in a variety of other primary sources. There is material on Sophonista Nott Moore (1800–1862) and her husband, Dr. Maurice Augustus Moore, in J. B. O. Landrum, *History of Spartanburg County* (Atlanta, 1900), 619–20. She was said to have been a brilliant conversationalist.

from November to March, and students normally attended in successive years. The schools were small; the better ones had seven faculty members and others less. They usually offered courses in chemistry, anatomy, and physiology and more specialized courses on the theory of medicine, medical practice, "materia medica," and surgery. At many schools little clinical experience was available in the first decades of the nineteenth century. Opportunities for dissection were limited and still met with clerical and popular objections, and many schools had no nearby hospital to offer students frequent experience with actual patients. Only in the larger cities like Philadelphia and New York did the presence of sizable hospitals and almshouses offer the student a diversity of practical experience, and even there the opportunities were often limited. For those who wished to obtain the widest experience in observing, practicing, and learning it was necessary to go abroad—particularly to the teaching hospitals of Paris.[34]

In the 1820s physicians were still painfully limited in the knowledge available to them. The causes of disease were unknown, and therapeutics were usually in the "heroic" mold—violent purges, frequent emetics, copious bloodletting, and huge doses of mercury in various forms. Surgery in these years before asepsis and anesthetics was often fatal.

When Nott graduated from South Carolina College in 1824, he began a medical apprenticeship in Columbia with Dr. James Davis. Working under Davis did not keep Nott long interested as a student. Although Davis was active in the founding of the Columbia lunatic asylum, his writing was usually on political rather than medical or scientific topics.[35] Nott quickly sought greater intellectual stimulation and decided to pursue his medical education in a more formal manner at a first-class institution. This decision made it necessary for him to leave the state, for medical education in South Carolina was only just becoming possible. In the

34. For medical education in the early nineteenth century see William G. Rothstein, *American Physicians in the Nineteenth Century: From Sect to Science* (Baltimore, 1972); Ronald L. Numbers (ed.), *The Education of American Physicians: Historical Essays* (Berkeley, 1980); Martin Kaufman, *American Medical Education: The Formative Years, 1796–1910* (Westport, Conn., 1976); William F. Norwood, *Medical Education in the United States Before the Civil War* (Philadelphia, 1944); Henry B. Shafer, *The American Medical Profession, 1783–1850* (New York, 1936). There is also very useful information in Russell M. Jones (ed.), *The Parisian Education of an American Surgeon: Letters of Jonathan Mason Warren, 1832–1835* (Philadelphia, 1978), introduction.

35. Emmett B. Carmichael, "Josiah Clark Nott," *Bulletin of the History of Medicine*, XXII (1948), 249; Joseph I. Waring, *A History of Medicine in South Carolina* (3 vols.; Charleston, 1964–71), I, 206–208; Columbia *Telescope*, April 22, 1831.

early 1820s Thomas Cooper had worked toward the founding of a medical college in South Carolina. He had hoped to attach it to his own college, but in 1823 the legislature had founded it as a separate institution in Charleston. No money was voted for it until 1825, and to obtain the best medical education the United States had to offer Nott had to travel north.[36] Philadelphia was the center of American medical education, but Nott, perhaps because of family connections, first decided to go to New York to attend the College of Physicians and Surgeons.

New York in the mid-1820s was nothing like the huge city in which Nott was to spend the last years of his life. Although growing rapidly, its population in 1825 was still only about 160,000. At the time Nott arrived, most of the population was still concentrated on the southern tip of Manhattan Island; Greenwich Village was just ceasing to be a village and was being linked to the city advancing north from the Battery. But compared to Columbia and the Pacolet River, New York was a teeming, bustling city, and it was in the midst of dramatic growth.[37] New York helped to give Nott a taste for city life that he was never to lose. On this occasion, however, his stay was short, for he arrived at a time of confusion and controversy for the College of Physicians and Surgeons.

After opening in 1807, the college quickly achieved a national reputation. Like most of the medical schools of these years, it offered limited formal training. Major advantages for the school were that clinical courses could be held at the New York Hospital and the Almshouse and that it had acquired several distinguished faculty members. Two of the faculty— Valentine Mott and David Hosack—had become well known in two of the areas in which Nott was later to achieve fame. Mott was one of the most skillful surgeons of the early nineteenth century and was interested in developments in French surgery; and Hosack devoted much attention to the questions of the origin and treatment of yellow fever. It was later said that Nott was particularly influenced by Mott during his brief stay in New York.[38]

36. Malone, *Public Life of Cooper,* 278–79.
37. See Charles Lockwood, *Manhattan Moves Uptown: An Illustrated History* (Boston, 1976), xviii, 6–57; Charles H. Haswell, *Reminiscences of an Octogenarian of the City of New York (1816 to 1860)* (New York, 1896), 172–82.
38. Francis R. Packard, *History of Medicine in the United States* (2 vols.; 1931; rpr. New York, 1963), I, 395–417; Christine C. Robbins, *David Hosack: Citizen of New York* (Philadelphia, 1964), 95–105; Norwood, *Medical Education,* 113–18; Shafer, *American Medical Profession,* 138–39; Carmichael, "Josiah Clark Nott," 249.

After experiencing Cooper's constant battles during his undergraduate years at South Carolina College, Nott must have found much that was familiar in the College of Physicians and Surgeons. When he arrived, the college was in the middle of a struggle between the trustees and the faculty over fees, funding, and examinations. The fight was so serious that it practically ruined a flourishing institution. In the spring of 1826, the president and faculty resigned and opened a rival medical college. The College of Physicians and Surgeons continued but in a sadly depleted state. There had been more than two hundred students in attendance in the 1825–1826 session, but only ninety returned in the fall of 1826.[39] Nott was one of those who decided to seek a more stable situation by going to the medical school of the University of Pennsylvania. In doing so he began to give a definite shape to his future career, for Philadelphia was already the main center of early American medicine and it was soon to become a center of early American ethnology. Nott's three years in Philadelphia gave him a medical and scientific bent that he never lost and helped develop an interest in French medicine that shaped his own medical practice. He visited Philadelphia regularly throughout his life, except when cut off by the Civil War, and he treasured his correspondence with its medical and ethnological leaders. Although Nott spent the most productive part of his life in Mobile, his intellectual horizons went far beyond the South to Philadelphia, Paris, London, and Berlin.

Although Philadelphia had in the past twenty years been surpassed in population and prosperity by New York, its quiet, confident stability often impressed visitors. Its regular streets were well-paved, the houses and sidewalks were usually of brick, and the shops were substantial and even elegant. The Quaker influence in the city was still strong, and after dark the streets in the main parts of the town were almost eerily silent, presenting a striking contrast to the noise and bustle of nighttime New York. On Sundays chains were thrown across many of the streets to prevent the passage of horses and carriages. More familiar to Nott were the servants, declared by an English visitor to be "universally" black or mulatto.[40]

39. Norwood, *Medical Education*, 120; Robbins, *Hosack*, 115–17.
40. Francis Trollope, *Domestic Manners of the Americans*, ed. Donald Smalley (New York, 1949), 260–61, 271–76; [Margaret Hall], *The Aristocratic Journey: Being the Outspoken Letters of Mrs. Basil Hall. Written During a Fourteen Months' Sojourn in America, 1827–1828*, ed. Una Pope-Hennessy (New York, 1931), 136–51.

The medical school of the University of Pennsylvania was the oldest and most famous in America. It had been founded before the Revolution as a separate college but in the 1790s had become part of the university. When Nott attended, the granting of a degree required at least two years' work as the private pupil of a practicing physician; attendance at two complete courses of lectures on anatomy, the institutes and practice of medicine, materia medica and pharmacy, chemistry, surgery, midwifery, and the diseases of women and children; and a course of clinical instruction at a hospital or almshouse. The candidate also had to present a satisfactory thesis and defend it in an oral examination. The thesis was to be in the candidate's own handwriting. "General bad spelling on a Thesis, or general inattention to the rules of grammar," were enough to "preclude a candidate from examination for a degree." Nott was able to complete his work in one year because a course of lectures in another approved medical school could count toward the degree.[41]

The faculty of the University of Pennsylvania medical school included some of the great figures of early American medicine. Best known at the time Nott attended was the famous surgeon Dr. Philip Syng Physick, who held the chair of anatomy. He had studied in Great Britain as well as in America and was an M.D. of Edinburgh. Physick's adjunct professor was Dr. William E. Horner. Horner, a Virginian, had a reputation as a first-class teacher of anatomy.[42] The ties of the medical school to Edinburgh were strong, for the professors of surgery, obstetrics, and materia medica had also spent some time in that city, but Nott, like many of the students of the 1820s and 1830s, was particularly influenced by those who were bringing the theories of French medicine to America. In the following decades, the French were to exert a strong influence on the best-trained American physicians.

Prominent among the younger teachers who looked to France for their inspiration was Dr. Samuel Jackson, and it was Jackson who exerted the most influence on Nott. Jackson, an extremely popular teacher and a brilliant conversationalist, was on the faculty of the Philadelphia College of

41. See George W. Corner, *Two Centuries of Medicine: A History of the School of Medicine, University of Pennsylvania* (Philadelphia, 1965); Packard, *History of Medicine*, I, 351–91; Norwood, *Medical Education*, 78–83; University of Pennsylvania, Medical Department, Rules and Regulations for Conferring the Degree of Doctor of Medicine, October 17, 1829, University of Pennsylvania Archives, Philadelphia.

42. Packard, *History of Medicine*, I, 387–88, 391; Samuel Jackson, *A Discourse Commemorative of the Late William E. Horner, M.D., Professor of Anatomy* (Philadelphia, 1853).

Pharmacy in the early 1820s, but Nott knew him as one of the attending physicians of the Philadelphia Almshouse, a post he assumed in 1822. Jackson also gave lectures there which attracted a great many students. In 1827 he became an assistant professor in the University of Pennsylvania medical school, lecturing on the institutes of medicine. Jackson in these years was a particularly strong adherent of François Joseph Victor Broussais and the French school of physiological medicine, and he fired Nott both with an interest in Broussais' doctrines and in the entire French physiological school.[43] The attack launched by that school on the earlier metaphysical emphases of medicine and its own stress on observation, analysis, and the pathology of disease proved particularly attractive to Nott. He had been well-prepared for this materialist approach to illness and the human body by his years under Thomas Cooper at South Carolina College.

Philadelphia had much to offer besides medicine and was a revelation to the young men from the up-country South who so often went there to complete their medical educations. Nott's younger brother Adolphus, who studied medicine there several years after Josiah, referred to Philadelphia as "that most delightful of cities." His advice to a prospective student was to "attend Jackson's lectures strictly" and to take all possible opportunities to make pathological observations by assisting at all the post-mortems. Also, by making a friend of the resident physician at the almshouse, Adolphus advised, he would be given the opportunity to attend at the surgical and children's wards and at all deliveries. Adolphus also told his friend where to live, what to eat, and what to see. His own Philadelphia lodgings were to be resorted to only if the landlady's niece was still there. If so, this was the place to go: "You will find my name a passport to you, and will admit you to more privileges than was ever dreamed of in your philosophy."[44]

Josiah Nott's first winter in Philadelphia was a fruitful one, for by March, 1826, he was ready to present himself for examination for his degree. His thesis was on the unglamorous topic of "costiveness" and needed some corrections after the final examination, but in mid-March

43. Joseph Carson, *A Discourse Commemorative of the Life and Character of Samuel Jackson, M.D.* (Philadelphia, 1872); Russell M. Jones, "American Doctors and the Parisian Medical World, 1830–1840," *Bulletin of the History of Medicine,* XLVII (1973), 43–44; James H. Cassedy, *American Medicine and Statistical Thinking, 1800–1860* (Cambridge, Mass., 1984), 58–59.

44. [Gustavus A. Nott] to James M. Gage, *c.* March [1838], in James M. Gage Papers, SHC.

he paid his $40 and received his degree. He now returned to Columbia and opened an office, but he was hopeful of returning to Philadelphia for further training through a year's internship at the Philadelphia Almshouse ("Old Blockley"). The origin of this public almshouse went back to the 1730s. By the early nineteenth century it included a hospital for the poor, a ward for pregnant, indigent women, and a section for the insane. One visitor in 1827 referred to it "as an immense building in which in winter there are from twelve to fifteen hundred persons." In the early 1820s the nonresident medical staff of the almshouse consisted of four general physicians, four surgeons, and two obstetricians. Some of the faculty of the University of Pennsylvania medical school served as staff members of the almshouse. Residencies for a year were eagerly sought by ambitious physicians to give them the opportunity to treat and observe a wide variety of patients and to work closely with the members of the staff. Lectures were given by staff members and were attended both by the residents and the numerous clinical pupils registered at the almshouse. Not all of the residents were graduate physicians, but this became more common in the 1820s. Even the graduate physicians at this time had to pay $200 for a residency. Competition was stiff, but Nott, as a graduate physician, had an advantage. Henry S. Levert, who was to be a colleague of Nott's in Mobile but who had not yet graduated, failed to gain a residency in the spring of 1827 but gained admission at the same time as Nott in the fall.[45] Nott's successful application meant that he gave up his brief attempt to begin a practice in Columbia and quickly returned to Philadelphia.

At the completion of his residency, Levert was to say that the year had been more profitably spent than any period of his life, and Nott's year was also of great value. He saw a host of patients, observed the application of the new French technique of localized bleeding, and was able to catch the eye of Dr. William Horner, the adjunct professor of anatomy at the University of Pennsylvania and a staff member at the almshouse. This acquaintance led to Nott being given the position of demonstrator of anat-

45. University of Pennsylvania Medical Department, Matriculation Register, 1826–27; Candidates for Degrees, Doctor of Medicine, 1827, University of Pennsylvania Archives; Waring, *History of Medicine in South Carolina*, II, 278; [Hall], *Aristocratic Journey*, 145 (quotation); Charles Lawrence (comp.), *History of the Philadelphia Almshouses and Hospitals* (1905; rpr. New York, 1976), 18–50; Packard, *History of Medicine*, I, 246–51; Norwood, *Medical Education*, 48–49; Henry S. Levert to Francis Levert, May 12, October 16, 1827, in Levert Family Papers, SHC; Carmichael, "Josiah Clark Nott," 249.

omy at the medical school for the 1828–1829 academic year. He now had the opportunity to work not only with Horner but also with the professor of anatomy Dr. Philip Syng Physick; it also gave him the continuous work in dissection so beloved by the French school.[46]

When in the spring of 1829 Nott finished his years of education in Philadelphia, he was far better prepared than most American physicians of his generation. His original apprenticeship had been shorter than most, but he had more than made up for this lack by his work with physicians in New York and Philadelphia, by his year of residency at the almshouse, and by his year of dissection at the medical school. He had also attended two sessions of lectures by some of the most prominent physicians in America. He would now use his knowledge and enthusiasm to create a successful practice in his own state.

46. Henry S. Levert to his mother, December 15, 1828, in Levert Family Papers; Carmichael, "Josiah Clark Nott," 249; Nott to Joseph Leidy, May 3, 1857, in Joseph Leidy Papers, CPP.

Chapter 2
THE YOUNG PHYSICIAN

In the spring of 1829, Nott returned to Columbia and opened an office. In the next six years he flourished as a physician, and he also revealed that his ambitions were greater than those of most local practitioners of the early nineteenth century. In this period of his career Nott shunned public controversy and dedicated himself wholly to medicine. His study and experience in Philadelphia had fired him with an interest in French medical theories, and he had become an enthusiastic convert to the medical doctrines of François Joseph Victor Broussais.

When Nott began his career, Broussais' doctrines were influencing the most advanced young American physicians. In 1828 Nott's older physician brother, William Blackstone Nott, had his eldest son christened as John Broussais Nott. Broussais stressed that general symptoms or fevers could be traced back to specific lesions, usually in the gastrointestinal tract. Pathology could be of vital assistance to the physician in showing the origin of irritation and the manner in which lesions had spread. Although Broussais had started by attacking the existing general theories of disease, he quickly arrived at a position of dogmatically stating that all illness, including fevers, tuberculosis, and mental disturbance, was the eventual result of irritation and lesions of the gastrointestinal tract. Because the harsh drugs typical of early eighteenth- and nineteenth-century medicine only increased the inflammation, Broussais reduced therapeutics to bleeding and a strict diet, mostly liquid. As he became more convinced of the truth of his theories, Broussais placed most of his faith in bloodletting by the use of leeches.[1]

1. Joseph I. Waring, *A History of Medicine in South Carolina* (3 vols.; Charleston, 1964–71), II, 278; Ervin H. Ackerknecht, *Medicine at the Paris Hospital, 1794–1848* (Baltimore, 1967),

In founding "physiological medicine" Broussais became famous not only as a medical theorist but also because his doctrines encouraged those who wished to discard metaphysical or spiritual explanations of human behavior. Broussais stressed that all could be explained by observation and logical analysis. He welcomed phrenological doctrines and lectured on them because the phrenologists presented seemingly rational, mechanistic explanations of human behavior. In 1832, when an American medical student commented on Paris physicians in a letter to his father, he said that "the great materialist here at present is Broussais." Thomas Cooper of South Carolina College was attracted to Broussais' theories, and in 1831 he published a translation of Broussais' work on irritation and insanity. He was particularly drawn to this work because of Broussais' rejection of metaphysical explanations of mental disturbance. By praising the physiological school and reprinting two of his own essays on materialism, Cooper again infuriated the South Carolina clergy.[2]

With two of his mentors—Cooper and Jackson—and his older brother deeply interested in Broussais and the French school, it is not surprising that Nott began his career as a serious author by attempting to disseminate Broussais' ideas in the United States. In 1831 he published a translation of J. M. A. Goupil's work on Broussais' theories under the title *An Exposition of the Principles of the New Medical Doctrine*. The book was printed at the office of the Columbia *Times and Gazette* and was dedicated to Dr. Samuel Jackson. In a generous dedication, Nott thanked Jackson for suggesting that he read the original, for introducing him to its doctrines in his lectures, and for being the first to "fight the battles of Broussais in the United States." Goupil's book was an attempt to summarize and explain Broussais' medical theories. In his introduction, Nott referred to it as the best elementary work of the physiological school. As a justification for presenting the translation to the public, Nott argued that although Broussais' name was familiar in the United States, few, particularly in the South, knew his doctrines. Nott said that he did not present

61–80; Russell M. Jones, "American Doctors and the Parisian Medical World, 1830–1840," *Bulletin of the History of Medicine*, XLVII (1973), 54. For John Broussais Nott, see typed MSS in University of South Carolina Archives, Columbia.

2. Jonathan Warren to his father, December 17, 1832, in Russell M. Jones (ed.), *The Parisian Education of an American Surgeon: Letters of Jonathan Mason Warren, 1832–1835* (Philadelphia, 1978), 94–95 and note; François Joseph Victor Broussais, *On Irritation and Insanity*, trans. Thomas Cooper (Columbia, 1831); Dumas Malone, *The Public Life of Thomas Cooper, 1783–1839* (1926; rpr. Columbia, 1961), 280, 347–48.

Broussais as perfect—like all geniuses, he generalized too much. "But," stated Nott, "I am persuaded he is nearer right than any one who has preceded him, and that no physician can read his works attentively without becoming a better pathologist and a better practitioner."[3] In placing "pathologist" before "practitioner" Nott revealed the extent to which, at this time in his career, he had absorbed the dedication of the French school to scientific medicine. Yet in spite of this fascination with medical theory, Nott was never to desert the practice of medicine to engage in purely scientific endeavors. He showed a willingness to modify or abandon medical theories as time and experience demonstrated their weaknesses.

Nott's practical side showed in the essay he appended to his translation, describing the keeping and use of the leeches so essential to Broussais' techniques. He pointed out that the localized bloodletting now used extensively in Europe and the larger American cities was almost unknown in the small towns and rural areas of the South. General bloodletting, by an incision in the arm, had of course long been in use, but Nott was referring to the new French technique of applying leeches as close to the site of the inflammation as possible. Nott discussed not only the use and advantages of leeches but also their catching and keeping. He said that the belief that only one type was suitable was wrong—any leech that would bite could be used. The Carolina leeches, which were abundant in freshwater ponds and streams, took less blood than the favored Spanish variety but caused less irritation by their bite. Boys could catch them by stirring up the water, or sometimes they were caught by spreading a sheep or other skin, raw side down, on the surface. Once caught, the leeches could be kept in tubs as long as the water was changed regularly. Nott had experience with leeches in Philadelphia, and he had obviously experimented with their catching, care, and use in South Carolina.

For physicians inexperienced with the extensive French use of leeches, Nott provided detailed instructions. The section of human skin to which the leeches were to be applied had to be cleaned—leeches, Nott pointed out, were very cleanly animals and would not bite unless the skin was clean and free from hair. Once applied, they were to be left on until they dropped off—if they were pulled off, they lost their teeth and could not be used again. So the leeches could be used again within a week or ten

3. J. M. A. Goupil, *An Exposition of the Principles of the New Medical Doctrine*, trans. Josiah C. Nott (Columbia, 1831), xvii.

days, Nott recommended that the blood be removed from them by means of an incision. Nott stressed that it was not just the act of bleeding the patient that was important but where the blood was taken from, for the "capillary system has laws peculiar to itself." There was now general agreement, he wrote, that the leeches were best applied as near as possible to the inflamed organ, or even directly on the inflamed tissue: for fevers affecting the stomach and head the leeches should be applied to the parts affected; for ear inflammations they should be put on the ear and neck; and similar direct applications should be used for inflammations on other parts of the body. For acute internal inflammation such as pleurisy or peritonitis that required quick results, Nott suggested that fifty or a hundred American leeches should be applied and bleeding encouraged by the use of warm fomentations after the leeches fell off. He said that though this might seem excessive, it was borne out by his several years' attendance and observation at the Philadelphia Almshouse. In some cases, particularly of chronic rather than acute inflammation, blood should be extracted by cupping rather than by leeches. In these cases cuts were made at the desired place and a cupping glass applied to create a partial vacuum. Nott preferred leeches because they produced less irritation to the skin.[4]

Although the localized application of leeches appeared useless to a later generation, and Nott himself was to move on to new theories, it was at the time viewed as an important medical advance. On occasion the new technique, however outlandish it might later have seemed, probably worked to the advantage of the patient. It usually took less blood than was taken by the free use of the knife, and along with the use of leeches Broussais had recommended sharply reducing the excessive, harsh medication that had often accompanied the earlier, draconian bleeding. The technique did not cure, but it was less likely to kill than the excessive use of lancet, purges, emetics, and preparations of mercury.

In publishing his work on French medical techniques and their American application Nott was in the van of scientific medicine in the South. Although Broussais was to be overshadowed and attacked by other French theorists in the 1830s, his emphasis on observation, detail, and pathology helped begin the process which in the next fifty years was to lead to a medical revolution and genuine breakthroughs in the diagnosis and treatment of disease.

When in May, 1832, Nott outlined his ideas on medicine to his old col-

4. *Ibid.*, appendix, 357–65.

lege friend and future South Carolina governor James Hammond, he further revealed why he had found Broussais' ideas so attractive. Hammond, who had no fortune or prominent family connections of his own, had married a rich heiress. Along with the heiress, he had acquired a large plantation near the South Carolina–Georgia border. To help make the plantation more efficient, Hammond introduced strict discipline and frequent floggings among the slaves and also decided to learn as much as he could about medicine so that he could have some idea of how to treat their ailments. He asked Nott to recommend a private course of study for this purpose.[5]

Nott tried to persuade Hammond that it was worth his while to undertake the reading necessary to acquire the rudiments of Broussais' system. Its principles, he argued, possessed all the logic of science, and its remedies were few and simple. It contrasted sharply with the old English system, he wrote, which had nothing of the simple order of science. The English system called for learning a list of diseases with an endless number of complicated prescriptions for each one; if one failed another was to be tried, and another, and another. This system, argued Nott, unlike that of Broussais, provided no distinct idea of the seat and nature of the disease to guide the physician.[6]

Broussais' idea that all disease could be explained on specific scientific principles was particularly attractive to Nott. Hammond had mentioned that he had broken two fevers by the use of calomel, the main form in which mercury was used in the early nineteenth century. Calomel was used in massive doses by nineteenth-century physicians, but Nott at this stage of his career made very little use of it. Nott warned Hammond against depending on his experience in this case. "Experience," wrote Nott, "has killed & still continues to kill its thousands." A physician, wrote Nott, prescribed a remedy, the patient recovered, and he could argue for the success of his treatment. But if the disease was not serious, the patient could have recovered under twenty different treatments, with each physician taking the credit. Most patients, argued Nott, would recover whatever the treatment, although the suffering and the duration of the illness would vary extensively.

The difficulty with becoming acquainted with Broussais' system, Nott

5. Drew Gilpin Faust, *James Henry Hammond and the Old South: A Design for Mastery* (Baton Rouge, 1982), 58–61, 69–78.
6. Nott to Hammond, June 11, 1832, in James Henry Hammond Papers, SCL.

conceded, was that one needed a sound grounding in anatomy and physiology. Anatomy was necessary for understanding physiology, which, he argued, was "the ground work of useful medical knowledge." Nott was a great enthusiast for physiology, which he termed "the most delightful of all studies." Throughout his career Nott was an ardent advocate of medical training as a route to a wider understanding of science and as a discipline of use to any civilized man. "Physiology," he wrote to Hammond, "embraces the only Metaphysics worth reading & no accomplished gentleman should be ignorant of it." Nott had difficulty believing that Hammond could possibly fail to relish the course of medical study he had outlined for him—"it does seem to me," he wrote, "that no man can fail to become fond of the study who can be fond of study of any kind." This enthusiasm for medicine stayed with Nott throughout his life. He believed that no one could fail to benefit from a scientific study of medicine, and he could never understand those who were not willing to do the necessary work. Though talent was of immense importance to a physician, he wrote, "it is far less valuable than Industry, close observation & Tact."[7]

In the early 1830s Nott began to build up a successful general practice in Columbia. As a member of a prominent South Carolina family and a well-trained doctor, Nott had no difficulty in gaining acceptance and patients. He treated a cross-section of South Carolinians, including both planters and their slaves, for, when necessary, southerners felt that they had to protect their property by having their slaves treated by a responsible physician. Some young physicians in the South survived partly because of the available business among the slaves, but Nott was also able to gain prompt acceptance as a physician to their powerful masters. When he wrote to James Hammond in 1832 he was sitting up with a patient at 2:00 A.M. on the first Wade Hampton's plantation near Columbia. Nott was Wade Hampton's personal physician in the last years of his life, as well as caring for Hampton's slaves. Hampton was one of the richest and most famous planters in America. Nott's connection with the Hampton family continued throughout his life. Within the year preceding Nott's death, he was called from New York to Baltimore to treat the third Wade Hampton's wife.[8]

7. *Ibid.*, and Nott to Hammond, May 6, 1832.
8. Nott to Hammond, [June 5, 1832], *ibid.*; Nott to Lyman C. Draper, August 11, 1870, in Draper Manuscripts, 13VV47, State Historical Society of Wisconsin, Madison; Michael P. Johnson and James L. Roark, *Black Masters: A Free Family of Color in the Old South* (New

From the beginning of his career Nott practiced medicine in the most general sense—combining internal medicine with any surgical procedures that were possible in the early nineteenth century. He also continued his interest in medical education and his strong academic bent. In 1833 he joined Dr. Robert W. Gibbes of Columbia in starting a preparatory school of medicine in the town. Gibbes was a young Charlestonian who had graduated from medical college there in 1830. He settled in Columbia, became a very successful physician, and was later well-known for his extensive natural history collection. Like Nott, he was to defend contemporary geology against religious objections, but he did it with much greater caution.[9]

In the announcement of the opening of their school Nott and Gibbes pointed out that most students entered medical school so ill-prepared that the first course of lectures was wasted on them. To alleviate this problem they proposed to offer preparatory lectures on anatomy, surgery, chemistry, and materia medica. Nott was to handle the anatomy and surgery and Gibbes the chemistry and materia medica. Nott had arranged for the construction of a building suitable for demonstrating anatomy, operative surgery, and the use of bandages, splints, and other medical apparatus. Clearly Nott wanted to go beyond general preparatory lectures to relive some of his busy and exciting days as a demonstrator of anatomy under Drs. Physick and Horner in Philadelphia. There were to be two courses of lectures each year, one beginning in November and the other in May. Nott always felt a strong desire to instruct, whether in person or through his writings.[10]

Nott was very much a South Carolinian as well as a physician, and while he was planning the opening of his medical preparatory school he was one of the attending surgeons at a duel fought near Columbia by two students of South Carolina College. Their argument began over who first took a dish of trout in the dining hall. Because they fought at only ten paces, the result was not surprising. One was shot in the abdomen, lin-

York, 1984), 139; Wade Hampton III to Dr. D. H. Trezevant, October 2, 1872, in Charles E. Cauthen (ed.), *Family Letters of the Three Wade Hamptons, 1782–1901* (Columbia, 1953), 144.

9. Sally G. Kohlstedt, *The Formation of the American Scientific Community: The American Association for the Advancement of Science, 1848–60* (Urbana, Ill., 1976), appendix; Columbia *Telescope*, October 8, 1833; Waring, *History of Medicine in South Carolina*, II, 89, 240; Richard M. Jellison and Phillip S. Swartz, "The Scientific Interests of Robert W. Gibbes," *South Carolina Historical Magazine*, LXVI (1965), 88.

10. Columbia *Telescope*, August 27, 1833.

gered for a day, and died. The other, Nott's patient, was shot through the thigh and suffered a dangerous fracture. Nott had him carried the fifteen miles into Columbia, and after waiting for two weeks because of fears of rupturing an artery, set the leg by using a jointed wooden frame which he devised. The patient was up and about by August, but later he fell and fractured the thigh again, and he died of a fever while a young medical student in Philadelphia. Nott apparently never fired a shot in anger in his life, but in his youth he absorbed and accepted many of the mores of his section. He fully accepted the concepts of honor and manhood that produced such a duel and eventually helped kill a generation of southerners, including two of his sons.[11]

By family and personal ties Nott was closely entwined with the controversial life of Columbia in the late 1820s and early 1830s. The tight-knit little community often buzzed with excitement as the South Carolina politicians clashed with the federal government over the tariff and bridled over possible northern interference with the institution of slavery. From the time of the passage of the "tariff of abominations" in 1828, South Carolina was swept by heated political discussions which culminated in 1832 in the nullification of the tariff of that year and the resignation of John C. Calhoun from the vice-presidency. After these years most South Carolinians profoundly distrusted the federal government and northern intentions, and distrust of northern intentions was accompanied by a rigorous defense of slavery.[12]

As the state capital and the site of the state college, Columbia assumed an importance and political sophistication out of all proportion to its size, and its very smallness ensured that its ruling elite constantly exchanged views. The total population of Columbia in 1830 was slightly over thirty-three hundred, including more than fifteen hundred slaves. The town was small but lively. When Karl Bernhard, Duke of Saxe-Weimer-Eisenach, visited Columbia in 1825, he said that "there seemed to be a great deal of life in the place," many well-provisioned stores, and "many elegant private houses."[13] Josiah's brother Henry Junius Nott,

11. Nott, "Description of a Modification of the Double Inclined Plane," *American Journal of the Medical Sciences*, o.s., XXIII (1838), 26–27; J. Marion Sims, *The Story of My Life* (1884; rpr. New York, 1968), 88–91; William E. Walker, "The South Carolina College Duel of 1833," *South Carolina Historical and Genealogical Magazine*, LXII (1951), 140–42.

12. See William W. Freehling, *Prelude to Civil War: The Nullification Controversy in South Carolina, 1816–1836* (1966; rpr. New York, 1968), 134–339.

13. Columbia, South Carolina, Census of 1830, RG 29, NA; Karl Bernhard, Duke of

who at times found life in Columbia tedious after several years in Europe, still was prepared to admit that "after all it is not a bad country where one can, on an average twice a week throughout the year, eat Scotch salmon, pates de foie gras, and tranches de Chevreuil moistened with Champagne, Chateaux Margaux, Johanisberger, not to mention such common things as Amontillado & Sercial."[14] The elite in Columbia had a social life that revolved around a fairly small number of families; and political, religious, and general intellectual discussion was an integral part of the constant round of dinners.

The Notts had been at the heart of Columbia affairs since Josiah's father, Abraham, had moved there in 1804. Abraham had been intendant (mayor) of the town in 1807 and was a trustee of the college from 1805 until his death. In the 1820s, as president of the South Carolina Court of Appeals, he was at the head of the legal profession in the state. It was said of him that he "brought into the social circle the keen, shrewd, and flashing intellect which distinguished him on the bench." In the late 1820s Abraham began to show signs of tuberculosis. It was a disease for which neither Josiah nor his older physician brother William could do anything, and their father died in June, 1830, while on his way from Columbia to his plantation in the Union District.[15] Josiah inherited the family home in Columbia on the condition that he pay $4,000 (without interest) into the estate before Abraham's youngest child reached the age of twenty-one. Abraham's oldest son, physician William Blackstone Nott, was already living in the Union District, and he was given the land on which he lived. Most of the estate, of which the most important part was the plantation on the Pacolet River, was left for the support of his wife and the education of his five youngest children. The three boys—James, Rufus, and Gustavus Adolphus—became physicians after first attending South Carolina College. Josiah's mother, Angelica, lived until the late 1840s. In her later years she spent much of her time in the up-country at Limestone

---

Saxe-Weimar-Eisenach, *Travels Through North America, During the Years 1825 and 1826* (2 vols.; Philadelphia, 1828), I, 208.

14. Henry J. Nott to Hugh S. Legaré, May 7, 1831, Henry Junius Nott Papers, SCL.

15. Helen K. Hennig (ed.), *Columbia: Capital City of South Carolina, 1786–1836* (Columbia, 1936), 70; John B. O'Neall, *Biographical Sketches of the Bench and Bar of South Carolina* (2 vols.; Charleston, 1859), I, 121–24; James D. Bailey, *History of Grindal Shoals and Some Early Adjacent Families* (Gaffney, SC., 1927), 71; Charleston *Courier,* June 25, 1830; W. C. Preston, *South Carolinian,* May 17, 1835, in Evert A. Duyckinck and George L. Duyckinck, *Cyclopaedia of American Literature* (2 vols.; New York, 1855), II, 250 (quotation).

Springs, where her son William Blackstone later practiced and spent much of his life.[16]

Though not the eldest son, Josiah had inherited the Columbia family home, and soon after his father's death he entered into the marriage that was practically essential for a young physician. He also established firm family ties to the South Carolina aristocracy. The Nott children had never experienced any difficulty in being accepted as dyed-in-the-wool southerners and prominent South Carolinians, but in 1832 through his marriage Josiah entered into an alliance with some of the most prominent families in the state. In March of that year he married Sarah (Sally) Cantey Deas, the daughter of James Sutherland Deas. Her cousin Lynch Harry Deas had been in Nott's graduating class at South Carolina College, and her father knew Josiah's father not only as a judge but also because they both had served as members of the South Carolina College Board of Trustees. James Deas was a prominent Camden planter and lawyer. His father, John, had come to South Carolina from Scotland in the mid-eighteenth century and had become a wealthy Charleston merchant. James had moved up-country to Camden after his admission to the bar in 1808. He married Margaret Chestnut, the daughter of the very wealthy first John Chestnut and Sarah Cantey. The Canteys and the Chestnuts were two of the most prominent families in the region; the Canteys had been in South Carolina since the seventeenth century. Nott's father-in-law had been extremely active in South Carolina politics, and as a member of the state senate from 1824 to 1832 had become one of the most important supporters of the nullification movement and states' rights. In the year of Nott's marriage Deas was engaged in a particularly bitter fight for his senate seat with his brother-in-law James Chestnut, who ran as a Unionist. Deas's defeat in this 1832 election embittered him and alienated him from his brother-in-law. Nott had married into a leading southern states' rights family, and, in spite of the bitterness between his father-in-law and James Chestnut, he now gained all the advantages of family ties to the Deases, the Canteys, and the Chestnuts. The Notts' first child, James Deas, was born in January, 1833, and a second, Edward Fisher, in the following year.[17]

16. Will of Abraham Nott, typed copy in the South Carolina Department of Archives; O'Neall, *Bench and Bar of South Carolina,* I, 123; manuscript obituary of William B. Nott (1795–1864), in Joseph Banks Lyle Papers, SCL.

17. Brent H. Holcomb, *Marriage and Death Notices from Camden, South Carolina, News-*

While Josiah Nott quietly laid a firm basis for his practice and future prosperity, he watched his brother Henry and his old mentor Thomas Cooper shake the close confines of Columbia with more of the religious controversy that had beset Cooper and South Carolina College in the early 1820s. Both Henry Nott and Thomas Cooper were to die before the decade was over, and in the following years Josiah Nott took pleasure in urging with even greater force the arguments for which they had been attacked by the orthodox clergy.

Henry Nott had begun his career by following his father's profession. After attending South Carolina College he had read law and in 1818 was admitted to the bar. For several years he was in partnership with David C. McCord, who later edited the Columbia *Telescope*. McCord was a close friend of Thomas Cooper and was one of the most ardent and outspoken states' righters in South Carolina. Law soon palled for Henry Nott. He was attracted to language and literature, and in 1821 he went to Europe for three years. He spent much of his time in France and Holland and while there married a native of Brussels. On returning to Columbia, he abandoned law and in 1825 took up the professorship of the elements of criticism, logic, and philosophy of languages in South Carolina College. Henry delighted in being irreverent, and he slipped easily into the free-thinking atmosphere encouraged by Thomas Cooper.[18] When New Englander Jared Sparks visited the college in 1826 and dined with a party that included Judge Abraham Nott and David McCord, he commented that "the conversation was that of men of intelligence, observation, and knowledge of the world." Henry Nott helped Sparks examine the state archives, and Cooper proposed a controversial article on the Pentateuch for Sparks's *North American Review*. After dining out at a Columbia home

papers, 1816–1865 (Easley, S.C., 1978), 53, 162; Thomas J. Kirkland and Robert M. Kennedy, *Historic Camden*, Pt. 2, *The Nineteenth Century* (Columbia, 1926), 85–86, 334, 376–78; *Roll of Students of S. Carolina College, 1805–1905* (Columbia, 1905); Joseph S. Ames, "Cantey Family," *South Carolina Historical and Genealogical Magazine*, XI (1910), 203–58; Edwin J. Scott, *Random Recollections of a Long Life, 1806–1876* (Columbia, 1884), 18; gravestones, First Presbyterian Church, Columbia, South Carolina, and Magnolia Cemetery, Mobile, Alabama.

18. Maximilian La Borde, *History of the South Carolina College* (2d ed.; Charleston, 1874), 209–17; Duyckinck and Duyckinck, *Cyclopaedia of American Literature*, II, 253–54; O'Neall, *Bench and Bar of South Carolina*, II, 509–10, 512–13; George A. Wauchope, *The Writers of South Carolina* (Columbia, 1910), 59, 303; Scott, *Random Recollections*, 56–58; Edwin A. Alderman and Joel C. Harris (eds.), *Library of Southern Literature*, IX (Atlanta, 1909), 3797–99; Daniel W. Hollis, *University of South Carolina*, I, *South Carolina College* (Columbia, 1951), 79–82; Malone, *Public Life of Cooper*, 325–28.

Sparks decided that since leaving Boston he had "not found a more intelligent, literary, and hospitable society than in this place." When Englishman George Featherstonehaugh visited Columbia and the college in
1836, after a decade of controversy in both the state and the college, he
reacted somewhat differently. After dining with Thomas Cooper and
some of the professors, he commented that what "particularly struck me
at this dinner was the total want of caution and reserve in the ultra opinions they expressed about religion and politics." [19]

Cooper's clashes with the clergy had continued since the days when
Josiah Nott had studied under him at the college, but he had survived as
president, largely because he continued to be an ardent defender of South
Carolina and its institutions. Beginning in 1827, Cooper vehemently attacked the tariff and even questioned the value of the Union. Even in this
most hotheaded of southern states Cooper became one of the most ardent defenders of states' rights. At the same time, Cooper continued his
attack on the idea of innate black equality that he had begun in the 1820s.
Cooper argued openly that blacks were "an inferior variety of the animal, man." [20]

As he got older Cooper showed a greater willingness openly to challenge the scientific validity of the Bible. Cooper was a born controversialist. He could never keep quiet, and he had no sense of caution. Attacks on him mounted, and in 1831 the South Carolina legislature passed a
resolution calling on the trustees of the college to investigate his actions.
His opponents were now particularly concerned that in talks at the college he had doubted the accuracy of the geological account given in
Genesis and had questioned the authority of Moses. The Presbyterian
clergy were also angered that he had attacked the idea of a paid clergy as
contrary to true religion and a drain on the nation's productivity and that
he had joined in the national controversy regarding the delivery of mail
on Sundays. The orthodox were trying to end mail deliveries on Sundays,
and Cooper in 1829 had published an anonymous pamphlet defending the
government from religious interference. Cooper's anonymous pamphlets
were usually easily recognized. [21]

19. "Sparks Journal of a Southern Tour in 1826," in Herbert B. Adams (ed.), *The Life and
Writings of Jared Sparks: Comprising Selections from His Journals and Correspondence* (2 vols.;
Boston, 1893), 436–42; George W. Featherstonehaugh, *Excursion Through the Slave States*
(1844; rpr. New York, 1968), 157.

20. Freehling, *Prelude to Civil War*, 128–30, 324; Malone, *Public Life of Cooper*, pp. 307–
308; *Southern Literary Journal*, I (1835), 192.

21. Malone, *Public Life of Cooper*, 337–50.

Cooper did not wait for the results of an investigation. In a vigorous, cleverly conceived pamphlet he discussed his own case, arguing that the effort to remove him as president of the college was part of the eternal effort to stifle free inquiry; his opponents, he wrote, were attempting to crush the freedom of religion guaranteed by the South Carolina Constitution. In this case, he said, the orthodox clergy who opposed him were also being used by the Unionist opponents of states' rights, who disliked his political opinions. Cooper then went on to repeat, in vigorous prose, the main ideas for which he had been attacked in the past ten years, arguing that Christianity formed no part of the law of the United States or South Carolina; that the setting aside of a Sabbath day was of human authority alone; that the New Testament forbade public prayers; that the New Testament did not sanction a paid clergy; that a paid clergy was a drain on the productivity of the nation; that the employment of a chaplain by Congress was "a fraud on the public treasury, and a disgrace to the national legislature"; that the five books of Moses (the Pentateuch) were not written by Moses in the state in which they now existed; and that the facts of geology clashed with the material in those books.[22]

Even though Cooper had no hesitation in admitting much of what he was accused of, he was eventually supported by the trustees. Students gave evidence in his behalf, and he was helped by his friends among the extreme states' righters. But the college was suffering from the continued controversy. Enrollment had declined, and continued to decline, and Cooper was eventually obliged quietly to retire. He gave up the presidency at the end of 1833.[23]

Cooper's retirement still did not bring peace to South Carolina College, and in 1834 Henry Nott found himself at the center of a controversy, which like those involving Thomas Cooper helped inspire Josiah Nott with a lifelong enmity for the clergy. In 1834 Henry Nott angered the South Carolina clergy and gave the public more reason to link the Notts with the irreligious ideas of Thomas Cooper. Henry had become a frequent contributor to the *Southern Review,* and in 1834 he published a more ambitious work, the *Novellettes of a Traveller,* a two-volume picaresque novel loosely woven around the adventures of Thomas Singularity, journeyman printer. The book was an immediate success, but it was attacked by the clergy and by some of the general religious community. It

22. *The Case of Thomas Cooper, M.D.* (Columbia, 1831), iii–vi, 1–6, 10–11, 28, 35–41.
23. *Dr. Cooper's Defense Before the Board of Trustees* (Columbia, 1832); Malone, *Public Life of Cooper,* 355–63.

was suggested that Henry Nott was irreligious and that his book was well-designed to corrupt youth. Although the criticism was exaggerated, Henry Nott clearly intended to dig at some of those in South Carolina who were easily offended. Eighteen years before, his father, Abraham, had caused an uproar in the state, and nearly lost an election as judge, when he had attacked a state legislative act concerning the judiciary by saying "that which was conceived in sin must be brought forth in iniquity." This paraphrase of a biblical phrase for a secular purpose caused considerable offense. In his novel, Henry Nott used almost the same phrase in his first pages.[24]

Most of Henry Nott's book was innocuous enough, but it contained sentiments that angered the straitlaced, particularly the clergy. Singularity, Nott declared, was a man who "exhibited the sublime and, in this age, rare spectacle of one who disdaining the vulgar and idle prejudices that trammel civilized society, dared both to think and act according to the pure dictates of reason." Singularity drank for the simple reason that he loved it: "As the Creator wills the happiness of his creatures, all inclinations are implanted to be gratified." That Singularity had been brought up according to no fixed principle was a cause for rejoicing, for "Virtue is only what people choose to call so!" Entire nations had sanctioned stealing, murder, and prostitution.[25]

One pamphleteer stated that it was "well known" that Henry Nott was "a most violent heretic." He wanted to know why the trustees ignored what all Nott's friends, acquaintances, and students at the college knew— that Henry Nott was "heretical, nay deistical." The pamphleteer's main criticism of the book was that it was simply a tale of low debaucheries, and he quoted the passage "all inclinations are implanted to be gratified." The book was said to be in the hands of every student in the college. For all his sins, the pamphleteer wrote, Thomas Cooper "is at least as orthodox as Professor Nott."[26]

The attack on Henry Nott was based on more than his novel, for it was

---

24. Alderman and Harris (eds.), *Library of Southern Literature*, IX, 3798–3801; O'Neall, *Bench and Bar*, I, 121–22 (quotation), II, 513; Bailey, *History of Grindal Shoals*, 60–61; Henry J. Nott, *Novellettes of a Traveller or, Odds and Ends from the Knapsack of Thomas Singularity, Journeyman Printer* (2 vols.; New York, 1834), I, 7. The phrase in James 1:15 is "when lust hath conceived it bringeth forth sin."

25. Nott, *Novellettes*, I, 6, 94.

26. "The Spy in Columbia," *The Mysteries of Government, or Favoritism Unveiled: A New-Years Present to the People of South Carolina* (n.p., 1835), 3–24.

known that he found Cooper's skepticism and freethinking to be compatible with his own ideas. In the spring of 1835, James Louis Pettigru stated in a letter to Hugh S. Legaré that "Nott is exceedingly odious to the religious public, and he bravely declares he would rather quit the College than degrade his freedom by going to church so much as once a day on Sunday." Both Pettigru and Legaré were close friends of Henry Nott. Several years before, Nott had sarcastically told Legaré in a letter that "to day being the Sabbath, as in duty bound I abstain from all secular employments, & eat dinner with Hampton." In the same letter he showed he was far removed from being a Sabbatarian when, daringly for the age, he joked about Legaré's sexual exploits with blacks. He described the rounds of dinners and entertainments that made Columbia bearable for a young man, but continued by saying that "for a Batchelor I confess there is something still wanting—You, however with the true philosophy, have always taken the goods the gods have provided you—And like Desdemona 'battened on a moor' in absence of better pasturage."[27]

That descendant of New England divines Abraham Nott and his Presbyterian wife, Angelica, had produced sons who delighted in scoffing at the orthodox religious establishment. Henry angered the clergy in the 1830s, Josiah was to infuriate them in the 1840s and 1850s, and their younger brother James, who graduated from South Carolina College in 1832, showed signs of the same lack of reverence for the orthodox and their beliefs. Writing to a friend in 1836, he cast his letter in the form of the "5th Chapter of Parables According to the Gospel of Cheves." Young Cheves was a prominent South Carolinian and a friend of the Notts. The letter began, "And it came to pass in the days of the parables that there was a poor miserable doctor who lived in the town of Columbia," and went on to describe how a friend had smuggled cigars into France in the legs of his boots. The letter indicates that parable letter writing had become popular among a group of friends.[28] It was innocent enough stuff, but the attitudes it revealed were not designed to endear the Notts to the Presbyterian clergy.

Columbia's strange mix of ardent states' rights, white fears of interference with slavery, and freethinking on religious matters left a clear

27. Pettigru to Legaré, May 31, 1835, in James P. Carson, *Life, Letters and Speeches of James Louis Pettigru, the Union Man of South Carolina* (Washington, D.C., 1920), 174; Henry J. Nott to Legaré, May 7, 1831, in Henry Junius Nott Papers.
28. James Nott to James M. Gage, September 1, 1836, in James M. Gage Papers, SHC.

mark on the mature Josiah Nott. South Carolina was strongly conservative in some matters but remarkably liberal in others. The states' rights position was advocated by many religious conservatives, but it was also defended by the radical and freethinking Thomas Cooper, his friends, and followers. For Cooper, states' rights meant resistance to centralized tyranny. Cooper's very presence as president of the state college testified to the complexity of South Carolina thought in these years. A man who had been considered too radical for Thomas Jefferson to appoint with ease to his University of Virginia became the acknowledged leader of South Carolina education. His unorthodoxy and anticlerical views were public knowledge, but he survived for fifteen years and even then was allowed to exit gracefully.

Josiah Nott found Cooper's mix of skepticism, belief in white superiority, and fervent defense of states' rights particularly attractive. The Nott boys had grown to manhood in a family of intellectual tolerance, wit, and controversial vigor. They were attracted to cosmopolitan ideas. But they also grew up in a state in which white dominance seemed essential to future social peace and economic prosperity. Josiah Nott emerged from this milieu to become a freethinker and a devout believer in the cause of science, but he also became a bigoted, narrow-minded racist. Nott's basic attitudes had been shaped by the mid-1830s, but his energies were still absorbed by establishing a practice, his marriage, and a desire to extend his medical knowledge. His fears for the South and the white race had not yet combined with his passion for science and new ideas to produce a vigorous controversialist. Still fired with the scientific interest in medicine that had been instilled in him in Philadelphia and that had persuaded him to present the medical ideas of Broussais to the American public, he decided in 1835 to further his education in Paris.

Paris was becoming the mecca for ambitious young American physicians in the 1830s, particularly for those like Nott who had enthusiastically adopted the doctrines of the French school. Many young doctors went to France as soon as they had obtained their American degree, but this would have been difficult for Nott. At the time he returned from Philadelphia to Columbia in 1829, his father was already suffering from the illness that led to his death, and in the following years Nott's private concerns kept him in South Carolina. The death of his father in 1830, his courtship of and eventual marriage to Sarah Deas in 1832, and his wife's two pregnancies in the next two years made it difficult to contemplate a year abroad. But there was little chance of his interest in France waning for two of his brothers went to study in Paris—William in 1833 and James in 1834. James was still there in the spring of 1835 when Josiah prepared for his journey. This was to be no student jaunt to Paris. Josiah took with him his wife, his two children, two of his medical students, and his two younger brothers—Adolphus and Rufus—who were also completing their training as physicians. The family links went even further, for one of his students was James Gage, the son of a family closely tied to the Notts in the Union District; Gage's brother Robert married Josiah's sister Eliza. Whether in Columbia, Paris, or Mobile, Nott was usually part of a closely connected web of relations.

Nott and his party left New York for Paris in the spring of 1835. Nott carried a letter of introduction to David Baillie Warden, an American citizen long resident in Paris, who made it his business to welcome and help American visitors. His sponsor said Nott was visiting Europe "chiefly for Professional improvement."[29] Nott also, of course, was to take the opportunity to see more of Paris and Europe than the hospitals.

During the 1830s, more than two hundred American medical men studied in Paris. Most of them had already graduated in the United States, although Nott, by establishing a successful practice in Columbia, had advanced further than the majority of American students. In addition to being on the cutting edge of medical theory, Paris had a host of practical advantages for foreign students. The city had a flourishing medical school with many courses of lectures and numerous hospitals with clinics and opportunities for observation. The lectures and clinics could be attended free by foreigners who were not signed up for study toward a degree. These could be supplemented with private lessons and opportunities for dissection, both of which could be obtained for reasonable fees.

The glory of Paris for American medical students was the opportunity to observe the actual practice of medicine at close hand by attending some of the numerous clinics in the Paris hospitals. Nott had obtained the best possible practical experience available in America at the Philadelphia Almshouse, but the work there was dwarfed by the Paris opportunities. The Paris hospitals were of particular importance because of the

29. The best source of information for Nott's year in Paris is the Gage Papers. There is also information in the Hammond Papers, SCL. See also J. A. Washington to David B. Warden, March 18, 1835, in David Baillie Warden Papers, Maryland Historical Society, Baltimore.

extent to which French medical theory of the 1830s stressed detailed examinations, autopsies, and the gathering of statistics. The greatest stress was on relating the findings obtained through detailed examinations to the lesions found in the autopsies and then compiling data from these findings. At the time of Nott's visit, Paris had a dozen hospitals, and in 1835 more than seventy thousand patients were treated at them. Apart from general hospitals, there were also specialist hospitals for children, obstetrics, venereal diseases, skin diseases, and mental disorders. The most famous of the hospitals were the Hôtel Dieu, noted for its surgery, La Pitié, and La Charité, but the Paris hospitals in general were the most active in the world in the 1830s.

By 1835 the influence of Nott's early idol Broussais had undergone a sharp decline in Paris. Younger physicians had revolted against Broussais' insistence on attributing practically all diseases to inflammation of the gastrointestinal tract, his dogmatism, and his excessive use of bleeding. "Eclectism" was the new mode; the leading physicians of the 1830s emphasized the detailed observation of patients, the connection of symptoms to evidence revealed by post-mortems, and the careful classification of specific diseases. The great emphasis was on statistics and numerical analysis. As the influence of Broussais declined, the dominating figure in Parisian medicine was Pierre-Charles-Alexandre Louis. He was particularly popular among the American students. The books that he wrote from 1825 to the mid-1830s were based on thousands of case histories. He identified and classified specific diseases and attacked Broussais' faith in bleeding, but he offered few solutions. Research and exact observation, not cures, were at the heart of the medicine of Louis and his followers. Louis' clinic at La Pitié was a center of attraction for American students in Paris in the mid-1830s.

Of the other Parisian physicians at this time the most successful and popular were Auguste François Chomel and Gabriel Andral. Chomel, who from 1827 was professor of clinical medicine at La Charité, was a strong supporter of the early work of Louis, and Louis gathered his data for his famous early works while in the wards at La Charité. Like Louis, Chomel believed firmly in observation and numerical analysis. Andral was a collegue of Louis at La Pitié, was also an "eclecticist," and was very popular among the American students. While Louis and his friends were at the height of their influence in the mid-1830s, still younger doctors were beginning to gain an enthusiastic following. Alfred-Armand-Louis-Marie Velpeau, who was the leading young French surgeon, began to work and teach at La Charité in 1835. Broussais still had his followers in Paris in the 1830s, but the earlier enthusiasm was much diminished, and he was not helped by his poor lecturing style.[30]

Nott and his party arrived in Le Havre from New York early in May, 1835, and traveled to Paris by way of Rouen. Even New York and Philadelphia had in no way prepared Nott for the sights and sounds of Europe. No reading, he told his friend Hammond, could prepare one for the rich variety of experiences that were to be encountered there. "The manners & customs of the people," he wrote, "& everything no matter how trivial interest you because it is Europe of which you have heard and read so much from early childhood." At Rouen, on the way to Paris, he was amazed by the size and richness of the cathedral. "When I first walked into this Church & looked around," he wrote, "I felt as if I was in the dwelling place of the Almighty himself." After settling his family in Paris, Nott took a quick trip to Liverpool on business for his father-in-law, James Deas. He traveled by way of Calais and Dover to London and then went north through the Midlands to Manchester and Liverpool. He was gone for less than two weeks and expressed his intention of settling down in Paris for a year's hard work. He said that his brain was already "all in confusion" and that the fault of most travelers was "to see too much & study too little."[31]

This intention of settling down in Paris was soon frustrated, for early in August the Notts' firstborn son, James Deas Nott, who was just eighteen months old, died. The death of young children was commonplace in the 1830s, but there are indications that the death of this first child was deeply felt. Although he was first buried in Paris, his parents had him exhumed in the following year, and they took his body with them on their return to America. In May, 1836, he was buried in Columbia. His epitaph, almost certainly written by Josiah, had the cadence and feeling that Nott was capable of on solemn occasions: "It is some consolation to those who loved him most to know that he sleeps in his native land amidst the tombs of his ancestors."[32] In the next thirty years the Notts were to bury six more of their children.

30. For medicine in Paris at this time see Ackerknecht, *Medicine at the Paris Hospital;* Jones (ed.), *Parisian Education*, introduction; Oliver Wendell Holmes, *Medical Essays, 1842–1882* (Boston, 1892), 426–36; William Osler, *An Alabama Student and Other Biographical Essays* (London, 1908), 5–10, 189–210; Russell M. Jones, "American Doctors and the Parisian Medical World, 1830–1840," *Bulletin of the History of Medicine*, XLVII (1973), 40–65.

31. Nott to James Hammond, May 28, 1835, in Hammond Papers, SCL.

32. Gravestone, First Presbyterian Church, Columbia, South Carolina.

It seems likely that it was the death of their first child that prompted Nott to take his wife on a visit to the British Isles. Nott's manner and style of traveling were clearly revealed later in his Paris year, when he gave detailed instructions for such a trip to his pupil James Gage. Gage was thinking of a trip to Ireland, even though Nott, with a generosity that was characteristic throughout his life, was advancing him money to make up for the nonarrival of a draft from his father. Gage's father was less open-handed than Nott and suggested to his son that perhaps it would be better to spend his money on surgical instruments than on a trip and warned him specifically that if he went to Ireland he was to avoid their relatives in Coleraine; they might want to come to America. Nott, however, as he demonstrated later with his own sons, never begrudged a youthful fling, and he tried to make sure that Gage would see what should be seen and that he would be no greenhorn while traveling.[33]

Nott visited England in the last years before the railroad replaced the coaches, and his instructions to Gage reflected this transition process. They also reflected Nott's eye for detail and the practical streak that was to stay with him throughout his life. The best route, he said, was Paris to Calais to Dover, and he tried to make sure that Gage would commit no obvious social errors. In France, he said, the coachman was to be tipped nothing, the conductor about five francs. In England, where the coachman usually drove a stretch of forty miles, he should be given a shilling; the conductor (when there was one) went eighty miles and should be given half a crown. The coachman was to be called "coachee" not "driver." At inns on the road, the waiter should be tipped sixpence, in hotels a shilling a day, and the maid and the boots sixpence a day. Nott always enjoyed giving detailed instructions.

In London Nott had stayed in Upper Norton Street, near the upper end of Regent Street, and he suggested that Gage stay along the same street. Nott had seen the main tourist sights, and he gave his pupil his usual practical suggestions. St. Paul's, the Customs House, and the Tower were to be seen in a group on one day, along with the pedestrian tunnel under the Thames (this was under construction at the time). For the rest, Nott recommended all the favorite tourist spots—the King's Palace, St. James Palace, Westminster Abbey, the House of Lords, Northumberland

33. Undated instructions in Nott's hand, in Gage Papers, are used for information in this and the following three paragraphs; also John Gage to James Gage, January 3, 1836, in Gage Papers.

House, the Guildhall, Apsley House, the National Gallery, Somerset House, the zoo in Regent's Park, and Hampton Court.

After London, Gage was told to follow Nott's route north to Liverpool in a series of coach stages, with a final short trip on the new railroad. He was to visit Windsor Castle before going on to Oxford. Coaches passed so often that Nott suggested that Gage should simply wait at the roadside with his trunk. After a guided tour of Oxford, Nott had gone on to Warwick and Kenilworth. Nott particularly liked Warwick Castle. Birmingham was to be visited "to get the *general* idea." The Birmingham of the mid-1830s was a far cry from Columbia and Union, and even New York and Philadelphia hardly prepared the American traveler for the shock of the new industrial England. Nott particularly urged Gage to leave Birmingham by the Wolverhampton Road so as not to miss "the greatest sight in England viz the *Coal Mines*." Manchester, Nott thought, was worth only a day. Then Gage was to take the railroad to Liverpool. Liverpool, Nott thought, had some things worth seeing—the City Hall (for its Lawrences and other paintings), the docks, and the "fine statue of Canning." In all the English cities Nott suggested walking through the fashionable streets to see the sights, and Gage was "to ask about every thing—there is no harm in it." The gregarious and assured Nott thought all others could proceed as easily and confidently as himself.

From Liverpool Nott had sailed to Ireland, and there he demonstrated sympathy for the European downtrodden that he never had for the slaves of the South. This sympathy was political rather than ethnic, for in spite of the Scotch-Irish origins of his mother Nott never identified himself with any of the inhabitants of Ireland. He later wrote of the Scotch-Irish, who dominated the area of the Union District in which he had spent many of his early years, that after generations of intermarriage "the majority in its population was stupid and debased in the extreme." He showed none of this scorn for the oppressed population he saw in Ireland in 1835.[34]

For Nott, from the backcountry of South Carolina, what was immediately striking in Ireland was the intensity of cultivation. In England and France, this had not struck him because, he said, there were so many woods and noble estates, "but in Ireland, hill & dale to the last inch, up

---

34. For this and the following two paragraphs see Nott to James Gage, September 19, 1835, in Gage Papers. For the quotation regarding the Union District population see Josiah C. Nott and George R. Gliddon, *Types of Mankind* (Philadelphia, 1854), 408.

to the cottage door, is in cultivation." The potatoes, he said, were "as large as pumpkins." Nott was impressed by Dublin, but he commented upon its extremes. He thought that the new part of Dublin was "splendid" and its public buildings "far superior to those of London." Yet in contrast, there was "a great deal of squalid wretchedness." The streets of Dublin and the rest of Ireland were thronged with beggars—"the people have been so ground down by oppression that it could not be otherwise." And even though Ireland's fetters would soon be broken, Nott argued, it would take years "for the mass of the people to recover from the ignorance & degradation into which they have been cast." Nott, like so many other southerners, had no thought that his comments on the contrasts of Ireland could have any relevance to his own section of the United States. At this time he simply assumed that comments on tyranny or oppression in Europe had no relevance to black slavery; later he was to spend much of his time trying to prove that the oppression of the blacks was not oppression but the best possible relationship between the white and black races.

From Dublin Nott went to Belfast and then on the lovely journey up the Clyde by way of Greenock to Glasgow and then on to Edinburgh. In Edinburgh Nott went to hear Irish nationalist Daniel O'Connell. For this he paid one shilling and sixpence. The audience was seated at long pine tables and served with "little hard sour apples, pears little better & cakes made with a little sugar & fennel seed." The Madeira that came with it, said Nott, would have defied even Broussais' analysis. O'Connell, he wrote, had "the look to me [of] a man from low society, who has forced himself up by dint of energy & talent." But his cause not his talent, thought Nott, had given him his great reputation—he had had the boldness to tell "the oppressors" of the wrongs of the people. Nott always ardently defended white political freedom and individual rights.

While Nott and his wife were in Great Britain, one of Nott's brothers, James, who had spent the previous year in Paris, returned to America. In New York, in a French restaurant, he ran into his brother-in-law Robert Gage, the brother of Nott's pupil James Gage. Henry Junius Nott was also in New York. This group, including Josiah, Adolphus, Rufus, and James Gage in Paris, shared their likes, dislikes, and political sentiments. Robert wrote to his brother in Paris to tell him that the country was in a ferment because "the daring and ingenious measures of the abolitionists begin to raise a storm in the south." The South's safety and liberty, he said, were in danger. There was a need for meetings and committees of vigilance in every quarter "to visit with the strong arm of the law & if it must be Lynches law every man who meddles with our private relations—& as a late resort to secede from the Union in one unbroken Phalanx when we are no longer safe under its Constitution & laws." These were extreme views for 1835, but of all the southern states they were most likely to be found in South Carolina, and they were particularly strong among Nott's friends and relations. Nott mixed with those who were on the extreme states' rights wing in South Carolina politics, and the extremists in South Carolina were the most extreme in the South. The reports sent to Paris from the South Carolina backcountry in the winter of 1835–1836 were that business was fine and cotton was selling high—"every body thrives hereabouts but the Drs," wrote Robert Gage, "they have no practice save Gonorhoeas." But in spite of the prosperity, Gage's father stressed the raging fuss about emancipation and said that the slaveholding states should not allow the issue to be discussed in Congress.[35]

Resistance and secession were in the air in South Carolina in the mid-1830s, and at the heart of the fears were blacks and the institution of slavery. Although business seemed good in the up-country, many in the state were disillusioned by both the political and the economic situation and were ready to move and make a fresh start in the rich lands of Alabama and Mississippi. In November, 1835, Hugh S. Legaré wrote to South Carolina from Brussels that while he was in Paris he had met some Carolinians "whose accounts of matters there were darker by far than my worst imaginings—and God knows that is saying every thing." Josiah Nott and his wife had spoken of "the whole country about the Wateree and Congaree, including that town and Columbia, as literally breaking up and moving off *en masse* to the West."[36] Nott was thinking of doing the same, but at least in the winter of 1835–1836 he could for a time forget the South's political problems as he threw himself into broadening his knowledge of medicine.

Nott left no detailed record of his Parisian medical studies, which began in earnest in November, 1835, although he later commented that he "attended the Hospitals everyday," and he was much influenced by the

35. Robert I. Gage to James Gage, August 31, November 12, 1835, and John Gage to James Gage, November 15, 1835, in Gage Papers.
36. Legaré to A. Huger, November 21, 1835, *Writings of Hugh Swinton Legaré,* ed. by His Sister (2 vols.; 1846; rpr. New York, 1970), 221.

great Louis. The general pattern for American students was well set by this time. The opportunities were great, and the days were long. Dr. John Bassett, a student from Alabama, who was there in 1836, and who, like Nott, was a practicing physician, described a spartan daily routine in a letter home: "I get up in the morning at six o'clock and am at La Charité by seven, follow Velpeau until eight, see him operate and lecture until after nine, breakfast at ten at a cafe. At eleven I am at a school of practical anatomy, where I dissect until two. Then I attend a class of practical surgery until three; then hear Broussais and Andral until five; then dine. At seven I attend Helmagrande's class of midwifery, which lasts until nine; then I come to my room and read or write until eleven, when I retire." [37]

Unlike Bassett, Nott had his wife and family with him, but for anyone who wished to imbibe the medical training and atmosphere of Paris the days were very full. Dr. Elisha Bartlett, who was in Paris in the 1820s, said, "We are continually engaged from half-past six in the morning until bed time. Visits are made at all the hospitals by candle-light, and a lecture delivered at most of them immediately after the visit." When Oliver Wendell Holmes was in Paris in the 1830s he spent "long hours" in the wards and autopsy room of La Pitié. Louis was the center of attraction there, and most American students tried to attend La Pitié for at least part of their stay. W. W. Gerhard, who graduated from the University of Pennsylvania in 1831 and immediately went to Paris, visited a clinic at Saltpêtrière and a surgical lecture at La Pitié before breakfasting at ten. The rest of the day until eight in the evening was divided between lectures at the school of medicine, a private course in anatomy, and a private clinic at La Charité. He said that he intended to vary his attendance at different hospitals during his stay. With two other Americans he had arranged to pay Louis for private lessons, and the same three had also arranged to study pathology at La Pitié three afternoons a week. [38]

In his year of study in Paris Nott was weaned from his youthful passion for the theories of Broussais. Louis and his followers were not only casting doubt on bleeding as a panacea, they were also challenging the efficacy of a host of harsh drugs so beloved of early nineteenth-century physicians.

37. Nott, *Two Lectures, on the Natural History of the Caucasian and Negro Races* (Mobile, 1844), 17; Nott to Doctor Louis, May 26, 1836, to Frederick May, May 26, 1836, in Hammond Papers, SCL; Bassett quoted in Osler, *An Alabama Student*, 7.
38. Osler, *An Alabama Student*, 7; "Elisha Bartlett: A Rhode Island Philosopher," *ibid.*, III–12; Holmes, *Medical Essays*, 431–33. For W. W. Gerhard see "The Influence of Louis on American Medicine," in Osler, *An Alabama Student*, 204–206.

Much of contemporary treatment was useless or even harmful, and therapeutic caution was often a help. Some, however, seemed to go as far as therapeutic nihilism, and to some Americans it appeared that the French were vitally interested in finding the specific location of the disease, or what had been its specific location, but less interested in effecting a cure. J. M. Warren, who studied in Paris in the 1830s, commented to his father about Parisian medicine that "it seems to be more an object to study the natural history of disease and to perform an operation beautifully and quickly than to save the life of a patient."[39] Nott never fell into this scientific trap, but his year in Paris, combined with his steadily accumulating experience, left him much less certain than he had been at the time of his early publications on Broussais.

A longtime colleague of Nott's, Dr. William H. Anderson, commented after Nott's death that he was extremely cautious in the use of drugs. Although at times Nott went to extremes in advocating specific remedies that seemed efficacious, once he discovered that the remedy was not what he had hoped he dropped it. "Having an accurate knowledge of pathological anatomy, and knowing too well the uncertainty of therapeutical remedies in profound changes of the tissues," Anderson said of Nott, "he was not much wedded to the use of drugs unless enlightened experience proved their unquestionable value. It may be safely said that he did not harm by rash and profuse medication." Nott also believed, said Anderson, in the influence of the mind over the body in disease and "often preferred to leave *nature* alone to work out for herself the grand problem of life and death." Nott had the ability to calm his patients by his presence, his manner, and, later in his life, his reputation. "A knowledge of this fact," said Anderson, "led him often to prescribe an inert and harmless pill or potion, when another physician . . . would, perhaps, have given an anodyne, the after effects of which would have been disagreeable or even hurtful."[40] Nott was far too good a physician to continue dosing patients with excessive amounts of drugs whose efficacy he had reason to doubt, but in his enthusiasm to find solutions he occasionally put all his hopes in

39. Warren to his father, April 18, 1833, in Jones (ed.), *Parisian Education*, 120. For the impact of Louis see *ibid.*, 44–46; Osler, "The Influence of Louis on American Medicine," in *An Alabama Student*, 189–210. For the general Parisian approach to therapeutics see Ackerknecht, *Medicine at the Paris Hospital*, 129–38.
40. William H. Anderson, *Biographical Sketch of Dr. J. C. Nott* (Mobile, 1877), 4–5. For a modern assessment of Nott as a physician see William B. Bean, M.D., "Josiah Clark Nott: A Southern Physician," *Bulletin of the New York Academy of Medicine*, 2d ser., L (1974), 529–35.

a new remedy. His work in Paris helped to give him the therapeutical skepticism that was necessary for effective medicine in an age of "heroic" dosing and doctors who often killed as well as cured, but he was certainly not a therapeutic nihilist and in his younger years used drugs freely.

Nott's stay in Paris, like his years in Philadelphia, helped give him intellectual horizons that stretched far beyond the South. From this time on he felt a close affinity with European physicians and scholars. When he later became interested in ethnology, his correspondents were in Paris, London, and Berlin as well as all over America. He felt that Alabama, where he was to spend much of his life, was a scientific backwater, and he eagerly awaited the parcels of books and the letters that tied him to a broader world of scholarship. In later life Nott drew on the ideas and writings of men in Europe and America to defend a southern way of life. In no way did he feel himself intellectually isolated or out of the main lines of European and transatlantic thought. In 1836 he needed this sense of belonging to a wider world of knowledge and science for he was about to exchange the medical ferment and stimulation of Paris for the good life and bustle of Mobile.

Chapter 3
MOBILE

The flow of South Carolinians to Alabama became a flood in the 1830s. In the years after the War of 1812 the cotton planters of the South opened up new lands from central Georgia to Texas. The years to 1837 saw unparalleled growth for the entire southwestern region, broken only by the setbacks following the 1819 depression. Feverish economic development reached its peak in the mid-1830s as new settlers rushed into the lands that had been torn from the Indians of the region. Between 1820 and 1840 Alabama's population grew from 128,000 to 591,000, Mississippi's from 75,000 to 376,000.[1]

Most emigrants moved west in the hope of greater prosperity and a better life, but among the elite of South Carolina there was also in the 1830s a sense of malaise after the feverish political excitement of the previous years; there was a feeling that South Carolina was passing out of the mainstream of events in the South. Henry Nott's friend and former partner, David J. McCord, an ardent states' rights advocate, complained from Columbia to James Hammond in January, 1836, that "I have never found life hang so heavily on my hands. For us lawyers, nothing remains to be done in the State. There is no business. Politics in a calm, society dull, and all things flat and unsavoury. I feel like volunteering to fight the Indians in Florida." The last course—to join in the Seminole War—was chosen by a number of prominent young men, and James Nott went as volunteer surgeon to a mounted regiment. Henry Nott was as disillusioned as his friend McCord. Though he saw consolation in South Carolina's prosperity, he despaired of the South's ultimate ability to maintain

1. U.S. Bureau of the Census, *Historical Statistics of the United States: Colonial Times to 1957* (Washington, D.C., 1960), 12.

slavery and its way of life. "I have made up my mind fully on the matter," he wrote, "& believe that all is lost. Europe is against us. . . . At the North I believe many are with us from mere good feelings, but without any perception of constitutional principle or unshaken resolution." He thought the South should battle every inch of ground in Congress and elsewhere, but its main objective should be to profit as much as possible from present prosperity.[2]

Among the disillusioned was Josiah Nott's father-in-law, James S. Deas. Deas's loss to his brother-in-law John Chestnut in the South Carolina State Senate race of 1832 had rankled, and while Josiah Nott and his family were in Europe he began to move his family to Alabama. He was to have a home in Mobile or its vicinity for most of the next thirty years, and this home became the center for a family network of several of his sons and daughters, including Sarah Deas Nott and her husband. Deas's various relations maintained their own homes but kept in close touch with their rich and influential patron. His wealth eased their path, and his name was frequently associated with their financial transactions.

Josiah Nott and his family returned to Columbia in the spring of 1836. In May they reburied their young son and quickly left for Mobile. At the end of the month Nott announced the opening of his office in the business section of the city, near the Custom House in Royal Street. He would be there, he said, from 8:00 A.M. until dark but would spend the nights at Spring Hill, a few miles to the west.[3] The South Carolinians were well acquainted with the problems of summer and autumn fevers in a low-lying coastal region, and at Columbia and in the up-country Nott and his friends had been used to the summer migrations of the planters from coastal South Carolina. Mobile, like Charleston, was a place to avoid in the sultry, mosquito-laden days of high summer and early fall.

By settling in Mobile Nott had chosen well for his future prosperity. Mobile was in a period of great growth in the years before the Civil War. It had been settled by the French as far back as the early eighteenth cen-

2. McCord to Hammond, January 24, 1836, in Ernest M. Lander (ed.), "Columbia in the Doldrums, 1836," *South Carolina Historical Magazine,* LXII (1961), 200; letter to David B. Warden, May 2, 1836, in David Baillie Warden Papers, Maryland Historical Society, Baltimore; Henry J. Nott to Hammond, March 8, 1836, James Henry Hammond Papers, LC; also see Henry J. Nott to William C. Preston, April 8, 1836, in Autograph Collection of Simon Gratz, HSP.

3. Gravestone, First Presbyterian Church, Columbia, South Carolina; Mobile *Register,* May 31, 1836. The Mobile *Register* has varying titles in these years, although the use of the word "*Register*" within the title is consistent. I have cited it throughout as Mobile *Register.*

tury, but its population had never exceeded 1,500 and usually was much less. After the settlement had been taken over by the Americans during the War of 1812, growth at first was slow—the population was estimated at 1,500 in 1820.[4] In that year it was described as "an old Spanish town," and its only church was Catholic. Growth was still slow in the early 1820s, and a fire destroyed much of the town in 1827. But from that time newcomers settled in ever-increasing numbers. By 1830, when the population was nearly 3,200, of whom 1,175 were slaves and 372 free blacks, the town was described as "an increasing place" and stated to be inferior only to Charleston and New Orleans as a port for the shipment of cotton.[5]

In the 1830s Mobile came into its own as one of the most bustling and lively towns in the South. Its population had increased to over 12,600 by 1840. In 1833 a local newspaper described the town's accommodations as filled to overflowing with newcomers; all the incoming ships and stages were crowded with passengers. A visitor at that time wrote of the beneficial effects of fires that had destroyed the earlier dwellings. The log huts had been replaced by "rows of fine brick houses." Instead of narrow, dirty streets there were now "wide and well-planned thoroughfares." Mobile was laid out on the west bank of the Mobile River. Broad streets ran from north to south parallel with the riverfront and were intersected by a series of streets running west out of the city. Cotton was brought downriver to the port and transshipped to oceangoing vessels in Mobile Bay. Large vessels could not come up as far as Mobile and had to lie at anchor in the bay.[6]

In the years immediately before Nott arrived, Mobile was in the midst

4. See Harriet E. Amos, "Social Life in an Antebellum Cotton Port: Mobile, Alabama, 1820–1860" (Ph.D. dissertation, Emory University, 1976), Appendix, 361; this is the best scholarly discussion of social life in Mobile in these years. Amos has since published a book on antebellum Mobile: *Cotton City: Urban Development in Antebellum Mobile* (University, Ala., 1985).

5. Adam Hodgson, *Remarks During a Journey Through North America in the Years 1819, 1820, and 1821* (1823; rpr. Westport, Conn., 1970), 155–56; [Margaret Hall], *The Aristocratic Journey: Being the Outspoken Letters of Mrs. Basil Hall Written During a Fourteen Months' Sojourn in America, 1827–1828*, ed. Una Pope-Hennessy (New York, 1931), 245; James Stuart, *Three Years in North America* (2 vols.; Edinburgh, 1833), II, 123; Weymouth T. Jordan, *Ante-Bellum Alabama: Town and Country* (Tallahassee, 1957), 1–12; Amos, "Social Life in an Antebellum Cotton Port," Appendix, 361.

6. Caldwell Delaney (ed.), *Craighead's Mobile: Being the Fugitive Writings of Erwin S. Craighead and Frank Craighead* (Mobile, 1968), 76; C. D. Arfwredson, *The United States and Canada in 1832, 1833, and 1834* (2 vols.; London, 1834), II, 44–45; Herbert A. Kellar (ed.), "A Journey Through the South in 1836: Diary of James D. Davidson," *Journal of Southern History*, I, (1935), 345–77.

of an unprecedented boom. One visitor wrote in the spring of 1834 that the city's population had grown from five thousand to sixty-two hundred in the past twelve months and that he had "not seen in any part of the Union . . . any town or city advancing so rapidly in wealth population and business." The same visitor was perhaps less than reliable, however, for he also said that he knew of no situation "more salubrious." Mobile had periodically been swept by yellow fever, and the worst was yet to come. In good years the problem was usually ignored, and in the mid-1830s Mobile was at its most optimistic. Local physician Solomon Mordecai told his father in January, 1836, that "Mobile is scarcely equalled by any city at the South in its prosperity." Thousands of immigrants had settled in the city in the past two or three years.[7]

Many visitors were fascinated by the charm as well as the growth and turmoil of Mobile. Some of its attraction was the product of French and Spanish influence—there was a greater urbanity, a sense of style, and certainly better food than in most western towns—but the charm extended beyond the customs of the inhabitants to the physical appearance of the area. A British visitor in the mid-1830s said that the older streets near the river were dirty and narrow, but as he moved westward, gently upward, into the newer parts of the town, he "was surprised at the peculiar beauty of the place," with its well-laid-out, broad streets covered with crushed oyster shells. He was struck by "the universal love of order, and the good taste which seemed to prevail." Irish comedian Tyrone Power, who acted in Mobile in the winter season of 1834–1835, thought the city "one of the most attractive spots I visited South of the Potomac." Power, like so many other visitors, was entranced by the flower-bestrewn paths that wound through the pine forests that bordered the city. New roads were being cut into some of these glades, and summer homes were being built among the trees. A young female visitor who was there in the same winter as Power thought that Mobile was a gay, lively town.[8]

Spring Hill, where James Deas built a large house and where Nott's family spent much time, was about five or six miles west of the center of

<hr/>

7. Frederick S. Blount to William A. Graham, April 22, 1834, J. G. de Roulhac Hamilton (ed.), *The Papers of William Alexander Graham* (4 vols.; Raleigh, N.C., 1957–61), I, 308–309; Solomon Mordecai to Jacob Mordecai, January 16, 1836, in Mordecai Family Papers, SHC.

8. George W. Featherstonehaugh, *Excursion Through the Slave States* (1844; rpr. New York, 1968), 142; Tyrone Power, *Impressions of America; During the Years 1833, 1834, and 1835* (2 vols.; London, 1836), II, 161–64, 211, 223–25; Eliza J. Witherspoon to William A. Graham, April 16, 1835, in Hamilton (ed.), *Papers of Graham*, I, 378–79.

town. It was on a plateau several hundred feet high, and its pine woods were far less plagued by heat and mosquitoes than the sultry riverside. It had long attracted Mobile residents who wished to reduce the danger of contracting yellow fever, and in the 1820s a road had been built from Dauphin Street on the outskirts of Mobile to Spring Hill. When built, it was smooth, clean, and white with its surface of crushed shells, but by the end of the 1830s it was in bad condition from the ever-increasing volume of traffic, as were many of the other roads so admired by early visitors to the town. When Nott moved to Mobile, there were two dozen or so families living at Spring Hill, about a third of them from South Carolina. The area was particularly attractive to Nott because it reminded him of the sand hills near Columbia where his brother Henry and many of his friends had owned homes.[9]

Over the next twenty-five years Mobile was a prosperous, ebullient city for its ruling white majority. But like the rest of the region, its prosperity was built on slaves. The cotton plantations that poured their crops downriver to Mobile depended on slave labor, and Mobile itself had a large black population. The number of slaves in the city never fell below 30 percent of the population in the years between 1830 and 1850, and even in 1860 a quarter of the population was slave. In 1840 more than half the households in the city contained blacks, and the demands of local industries and riverside merchants swelled the number of slaves owned in the city. Mobile was also the center of the Alabama slave trade. Slaves from the older South were sent by sea to Mobile and bought there by planters from the surrounding region. In the spring of 1842 there was a complaint in the Mobile *Register* that an ordinance was needed to prohibit "the unseemly parade daily through our principal streets, and exhibition at our most public corners of slaves." The writer suggested that the town needed a central place, as in Charleston, where purchases could be made. Later in the decade, and for much of the 1850s, most of the city's traffic in slaves took place in a slave market on Royal Street, not far from the river.[10]

An unusual feature of black-white relations in Mobile was a population of free blacks with extraordinary privileges. In 1840 there were more than

9. Sub Rosa [Paul Ravesies], *Scenes and Settlers of Alabama* (Mobile, 1885), 26–27; Amos, "Social Life in an Antebellum Cotton Port," 19–20; Mobile *Register,* November 23, December 31, 1840; Josiah C. Nott to James Gage, July 28, 1836, in James M. Gage Papers, SHC.

10. Richard E. Wade, *Slavery in the Cities: The South, 1820–1860* (New York, 1964); Amos, "Social Life in an Antebellum Cotton Port," 322–24; Mobile *Register,* March 30, 1842.

five hundred free blacks in the town, nearly all of them mulattoes. In the Adams-Onis treaty of 1819, by which the United States formally acquired this region along with the rest of the Floridas, it was stated that the inhabitants of this former Spanish territory should be granted all the rights of citizens of the United States; among the "inhabitants" were several hundred free blacks. The descendants of these free blacks retained their rights to an education—very few free black Mobile adults were illiterate in 1850—and in general they thought of themselves as distinct from the black slaves by whom they were surrounded.[11]

Still one other population group was present in antebellum Mobile—the Choctaw Indians. Josiah Nott eventually used them to support his racial theories. Although most of the Indian inhabitants of the region had been removed to the West by the time that Nott arrived in Mobile in 1836, there were still Choctaws living in poverty-stricken circumstances in the woods on the outskirts of town. Throughout the antebellum years Choctaw women were to be seen in the town carrying bundles of wood from door to door for sale. Foreign travelers were often taken to see the Indian encampment, and they usually uttered a few clichés about the sad degradation of once proud warriors.[12]

Black, white, red, and a variety of intermediate mixtures were to be seen on the streets of Mobile. In his ethnological writings Nott was often to draw purportedly scientific conclusions from his observations of the customs and characteristics of the different races. Nott himself was a slaveowner. In 1840 his household consisted of himself, his wife, three sons (two of them born since his arrival in Mobile), and nine slaves, only three of them over twenty-four years old.[13] Later, at the end of the 1840s, Nott was to open an infirmary for blacks near the slave market on Royal Street. Slavery and white-black relations were entwined with Nott's private life, his practice, and the life of his city and his region. As yet, he

11. James B. Sellers, *Slavery in Alabama* (University, Ala., 1950), 384–88; Amos, "Social Life in an Antebellum Cotton Port," 340–41; Ira Berlin, *Slaves Without Masters: The Free Negro in the Antebellum South* (1974; rpr. New York, 1976), 108–109, 131, 148, 278, 388–89.

12. Many of the travelers to Mobile in the antebellum years mention the Choctaws. There are good descriptions in Fredrika Bremer, *The Homes of the New World,* trans. Mary Howitt (3 vols.; London, 1853), III, 19–20; [Hon. Victoria Welby-Gregory], *A Young Traveller's Journal of a Tour in North and South America During the Year 1850* (London, 1852), 137–54; J. W. Hengiston, "Mobile—Pensacola and the Floridas," *New Monthly Magazine* (London), XCIII (1853), 370–71.

13. Mobile, Census of 1840, in RG 29, NA. In a letter to James Hammond in 1833 Nott implied that he was not the most rigorous of slave masters. In offering a slave for sale to

appeared to take most of this for granted, but as northern attacks on slavery increased he was ready to defend the institutions and way of life that helped to make life in Mobile so pleasant for its white elite.

As in Columbia, Nott quickly threw himself into the development of his medical practice, and by February, 1837, was able to say, "I have made a very fair start in the professional way & shall do well I think." He was an exceptionally well-trained doctor, and he was always a glutton for work. Mobile had a mixture of old-style physicians with little formal training and some of the new, enthusiastic graduates of the 1820s and 1830s. Soon after arriving in Mobile, Nott wrote to his old pupil and friend James Gage that books were apparently not necessary for the medical profession. He said that a physician had boasted to him the other day of not having read a book in twenty years, though he was making ten or twelve thousand dollars a year. Four or five others, Nott wrote, were "making fortunes by the intrepidity of ignorance." Nott, however, allied himself with the young physicians who were in touch with the latest ideas. Among this group was Dr. Richard Lee Fearn, a Virginian and a classmate of Nott at the University of Pennsylvania, who had moved to Mobile several years earlier. In his first years in Mobile Nott entered into a partnership with Fearn, which proved extremely useful to Nott because Fearn was surgeon to the Mobile City Hospital. The Mobile Board of Aldermen agreed that Fearn could divide his duties with his new partner. A few months after his arrival, Nott commented that his agreement with Fearn regarding the hospital gave them "a good deal of important surgery"—amputations, eye cases, and a variety of injuries.[14]

At first Nott found a marked difference between his general practice in Mobile and in Columbia. In Columbia he knew everybody, and many of his patients were his good friends. He treated them, but he also spent a good deal of time with them. In Mobile he noticed at first that "it is a mere money transaction"; he presented his bill and left like "a tailor." Because Mobile was growing with such amazing speed, said Nott, half of the families had no regular physician—they took the first that came to

---

Hammond, Nott said: "My objection to him is that he will occasionally drink, & living in Columbia with as little discipline as I use he will be ruined—I do not know a negro more easily governed" (Nott to Hammond, January 10, 1833, in Hammond Papers, SCL).

14. Nott to James Hammond, February 15, 1837, in Hammond Papers, SCL; Nott to Gage, July 28, November 5, 1836, in Gage Papers; W. J. Maxwell, comp., *General Alumni Catalogue of the University of Pennsylvania* (Philadelphia, 1917); Mobile *Register,* June 7, 1839.

hand. Nott's relationship with his patients was soon to change, for he quickly gained a body of devoted patients, and he was a man who liked good society and good talk. Mobile was to provide patients, good society, and good talk in abundance.[15]

Although the French influence was still strong in Mobile when Nott arrived—he said he was obliged to speak as much French as in Paris—his friends were usually to be found among the newcomers from the South Atlantic states, particularly South Carolina. Nott thought that there was some "very good society" in the town but claimed that he was pleased that he did not have the constant demands on his time that had been made by his family and social circle in the close-knit community of Columbia. After less than a year in the city, he told his friend Hammond that Mobile was "decidedly a pleasant place—good society is coming from all quarters & there is something exhilarating in the prosperity & activity of everything about us, when compared to the lifeless despondency of Carolina and the other old states." Although the "ruling influence" in the city was still that of "rascality," produced by the widespread spirit of speculation, Nott believed that it was possible to find good society.[16]

At first Nott's family found the transition to Mobile a little more difficult than he did. They had arrived at the beginning of the summer when many who could afford to leave Mobile went to any one of a variety of southern and northern spas and resorts. The suburbs of Mobile might have been beautiful, but after France they were unexciting. Nott also missed Paris. Although he claimed to Hammond that Paris was a charming place only when one became "habituated to the dishonesty & bestiality of its inhabitants," he also acknowledged that "all that this world affords is there." The contrast with Paris was sharp, but the Notts soon slipped easily into Mobile's expanding elite, and their immediate loneliness was eased by the variety of family ties they had in the city. Mobile was never the intensely close-knit community that Columbia had been, but the Notts and their like made a small, comfortable world for themselves among their friends and relatives from South Carolina and similar states.

One social obligation that Nott was never happy with was church

15. Nott to James Gage, July 28, 1836, in Gage Papers.
16. For the material in this and the following paragraph see *ibid.* and Nott to Hammond, February 15, 1837, in Hammond Papers, SCL.

membership—the wife of one of his physician colleagues later wrote in her journal that he was "a disbeliever in religion"—but his wife used the opportunity of the move to Mobile to become a member of the Episcopal church. The Deases had originally been Presbyterians, and in the 1820s James Deas had been a pew holder in the Presbyterian church in Camden, South Carolina. The Episcopal church had been unpopular in up-country South Carolina in the years after the Revolution, but in 1832 an Episcopal church was built in Camden, and John Deas, in a move that was probably social as well as religious, became one of the first vestrymen. When the Notts moved to Mobile in 1836, Sarah Nott joined her father, James Deas, in membership in Christ Episcopal Church. In February, 1837, she went through the rite of adult baptism on the same day as Ned, her father's slave. Josiah Nott apparently never became a communicant, although Christ Church remained the Notts' family church while they were in Mobile, and their children were baptized there.[17] For Nott, a family affiliation with the Episcopalians was undoubtedly more satisfactory than ties with the more ardent Presbyterians, with whom he was often to clash in his writings and by whom he was often attacked.

Nott's prospects seemed particularly promising in the first months after his arrival in Mobile. Like many of the other professional men who arrived in these years, he was amazed by the amount of money that could be made. "Mobile," he wrote, "is essentially a money making place." After six months' residence Nott estimated that in the next year he would make from $8,000 to $10,000. This was no wild exaggeration. Dr. Henry S. Levert, a contemporary of Nott's in Philadelphia, who had also settled in Mobile, estimated in the fall of 1836 that the income from his practice in the course of the year should amount to $15,000 to $20,000.[18]

The rich prospects were somewhat offset by the soaring costs. Writing to young James Gage, who had just qualified as a physician, Nott suggested that prices in Mobile would be too great for a young man. A home could not be rented for less than $800 to $1,600 a year, and an office on a business street would cost at least $1,000 to $1,200—"the Drs. & law-

17. Sarah Gayle Crawford Journal, October 22, 1853, in Sarah Ann and William B. Crawford Papers, William Stanley Hoole Special Collections Library, University of Alabama, Tuscaloosa; Thomas J. Kirkland and Robert M. Kennedy, *Historic Camden*, Pt. 2, *Nineteenth Century* (Columbia, 1926), 282–83, 295; Christ Episcopal Church, Mobile, Parish Records, copies in Local History Room, Mobile Public Library, Mobile, Ala.

18. Nott to James Gage, July 28, November 5, 1836, in Gage Papers; Levert to Francis J. Levert, September 9, 1836, in Levert Family Papers, SHC.

yers," he wrote, "are in the habit of huddling together like swine to save rent." Undoubtedly this was another reason for Nott's partnership with Fearn in his early years in the city. When Charleston lawyer Philip Phillips arrived in the city in 1835, he was shocked to discover that the office that had been rented for him and his partner would cost $1,500 a year. "I was staggered," he later wrote, "by what seemed to me an unheard-of price for a lawyer's office." Physician Solomon Mordecai wrote to his sister in June, 1836, that the expenses of living in Mobile were "great beyond what your most extravagant ideas could fancy them." Though prices were incredibly high, most well-off residents were using what money they could raise to invest in property. Mordecai wrote that no one could get rich in Mobile "who does not embark in speculation in real estate, which has turned into gold in the hands of all who have touched it." Helped by James Deas, Nott bought two tracts of land for a total of more than $16,000 in 1836. He had plans to build a private hospital with Dr. Fearn, which, he wrote, would bring both money and reputation. In the winter of 1836–1837 Dr. Henry Levert was building a private hospital, which he estimated would cost $30,000, exclusive of the land, but he expected it to be very profitable.[19]

Mobile was destined to be a very prosperous town in the years before the Civil War, but the dreams of sudden wealth that hovered over the city when Nott arrived in 1836 evaporated within a year with the coming of a nationwide depression. By the spring of 1837 Mobile was in the midst of a major slump. For the rest of the decade and into the early 1840s times were hard. Doctors were still needed, but they experienced great difficulty in collecting their bills. Nott was financially sound, but his hopes of extraordinary income and a new private hospital had to be deferred.

To add to his worries, Nott in 1837 had to absorb the shock of a family tragedy. That summer Nott went north, and in New York he met his brother Henry. Henry had come to the city to see his young daughter, who lived with a family there, and to arrange for the publication of another book. Early in the fall Josiah returned to Mobile, and Henry and his wife, leaving their young daughter in New York, sailed for Charleston in the steam packet *Home*. Leaving New York, the *Home* ran onto a

19. Nott to Gage, November 5, 1836, in Gage Papers; Manuscript Autobiography of Philip Phillips, Box 13, in Philip Phillips Family Papers, LC; Solomon Mordecai to Ellen Mordecai, June 17, August 7, 1836, in Mordecai Family Papers, SHC; Nott purchases in Deed Books, Mobile County Court House, Mobile, Ala.; Levert to Francis Levert, March 20, 1837, in Levert Family Papers.

shoal. She got off, but on the following day her boilers gave out as she ran into a gale. Off Cape Hatteras, with the ship leaking badly and passengers and crew desperately manning the pumps, her captain decided to try to beach her. The attempt failed. She ran on a reef off Ocracoke Island and broke in pieces. An attempt was made to launch the boats, but they capsized, throwing their passengers into the water. Many of the other passengers and crew were washed into the sea, "their shrieks and cries . . . appalling and heart-rending beyond description." Of eighty or ninety passengers and a crew of more than forty only about one-third were saved; among the drowned were Henry Nott and his wife. It was said that he could have saved himself but chose to remain with his wife. Three months later, in January, 1838, Josiah and his wife named their new son Henry Junius.[20]

In 1838 and 1839 a great majority of the supposedly prosperous citizens of Mobile were experiencing great difficulty in either paying their bills or collecting what was due them. Late in the summer of 1838, Nott wrote that "this is the hardest country to get money in You ever saw. I think I shall make some money some of these days if I live, but it will be when people of substance take the place of the bankrupts." On paper he was now earning $50 a day. It would be more, he wrote, but the town was healthy. He hoped that within a few weeks his earnings would be $75 to $100 a day. The problem, however, was collecting the money that was owed. "It would do you good," he wrote, "to see fellows here who wont pay a Dr $5, betting $500 on an election or horse race, getting drunk on the *best* every day & driving the fastest trotting horses in town." The problems in the Mobile economy lingered. Dr. Henry Levert wrote in May, 1839, that there was not enough money in circulation in Mobile to furnish a family with market money, and it was impossible to collect bills. "I have bills of from $10 to fifty dollars against persons who are worth $50,000, and it is impossible to collect them." Levert said that he had between $25,000 and $30,000 owed to him but was unable to collect $100. His property was unsalable in the prevailing conditions.[21]

The panic of 1837 dampened the optimism with which Nott had begun

20. Nott to Lyman C. Draper, August 26, 1870, in Draper Manuscripts, State Historical Society of Wisconsin, Madison; Maximilian La Borde, *History of the South Carolina College* (2d ed.; Charleston, 1874), 215; E. A. Duyckinck and G. L. Duyckinck, *Cyclopaedia of American Literature* (2 vols.; Philadelphia, 1855), II, 253–54; Charleston *Courier*, October 13, 17, 19, 20, 1837; Charles Ellms, *The Tragedy of the Seas* (Philadelphia, 1848), 69 (quotation).

21. Nott to James Gage, September 8, 1833, in Gage Papers; Levert to Francis Levert, January 18, May 1, 1839, in Levert Family Papers.

his career in Mobile, particularly as it coincided with the loss of $10,000. Nott discovered that the title to a home he had bought on arriving in Mobile was flawed, and although he had hopes of recovering the money he was at least temporarily and perhaps permanently out of pocket to that amount. Nott was more hopeful about the future prospects of land he had bought in northwestern Louisiana on the Red River. The prime mover in buying land in that region had been Nott's father-in-law, James Deas, who had bought some twelve thousand acres. Two of Deas's sons-in-law—Nott and John Middleton Huger—had bought land alongside Deas's acreage. All three hoped to develop cotton plantations. For a time in the late 1830s Nott gave some thought to abandoning the profession of medicine in Mobile and locating as a plantation owner along the Red River. His primary reason was a well-grounded fear about the health of Mobile in the summer months. Mobile was periodically swept by yellow fever, and there were epidemics in 1837 and 1839. He told James Hammond in the summer of 1840 that although his practice was good and Mobile was for most of the year a very pleasant place of residence, the city had a severe drawback: "Here is my great trouble & it is a source of unhappiness to me—it is a very sickly place & I look forward to every summer with dread—My wife, my children & my self are in danger & I would make almost any sacrifice to get away."[22]

In the 1840s, when Mobile boomed again, Nott's practice flourished, and yellow fever seemed to subside, Nott buried his fears and his thoughts of moving. In the 1850s, when yellow fever brought devastation to the city and to his family, he must often have remembered his early determination to seek a safer spot in which to live. Nott soon abandoned any thoughts of moving. His brother Rufus was to become a planter, first on the Red River and later in Texas, but Nott was to devote his life to the practice of medicine, to teaching, and to writing both on medicine and on race.

The hard times did not reduce Nott's usual financial generosity. He had always been free with his money, and as late as the fall of 1836 John Gage had still not repaid the money that Nott had advanced to his son James when he was Nott's pupil in Paris. Nott had never pressed this matter and referred to it only when James himself wrote and asked if it had been repaid. Nott replied that the account had not been settled and suggested that James should give his father a hint. In the middle of the

22. Nott to Hammond, July 21, August 17, 1840, in Hammond Papers, SCL.

panic of 1837, Nott also used his own money to avoid difficulties for his partner, Richard Fearn. In the spring of 1838, Fearn had taken his wife to the Virginia Springs for her health. They were still there in September. Nott had to handle Fearn's personal investments. Fearn had a dozen slaves hired out in Mobile, and Nott was responsible for dealing with their employers and collecting the money for their hire. This proved to be practically impossible—"no body paid a damd cent," wrote Nott. He was also supposed to pay interest and renew notes as they came due with Fearn's income, but, because no one was paying, Nott was advancing his own money to help his partner. Fearn's problems were extensive at this time. He had been speculating in real estate and owed some $20,000 as a result of the collapse in the city. Fearn weathered these hard years, continued to speculate in real estate, and eventually retired from medical practice to manage what became lucrative investments.[23]

In these grim days of the late 1830s Nott was also providing money and support to some of his brothers. He commented in August, 1840, that his financial burdens had been increased in the past few years because he had advanced several thousand dollars to his younger brothers. Two years earlier he had said that he was sending money to his brother Adolphus, who was "sitting down in New Orleans smoking segars & keeping Cool, without any practice or money but what I sent him." Adolphus Nott was eventually to become a successful New Orleans physician, but he was never to achieve Josiah's fame. Josiah's sense of family obligation was strong, and while supporting Adolphus he also proposed to his brother James, who was having little success as a physician in South Carolina, that he should come to Mobile. "I think I can take Jim up in a way which will be advantageous to him," he wrote to a friend, "without feeling it myself." Dr. James Nott did join his brother in Mobile for several years. Later he went to California, practiced in San Francisco for several years, and died as a comparatively young man after returning east.[24]

Josiah's brother Rufus, yet another Nott physician, was also interested in moving from South Carolina, and in the summer of 1840 Josiah paid a brief visit to South Carolina to discuss the possibility of Rufus buying

23. Nott to Gage, November 5, 1836, September 8, 1838, in Gage Papers. For Fearn in later years see Herbert J. Peabody to [Samuel St. John], September 20, 1858, in Herbert C. Peabody Letters, SHC.

24. Nott to Hammond, August 17, 1840, in Hammond Papers, SCL; Nott to James Gage, September 8, 1838, in Gage Papers. There is information on James Nott in the University of South Carolina Archives.

half of Nott's plantation, moving to the Red River, and making an arrangement for Rufus' slaves to be used on Josiah's land. Rufus was interested, and in the early 1840s he moved to the Red River.

Nott's visit to Columbia to see his brother at first conjured up a romantic nostalgia as he "walked amidst the scenes of childhood & youth," but his feelings of regret were soon overcome by his conviction that he had been wise to leave a state that he felt was economically exhausted and politically divided. Nott had visited his lands on the Red River during the previous winter, and now he was struck by the contrast with the "worn out" lands of South Carolina. He was also shocked that many of his old friends were divided on political questions in the state and were lampooning their mutual friend James Hammond, who was a candidate for governor. "Damn politics," Nott told Hammond, "quit it & be an honest man & a gentleman." After his quick visit to South Carolina, Nott appeared to become more reconciled to his life in Mobile.[25]

The panic of 1837 and Nott's various obligations to friends and relatives did not place him in financial difficulties. He was able to say in the summer of 1840 that he was still in about the same financial state as when he left South Carolina. And that this condition was quite comfortable was shown not only because he was able to back his brothers but also because in these years of depression he was able to continue an earlier interest in horses and horse racing. In the years before he left South Carolina, Nott and his circle had been much involved with horses. South Carolinians had long supported horse racing and had a fervent interest in good stock. Josiah's brother Dr. William Nott was described in 1835 as "insane on horses" and Josiah's "young Monr Tonson" as "the finest foal I have ever seen on the Earth." Nott's marriage encouraged him in this interest, for horse racing had always been popular in Camden, the home of his wife's family, and his father-in-law had been a steward of the Camden Jockey Club.[26]

When Nott went to Mobile, he took some of his race horses with him, and he exchanged five of them, including the superb Monr Tonson (now with a blemish on one eye), for a town lot worth $4,000. In the fall of 1836, Nott had one filly in training but hoped to put her to a famous stal-

25. Nott to Hammond, July 21, August 17, 1840, in Hammond Papers, SCL. There is material on Rufus Nott in the University of South Carolina Archives. See also J. Marion Sims, *The Story of My Life* (1884; rpr. New York, 1968), 102–104.

26. Robert I. Gage to James Gage, May 1, 1835, in Gage Papers; Kirkland and Kennedy, *Historic Camden*, Pt. 2, 52–53.

lion near Montgomery, for in foal to this "Chateau Margaux" she would be worth $2,000. Nott's enthusiasm reached a peak in his first two or three years in Mobile; after that, the demands of his career took over. In 1838 Nott twice wrote to the *Spirit of the Times,* the famous sporting newspaper published in New York. He argued that America needed improvement in its horses and its jockeys. English experience, he argued, could be used to bring more scientific breeding to America. He said that he corresponded with English racing enthusiasts and that he was one of the few men in Alabama who subscribed to the English *Racing Calendar.* American jockeys, said Nott, "generally are unquestionably much inferior to those of England." In America such lightweights were carried that owners were obliged to get young riders. Moreover, argued Nott, in the South these were most commonly blacks, "who cannot recollect more than one direction at a time—their skill lies mainly in *judicious use of whip and spur.*"[27] Within ten years Nott was to develop his assumptions about blacks into full-scale arguments.

In his first years in Mobile, Nott was optimistic that money could be made from horse breeding. In the fall of 1838, in the midst of the depression, his bloodstock was thriving, and he had two fillies in training for a coming race. He told Robert Gage that if he had $20,000 to lay out in a breeding farm in the Mobile area he could make a fortune by importing English horses. Of the $20,000, $5,000 would go for an English stallion, which would more than clear its cost every year; $10,000 for ten imported mares, each of which would produce a foal a year worth $1,000; and $5,000 for a little farm and three or four slaves. "The mania for racing & stock here is tremendous," he wrote, "& as soon as they get out of debt every body will go into it—but they know good things & will have none other."[28]

Nott's dream of money from horse breeding faded in the 1840s. The demands of his practice and his increasingly important career as an author gave him much less time to devote to other pursuits. Both Nott and his father-in-law were members of the Mobile Jockey Club, which opened a new course and club-stand outside the city in 1837, but, unlike his partner, Fearn, he was too devoted to his professional and scientific interests

27. Nott to James Gage, November 5, 1836, in Gage Papers; *Spirit of the Times* (New York), June 9, 1838. In another letter, published on August 18, 1838, Nott tried to echo the comic style of his dead brother, Henry. He described how an Irishman had been ridden on a rail in Mobile after taking his stepmother from his father and marrying her.

28. Nott to James Gage, September 8, 1838, in Gage Papers.

to spend much time in the speculative activities that flourished in the again booming city of Mobile.[29]

The frenetic boom and construction of the mid-1830s had created a substantial and in parts elegant town. Government Street, where many of the most substantial private houses were located, was said in the spring of 1839 to be "as handsome an avenue as is to be seen in the country, exceeding a mile in length, from 100 to 120 feet, lined with rows of trees on either hand, protected by an excellent flag-pavement at the sides, and already ornamented with exceedingly handsome public structures, and private mansions and dwellings." But in the early fall of the year Mobile's continuing financial problems were compounded when a series of fires swept through the center of the town. At least part of the problem was caused by arsonists, who committed robberies during the ensuing chaos. Nott's office was destroyed, but fortunately not much was lost. In early October Nott advised a Mobile lawyer friend who was in Pascagoula to return to Mobile. The risk from yellow fever was now slight, he said, but fires were raging every night and the risks to property were great. "We can *now*," he wrote, "see another fire burning in town," and as he was writing the letter a stage driver arrived at Spring Hill with the news that when he left the town the Government Street theater and the buildings around it were on fire. Nott estimated that at least five hundred houses had been burned, in addition to the City Hall, the Planters Bank, and one of the main hotels. He advised his friend to return to look after his possessions; Nott himself was at Spring Hill every night to visit patients, and he knew no place of safety in the town. Once again Fearn was absent, and when their office had burned, Nott's slaves had "worked manfully" to bring out their papers.[30]

In the early 1840s Mobile gradually regained its prosperity, and by the middle years of the decade the city was again experiencing tumultuous economic growth. A visitor in 1845 wrote that no one in the North, unless in the factories, could have any idea of the amount of cotton shipped from Mobile. "Several steamboat loads arrive here daily," he wrote, "and a hundred large vessels lie down in the Bay loading with cotton which is

29. Mobile *Register,* March 24, 1837; *Alabama Planter* (Mobile), December 22, 1851; undated note by Nott in the Squier Papers, LC.

30. James S. Buckingham, *The Slave States of America* (2 vols.; 1842; rpr. New York, 1968), I, 282; Bernard A. Reynolds, *Sketches of Mobile* (Mobile, 1868), 21; Noah M. Ludlow, *Dramatic Life as I Found It* (1880; rpr. New York, 1966), 514–16; Nott to Joseph W. Lesesne, October 9, 1839, in Joseph W. Lesesne Papers, SHC.

taken down in lighters besides smaller vessels which load at Mobile." The wharves of the town were crowded with cotton that was brought down the river. By 1844 and 1845 signs of prosperity were again everywhere in the city, and the old financial optimism had returned. A visiting Tennessee lawyer said that from what lawyers had told him he had no doubt that $10,000 could be made in the first year.[31]

The lively atmosphere and the excellent food and drink again began to be mentioned in the comments of Mobile's visitors. Even when overwhelmingly American, the town continued to be spiced by a lingering French and Spanish influence. A visiting clergyman found that the "tone of society" in the city was "very gay and to a certain extent dissipated; altho' there are many here who prefer literature & its rational enjoyments to the theatre & gay revels." As a port town Mobile had many temporary visitors, and near the waterfront there was an abundance of oyster houses, saloons, and brothels along the dirty, cluttered streets. Violence was common, and guns and knives were often carried. When William Macready performed *Hamlet* in Mobile in 1844 he commented that "many *rowdy* people were there, women of the town." Yet Macready was delighted with most that he saw of Mobile. He enjoyed driving in the outskirts with the "very pretty suburban villas with their many flowers and richly blossoming peach-trees, oranges in blossom, fig, and various ornamental shrubs." He also wrote with pleasure of a dinner with a group that included Nott; Nott later corresponded with him.[32]

Nott's status as a physician grew rapidly in the late 1830s and early 1840s. His practice was flourishing, and he began to take the lead in organizing the best-qualified Mobile physicians to defend the exclusiveness of their profession. In June, 1841, the Mobile Medical Society was organized in the office of Nott and Fearn. The moving spirit behind the new organization was Nott, and at this first meeting he offered a set of nine resolutions designed to shape the new society. Nott wanted to increase the professionalism of medical practice in Mobile and to take all possible steps to exclude the unqualified from the practice of medicine.

31. Matthias H. Welles to George H. Welles, February 8, [1845], in Mobile Letters, SHC; Spencer Jarnagin to his mother, December 2, 1845, in Spencer Jarnagin Papers, SHC.
32. Lester B. Shippe (ed.), *Bishop Whipple's Southern Diary, 1843–1844* (Minneapolis, 1937), 90; Sir Frederick Pollock (ed.), *Macready's Reminiscences, and Selections from His Diaries and Letters* (London, 1875), 553; also Buckingham, *Slave States*, I, 284–86; Albrecht K. Koch, *Journey Through a Part of the United States of North America in the Years 1844 to 1846*, ed. and trans. Ernst A. Stadler (Carbondale, Ill., 1972), 109.

The subscription of the new society was set at $10, and as soon as this money was collected it was to be applied to the purchase of foreign and American periodicals for the use of the members. A committee of three was to be appointed to draft a code of laws for the society. This same committee was to draft a revision of the Alabama laws regarding the practice of medicine and apothecaries and to frame an appropriate bill for the next session of the Alabama legislature. The bill was to deal with the practice of medicine and the profession of apothecary in Mobile County in such a manner as to maintain the dignity of the medical profession "and to guard the community against ignorance and imposition." The three-man drafting committee, which consisted of Drs. Nott, Henry S. Levert, and William B. Crawford, was also given the task of selecting the periodicals to be purchased.[33] Nott intended to exert a strong guiding hand on the affairs of the society.

In shaping a professional organization in Mobile, Nott was reflecting the extent to which regularly trained physicians in the United States in the 1840s were attempting to resist the advance of the unauthorized practice of medicine. Regularly trained physicians were disturbed by the degree to which the general public was placing its faith in either untrained or unorthodox physicians. The inability of even the best-trained physicians to understand the causes of disease and their dependence on harsh purgatives, emetics, and copious bloodletting made many eager to seek the services of those who offered less draconian, and therefore in many cases less dangerous, treatments. Two movements that gained particular strength in the 1830s and 1840s were homeopathy and Thomsonianism or botanic medicine.

Homeopathy was based on the theory that a medicine that would produce certain symptoms in a healthy person could cure the same symptoms in one who was sick. The doses given were minute and were often combined with rest, cleanliness, and a proper diet. Thomsonianism, or botanic medicine, stemmed from the practice and writings of Samuel Thomson (1769–1843). Unlike homeopathy, which involved regular doctors, Thomsonianism encouraged home treatment and practitioners who had not gone through a regular course of medical training. Drawing on "natural" herbal remedies, Thomson attacked heroic medicine, particularly bleeding, although he continued the use of purges. There had always

33. *New Orleans Medical and Surgical Journal,* I (1844), 98–100.

been practitioners and private individuals who had practiced "botanic" medicine, and Thomsonianism fell on fertile ground among a general public that distrusted the harsh treatments of regular practitioners. Thomson was an excellent entrepreneur, and by 1833 he employed twenty-one agents in Alabama; botanic medicine was extremely popular in the state.[34] In 1838 a young woman who had moved west from South Carolina to settle in Alabama wrote to her sister that their father "thinks some of these Botanic Dr's out here, could cure you, as they perform such great cures. I believe he has heard that they do cure coughs and consumption."[35] Back in South Carolina, Nott's friend James Hammond, who in the early 1830s had called on Nott for advice on the medical treatment of his slaves, had by 1834 begun to use botanic medicine to treat their ills.[36]

Nott's committee quickly tackled its various tasks. Within ten days the group had drafted a constitution for the society and prepared a bill for the 1841–1842 session of the legislature; in the form in which it was finally passed, it achieved some but by no means all of what the committee wanted. Alabama was divided into five medical districts. To practice medicine, a doctor had to be licensed by the medical board of the district in which he intended to practice. For Mobile the powers of the medical board were to be vested in the new Mobile Medical Society; the society would provide the board for the Fifth District. When an applicant wished either to practice medicine or to be an apothecary in the Fifth District, he was to apply to the president of the Mobile Medical Society. The president would appoint a committee made up of six members of the society to examine the applicant. For violations of this act a fine of $500 could be levied. Half of the fine was to go to the informer, or to the medical society of the district if the medical board or a member of the society informed. The act also made it easier for physicians to collect their bills. If a

34. See William G. Rothstein, *American Physicians in the Nineteenth Century: From Sect to Science* (Baltimore, 1972), 125–74; Joseph F. Kett, *The Formation of the American Medical Profession: The Role of Institutions, 1780–1860* (New Haven, 1968), vii, 13, 20–23, 97–142; Martin Kaufman, *American Medical Education: The Formative Years, 1765–1910* (Westport, Conn., 1976), 62–71; John S. Haller, Jr., *American Medicine in Transitions, 1840–1910* (Urbana, Ill., 1981), 105–29.

35. Sarah L. Fountain to Hannah L. Coker, February 15, 1838, in Fletcher M. Green (ed.), *The Lides Go South . . . and West: The Record of a Planter Migration in 1835* (Columbia, 1952), 25. For the "irregular" practice of medicine in Alabama see Howard L. Holley, *The History of Medicine in Alabama* (Birmingham, 1982), 9, 241–47, 256–57.

36. Drew Gilpin Faust, *James Henry Hammond and the Old South: A Design for Mastery* (Baton Rouge, 1982), 78–79.

physician brought an action for payment, his book of original entries, sworn to by the physician, would be accepted as evidence.

The bill aided regular physicians in Mobile and Alabama, but the legislature added a condition that reduced its value to them—it was enacted with the proviso that there would be no interference with those practicing the *"Botanic System."* Botanic medicine had a considerable following in Alabama, and the legislators had no desire to lose one possible route to health. But the Mobile Medical Society, which had about twenty active members in the 1840s, had made a good beginning. Its members were the elite of the medical profession in Mobile. They subscribed to the leading medical journals of France, England, Ireland, Scotland, and the United States, and they held monthly meetings to discuss cases and topics of general interest. Also, in addition to supplying the medical board for the district, the president, vice-president, and secretary of the society in each year constituted the Board of Health for the city.[37]

When in 1842 the Mobile city directory published a list of those acknowledged to be authorized physicians it included twenty-five, of whom fourteen had M.D. degrees. The entry warned against "persons who scorn the learning and attainments of well educated Physicians" and "confide their lives where they would not trust a dollar."[38] The leadership that Nott exerted in Mobile was always in favor of the professionalization of medicine and of basing it on the latest research. It was typical of Nott that the new organization should on one hand strive to exclude unlicensed practitioners and on the other subscribe to the leading European and American medical journals.

In the years after his arrival in Mobile, Nott gradually became a regular contributor to American medical journals. His contributions showed him to be a wide-ranging, eclectic physician and surgeon whose interests ranged from early psychiatry to the construction of various items of medical hardware. In 1838 his suggestion for a new and improved jointed splint for leg fractures was published in the *American Journal of the Medical Sciences.* It was an extremely practical article, describing how to make the splint in some detail and indicating the ways in which it could be used

37. *New Orleans Medical and Surgical Journal,* I (1844), 100–102; *Southern Medical Reports,* I (1849), 287–301; Mobile Medical Society to the Mayor and Aldermen of Mobile, June 21, 1841, in Mobile City Records, transcripts, Local History Room, Mobile Public Library.

38. *Wood's Mobile Directory, 1842* (Mobile, 1842), 6.

in fractures in different parts of the leg. Of the four cases he used to illustrate the effectiveness of the splint, three had been in Mobile. In one of these cases, both Nott and Fearn had attended a slave who had suffered a double fracture of his leg by falling through a trapdoor on the second floor of a warehouse. From the description given by Nott, it is clear that both Nott and Fearn were in regular attendance on the patient for a week following the accident. Nott indicated that the patient was walking on crutches on the forty-second day after the accident and that after three months he was able to walk unaided to the office. As in Columbia, Nott's practice in Mobile included both slave and free.[39]

Although Nott practiced as a general physician, his reputation as a surgeon grew rapidly. After his death in the 1870s, it was written that "Doctor Nott performed successfully all the capital operations in surgery; originating some, improving the usual procedure of others, and performing all with dexterity, boldness, and astonishing self-reliance." It was said that he was particularly effective at times of surgical crisis or accident—he did not lose his "judgment or his administrative ability" when younger men panicked.[40] It was in the 1840s that Nott began to lay the basis for this reputation.

As early as 1841 Nott's advice was being sought from areas outside Mobile. In June of that year he strongly advised against surgery in the case of a woman with a large abdominal tumor. He said that the tumor was so large, was so firmly attached to important organs, and had caused so much inflammation in the abdomen "that the knife would be like putting fire to a magazine!" He said there was no instance on record of a surgeon being "cruel enough" to attempt an operation in such a case. "I would," he wrote, "with great willingness come up and bestow time and attention on the case if I could see any prospect of relief." Nott himself was having some difficulty at this time with what he believed was a form of rheumatism, and he made arrangements to spend the summer of 1841 at the Virginia Springs. Clearly the panic of 1837 had left him with no serious financial difficulties. The Virginia Springs in the Alleghenies were famous for their curative qualities and were a fashionable summer resort for southern planters and their families.[41]

39. Nott, "Description of a Modification of the Double Inclined Plane," *American Journal of the Medical Sciences,* o.s., XXIII (1838), 21–29.

40. William H. Anderson, *Biographical Sketch of Dr. J. C. Nott* (Mobile, 1877), 5–6.

41. Letter of Josiah C. Nott, June 24, 1841, in *De Historia Medicinae* (Alabama), III

While Nott exhibited the strong, decisive, practical streak that was essential for the surgeon in these years without anesthesia, he showed in the early 1840s that his medical interests extended across the entire field of medicine. It was in these years that Nott developed an interest in possible treatments—ranging from surgery to hypnosis—for a variety of nervous disorders.

In May, 1844, Nott published an article in the *New Orleans Medical and Surgical Journal* arguing that physicians paid too little attention to the importance of the nervous system in illness. Physicians, he wrote, needed to remember that "the seat of pain is not necessarily the seat of the disease," and he illustrated his argument with two cases from his own practice. In the first of these he eventually had traced a variety of acute pains in a woman to a decayed molar. The second was more significant in that he described an original procedure he had devised for treating what was later called coccygodynia; he was the first to describe this condition and to remove the coccyx as a cure. In treating a young woman who had been generally ill and suffering from "neuralgia" for ten months, Nott examined the length of her spine and found that the point of the coccyx was extremely sensitive. To deal with this, Nott operated to remove the two end bones of the coccyx. He found that the last one was carious and hollowed out "to a mere shell." The operation, carried out, of course, without anesthetic, caused the patient extreme pain, which continued for several hours. Nott gave morphine and other anodynes in large amounts, but they gave little relief.

The patient recovered from the immediate effects of the operation and was generally much better, but two months after the operation she was again seized by extreme pain, which reoccurred for several days in each of the next two months. Nott decided that the problem was neuralgic and that all the difficulty stemmed from the diseased coccyx. In an attempt to stop the immediate pain, he gave anodynes both orally and by injection, but they had little effect and the attacks usually passed off of their own accord. Nott then put his patient on a course of citrate of iron, five grains three times a day for a month, and for the second month continued the dosage only twice a day. He reported that when he last saw her, this treat-

---

(April, 1959), 13–14; Lawrence F. Brewster, *Summer Migrations and Resorts of South Carolina Low-Country Planters* (Durham, N.C., 1947), 90–100; Perceval Reniers, *The Springs of Virginia: Life, Love, and Death at the Waters, 1775–1900* (Chapel Hill, 1941), 25–26.

ment had proved effective, and she had suffered no attacks for three months.[42]

At the same time that Nott was using surgery and drugs to deal with his acute case of "neuralgia," he was in the midst of experiments on mesmerism and its use in the treatment of nervous disorders. Nott first described his work in February, 1846, in a lecture to the Franklin Society of Mobile. The society, which had been in existence since before Nott had arrived in the town, provided a center for scientific and cultural activities. Its members had originally met in a room of the Barton Academy, but by 1846 they had a hall with a reading room and library in St. Joseph's Street. The Mobile *Register* commented in the spring of 1846 that the society had fallen into the good hands of a number of young gentlemen who were zealous in their pursuit of literature and science. Both local and national speakers appeared before the society. For Nott's talk, "The Phenomena of Mesmerism," an admission fee of twenty-five cents was charged to go toward expenses and to increase the society's library.[43]

Nott's interest in mesmerism or "animal magnetism" had begun in 1843. He later said that he had been persuaded to experiment by a letter he had received from his old friend and partner, Dr. Robert W. Gibbes of Columbia, South Carolina. Gibbes had described the success of certain of his experiments in mesmerism, and Nott, who trusted Gibbes, decided he should test a subject in which he had previously disbelieved. One wonders if Nott's curiosity had not also been whetted by two public demonstrations of mesmerism in Mobile in the early months of 1843. In January of that year, Dr. Moore "excited the astonishment and admiration of the audience" with experiments on several nights, and in May a Mr. Fisk not only lectured on the subject but also played cards with a woman who had supposedly been both blindfolded and mesmerized.[44]

Mesmerism or animal magnetism had been controversial since its formal development by Dr. Franz Anton Mesmer in the eighteenth century. Mesmer had originally argued that "animal magnetism" was a universal fluid and that health depended on the maintenance of a correct balance of

42. Nott, "Facts Illustrative of the Practical Importance of a Knowledge of the Anatomy and Physiology of the Nervous System," *New Orleans Medical and Surgical Journal*, I (1844), 57–60.

43. For the Franklin Society see Amos, "Social Life in an Antebellum Cotton Port," 318–19; Delaney (ed.), *Craighead's Mobile*, 48; Ludlow, *Dramatic Life*, 431, 434; Buckingham, *Slave States*, I, 282; Mobile *Register*, December 25, 1845, February 17, 18, March 28, 1846.

44. Mobile *Register*, January 12, 13, 25, May 10, 1843.

the fluid in the human body. At first, Mesmer had used magnets to add or withdraw the fluid as necessary, but later he dispensed with the magnets and argued that they merely acted as conductors. Mesmer's theories became highly controversial and were easily satirized, particularly as in his last years he developed an interest in clairvoyance. Those who supported him emphasized the scientific nature of his work and were attracted by the idea that his healing efforts supposedly depended on the presence of a specific fluid rather than on occult procedures. In reality, Mesmer's cures were achieved in the area of psychosomatic medicine. He used hypnotism and the power of suggestion to cure a variety of psychosomatic illnesses. Yet in an age when many doctors were anxious to place medicine on a sound scientific footing, they were happier to find specific physical reasons for any aspect of the success of Mesmer and his followers. In the first decades of the nineteenth century, Mesmer's ideas were generally in disrepute, particularly because they had been taken over by a variety of quacks and showmen.[45]

Nott wrote that until early 1843 he had been "as obstinate a disbeliever in mesmerism as any man in the world," but after deciding to test it he threw himself into the work with enthusiasm. He tested mesmeristic phenomena on more than fifty subjects over the next three years. These included some of the "most respectable gentlemen and ladies of Mobile," some children ten or twelve years old, and some blacks. The last two categories were included because of the subjects' supposed lack of knowledge of the phenomena of mesmerism, which meant that they would be less likely to fake their responses. For most of this period Nott was simply trying to produce the phenomena he had read about in the literature, but in the last few months of his experiments he also tried to use animal magnetism for the purpose of healing. Most of his experiments were conducted in the private homes of his patients.[46]

The report on his experiments, which Nott published in a medical journal after delivering the gist of it to the Franklin Society, generally testified to his good sense and openness on medical matters. His general conclusion was that the subject had been too long in the hands of charla-

45. Vincent Buranelli, *The Wizard from Vienna: Franz Anton Mesmer* (New York, 1975), 17, 39, 62–77, 115–16, 205–10. For mesmerism in America see Robert C. Fuller, *Mesmerism and the American Cure of Souls* (Philadelphia, 1982).

46. The material in this and the following paragraphs is from Nott, "A Lecture on Animal Magnetism, delivered by request, before the Mobile Franklin Society, 18th Feb., 1846," *Southern Journal of Medicine and Pharmacy* (Charleston), I (1846), 261–89.

tans and that there was "truth, and useful truth in mesmerism." He had not been able to produce clairvoyance or the more remarkable phenomena claimed for the subject (though he said there was evidence in the literature to support such phenomena), but he had been able to produce "a peculiar sleep, catalepsy, various degrees of insensibility to pain, the relief of many neuralgic pains, and contraction or relaxation of muscles at pleasure" in a number of individuals. The subject, he thought, had been confused by amateur practitioners, for as mesmeric phenomena "all emanate from the nervous system" only a physiologist or pathologist was capable of investigating them effectively.

Nott's general inclination was to support those who believed that some specific physical factor—a magnetic field—accounted for the phenomena of mesmerism. His interests had long inclined to a material interpretation of medicine and the universe, and he believed that somehow galvanism, electricity, magnetism, and mesmerism were all linked. The human body, he believed, was magnetic, and although most of his experiments were in reality simply efforts at psychosomatic medicine, he had on at least one occasion treated a case of female hysteria by placing a large horseshoe magnet by the bed. The success he said he had achieved in this case undoubtedly stemmed from the same power of suggestion and autosuggestion that he had used in most of the other cases reported on in this article on mesmerism. Yet, though Nott was inclined to believe that there was some unknown fluid that accounted for the phenomena, he was prepared to admit that "imagination" alone could work powerful effects. He concluded that if certain of the phenomena were true, "it is perhaps of little importance whether we attribute them to animal magnetism or the imagination." If others preferred to describe what was happening by the term "imagination" rather than "mesmerism," he argued, let them use it: "If the imagination is so easily brought into action in many persons, if it can exert such powerful influence over the body; if it can be so controlled as to cure many diseases which are difficult to cure by other means, then I say it is clearly a subject none the less worthy of investigation."

The methods Nott used, and the nature of his success, are made clear by his article. In many cases Nott was actually treating a variety of psychological problems by means of hypnotism or simply by suggestion and a calming, tactile therapy. Most of his patients treated in this way were women. His technique was to sit facing the patient, to take her hands, and to ask her to look steadily into one of his eyes. Nott then stared steadily at the patient and fixed his own "*will* by saying mentally *sleep, sleep,*

sleep." After a few minutes, if the patient was susceptible, she would begin to show signs of drowsing. Nott then removed one of his hands and placed it on the patient's head, still gazing at the patient until her eyes closed. He then passed his hands down the sides of her head and face along the arms to the tips of her fingers. The whole process took from two or three to ten minutes. It was possible to check for mesmeric sleep, Nott reported, by raising one of the patient's arms to a horizontal position—it would remain there indefinitely.

Nott emphasized that this technique usually did not work in the case of robust, healthy persons, and in some cases it merely produced drowsiness without sleep, but in more than fifty persons of "temperaments more or less nervous" he had induced sleep. He also stated that even in this sleep patient reactions were varied—some were insensible to pain, some not; in some cases muscles were rigid, in some cases not. Nott said he had found no proof of clairvoyance, though he thought it possible; he had never been able to produce an influence of the will, though, he said, he had tried it repeatedly; and in only two cases had he seen "magnetic attraction," with a patient's head or hands following his hand even when the patient was blindfolded. After nearly three years of testing his powers, Nott experimented with using his induced sleep for remedial purposes. Several times within two months he extracted teeth from patients who were in this mesmeric sleep; on two occasions he had the teeth extracted by a dentist while the patients were under his influence. He also described a case in which he was called to the wife of a local Spanish teacher. She had an excruciating pain in the back of her neck, and her muscles were so rigid she dared not move. Nott put her under, passed his hands down the side of her neck, and was able to turn her neck from side to side. She slept for an hour and awoke "perfectly relieved." There was some reoccurrence, but further treatments cured her.

In many cases, however, Nott did not have to use hypnotism. He stressed that the most extensive use he had made of mesmeric techniques was "in the nervous headaches of females, and I declare that my success had been so great and unexpected, that I can scarcely credit my own senses." He said that he was able to provide relief in nineteen out of twenty cases, and in most of these it was not necessary to induce sleep. He simply drew his hands slowly from the top of the head over the temples and repeated the action for a few minutes. He suggested that any physician could test this technique if he selected "half a dozen nervous females." Nott asserted that in spite of the attacks on mesmerism as impossible, "the sleep, catalepsy, insensibility to pain, the relief of pain, and some of its other phenomena *are nevertheless true*." Mesmerism, he said, was of great use in the treatment of nervous disorders. "I can produce very decided and satisfactory impressions on more than half of the ladies of the better class of society, whose mode of life is calculated to make them more or less nervous," said Nott. "The majority of these may be put to sleep or relieved of headaches in five minutes."

In the ten years after his arrival in Mobile Nott had established a successful practice while becoming a member of the town's elite. He was a confident, energetic, and able doctor who always kept abreast of the latest developments in the medical art, and his powers of conversation and wit, and his South Carolina connections, made him welcome in the best houses of Mobile. Nott was never particularly active in nonmedical municipal concerns, but even in these early years his local eminence was becoming obvious; his name usually appeared among the committee members designated to make the arrangements for the reception of visiting dignitaries. Nott was a Democrat but was little involved in party politics. He had friends from both parties and was usually content to defend his ideas through his writings. He was often concerned with questions of public health in Mobile, and for a time he served on the board of Mobile school commissioners, but for the most part he did not have the time or the inclination for a public life separate from his medicine and writing.[47]

By the mid-1840s, with Mobile again prosperous and Nott's practice a definite success, Nott decided to make arrangements for a permanent home and office in the center of the city. In the spring of 1844 he bought at public auction land approximately ninety feet square on the corner of St. Francis and St. Joseph streets. He paid $4,100, of which a quarter was down and the rest in installments.[48] Here Nott was to have his home and office for more than twenty years. By this time, Nott was not only firmly established in his business and personal life, he was also set in his beliefs. He was a man of extremely strong opinions, and he was now ready to express them on a variety of subjects. In his article on mesmerism, which was published in 1846, he went out of his way in a footnote to attack those who wrote on subjects without knowing anything about them.

47. Mobile *Register,* January 2, 1838, April 6, 1842, January 24, February 27, April 6, 15, 1843.
48. Deed Books, in Mobile County Court House, Mobile.

"Such writings fall upon my ear," he wrote, "like Broussais' theory and treatment of bilious fever, or the fine abstractions of an abolitionist. Where writers are not acquainted with the facts they cannot instruct us."[49] This statement revealed not only Nott's disillusionment with Broussais, the idol of his youth, but also a new preoccupation with the external dangers to the South and slavery. Nott had already begun to turn his scientific and research interest to the problem of race and its impact on southern and world history. He believed that he was being a fearless scientist following his research where it might take him. In reality, he was a man of his time and his peculiar environment using his talents to defend the way of life he knew and loved.

49. Nott, "A Lecture on Animal Magnetism," 281.

Chapter 4
SEPARATE ORIGINS

Until the early 1840s Nott avoided public commitment on anything but medical matters. This was now to change. Medicine continued to occupy most of Nott's time, but for the rest of his life his greatest fame was to be as an ethnologist writing on race. Nott had inherited a powerful intellect from his New England forebears, but it was an intellect born and nurtured in exotic South Carolina soil and shaped by a questioning family and education at freethinking South Carolina College. Nott was to become a fervent southern polemicist who defended white supremacy with all the zeal of a South Carolina slaveowner while urging the freedom of scientific inquiry from religious orthodoxy.

One of Nott's beliefs—that blacks were permanently inferior to whites—was an orthodox position in the South in the years leading to the Civil War. By itself his espousal of this idea would have brought little but praise for Nott in the society in which he lived. Surprisingly, however, Nott's ideas on race were acceptable and even welcomed outside the South—in the North and in Europe. Nott believed that the future progress of the United States and world civilization depended on government by white races untainted by racial mixing. He always devoted most of his scholarly attention on racial matters to the origin and nature of racial differences rather than to any simple defense of slavery. He wanted to educate both North and South to what he believed was scientific truth—that the black race was incapable of living with whites in a condition of freedom.

Nott caused controversy not by defending racial inequality but by one of the ways in which he chose to defend it. Like Thomas Cooper, Nott denied the scientific validity of the account of creation and early human history given in Genesis. For Nott, the permanent inferiority of blacks stemmed from creation itself; God had made blacks separate and unequal. Nott could have said much of what he wanted to say without attacking the use of the Bible for scientific purposes. Most of his scientific friends, both in the North and the South, reached much the same conclusions about black incapacity, but many of these friends found ways to pay lip service to religious orthodoxy while writing works that in effect challenged the scientific validity of Genesis. Nott, however, did not equivocate. Although he often protested that he wanted no public controversy, in reality he delighted in raising clerical hackles. He wanted to argue that the world was inhabited by a variety of inferior and superior races, but he also wanted to defend the independence of science against any attempt of the clergy to determine the course of scientific investigation. The accusations of irreligion that had been launched against Thomas Cooper and Henry Nott in South Carolina arose with even greater vigor against Josiah Nott, for he was to be far more daring in his views on science and religion than either of them.

When Nott began to write on race in the 1840s, his ideas, although expressed with his own idiosyncratic style, vigor, and extremism, represented the merging of two broad streams of thought within a distinctly southern setting. The eighteenth-century rationalism and materialism that had been influential in the South in the forty years after the American Revolution and flourished at South Carolina College with Thomas Cooper in the 1820s were in Nott to be blended with an ardent enthusiasm for the burgeoning scientific racism of the nineteenth century.

At the heart of Nott's motivation was the desire to defend the way of life he knew and enjoyed. Nott, like most other southerners of his generation, could not conceive of a society in which millions of blacks would mix in freedom with whites. He was far too knowledgeable to believe those who argued that freedom could be followed by mass overseas colonization. The ending of slavery would mean that in many parts of the South blacks would equal to or outnumber whites. To Nott this prospect was disastrous to contemplate—economically, socially, and politically. Another southern physician and a friend of Nott, Richard D. Arnold, expressed this point of view simply in 1837: "The institution of Slavery, although indefensible on the ground of abstract rights, can be defended and well defended upon this, that so intimately is it mingled with our social conditions, so deeply has it taken root, that it would be impossible to eradicate it without upturning the foundations of that condition."[1] By the 1840s abolitionists and a variety of other reformers in America and Europe were arguing that slavery had to end. As these antislavery arguments grew, Nott became increasingly exasperated at the inconsistency of European and northern reformers telling the South that slavery would have to end while northern and European scientists were engaged in proving the innate inequality of the races of mankind and the necessity of white supremacy for future world progress.

In the years between 1830 and 1860, western Europeans and Americans abandoned the theoretical belief in innate human equality that had dominated eighteenth-century thought. Nott was more outspoken and vituperative than most, but his views on racial difference won him the respect and friendship of some of the most important scientists in America and Europe. By the 1840s the most respected racial theorists believed that there were permanent differences between the races and that races could be categorized by innate ability. Most still publicly asserted, and many believed, that all human beings were descended from Adam and Eve, but the idea of separate creations for different races had already been defended strongly by some writers and was to become dominant among the most important American racial theorists by 1850. The process of separating human beings into separate, unequal races had its origins in pre-nineteenth-century thought, but only in the 1840s and 1850s did the advocates of the new racial hierarchies sweep all before them.[2]

By the time Nott wrote on racial differences, the topic had become of vital importance to a variety of writers. For more than a decade southerners had been using the new ideas to defend their institution of slavery, and by 1843 northerners were showing that the scientific defense of slavery was one aspect, not the root cause, of a variety of new racial theories. Southern assertions of innate black inferiority had become commonplace

1. Richard Arnold to Chandler Robbins, August 15, 1837, in Richard H. Shryock (ed.), *Letters of Richard D. Arnold, M.D., 1808–1876* (Durham, N.C., 1929), 14.

2. For the development of scientific racism in America after 1815 see William Stanton, *The Leopard's Spots: Scientific Attitudes Toward Race in America, 1815–59* (Chicago, 1960). Stanton gives a comprehensive account of the state of scholarly research in these years. His work includes the best account of Nott as an ethnologist, although Stanton minimizes the impact of the new racial ideas on popular thought. See also C. Loring Brace, "The 'Ethnology' of Josiah Clark Nott," *Bulletin of the New York Academy of Medicine*, 2d Ser., L (1974), 509–28. For the impact of the new ideas on American society see Reginald Horsman, *Race and Manifest Destiny: The Origins of American Racial Anglo-Saxonism* (Cambridge, Mass., 1981).

by the time Nott joined the argument. South Carolina had been a fertile breeding ground for the new ideas. As early as 1826, Thomas Cooper had stated that he had not the slightest doubt that blacks were "an inferior variety of the human species, and not capable of the same improvement as the whites," and he continued to maintain that position until his death.[3] In the 1830s a whole series of southerners defended essentially the same position, and some went even further to argue that the supposed permanent inferiority of blacks had its roots in an origin separate from that of the white race.

Beginning with the rather cautious pamphlet of Thomas R. Dew in 1832, in which he argued that slavery had to be perpetuated because mass colonization of free blacks was impracticable, not a year passed without a southern pamphlet or periodical attacking the idea of black equality. Even those who continued to maintain the common descent of human beings from Adam and Eve had no doubt that blacks were innately inferior to whites. Some, like J. Jacobus Flournoy, used the argument that the black race was descended from Ham and different from the rest of mankind because twice fallen; others, such as Robert G. Harper, were content to maintain that blacks were "an inferior variety of the human race."[4]

Polygenesis, the idea of multiple creations, was first publicly defended in the United States in 1830 in a pamphlet by Charles Caldwell. He argued that there were four distinct human species—Caucasian, Mongolian, Indian, and African—and that the Indian and the African were "inferiorly organized and endowed." His arguments stressed the differences between the accepted biblical chronology and what was known about the early history of the Middle and Near East. Caldwell's arguments shocked some, but he also had supporters, particularly in the South. Richard H. Colfax argued in 1833 that there were at least two distinct species, and J. H. Guenebault in 1837 published a translation of Frenchman J. J. Virey's arguments defending polygenesis.[5] Arguing that there had been separate

3. Cooper's letter is quoted in William S. Jenkins, *Pro-Slavery Thought in the Old South* (1935; rpr. Gloucester, Mass., 1960), 252. See also *Southern Literary Journal*, I (1835), 192.

4. Thomas R. Dew, *Review of the Debate in the Virginia Legislature of 1831 and 1832* (Richmond, 1832); J. Jacobus Flournoy, *An Essay on the Origins, Habits, &c, of the Negro Race: Incidental to the Propriety of Having Nothing to do with Negroes* (New York, 1835); *Southern Literary Journal*, n.s., III (1838), 168 (quotation).

5. Charles Caldwell, *Thoughts on the Original Unity of the Human Race* (New York, 1830), 72–74, 135, 173; see also Harriot W. Warner (ed.), *Autobiography of Charles Caldwell, M.D.*

creations was still highly controversial, for whatever clergymen believed about racial differences they were adamant in supporting the literal truth of the Bible. In the twenty years before the Civil War, as polygenesis came to be accepted by most of the main American racial theorists, clergymen in the South bridled at such religious skepticism while accepting the argument that blacks were a permanently inferior race.

American arguments for innate racial difference began the process of achieving general respectability with the publication in 1839 of Samuel George Morton's first major work. In the 1840s Morton became the central figure in what became known as the American school of ethnology. His main followers—who often went beyond him in the vigor of their arguments—were to be Nott, English-born Egyptologist George Gliddon, and archaeologist Ephraim G. Squier. Within this group Nott was to find friends and a comfortable intellectual home. Morton was a Philadelphia physician who in the years from 1839 to his death in 1851 became one of the world's leading craniologists. Much of his work was based on the extensive collection of skulls that he gathered in Philadelphia. Morton was a cautious scientist who knew that his defense of racial diversity threatened orthodox religious belief. He let others draw conclusions from what he wrote, but not until near the end of his life did he openly support the polygenetic position.[6]

The core of Morton's 1839 book, *Crania Americana,* was a detailed comparison of the Indians of North and South America, but he prefaced this study with a general essay on human races and concluded it with an essay on race by the phrenologist George Combe. Although Morton wrote nothing directly attacking the biblical story of Adam and Eve, he insisted that the earliest recorded accounts indicated the existence of distinct races with precisely the same basic characteristics as they had in the nineteenth century. Environmental forces, he argued, could not account for the differences between the races, and he emphasized that the Caucasian race was superior in its endowments. The blacks were "the lowest grade of humanity." In the main part of his book Morton reached the

---

(Philadelphia, 1855); Richard H. Colfax, *Evidence Against the Views of the Abolitionists, Consisting of Physical and Moral Proofs, of the Natural Inferiority of the Negroes* (New York, 1833), 7–8; J. H. Guenebault, *Natural History of the Negro Race* (Charleston, 1837).

6. The best account of the American school of ethnology is in Stanton, *Leopard's Spots.* See also D. A. Swan, "The American School of Ethnology," *Mankind Quarterly,* XII (1971), 78–98, and Stephen Jay Gould, *The Mismeasure of Man* (New York, 1981), 50–69. Gould discusses the weaknesses in Morton's research techniques.

conclusion that all the American Indians were composed of one race, which was essentially different from all others, including the Mongolian. Morton's book was greeted as a classic work. Even the clergy had little to attack because Morton was careful to avoid a direct challenge to the Mosaic account of creation. Although the book was accused of being irreligious, it did not stir up any general controversy.[7]

Morton's work was the turning point, and in the early 1840s the dividing of the human family into distinct superior and inferior races proceeded rapidly in the United States. Southern apologists for slavery naturally seized upon this defense by informed scientific opinion throughout America of the idea that a wide gulf separated an inferior black race from the superior Caucasians.

One of the great stumbling blocks for those who wished to argue that blacks were a separate species was the hypothesis, given its most elaborate statement by George-Louis Leclerc, Comte de Buffon in the eighteenth century, that hybrids produced by the mating of separate species could not produce fertile offspring.[8] If it could be shown that mulattoes were hybrids, then it could be contended that blacks were not descended from Adam and Eve. In 1843 Nott entered the public racial argument by contending that there was evidence to show that mulattoes were less fertile than either of the races that produced them. His short article in the *American Journal of the Medical Sciences* did not equivocate in its title: "The Mulatto a Hybrid—probable extermination of the two races if the Whites and Blacks are allowed to intermarry."

Nott's interest had been stimulated by an article the previous year in the *Boston Medical and Surgical Journal,* which argued that although pure Africans were the longest-lived of any people, mulattoes lived the shortest time of any members of the human race. Some southerners had already used the 1840 census to try to show that free blacks in the North were much less healthy and much more liable to early death than blacks in slavery, but Nott was particularly delighted that such an argument had been published in a New England journal—"the writer," he said, "cannot

7. Samuel George Morton, *Crania Americana; or, A Comparative View of the Skulls of Various Aboriginal Nations of North and South America. To Which Is Prefixed an Essay on the Varieties of the Human Species* (Philadelphia, 1839), 1–6, 260. See Stanton, *Leopard's Spots,* 39–40, for the limited nature of the attack on Morton.
8. Arthur O. Lovejoy, "Buffon and the Problem of Species," in Bentley Glass, Owsei Temkin, and William L. Stauss, Jr. (eds.), *Forerunners of Darwin, 1745–1859* (Baltimore, 1959), 84–113.

be charged with sectional prejudice, or the influence of self-interest." Encouraged by this northern argument, Nott now presented his own observations based, he wrote, on fifteen years of medical practice 'in situations where the population is pretty equally divided between the blacks and whites."[9] Nott's observations, like so many other medical and scientific observations in both North and South in these years, were clearly based not so much on empirical data as on preconceived ideas.

The supposed evidence advanced by Nott strongly supported the idea that mulattoes were hybrids. He argued that mulattoes were less capable of endurance and shorter-lived than blacks and whites; that mulatto women were particularly delicate and susceptible to female diseases, "bad breeders and bad nurses," often incapable of conception, frequently subject to miscarriages, and producers of children who were short-lived; that mulattoes who intermarried were less prolific than those who married one of the parent stocks; and that blacks and mulattoes were practically immune from yellow fever in the Mobile epidemics of 1837, 1839, and 1842. Nott admitted that there were exceptions to his "truths" and that he had no statistics to back them up. The statements, he wrote, would have to depend "upon my veracity alone." As a southern gentleman, Nott expected to be believed.

After his assertions based on his supposed observation of mulattoes, Nott added some general reflections on the human race and on species. He suggested, unsensationally but in a way that would shock the religious, that the five main races—Caucasian, Ethiopian, Mongol, Malay, and American—might have been either distinct creations or varieties of the same species, but he was confident that "*the Anglo-Saxon and Negro races are, according to common acceptation of the terms, distinct species, and that the offspring of the two is a Hybrid.*" Nott pressed on with assertions that had nothing to do with scientific observation. He compared the Caucasian female "with her rose and lily skin, Venus form, and well chiseled features" with "the African wench, with her black and odorous skin, woolly head and animal features." He asked the reader to compare their intellectual and moral qualities and their entire anatomical structure and decide whether they did not differ as much from each other as a swan from a goose or a horse from an ass. Why this was so he left moot—the

9. Nott, "The Mulatto a Hybrid—Probable Extermination of the Two Races if the Whites and Blacks are Allowed to Intermarry," *American Journal of the Medical Sciences,* n.s., VI (1843), 252–53. The quotations in the following paragraphs are from this article.

Creator at some period of time, he said, had so made or changed them.

Nature, wrote Nott, exhibited a great variety of hybrids, and human hybrids might also have their own peculiar laws. Might it not be the case that "the Mulatto or Hybrid is a degenerate, unnatural offspring, doomed by nature to work out its own destruction?" To back up his arguments he cited earlier historians of Jamaica who had argued that mulattoes were less prolific when married to each other than when they were married to blacks or whites, and he used Virey's contention that connections between Europeans and Australian aborigines were seldom prolific. Nott was always an avid reader, and his later articles and books are filled with citations to authorities who could be used to support his point of view.

Nott's conclusion was that there were fundamental physiological differences between blacks and whites. "It is well settled by anatomists and physiologists," he wrote, "that the brain of the Negro compared with the Caucasian is smaller by a full tenth, that its nerves are larger, the head differently shaped, the facial angle less, and the intellectual powers comparatively defective." Typically, Nott ended his article with an apology that it was written in haste and with the assertion that he was merely attempting to "start the ball" on this subject in the hope that someone with more ability and leisure would take it up. This was more an exercise in disarming possible criticism than innate modesty.[10]

This first essay on hybridity was cautious compared to most of Nott's later writings. He had suggested the possibility that blacks and whites were of separate species and that there could have been more than one creation, but his assertions were guarded. Soon, however, he threw caution to the winds in presenting his racial views to the citizens of his own city. In the winter of 1843–1844 Nott gave two lectures in Mobile on the natural history of the Caucasian and Negro races. The Mobile Franklin Society had helped to excite a taste for scholarly presentations, and at this time several prominent citizens were asked to give lectures on subjects of their own choosing. Nott's lectures on race, in which he chose to address some of the religious problems head-on, brought criticism and controversy, and Nott quickly had his lectures and a defense published by a local printer. In this published version of his lectures, which attracted national and even international interest, Nott indicated that he had made use of the writings of James Prichard, Charles Caldwell, George Gliddon, and Samuel Morton. He made use of some of Prichard's details, but he

10. *Ibid.*, 253–56.

strongly attacked Prichard's contention that human beings consisted of one species.[11]

Nott directly addressed the religious difficulties in his introduction. It was natural, he said, in looking at the various human types, to ask, "*are all these derived from one pair, or are they of distinct origins?*" Yet this question was difficult to approach, he argued, because of the religious objections that had already impeded the advance of astronomy and geology. Discoveries inconsistent with the Mosaic account of creation had been attacked and the discoverers persecuted. The unity of the human race, wrote Nott, was a question for natural history, and religion should have no part in it. "*My* object is truth," he wrote, "and I care not which way the question is decided, provided the discussion is a correct one." Astronomy and geology had already cast doubt on the scientific validity of the Bible and had required a rethinking of the Mosaic account. Similar doubts arose when the history of animal life was considered. The Ark could not have contained pairs of all the animals on earth—it could have had only the animals in the area where Noah lived. Similarly, the account of human origins given by Moses was "*imperfect.*" Geology and natural history could be merged with Christianity, if the words and works of God were properly understood.

After these fighting preliminaries, Nott announced that he intended to challenge the Mosaic account of Adam and Eve by maintaining that "there is a Genus Man, comprising two or more species." Unlike Morton, who simply advanced supposed proofs to demonstrate the ancient and contemporary gulfs between human races, Nott was prepared to show why and how the biblical account of human origins was wrong. Like Caldwell in his 1830 pamphlet, Nott laid great stress on the problems inherent in accepted biblical chronology. This chronology, he argued, had not been divinely inspired but had been appended to the Bible by later commentators. There were hundreds of different compilations, and there was even a difference of ten years in suggested dates for the birth of Christ. The most common accepted dates, those of Archbishop James Ussher, put the creation of the globe at 4004 B.C. and the flood at 2348 B.C. Modern science, said Nott, had demonstrated "beyond the possibility of a doubt" that these dates were too recent, probably by thousands of years.[12]

To challenge biblical chronology Nott made extensive use of recent re-

---

11. Nott, *Two Lectures, on the Natural History of the Caucasian and Negro Races* (Mobile, 1844).

12. *Ibid.*, 3–9.

search on ancient Egypt. Monumental evidence demonstrated that blacks and whites had existed in Egypt within a few years of Ussher's date for the flood, and there was reason to believe, wrote Nott, that the blacks did not descend from Noah's family. Blacks in ancient Egypt, as in modern America, were servants and slaves, and those historians who had once believed that the ancient Egyptians were black were wrong. The ancient Egyptians were Caucasians. From all this Nott drew the conclusion that the flood must either have been at a much earlier date or of limited extent. There were even trees in Africa and central America that were six thousand years old.[13]

Having attacked the idea that the Bible could be used as scientific evidence for the early origin and descent of man, Nott advanced the theory that there was "a Genus *Homo*" with different species and varieties and that the human race was descended from several or many original pairs. These original stocks were placed "in the climate and situation best suited to their organization." In a private letter in the following year, Nott was to write that "Nature has formed plants, animals, Birds, Fishes, insects & for each Zone where alone they can flourish." Nott was here anticipating the theories that achieved fame when put forward by Swiss scientist Louis Agassiz. Only after coming to America in 1846 did Agassiz extend his theory of zoological provinces to encompass a polygenetic argument for the origin of human beings.[14] Nott made it clear in these lectures and pamphlet that he believed that the account of human origins given in the Bible related only to a small area of the globe and that even for this restricted area the chronology usually given for the biblical account was wrong.

Nott used his hypothesis of separate creations and distinct human species as a basis for comparing the characteristics and innate abilities of the black and white races. The blacks, he said, were an inferior race intermediate between the Caucasians and the apes; they were permanently inferior because their brains were smaller. He brought in much of the material from his earlier article on mulattoes in an attempt to show that breeding across the races produced a weak hybrid; one hundred white men and one hundred black women isolated on a desert island, he argued, would in time become extinct.

13. *Ibid.*, 10–11.
14. *Ibid.*, 17–18; Nott to James Hammond, August 12, 1845, in Hammond Papers, LC. For Agassiz' theories see Edward Lurie, *Louis Agassiz: A Life in Science* (Chicago, 1960), 256–65.

Racial mixing not only weakened the individual, Nott stated, it also ruined the society. Egypt, he said, had fallen from her high position because of racial mixture—"the black stain." The "adulteration of blood," he wrote, was the reason why Egypt and the Barbary States could never rise again, until the present races were exterminated and the Caucasians substituted. Civilization had always depended on the Caucasian race and could survive only if the Caucasian strain was unadulterated by weaker strains. Nott dismissed the abilities not just of blacks but of all the nonwhite races. "History and observation, both teach," he wrote, "that . . . the Mongol, the Malay, the Indian and Negro, are now and have been in all ages and places, inferior to the Caucasian." At best, he argued, the Chinese could be considered as intermediate links between blacks and Caucasians.[15]

Nott was particularly scathing about the abilities of the Indians of the Americas. Even in discussing the highly developed Indians of Central America at the time of Spanish contact, Nott was outrageous in his assertions. "Every thing proves," he wrote, "that they were miserable imbeciles, very far below the Chinese of the present day in every particular." Their architectural prowess, he argued, proved nothing: "Every thing in the history of the Bee shows a reasoning power little short of that of a Mexican."[16] These assertions appeared in a pamphlet that helped Nott win the friendship and support of the famous Morton in Philadelphia, as well as the support and encouragement of a number of prominent European scientists.

When Nott wrote on race, he abandoned the scientific tolerance and good sense that usually pervaded his medical writings. His gift for vigorous and colorful language and his delight in controversy gave most of his writings on race a fervent and impassioned quality, particularly in the writings that were first given as lectures. He delighted in conversation, in repartee, and in the effect of what he was saying, and when he moved from the dinner table to the lecture platform he obviously delighted in the audience's response to his dogmatic and assured statements. "Can any reasoning mind believe," he asked, "that the Negro and Indian have always been the victim of circumstances? No, nature had endowed them with an inferior organization, and all the powers of earth cannot elevate them above their destiny."[17]

15. Nott, *Two Lectures*, 16, 23–24; 35.
16. *Ibid.*, 36–37.
17. *Ibid.*, 38.

Particularly noticeable in these first main racial arguments of Nott was his delight in sweeping generalizations. His attitudes toward blacks and other races were already well-shaped by the time of his first writings, and he was always on the lookout for evidence that could be used to support these preconceived racial theories and prejudices. Although Samuel Morton's research methods were badly flawed, he used seemingly careful comparisons of cranial capacity to support his conclusions. Nott simply wrote about what he had come to believe after a young manhood spent mainly in South Carolina and Alabama, and he largely supported his generalizations with selective historical materials. He told his friend James Hammond that "the negro question was the one I wished to bring out & embalmed it in Egyptian Ethnography &c to excite a little more interest."[18] This statement was not quite as candid as it seems, for Nott knew that Hammond was much more interested in defenses of slavery than he was in challenging the religious control of the early history of human beings. Nott had a dual objective in these first lectures. He was tacitly defending the southern institution of slavery and the subordination of blacks, but he was also challenging the right of the clergy to dismiss scientific investigation that clashed with the biblical account of human origins. Nott spoke from the heart in these first lectures on race. He was to spend much of his career as an ethnologist trying to find proofs for the opinions he had advanced with confidence in his first writings.

Although Nott constantly argued that he was advancing the cause of science against those who would pervert it, there was no scientific method in either his article on hybridity or his lectures on race. They were very much pieces based on his general reading and the prejudices he had formed in his daily life. He told Hammond that he had written the lectures "with about as little care as I write you, save the main points of the discussion."[19] There was much truth in this—Nott had a large and expanding medical practice, and he usually wrote in haste and without adequate preparation—but Nott also exaggerated these qualities in his work. Although he constantly said he was advancing the cause of scientific truth, he liked to be thought of as a southern gentleman, living in a town without adequate libraries or bookstores, who dashed off thought-provoking pieces to stimulate discussion. He felt less vulnerable when he could ap-

18. Nott to Hammond, August 12, 1845, in Hammond Papers, LC.
19. *Ibid.*

pear to be more casual, and he could in this way explain away the various inconsistencies and many typographical errors in his published work.

The stir and attention that his lectures caused encouraged Nott to plunge far more deeply into all the relevant writings on race. In the months following the publication of his lectures, he ordered books from the North and from Europe and constantly complained about the lack of good libraries in Mobile. Within eighteen months he was admitting that he now knew a lot more about race and related matters than he had when he wrote his lectures.[20] This extensive reading had little effect on his views.

Nott was already a prominent local physician before he began to write on race, but now he achieved local fame and national attention and a notoriety among those who disagreed with him. A northern visitor to Mobile, a guest of a minister who was later to challenge Nott's ideas in writing, noted in his diary his impressions of the published lectures and their author. He suggested that the essays were "the first attempt of a young medical man, just begining the world, to commend himself to his employers, by advocating their most obstinate prejudices, and giving them the benefit of professional pleading." He was shocked that Nott had announced his faith in the existence of living trees that antedated the flood.[21]

Nott had written in the appendix to his published lectures that he was "amazed" at the local objections to his views and said that he would add to his "crime of *heresy,* by turning Judas and betraying my teachers." He then listed distinguished scholars in various parts of America and Europe who "have passed for good christians in other parts of the world, but who would be counted as heretics in Mobile."[22] These were not defenders of polygenesis but merely those whose arguments in geology and natural history had led Nott to dismiss the Bible as a source of scientific truth.

The initial clerical disapproval of Nott's religious views was soon more than offset for Nott by the national and even international notice that the publication of his lectures brought him and by the local pride at having a

20. See Nott to Samuel G. Morton, October 15, 1844, February 20, September 4, 1845, in Samuel George Morton Papers, HSP; Nott to James Hammond, July 25, August 12, September 4, 1845, in Hammond Papers, LC.

21. Rev. G. Lewis, *Impressions of America and the American Churches: From Journal of the Rev. G. Lewis* (Edinburgh, 1845), 184–86.

22. Nott, *Two Lectures,* 43–45.

vigorous defender of white supremacy and a man who had attracted national attention. Nott asserted in October, 1844, that his lectures had done him much good in Mobile by giving him a "reputation for infinitely more talent & knowledge than I possess." By early 1845 he was even more confident. He said that public opinion in Mobile was backing him and that the pamphlet had doubled his practice.[23]

What particularly delighted Nott about the reaction to his lectures was that it brought him into close contact through correspondence, and eventually in person, with leading scientists and other writers on race in America and Europe. The most important sign that Nott was to be taken with utmost seriousness outside the South was that Samuel G. Morton wrote to him after reading his first efforts on race with the comment, "I have read your remarks on the mulatto race with much pleasure and instruction," and he sent Nott some of his own publications. This praise was of great importance to Nott because Morton was a northerner, and his *Crania Americana* had made him the foremost American scientist writing about racial matters. The book had been reviewed as the best work on the history of man ever published in America. Morton continued to add to his reputation in the 1840s, and he was well-known and highly respected in Europe as well as in the United States. A meeting of the French Ethnological Society was devoted to the *Crania Americana*, and the distinguished Swedish anatomist Andreas Retzius told Morton in 1847 that he had done more for ethnography than any living physiologist.[24] The correspondence between Morton and Nott that began with Morton's favorable comments on Nott's work continued until Morton's death, and beginning in 1845 Nott usually visited Morton in Philadelphia when he went to the North.

Another correspondent, and eventually a fairly close friend, that Nott gained at this time was George R. Gliddon, an Englishman who for many years had lived in Egypt and the Middle East. Gliddon had begun to correspond with Morton in the late 1830s when Morton had asked him to supply Egyptian skulls. In the 1840s Gliddon wrote a number of works on ancient Egypt, studied with famous European Egyptologists, and toured the United States giving popular lectures on Egyptology. Gliddon

23. Nott to Morton, October 15, 1844, February 20, 1845, in Morton Papers, HSP.
24. Morton quoted in "Dr. Nott's Reply to 'C'," *Southern Quarterly Review*, VIII (1845), 160; *American Journal of Science and Arts*, XXXVIII (1840), 341; Richard K. Haight to Morton, May 11, 1844, Andreas Retzius to Morton, April 3, 1847, in Morton Papers, HSP.

was a man of infectious enthusiasms, who eventually delighted as much as Nott in baiting the clergy. He kept up a constant and extensive correspondence in the United States, partially because he was a gregarious, gossipy person and partially to ensure the success of his lecture tours. He used his many American contacts to arrange lecture dates in their home towns and to provide accommodations and hospitality during his stay. He was often short of money, and he leaned on the generosity of his American friends, including Nott.[25]

In the early 1840s Gliddon, who in his private correspondence was fond of outrageous statements in the Nott style, was extremely cautious in his public lectures. Theodore Parker said that Gliddon confirmed all the stories of the Old Testament in his public lectures "but does not believe a word of them in private." He was soon to discard this public caution. He was delighted with Nott's lectures, began to correspond with him, and encouraged him to continue and increase his attacks on clerical attempts to interfere with scientific research. In writing to Nott about his published lectures on race, he recommended a batch of new books on the subject, books in which, he wrote, a parson stands "no more chance than a stump tailed Bull in fly time." Gliddon filled his letters with dogmatic assertions, long accounts of the chronology and racial history of ancient Egypt, long lists of books, and a series of underlinings and exclamation points. He had earlier referred Morton to various writings with the comment, "You will learn much about [the] Antiquity of *Niggers!*" In the early 1840s Gliddon helped inform Americans, including Morton and Nott, about the new European research that was revolutionizing the history of ancient Egypt. The southerners were, of course, primarily delighted with the news that whites and blacks existed as distinct races in the distant past, and in 1844 John C. Calhoun met with Gliddon in Washington to obtain the latest information on the ancient separation of races.[26]

Morton was never as lacking in caution as Gliddon and Nott, but in the mid-1840s he was pleased to find enthusiastic allies who would help divert the barbs of the parsons, for he was edging toward a defense of the

25. The best account of Gliddon is in Stanton, *Leopard's Spots.*
26. Theodore Parker to Caroline Healey, April 4, 1843, in John Weiss, *Life and Correspondence of Theodore Parker* (2 vols.; New York, 1864), I, 353; Nott to Hammond, August 12, 1845, in Hammond Papers, LC; Gliddon to Morton, April 1, 1844, in Morton Papers, HSP; Nott and Gliddon, *Types of Mankind* (Philadelphia, 1854), 50–52.

idea of multiple creations as a basis of racial diversity. In the 1844 published version of a lecture he had delivered two years earlier, Morton argued that distinct races existed at the time of the primitive dispersal of the
human species, and this was fully compatible with the Bible. More sig-
nificantly, in 1844 Morton published his second major work—the *Crania Aegyptica*. Morton, like Nott, concluded that those who had argued
that the ancient Egyptians were black were wrong. His cranial research
had established that they were Caucasians. "Negroes were numerous in
Egypt," he wrote, "but their social position in ancient times was the same
that it now is, that of servants and slaves." Morton still avoided any direct
conflict with the biblical account of creation, but he asserted that "the
physical or organic characters which distinguish the several races of men,
are as old as the oldest records of our species." Southerners were delighted
that Morton had stressed that the lowly position of blacks stretched back
into the mists of history. One southerner wrote from Charleston after
reading the book that "in the South, we shall not be so much frightened
hereafter by the voices of Europe or of Northern America." He said that
he hoped to give the book to John C. Calhoun, who would "appreciate
the powerful support which may be deduced from it, of our peculiar institutions, here." [27]

Nott was delighted with the book. He believed that Morton's researches
had proved the errors of the usual biblical chronologies, though he admitted that "it may not be very *politic* to say so in these days of Christian
intollerance [sic]." The Bible, Nott wrote to Morton, is of divine origin,
but "it shows no knowledge beyond the *human* knowledge of the day &
its great ends do not require any other." Nott also took the opportunity
presented by Morton's new book to point out to him that Nott's own
observation of mulattoes tended to prove the original separation of races.
The lack of statistical data to back up his assertions should not invalidate
them, he argued, for he sought scientific truth and was "as free from sectional feeling or prejudice on this point as an oak tree." [28]

In February, 1845, Nott's determination to marshal more knowledge on
racial matters increased sharply. He heard from the editor of the *Southern*

27. Morton, *An Inquiry into the Distinctive Characteristics of the Aboriginal Race of America* (2d ed.; Philadelphia, 1844), 36; Morton, *Crania Aegyptica; or, Observations on Egyptian
Ethnography, Derived from Anatomy, History and the Monuments* (Philadelphia, 1844), 65–66;
William B. Hodgson to Morton, March 29, 1844, in Morton Papers, HSP.
28. Nott to Morton, October 15, 1844, in Morton Papers, HSP.

Quarterly Review that an Episcopal minister and botanist, Moses Ashley Curtis, a native of Massachusetts who lived in North Carolina, had written an article attacking Nott's lectures for the April number of the review. Nott immediately wrote to Morton asking for any information he could send that would help him to reply. To supplement his own modest collection of books, he told Morton, he would not be stopped "by any moderate expense." He was obviously a little worried about the effect that a strong attack might have on his reputation and wrote that he expected to be "skinned alive for not believing as the Presbyterians believe, the facts of science to the Contrary notwithstanding." His opponent, instead of writing like a gentleman, could be expected to "prove scientific points as parsons generally do, by proving one end of the Bible out of the other."[29] In spite of his own virulence on racial matters, Nott constantly raised nonexistent differences between gentlemanly and nongentlemanly forms of argument.

Curtis was in fact more moderate in language than Nott. In his article he emphasized the widely varying impacts that the environment could have on human beings, and he also stressed that plants and animals could adapt to extremely different regions of the world; there was no need to assume different creations in different regions. Curtis was on extremely safe ground in pointing out that, contrary to Nott's assertions, mulattoes were prolific. He concluded therefore that they were not hybrids and that blacks and whites belonged to the same species. Curtis' general judgment of Nott and his lectures coincided remarkably closely with Nott's own private statements regarding the hurried and ill-prepared way in which he had put the lectures together. "On perusing the pamphlet," wrote Curtis, "we came to the conclusion that the writer was a young man, too eager for taking rank among savans to wait for a due digestion of his varied reading, too impatient for the slow toil of laying deep and sure the foundations of an impregnable reputation."[30]

Although Curtis' reply to Nott was not cast in extreme terms, Nott thought that it showed "a great want of gentlemanly fairness & temper." He told Morton that he could not allow this critique to pass without reply, for to do so would injure him. Once again, he said, time was a problem—his practice prevented him from putting in sustained work on

29. Nott to Morton, February 20, 1845, *ibid.*
30. Moses A. Curtis, "Unity of Races," *Southern Quarterly Review,* VII (1845), 372–448, 447 (quotation).

his article for the *Quarterly*—but by July Nott was in print again, publishing the first part of a reply that was completed in the journal early in the following year. In essence the article was a defense of his original lectures, particularly of that section in which he had made a chronological challenge to the account of human origins given in Genesis, but Nott also used his reply to link his name with that of the famous Morton by quoting from Morton's favorable letter about his lectures. To Morton, Nott protested that Curtis' "ungentlemanly" attack had meant that he had to reply with less admissions of uncertainty than otherwise would have been the case for Curtis would take advantage of such confessions "& backed by the Bigotry of the church would place me before the ignorant *Mass,* in a very ridiculous position." Accordingly, Nott argued, he had assumed "a much more confident & *impudent* tone than I otherwise should."[31] As Nott's original pamphlet had been presented to the world filled with dogmatic and wild generalizations, it is difficult to conceive that the rather inoffensive Curtis had stirred Nott to confidence and impudence.

Nott had joined the racial argument at an opportune time. Race was a topic of wide public concern in the North and in Europe as well as in the South, and by dogmatically challenging Genesis, defending free inquiry, and arguing for separate creations, Nott had grasped the nettle that Morton and the more cautious scientists had been skirting. When Gliddon wrote to Morton from Paris, he asked to be remembered to "our *Mobile* Champion."[32] To a later generation Nott's views on Caucasians, blacks, and Indians are wildly racist and obviously nonscientific—the extreme ravings of an ardent southern publicist—but at the time they were far more than that. It soon became apparent that Nott was reaching conclusions on race and the scientific weaknesses of the Bible that many intellectuals outside the South—in the North and western Europe—found acceptable and scientifically sound. In his day Nott was anything but a crank. He was a respectable scientist who was controversial not because of his extreme and even violent views on race but because he had made no attempt to disguise his desire to see the Bible abandoned as a source of scientific knowledge. To dismiss Nott as a fringe southern polemicist with outlandish racial views is to ignore the respect with which his views were treated in the North and in Europe.

The excitement generated by his clash with Curtis stimulated Nott to

31. Nott to Morton, May 19, June 1, 1845, in Morton Papers, HSP.
32. Gliddon to Morton, October 31, 1845, *ibid.*

an extensive correspondence on racial matters in the summer of 1845. Having gained the notice of Morton, Nott was anxious to continue and expand their relationship. He knew full well that to gain the friendship and help of the foremost northern writer on ethnology was a major triumph for a southerner anxious to defend racial inequality, and his letters to Morton were far less dogmatic than those to his southern friends. Morton had suggested that some of Nott's assertions were not yet capable of proof and that some of the races intermediate between black and white had originally been formed by a mixture of the two. Nott was quick to agree with this possibility. He also qualified his remarks on the inability of mulattoes to breed fertile offspring—and at the same time gave a special status to northern Europeans—by suggesting that blacks who intermixed with the French and Spanish produced mulattoes who lived longer and were more prolific than were the offspring of an Anglo-Saxon–black mixture. This, he suggested, was because the southern Europeans had greater "affinity of blood" with Africans than the northern Europeans.[33]

Nott had always been a bookish man, and he was fond of quoting from his favorite books—both literary and scientific—but the attention given to his lectures and the quarrel with Curtis took him on a far more ambitious course of acquiring books that was to stay with him throughout his life. As a young man he had read for pleasure as well as for medical training, but from this time he devoted most of his library to books on race and ethnology and to professional medical literature. He was willing to give his northern correspondents any help they required in the South— he was collecting alligator heads for Morton in 1845 and later was to collect specimens for Louis Agassiz—but in return he had no compunction in asking his northern correspondents, including Morton, to combine with their booksellers in sending him lists of books on particular topics that would aid his racial research. "All I can hope to do in Mobile," he told Morton, "is to get information enough on a subject to display my ignorance—I went a few days ago to look for Baron Munchausen and Robinson Crusoe for one of my little boys & could not find them!"[34]

To Morton, Nott continued to be reasonably cautious, somewhat deferential, and falsely retiring—he told him "all I care about is the title of

33. Nott to Morton, July 15, 1845, *ibid.*
34. Nott to Morton, September 4, 1845, *ibid.;* Nott to Joseph Leidy, March 15, 1856, in Joseph Leidy Papers, ANSP.

Gentleman"—but to his old friend James Hammond, who had recently finished a term as governor of South Carolina, Nott was his usual confident, outrageous self. He had a particular interest in Hammond in the summer of 1845 because the former governor had just published a defense of slavery that was to become widely sold and extremely popular in the South. Nott was delighted with the newspaper extracts he had seen and told Hammond that on this subject "we cannot be too vigilant." He also took the opportunity to present his own view of the quarrel with Curtis. Nott was not optimistic that either Hammond's or his own arguments would have any quick effect on the abolitionists. "Abolition," he wrote, "is one of those unfortunate questions which present one face to the philosophers & another to the mass." Nott believed that many outside the South were simply unable to comprehend the immediate and practical problems that abolition would bring. He hoped that his own racial arguments would eventually cause a rethinking, but he was never optimistic that those outside the South would understand what was at stake. He made it clear in writing to Hammond that he believed his doctrine of separate creations was of vital importance to the argument. To Nott it was essential to knock down any religious belief that blacks and whites were brothers and sisters under the skin. "Just get the dam'd stupid crowd safely around Moses," he told Hammond, "and the difficulty is at an end."[35]

To Hammond, as to Morton, Nott revealed the extent to which he believed himself linked to an older, gentlemanly tradition that was being threatened by a variety of new tendencies, including abolitionism. In the next thirty years Nott often referred to the world as a sordid, money-grubbing, power-mad arena that was no fit place for a gentleman. Although he took this stance, he also had a keen eye for the extension of his medical practice and an obvious delight in public controversy. Nott liked to think of himself as a gentleman defending an established order even while he was attempting to shatter orthodox religious opinion. In response to Hammond's suggestion of weariness with the honor of public office, Nott reminded him of what he had told him when he had first sought the governor's chair: "Politics is no calling for a Gentleman now a days—You do things yet with *some* decency in Carolina, but in Washington & every where else it is all *filth*." Cynicism was often a pose for Nott.

35. Nott to Morton, July 15, 1845, in Morton Papers, HSP; Nott to Hammond, July 10, 25, 1845, in Hammond Papers, LC.

He was not really believable when he wrote to Hammond, "Damn the Reviewers, let them have their own way—they cannot hurt *my* reputation much or feelings either, for I never aspired to any celebrity beyond that which could be useful to me in the community in which I live—I want reputation which will pay—that *Almighty dollar* is the thing at last."[36] In reality, Nott sought the admiration and respect of the international scientists and scholars he himself admired, and he fought passionately for what he believed in. In his medical practice it made him a fine doctor; in ethnological arguments it made him an arrant racist.

Nott was more open with Hammond than with Morton about the delight his new fame had brought him. "My Nigger hallucinations," he wrote, "have given me much more notoriety than I had any idea of." He told Hammond about the friendly overtures he had received from Morton and Gliddon and said that the latter had convinced him that Egyptology would soon irrevocably shatter accepted biblical chronology. Although there had been local criticism at first, he wrote, "no body finds fault with me in Mobile now." To add to his pleasure, his lectures had already brought a foreign response. The famous actor William C. Macready, who played in Mobile in 1844, had dined with Nott, read his lectures, and taken a copy to England. He gave it to John Elliotson, a prominent English physiologist. Elliotson wrote to Nott saying that he would make use of the work in the next edition of his translation of Johann Friedrich Blumenbach's physiology, which Elliotson had published with extensive notes. Nott's work also rapidly became known in Paris. Here Gliddon was of great help. He discussed Nott's writing with interested Parisians and told Morton of his own admiration of Nott's "fearless defense of *Science* from ecclesiastical *stiflings*." Gliddon was a passionate friend or foe, and before he ever met Nott he wrote of him with the warmth of genuine friendship.[37]

The quarrel with Curtis lingered into 1846 and continued to give wide publicity to Nott's views. In January the *Southern Quarterly Review* published the second part of Nott's answer to Curtis' attack. This was largely a restatement of his previous arguments, but as usual he backed his position by bringing in the name and evidence of his latest correspondent. Gliddon's authority was used in support of the antiquity of separate races

36. Nott to Hammond, July 25, September 4, 1845, in Hammond Papers, LC.

37. Nott to Hammond, August 12, September 4, 1845; *ibid.;* Gliddon to Morton, October 31, 1845, January 28, April 24, 1846, in Morton Papers, HSP.

in Egypt. Nott again clearly demonstrated that his views on race encompassed far more than a simple defense of slavery. He said that the American Indians were doomed to disappearance. Their "capacity" was limited, he wrote, "and incapable of development." After a few generations, all the Indians would have gone: "Their destiny, in another world, rests in the hands of an Omnipotent god, whose laws we have no right to call in question. A powerful argument against their Adamic origin is the impossibility of civilizing or christianizing them." The juxtaposition of these two sentences was well-designed to infuriate the clergy. Curtis replied yet again, but there was little more to be said; unwittingly, Curtis had widely publicized Nott's views.[38]

Nott's contacts within the wider scientific world became more solid in the winter of 1845–1846. In the fall he traveled to the North and took the opportunity to visit Morton in Philadelphia. Personal contact usually increased Nott's influence, and this visit was no exception. In person, Nott could be a scintillating man; he made friends with ease. At this time Morton arranged for Nott to be made a corresponding member of the Academy of Natural Sciences. On his return to Mobile, Nott entertained the visiting English geologist Charles Lyell. Nott in person did not usually exhibit the uncompromising arrogance he showed in print. Lyell argued that in a few generations blacks could be brought up to whites in intelligence. Nott tried to convince him otherwise but bore Lyell no grudge. He told Morton that he liked Lyell very much and that he was "an honest seeker after truth." But because he was traveling so fast, he would probably write "a good deal of trash."[39]

The brief article on mulattoes and the two lectures on race had made a striking impact. They had been received not as the typical productions of a southern slavery apologist but as the major contribution of a man of science. Of vital importance in achieving this response was Nott's emphasis on broad racial themes rather than on slavery itself, but most important was that he had chosen to urge the independence of science from the limitations of clerical interpretations of the Bible. When Caldwell had defended separate creations in 1830, he had stood in isolation, but by the time Nott began to write, the surging interest in racial classification and differentiation made Nott's theories readily acceptable. More cautious scientists might not want to defend a theory of separate creations, but

38. *Southern Quarterly Review,* IX (1846), 1–57, 372–91.
39. Nott to Morton, February 23, 1846, in Morton Papers, HSP.

they were anxious that it should be made clear that racial differentiation went so far into the past that it cast doubt on accepted biblical chronology and the biblical account of the origin of human beings. In achieving immediate notoriety and prominence Nott was also helped by the particular friends and enemies he made. Morton gave him respectability, Gliddon publicized him, and Curtis allowed his views to be reiterated in the influential *Southern Quarterly Review*. When in the second half of the 1840s the scientific argument over the origin and nature of racial differences reached a peak in the United States, Nott was at the heart of the storm. He had begun with the object of defending the southern way of life, but this particular argument was subsumed in a series of discussions about the importance of race in history and in contemporary America and in a major quarrel over the fallibility of the Bible as a source of scientific fact.

Chapter 5
A NATIONAL FIGURE

In the years between 1846 and 1850 the most important American scientists interested in racial diversity reached the conclusion that there had been separate creations in different areas of the globe; Adam and Eve were not unique. For Nott these were exciting years. Although clerics continued to resent his lack of reverence for the Bible and his delight in pointing out the scientific inconsistencies in the account of human origins given in Genesis, the most respected northern racial theorists joined with him in asserting that all human races could not have descended from a single pair. Morton gradually revealed his belief in multiple creations in the second half of the decade, and there were a number of important recruits to the cause of pluralism. By far the most influential of these was the Swiss-born zoologist Louis Agassiz.

Agassiz had won a major scientific reputation in Europe before coming to the United States in 1846. Recently he had argued that the world had a number of distinct zoological provinces each with its own particular plant and animal life. The only exception, he had argued, was the human race, which was a single species spread over the surface of the globe. After arriving in the United States and settling in Boston, Agassiz steadily moved toward the idea that his hypothesis of creations in separate zoological provinces applied to human as well as to other animal life. For Agassiz this was a major personal as well as professional decision, for he held strong religious beliefs.[1]

Agassiz showed signs of abandoning unity from the first months after his arrival in the United States, although it was to be 1850 before he threw

1. See Edward Lurie, *Louis Agassiz: A Life in Science* (Chicago, 1960), 256–59.

caution to the winds by publicly defending polygenetic views. In the fall of 1846 he visited Philadelphia to see Morton and was shocked by his first sight of blacks. Referring to "this degraded and degenerate race," he wrote to his mother that it was impossible for him to repress his feeling "that they were not of the same blood as we are."[2] This personal aversion stayed with Agassiz and influenced his scientific conclusions. Later, in the Civil War, he told a correspondent who advocated racial amalgamation as a solution to America's racial tensions that "the idea of amalgamation is most repugnant to my feelings. I hold it to be a perversion of every natural sentiment." The population arising from an amalgamation of races, argued Agassiz, was always degenerate.[3] In 1846 Agassiz was not yet in Nott's camp, but in the following years he moved away from a belief in the unity of the human race.

While Agassiz prepared to fit human races within his scheme of zoological provinces, Morton was in the process of making overt what had been implicit in his writings since the publication of his *Crania Americana* in 1839. In 1846 he sent a paper to the American Ethnological Society in which he argued that the American Indians were one race but that they might have originated from any number of pairs. Writing to archaeologist Ephraim G. Squier, who through his study of Indian mounds was proving the great antiquity of Indians in America, Morton said that there "may have been fifty pairs for all I know to the contrary" and that the Indian race was "indigenous to the American continent; having been planted there by the hand of Omnipotence."[4]

In the fall of 1846 Morton also joined the hybridity argument in a far more systematic way than Nott and with a different emphasis. In a long paper delivered at the Academy of Natural Sciences in Philadelphia, Morton argued that the infertility of crosses was not the proper mark of distinction between species. He asserted that there were numerous examples of distinct species crossing to produce fertile hybrids. Thus, he said, it was inaccurate to argue that the fertility of those produced by the crossing of different human races meant that all humans were of one species.

2. Quoted in *ibid.*, 256. See also Asa Gray to Morton, October 13, 1846, in Morton Papers, HSP.
3. Agassiz to Samuel G. Howe, August 9, 10, 1863, in Louis Agassiz Papers, Houghton Library, Harvard University, Cambridge, Massachusetts.
4. William Stanton, *The Leopard's Spots: Scientific Attitudes Toward Race in America, 1815–59* (Chicago, 1960), 97; Morton to Squier, December 8, 1846, April 10, 1847, in Squier Papers, LC.

Morton was taking a much different, and more defensible, ground than Nott, who was arguing that mulattoes became infertile. Both Morton and Agassiz used Nott's idea, however, to the extent that they argued that breeding between races produced individuals who were less fertile. As late as 1863 Agassiz argued that among the characteristics of half-breeds was "their sterility or at least their reduced fecundity."[5]

Although Morton's position on hybridity differed from his own, Nott was delighted that Morton's researches were leading him further in the direction of a vigorous defense of racial diversity. Writing to Morton in the spring of 1847, Nott agreed with his contention that climate might have much to do with the fecundity of particular hybrids. Nott was able to use Morton's hybridity article in his next contribution to the racial controversy, an article on the mortality of southern slave populations, which he published in *De Bow's Review*. James D. B. De Bow, a South Carolinian, had founded his famous journal in his own state but had quickly moved it to New Orleans. There it became one of the best known of southern periodicals. De Bow became a good friend and an ardent supporter of Nott and often publicized his ideas. In his article for De Bow, Nott revealed himself far more as an outright defender of slavery than he had in his earlier publications. He argued that attempts at bettering the condition of the slaves were useless. The Negro, said Nott "attains his greatest perfection, physical and moral, and also his greatest longevity, in a state of slavery." Emancipation was doomed to failure, for outside of slavery blacks relapsed into a state of barbarism.[6]

In a letter appended to his article, Nott more directly took up the challenge of the abolitionists. The basic question that had to be answered, he wrote, was who would be helped by emancipation. Clearly it would not help whites, for emancipation would ruin the great staple crop production of the South. Would it help the blacks? Nott's answer was a resounding no. Southern blacks, he wrote, were better off than blacks in Africa, the West Indies, or the North. Arguments about unity or pluralism, he said, were irrelevant to the question of the necessity of slavery. No one who wrote on the subject of the natural history of man, whether attack-

---

5. Stanton, *Leopard's Spots,* 113–18; Agassiz to Samuel G. Howe, August 9, 1863, in Agassiz Papers.
6. Nott to Morton, June 1, 1847, in Morton Papers, HSP. For De Bow see Ottis C. Skipper, *J. D. B. De Bow: Magazinist of the Old South* (Athens, Ga., 1958); Nott, "Statistics of Southern Slave Populations with Especial Reference to Life Insurance and the Question of Slavery and the Slave States," *De Bow's Review,* IV (1847), 280.

ing or defending the original unity of human beings, maintained the intellectual equality of blacks and whites. History, wrote Nott, gave positive proof that there was no way to enlarge the brain of a race and expand its intellect through education. Caucasian heads had always been as they were in the nineteenth century—the head was ready formed, and "when the spark is applied the intellect blazes forth." Black heads and brains were still as they were in ancient Egypt—inferior in intellectual capacity. This condition could not be changed. The species, argued Nott, was irrevocably fixed in its inferiority. Similarly, the Indian, though "untamable, carnivorous," and unlike the "mild and docile" Negro, was incapable of change. The Indian race "must soon be extinct—even the pure blood Mexicans, who I have no question are a different race from the aboriginal savage, are going down in darkness to their long home."[7]

Nott's confidence in his defense of slavery grew rapidly in the following years, helped by Morton's writings on hybridity, by the news from Charleston late in 1847 that Agassiz was defending the diversity of races in his lectures, and by George Gliddon's visit to Mobile early in 1848. Nott had arranged for Gliddon to give a series of nine lectures in Mobile under the sponsorship of the Franklin society. The two men were instant friends. Gliddon dined frequently in Nott's home and was delighted with his host. He wrote to tell Morton that Nott was "a *prince* of a fellow, as well as a *savant*." In his turn, Nott was highly impressed by Gliddon and by his lectures on ancient Egypt. When Gliddon left for New Orleans, Nott sent with him a letter of recommendation to James De Bow, stating that more could be learned from Gliddon in a few weeks than from any other source. Gliddon, of course, had told Nott what he wanted to hear about the ancient diversity of races in Egypt. Nott told De Bow that Gliddon knocked unity "into a cocked hat," carrying chronology far beyond the dreams of Noah and Adam.[8]

Nott's desire to show the antiquity of racial diversity and to prove the inaccuracy of accepted Old Testament chronology was given another boost in 1848 by the publication of Ephraim G. Squier's *Ancient Monuments of the Mississippi Valley* (written jointly with Dr. Edwin H. Davis). Nott now gained another correspondent and friend. Several years earlier,

7. Nott, "Statistics of Southern Slave Populations," 277–80, 288–89.
8. See Gliddon to Morton, January 9, February 3, 1848, in Morton Papers, HSP; Nott to De Bow, March 2, 1848, in James D. B. De Bow Papers, William R. Perkins Library, Duke University, Durham, North Carolina.

Squier had begun to investigate the Indian mounds at Chillicothe, Ohio. He had attracted Morton's attention because his work quickly showed the great antiquity of Indian life in the United States and thus threw new doubts on biblical chronology. Squier was even more cautious on religious matters than Morton, and he let others draw their own conclusions about racial origins from his work, but he was quickly taken into Morton's circle.[9] In the summer of 1848 he initiated a correspondence with Nott. As usual, Nott was delighted to be noticed, and with Squier, as with Gliddon, Nott had a relaxed informality that he never assumed in his correspondence with Morton.

Even when writing to a brand-new acquaintance, Nott had no qualms about scoffing at orthodox religion and emphasizing his commitment to the overturning of the account of human origins given in Genesis. In his first letter to Squier he expressed the hope that Squier's researches into the ancient American mounds would give the "coup de grace" to Moses. "I have no disposition to meddle with religion," wrote Nott, "as long as it is confined to its proper sphere, but we must not allow worn out legends to obstruct the path of science." Later, after reading several issues of a new English ethnological journal edited by Luke Burke, he expressed his delight that challenges to Old Testament chronology and science had become commonplace. Moses, he thought, would have to take rank "amongst the lesser heathen Gods." Nott prided himself that he was even bolder than Luke Burke: "I attack the authenticity of the Pentateuch directly & quote 'all the parsons this side of Hell' to sustain me."[10]

The five years since Nott had published his brief article on hybridity had seen a stream of publications endorsing his view of the ancient, deep, and irrevocable divisions between races. He was gratified by this support and by the manner in which his name and fame had spread beyond Mobile. His delight bubbles through in his letters. He could hardly believe that a brief article on hybridity and the forthright lectures on race had achieved so much so rapidly. He had begun as an obscure physician, he told Squier, "& I am now in Scientific correspondence with all Creation."[11]

In both his private letters and his publications Nott in the 1840s

9. For Squier see Stanton, *Leopard's Spots,* 82–88.
10. Nott to Squier, August 18, September 7, 1848, in Squier Papers, LC.
11. Nott to Squier, September 30, 1848, *ibid*. This letter is also the source for the next two paragraphs.

showed as much interest in attacking religious orthodoxy as in defending slavery. He was determined to free science from any necessity to restrict its arguments for fear of religious objections, but he also delighted in irritating the clergy and shocking the orthodox. If he ever lied, he told Squier, "I hope the Devil may gather me to his bosom"—"I have a great respect for his Sable Majesty. I regard him as a bold and manly fellow, & a gentleman—these are rare qualities in our Mythology." The authority of the Old Testament in scientific matters had nearly gone, wrote Nott, "and the parsons must look out for a new humbug." He was thankful, he said, that he lived in the glorious nineteenth century.

Nott liked to regard his writings as disinterested scientific endeavors, but in reality they were special pleadings of major political importance in the South. Many southerners as well as northerners were irritated by his scoffing attitude toward religion, but most were willing to ignore his irreverence because of the importance of his ideas for the defense of slavery. In the fall of 1848 Nott received an invitation that demonstrated the extent to which his writings were entwined with the political history of the South in these years. Nott's friend James De Bow, who along with his review editorship held the chair of political economy in the University of Louisiana at New Orleans, invited Nott to go to New Orleans while the legislature was in session and, as Nott phrased it, "deliver a lecture for him on Niggerology." In telling Squier of this invitation, Nott commented in typical style, saying that he expected "to have some rare sport." He was going to tell his audience of the number of "heathens" (including Morton) who supported his views and above all of "that infamous sinner Squier who has the hardihood to assert" that the Indians were making hills in the valley "before Eve was convicted & punished for stealing apples." Nott's friends and correspondents never knew how seriously to take him, and undoubtedly Squier shuddered a little at the possibility of being too closely associated with Nott's parson-baiting.

The new confidence that Nott had gained from his support in the North, and even in Europe, gave a more assured and less frenetic tone to the two lectures he delivered in New Orleans. In the prefatory letter to De Bow that introduced the published version of the lectures, Nott emphasized that almost all the recent works on ethnology had challenged the idea of the unity of species and that the main defense for unity came from a forced construction of the Bible—"a persistence in this error is calculated to subvert and not to uphold our religion." Nott had no hesitation in asserting that the "Almighty in his wisdom has peopled our vast planet from many distant centres, instead of one, and with races or species originally and radically distinct."[12]

In the main body of the lectures Nott calmly challenged the Bible as a scientific source. He had four basic premises: that the Pentateuch, if written by Moses, had not reached the present in authentic form; that the text of the Bible had been corrupted by transcribers; that the mission of the inspired writers was moral not scientific; and that the weight of evidence in the Bible was opposed to the unity of species.[13]

Along with the arguments for original diversity, Nott vigorously defended the position that the different races had vastly different innate abilities. The Caucasian was the civilizing race because "the Caucasian brain has always been fully developed and ready for immediate action when placed under favorable circumstances." Even among the Caucasians Nott was now prepared to draw distinctions. "The ancient Germans," he wrote, "may be regarded as the parent stock from which the highest modern civilization has sprung. The best blood of France and England is German; the ruling caste in Russia is German; and look at the United States, and contrast our people with the dark-skinned Spaniards. It is clear that the dark-skinned Celts are fading away before the superior race, and that they must eventually be absorbed."[14]

If even the "dark-skinned Celts" were fading away before the descendants of the ancient Germans, Nott could see no hope of progress, or in some cases even survival, for the nonwhite races of the world. Morton, he said, had demonstrated that the cranial capacity of the dark-skinned races was less than that of pure whites and that this deficiency was most marked in those parts of the brain controlling the moral and intellectual faculties. All attempts by Caucasians to civilize the nonwhite races had failed. This failure had been complete, and it might well be asked "whether we are not warring against the immutable laws of Nature, by endeavoring to elevate the intellectual condition of the dark, to that of the fair races." For Nott, the conclusion was clear. Slavery was the only possible relationship between blacks and whites in the South, and in the rest of the world the white race would eventually "hold every foot of the earth where it can live and prosper."[15]

12. Nott, *Two Lectures on the Connection Between the Biblical and Physical History of Man* (New York, 1849), 5–8.
13. *Ibid.*, 16–17.
14. *Ibid.*, 37.
15. *Ibid.*, 17–18, 36.

When Nott wrote his 1848 lectures he was far more knowledgeable about contemporary ethnological writing than he had been at the time of his first lectures on race less than five years before, and he was anxious that his latest effort should have a wide distribution. After delivering the lectures in December, he quickly expanded them and began inquiries in the hope of publishing them in the North. Although he could have had them published quickly in Mobile or New Orleans, Nott wanted the greater respectability of Philadelphia or New York. His efforts to interest Lea & Blanchard in Philadelphia failed. They declined to publish the lectures "upon conscientious grounds" because they were concerned at Nott's open rejection of Genesis. Nott then wrote to Squier in New York saying that if he could find a publisher Nott would, if necessary, guarantee the publisher against loss. He thought that the pamphlets would sell well, particularly in the South, although "I have never wrote to please the Crowd, but for the advancement of truth." Nott, however, was hopeful that he might make a little money on the book. He was now buying books from the North and abroad with even greater enthusiasm, and in the previous year a shipwreck had resulted in the loss of books worth $300.[16]

Squier was willing to help Nott, and, acting through his friend John R. Bartlett, the corresponding secretary of the American Ethnological Society, he arranged for the book to be published by Bartlett and Welford in New York. Nott agreed to subsidize the publication, although he was confident that he would regain his money through good sales. The publishers were also optimistic and arranged to stereotype the volume so that additional press runs could be made without difficulty. Nott was afraid that stereotyping might make it appear that he had too rosy a view of the importance and likely sales of the work, and he asked the printer to omit that fact from the title page for otherwise "it might look as if I placed too high an estimate on my 'dirty linen!'"[17]

It was obvious that the book would produce strong clerical reactions, and Nott was delighted at the prospect of another fight. "I am ready & willing to be skinned for the good of morality, religion & science," he told Bartlett. "Gallileo, Christ &c have run the gauntlet," he wrote, and he thought he could do the same. To Morton, Nott wrote to say that the

16. Nott to Squier, February 14, 1849, in Squier Papers, LC.
17. Nott to Squier, March 8, 1849; *ibid.*; Nott to John R. Bartlett, May 12, June 8, 1849, in John R. Bartlett Papers, John Carter Brown Library, Brown University, Providence, Rhode Island.

book should do some good to "the cause of truth," although he expected to be attacked more strongly than at the time of his first pamphlet. His medical practice, however, was still being helped rather than hindered by his fame as a racial theorist, and he was now "the big gun of the profession here." In reality his expanding practice in Mobile stemmed more from his ability and energy as a doctor than from his writings on race.[18]

Various problems in transferring funds and in printing delayed the pamphlet's appearance and brought Nott to a high pitch of impatience, but by August, 1849, the volume was out. Nott waited with almost eager anticipation for the attacks of the clergy. Nott was anticlerical in a way that was more common in the eighteenth than in the nineteenth century. "Religion you know is a funny thing," he commented to Squier, "a man's conscience is always on the side of his interest." Nott told of dining in New Orleans with a clergyman who had published a book defending scriptural chronology: "I wish you could have seen the reverential, thanksgiving air with which he exposed the whites of his eyes as he turned down his throat the last drops of Hock."[19]

The New Orleans lectures sold well in Charleston, Mobile, and New Orleans, Charleston alone taking two hundred copies, and though there was little demand in the North, Nott was extremely pleased at Morton's reaction. The Philadelphian wrote to tell him that he had "read and re-read your *Two Lectures* with great pleasure and instruction" and that he was delighted with some of Nott's aphorisms. The clergy was less delighted. Even Gliddon, who was often scurrilous in attacking the clergy in private and who agreed with Morton that the book was "done with a master-hand," thought that Nott had gone out of his way to attack Scripture. Gliddon was a little worried that his private opinions had been made too obvious by Nott's use of his work. "Still," Gliddon told Morton, "I privately endorse all Nott says."[20] Gliddon's income depended on his American lecture tours, and though in private letters he encouraged Nott in his exuberant anticlerial language, he was careful to avoid openly antagonizing the clergy. Not until the early 1850s did Gliddon throw off his caution, and then it was Nott who feared that Gliddon had gone too far.

18. Nott to Bartlett, June 8, 1849, in Bartlett Papers; Nott to Morton, June 27, 1849, in Morton Papers, HSP.
19. Nott to Squier, August 6, 1849, in Squier Papers, LC.
20. Nott to Morton, September 1, 27, 1849, Gliddon to Morton, January 31, 1850, in Morton Papers, HSP; Morton to Nott, January 29, 1850 (extract), in Nott and Gliddon, *Types of Mankind*, xlix—l; Mobile *Register*, January 12, 1850.

In the months after the publication of his book, Nott was surprised, even disappointed, at the lack of attacks. Even the *American Whig Review* conceded that the reader would find "much to elicit thought" in the book and merely added that "the author does not treat the historical character of Scripture with the respect usually given it by the most learned and valuable authorities." Yet the calm was deceptive. The clergy was annoyed, and in Nott's home state of South Carolina some were preparing to launch an attack.[21] Chief among these was the Reverend John Bachman of Charleston, who had the scientific credentials to take on not only Nott but also bigger game—Morton himself.

Bachman, who had been born in the state of New York, had for many years been the minister of St. John's Lutheran Church in Charleston. He had received a Ph.D. from the University of Berlin in 1838 and had become well-known as an ornithologist. In the spring of 1848 he had become professor of natural history in the College of Charleston. Charleston was a lively scientific center in these years, and as the unity question flared the Charleston Literary Club took up the question as a major topic of discussion.[22]

In the course of the 1840s Bachman had become increasingly disturbed at the disregard the leading writers showed for the authority of the Bible in their attack on the unity of the human race. His concern was enough to take him away from his main scientific interests to enter the quarrel over human origins. In the late summer of 1849, the Charleston Literary Club asked him to review Nott's new work at one of its meetings. His adverse review and defense of pluralism led to other meetings at which defenders of pluralism took issue with Bachman. It was said at this time in Charleston that the question of unity "has of late occasioned a good deal of conversation about town." In October, Bachman wrote to Morton, telling him of the Charleston discussions, expressing disagreement with his views on hybridity, and warning him that he intended to publish on the subject. The letter was balanced and reasonably expressed, and

21. *American Whig Review*, X (1849), 439–40; Robert W. Gibbes to Morton, January 21, 1850, in Morton Papers, HSP.
22. For Bachman see [C. L. Bachman, ed.], *John Bachman* (Charleston, 1888); John F. Ficken, *A Sketch of the Life and Labors of John Bachman* (Charleston, 1924); and Stanton, *Leopard's Spots*, 123–25. Also, for Bachman and the Charleston intellectual community, see Thomas C. Johnson, *Scientific Interests in the Old South* (New York, 1936). There are notes on Bachman's connection with the College of Charleston in the John Bachman Papers, Charleston Museum, Charleston, South Carolina.

Bachman insisted that his questioning of Morton's views of hybridity did not affect his general regard for Morton's work.[23]

Charleston and the South were to have ample opportunity to take sides in the controversy, and Nott was to have more of the notoriety he obviously desired, for while Bachman worked on articles and a book, the newly formed American Association for the Advancement of Science prepared to take up the question at its annual meeting in Charleston in March, 1850. Nott did not have to wait that long for his name to be again thrust before the public, for in January of that year the Reverend Thomas Smyth of Charleston launched the first blow against Nott in an issue of the *Southern Presbyterian Review*, a journal that was published in Nott's home town of Columbia. Smyth defended the unity of the human race and the authority of the Bible and took issue with both Nott and Morton. Nott's old friend Robert W. Gibbes of Columbia wrote to Morton that Nott has brought down "the wrath of the clergy in S.C."[24] Nott was now engaged in happy, open conflict with those who had long ago caused his father a great deal of trouble for an offhand remark, who had clashed with his dead brother, Henry Junius Nott, and who had launched determined attacks on his old teacher Thomas Cooper. The clergy was angry, but most scientists sided with Nott, and in the following months Nott was able to rejoice in what he viewed, with good reason, as the rout of his opponents.

Nott had been invited to submit a paper to the American Association for the Advancement of Science meeting in Charleston, and he had decided to write on the history of the Jews. He had begun the article in the previous fall with the object of showing that the Jewish physical makeup had remained the same throughout the ages and that nowhere had climate or environment been sufficient to eradicate the original type. Nott could not spare the time from his practice to visit Charleston so his paper was read for him. At the momentous session, attended by Agassiz and Bachman, Nott's paper reiterated his arguments for the antiquity of human diversty. He stressed that the Jews had retained their type unchanged for four thousand years in all parts of the globe. With the confidence born of influential scientific support, Nott dismissed contrary evidence advanced

23. Letter to Lewis R. Gibbes, September 29, 1849, in Lewis R. Gibbes Papers, LC; Bachman to Morton, October 15, 1849, in Morton Papers, HSP; Stanton, *Leopard's Spots*, 124–25.

24. Robert W. Gibbes to Morton, January 21, 1850, Nott to Morton, March 1, 1850, in Morton Papers, HSP.

by James Prichard in his *Physical History of Man*. Nott had previously treated the great English ethnologist, the foremost scientific defender of unity in the world, with respect, but not now. "We are prepared to show," observed Nott in a note to the published proceedings of the meetings, "that no book in the language, contains more false facts and forced conclusions, than PRICHARD's celebrated work on Mankind." Nott also went beyond his professed subject of the Jews to comment on the permanence of type among the Gypsies and Magyars and mentioned in passing that one could also find similar examples of permanence of type in China, Egypt, America, and elsewhere.[25]

Bachman could hardly have been too disturbed at Nott's paper—it was far less vehement on religious questions than most of Nott's other works— but far more serious, indeed devastating, was Agassiz' reaction. Agassiz rose at the conclusion of the reading of Nott's paper and said that he wished to clarify his views on the unity of the human race, "or rather with regard to the diversity of the different races of men." Races, Agassiz said, "did not originate from a common centre, nor from a single pair." Among the corroborating facts was the permanence of difference between the Caucasians and Negroes since the remotest times.[26]

Many in the South were delighted at Agassiz' announcement, but it was a major shock to Bachman and to most clergymen. Agassiz was no southern apologist. He was an internationally respected scientist of the very first rank and was already a star of the American scientific establishment. In the following months, Agassiz was to write vigorously in defense of the plurality of human origins. In Mobile, Nott could not contain his delight. "With Agassiz in the war the battle is ours," he wrote to Morton, "—this was an immense accession for we shall not only have *his* name, but the timid will come out from their hiding places."[27]

After the Charleston meeting, Agassiz spent a week with Robert W. Gibbes in Columbia. Gibbes took him to several plantations in the Columbia region, and Agassiz examined a variety of slaves from different African tribes. "He found enough," wrote Gibbes, "to satisfy him that they have differences from other races." Agassiz asked for daguerrotypes

25. Nott to Morton, October 21, 1849, January 16, 1850, *ibid.*; Nott, "An Examination of the Physical History of the Jews, in its bearings on the Question of the unity of the Races," in *Proceedings of the American Association for the Advancement of Science. Third Meeting. Held at Charleston, S.C., March 1850* (Charleston, 1850), 98–106, 101 (quotation).
26. Nott, "Examination of the Physical History," 106–107.
27. Nott to Morton, May 4, 1850, in Morton Papers, HSP.

of native Africans of the various tribes, and Gibbes arranged for these to be sent to him.[28] The Boston scientist was now prepared to side himself completely with Nott and Morton, and in July he published an article in the *Christian Examiner* on the diversity of the origin of human races. He argued, in terms well-phrased to delight Nott, that scientists had the right to investigate questions growing out of the physical relations of man "without reference to either politics or religion." The acceptance of the unity of mankind under God, stated Agassiz, did not preclude a belief in the diversity of the origin of human races.[29]

Agassiz not only defended separate creations for human races, he also argued that scientists had the obligation to assess the relative rank of human races. It would be "mock philanthropy and mock philosophy," he argued, "to assume that all races have the same abilities, enjoy the same powers, and show the same natural dispositions, and that in consequence of this equality they are entitled to the same position in human society." Five thousand years ago blacks had differed as much from whites as they did in the nineteenth century. In dealing with the "inferior races" it was essential to take into account "the real differences existing between us."[30] Agassiz' language was more moderate than Nott's, but in his way he was giving just as much comfort to southern slaveholders, indeed more, because he was one of the most respected of northern scientists and had no stake in the perpetuation of slavery.

The defenders of unity did not yield ground without a fight. In 1850 Bachman published a book defending unity and, in article form, took issue with Morton's theories of hybridity. Bachman defended the account of human origins given in Genesis and argued that all the races of the world were simply varieties of one species. Morton answered Bachman and agreed with Agassiz' argument that races were separate species created for specific zoological provinces. The account in Genesis referred to one province, not all.[31]

In 1850 the question of the unity of man was of wide popular interest.

28. Robert W. Gibbes to Morton, March 31, June 17, 1850, *ibid.* In 1976 these daguerrotypes were found in an attic of the Peabody Museum at Harvard University; see Mary Jean Madigan and Susan Colgan, *Prints and Photographs* (New York, 1983), 107.
29. Agassiz, "The Diversity of Origin of the Human Races," *Christian Examiner,* XLI (1850), 110, 135n.
30. *Ibid.,* 142–44.
31. For Bachman's views and the dispute with Morton, see Stanton, *Leopard's Spots,* 125–43.

William Gilmore Simms, editor of the *Southern Quarterly Review,* told one writer to send his article on race as soon as possible because "the subject is one at the moment of considerable interest." Throughout the year the books and articles of the specialists were discussed in review articles in the main periodicals, and it was clear that except in specifically religious periodicals the pluralists were carrying the day. Unlike Nott, Morton and Agassiz could not be dismissed as southern polemicists. In April the *Democratic Review* commented that "few or none now seriously adhere to the theory of the *unity* of races."[32]

New England journals, though testifying to the general interest in the race and unity question, were less willing to accept the word of America's scientists. The *New Englander* regretted Agassiz' polygenetic views and was disturbed by the assumption that large parts of the world were incapable of civilization on the American model; the author was obviously perturbed by "the high authority of Agassiz."[33] Yet, although most ministers continued to defend the unity of man, and some even defended the capacity of nonwhite races, influential American scientific opinion now generally agreed that human races had separate origins, and there was even stronger agreement that the world was divided into inferior and superior races, whatever their origin.

The results of the Charleston meeting vindicated Nott, and at home in Mobile, busily immersed in his medical practice, he still found time to work on new articles and to fire off exuberant letters to his friends. He received Bachman's book and Agassiz' first *Christian Examiner* article on the same day in May and quickly skimmed through both. Bachman, he said, "writes like a Blackguard," Agassiz, like "a *gentleman.*" His satisfaction at being vindicated was very great. "I feel," he wrote to Morton, "as if my function was fulfilled—the devil has been pushing me on in spite of myself, to *agitate,* & I have been thumped & pummeled on every side, but thank the Lord I have succeeded in getting some of the rest of you into the fight, & you can't get out now until the field is won." With Agassiz on his side, Nott was ready to claim victory. He was now confident enough to tell Morton, one of the few men he deferred to, that he

---

32. W. G. Simms to John Y. Bassett, June 1, 1850, in John Y. Bassett Papers, SHC; *Democratic Review,* XXVI (1850), 328, 571; *De Bow's Review,* IX (1850), 231. Also Reginald Horsman, *Race and Manifest Destiny: The Origins of American Racial Anglo-Saxonism* (Cambridge, Mass., 1981), 139–57.
33. *New Englander,* VIII (1850), 542–84, 578 (quotation).

should stop cramming a variety of races, including the Hindu, Egyptian, and Hebrew, under the single name of Caucasian. Some of these races, he said, existed in the most distant past. Later in May, after seeing Morton's response to Bachman on hybridity, Nott told him "it made me feel good all over—I like to see a man stand up like a gentleman for what he believes to be true, but when one makes a blackguard of himself like Old Bachman, I like to see him cut into sausage meat." [34]

To Squier, Nott was equally exuberant and willing to write about religion and its ministers in a manner that was rare in 1850. He joked with Squier about his religiously working on the serpent mounds of the Ohio Valley and hoped that he would soon see the error of his ways and turn his thoughts to "Jesus Christ & Co." Bachman he referred to as "a man of Science, but a biggoted [sic] Old Lutheran." [35]

Nott thrived emotionally on the controversy he stirred up in the 1840s. His writings on race rewarded him in a variety of ways. He had gained the respect and friendship of scientists throughout America and Europe; he believed that he was succeeding in freeing science from those who said it must conform to the limits of the Bible; and he was defending slavery and a way of life he wanted to protect. In writing to his friends after Agassiz' cooperation in 1850, he tried to maintain that he had served his purpose of bringing the question before the public and that he could now sit on the fence and watch, but he did not mean it. He was busily getting other articles ready for the press, and even in victory he approached the question more as a polemicist than as a man of science. "I will give them hell before we stop," he told Squier. [36]

Nott's aims of establishing scientific truth as he saw it and gaining recognition that the ending of slavery in the South would be disastrous for both blacks and whites were complicated by his marked pessimism regarding human nature and rationality. He firmly believed that there were many distinct races, with vastly different abilities and potential, but he was not at all sure that the world was prepared to listen to what he perceived as the truth. He often thought of himself as a scientific realist contending with fuzzy-minded philanthropists and amateurs.

When in the spring of 1850 Nott heard that his old friend James Hammond of South Carolina was hoping to return to politics, he wrote a

34. Nott to Morton, May 4, 26, 1850, in Morton Papers, HSP.
35. Nott to Squier, May 4, 1850, in Squier Papers, LC.
36. Ibid.; also Nott to John R. Bartlett, June 28, 1850, in Bartlett Papers.

letter to him which revealed his doubts about his ability to influence the masses. "Human nature is a bad thing," he told Hammond, "& I fear it will never be much better. The great mass of mankind must always be too ignorant to reason about Religion, Laws, Government, & must ever be the victims of ignorance, folly & passion." Every college, he said, should have a professorship devoted to teaching boys their ignorance. Accurate knowledge was the exception. "It is rare," he wrote, "to see a man reason well who has not studied well some branch of *exact science*." This was to be Nott's cry for the rest of his life: ignorance was far more common than knowledge, and people and nations had the greatest difficulty in acting in their own best interests.[37]

Nott encouraged Hammond to reenter politics. South Carolina needed good minds to lead her—"even if the *love* of the people should not call you out, their *selfishness* will." Nott was an elitist as well as a racist. He thought whole races unfit to participate in nineteenth-century civilization, but he also had doubts about the abilities and judgment of many within his favored white race. Only those who were gifted, thought Nott, could meet the world's challenge. "The natural element of every active mind is *action*," he told Hammond, "& *you* cannot be content to lie & rust while the crowd without is carrying on the work which nature has assigned our generation." Of all things, human beings desired power, Nott argued, though success that had to be attained by struggle was worth little unless a man was fighting "for justice & truth."

Even with his friends Nott had a confident arrogance, and he risked annoying Hammond by giving some useful but candid practical advice. "The love of filthy lucre," he told him, "of which you discourse so philosophically, has been put down as your crying sin—I have been told stories about squabbling with small dealers about small bills—such things sound badly, will kill any man, & should be guarded against." One wonders if Nott was perhaps hinting that Hammond, a man from a relatively obscure family who had married an heiress, had to try harder to act like a gentleman.

Nott's assessment of Hammond's ambitions and purposes led him to comment on his own purposes, which he did perhaps a little more honestly than in writing to some of his less intimate correspondents. He said

37. Nott to Hammond, June 3, 1850, in Hammond Papers, LC. This letter is also the source for the material in the next three paragraphs.

that he viewed himself as belonging to the class of "*agitators*," who speeded the world along—"this may be my principal merit—I stand *abuse* well, & no cause can prosper without it—I may have made some *miss-licks*, but I feel an honest conviction I have struck in the right direction."

In spite of his frequent protestations that he was now ready to sit on the fence, Nott was eager for the fray; articles flowed from his pen in the months following Agassiz' open avowal of pluralism. He had the friendship and support of both James De Bow of *De Bow's Review* and William Gilmore Simms of the *Southern Quarterly Review*. Both were eager to publish his work, and both wrote of him with the highest praise. In 1850 Simms printed the full version of the article on the history of the Jews that Nott had written for the Charleston meeting and his article on ancient and scriptural chronology, and early in the following year De Bow printed a new Nott article on the old subject of human diversity.[38]

The article on scriptural chronology was mostly a response to the clerical attacks on the two lectures Nott had first delivered in New Orleans, although it also gave him the opportunity to point out that Agassiz was now fully in his camp. His object in his two lectures, he wrote, had been to "cut the natural history of man loose from the Bible." This had been done. It was now impossible, he believed, to defend the scientific truth of Genesis. The discoveries in Egypt of the antiquity of distinct races had shattered any accepted biblical chronology. For Nott the physical history of mankind was "wholly irreconcilable with the account given in the Book of Genesis." The diverse races of the world were not all descended from Noah's family. The writers of the Bible were limited in their knowledge to a small portion of the earth bordering on the Mediterranean. The world contained a variety of races, of distinct origins, and these races differed "in physical organization, in intellectual and moral perfectibility." This fact was of vital practical importance, he argued, for a number of contemporary issues, including blacks in the United States, the American Indian, and the condition of the West Indies.[39]

Nott's article for De Bow in February, 1851, was an extended review of Bachman's book on unity. Writing to South Carolina scientist Lewis R. Gibbes about the article, Nott argued that the book had been ruined by Bachman's "uncompromising biggotry [sic]." He had little patience, he

38. Nott, "Physical History of the Jewish Race," *Southern Quarterly Review*, XVII (1850), 426–51; Nott, "Ancient and Scriptural Chronology," *ibid.*, 385–426; "Diversity of the Human Race," *De Bow's Review*, X (1851), 113–32.

39. Nott, "Ancient and Scriptural Chronology," 387, 391–92, 423–25.

wrote, with "such prostitutors of Science as him & Smythe." Nott showed little tolerance in this review. In disagreeing with most aspects of Bachman's work, he reiterated his reasons for arguing that races had been distinct since their first creation and once again defended his old argument that crosses between blacks and the pure white stock ("by which we mean the descendants of the early Germans") did not produce an indefinitely prolific variety.[40]

After gaining the overt support of Morton and Agassiz, Nott showed an increasing impatience at the efforts of the clergy to resist the new scientific accounts of the original diversity of human beings, and he revealed a deep-seated anticlericalism that went far beyond the quarrel over the scientific reliability of Genesis. In referring to Bachman's book, he told Morton that he was "sick, tired, and disgusted with fighting dishonest parsons."[41] To Nott, those who, like Bachman, knew that parts of the Bible could not be true scientifically but still refused to point out its inaccuracies were hypocrites. From 1850 he showed a much greater willingness to scoff at the clergy and even at the Bible in public as well as in his private letters. He also began a public controversy with one of the most prominent clergymen in Mobile—William T. Hamilton.

The Reverend Dr. William Hamilton, who was a personal acquaintance of Nott, had been pastor of the Government Street Presbyterian Church in Mobile since 1833. He was English-born but had been in the United States for many years. He had a high reputation in Mobile, and visitors to the city were often taken to hear him preach in his style of "fervent and masculine eloquence." One traveler referred to him as "one of the best preachers in the United States."[42] In August, 1850, Hamilton published in a Mobile newspaper three long letters taking issue with Agassiz' defense of polygenesis in the pages of the *Christian Examiner.* Hamilton also reviewed Nott's *Two Lectures* and Bachman's work on unity in a New Orleans Presbyterian newspaper. Nott's reply to Hamilton produced a rebuttal. In his writings Hamilton defended the biblical account of creation and argued that the varieties of races were produced by a direct miracle at the time of the Tower of Babel. Hamilton's conclu-

40. Nott to Lewis R. Gibbes, November 21, 1850, in Lewis R. Gibbes papers, LC; Nott, "Diversity of the Human Race," 114, 128.

41. Nott to Morton, July 25, 1850, in Morton Papers, HSP.

42. Mobile *Register,* February 23, 1841; Albrecht K. Koch, *Journey Through a Part of the United States of North America in the Years 1844 to 1846,* ed. and trans. Ernst A. Stadler (Carbondale, Ill., 1972), 89. For Hamilton see Thomas M. Owen, *History of Alabama and Dictionary of Alabama Biography* (4 vols.; Chicago, 1921), III, 734–35.

sion was that "there is, and there can be, *no tenable middle ground between absolute infidelity and absolute belief!*"[43]

In arguing with Hamilton, Nott chose less to repeat his now familiar arguments for original diversity and the basic errors of biblical chronology than to attack the damage caused by a false reliance on the literal truth of the Bible and by the protestations of ministers and theologians. "The fact is," he wrote, "it is not part of the design of the scriptures to teach science, and incalculable injury has been done to the advance of Christianity by making it responsible for the palpable errors of Genesis." Nott was now prepared to go beyond his old attack on Genesis. He also pointed out the discrepancies between the accounts of Matthew and Paul. "I am disposed to attribute them," he wrote, "to a want of full inspiration, or to a want of strict authenticity in the text."[44]

In his articles Hamilton had taken issue with the now common scientific assertion that the Bible and the events described in it referred only to the people in one small part of the globe. Hamilton had expressed shock at the idea of shutting out nine-tenths of the world's population from Christian hope and Christ's sacrifice. Nott in his reply turned to humor designed to shock and offend the orthodox. After saying that he was too confident of "the wisdom, justice and mercy of the Almighty" to worry with Hamilton about the excluded nine-tenths, he suggested that it was possible that the dark races did not fall through Adam "and therefore may have a better chance than some of the rest of us." In any case, wrote Nott, "I must in candor say I would rather take my chance with the darkies, than to be tried under the code preached by some, of eternal punishment with fire and brimstone for the sins committed in our brief three score and ten years." He might accept this idea, he said, if the term of punishment was cut to ten million years, "or any thing reasonable." All this was going beyond challenging the scientific accuracy of the Bible to challenging Christianity itself. Nott admitted that some were attacking him as an enemy of morality and religion, but he said that those who insisted on forcing false constructions on the Bible were doing more harm to religion and morality "than ever have been inflicted by Paine, Voltaire, Hume and all this school."[45]

Nott clearly felt confident enough of his national and international status and of the strength of his medical practice to ignore the feelings of

43. *Alabama Planter* (Mobile), September 9, 1850.
44. *Ibid.*, August 12, 19, 1850.
45. *Ibid.*, August 19, 1850.

the orthodox and to joke about matters they thought of only with the greatest seriousness. He was now an important man in Mobile, and he knew it. The Mobilians were happy to support him, not only because he was a good physician but because they respected his fame as a scientist and realized that his arguments were a major weapon in the southern defense of slavery. By 1850 the sectional split was beginning to absorb most of the energies of southern politicians and patriots. Mobile, like the rest of the South, now had its group of extremists who were less interested in compromise than in a victory for the southern position on a variety of issues. Nott, who had previously shunned overt political commitment, openly committed himself to the extreme states' rights position.

In the fall of 1850 a southern rights meeting was held in Mobile; it was described as one of the largest meetings ever held in the town. The meeting was called to form an association to present a united front of opposition to the Compromise of 1850; its participants objected to the general threat to the slave system, to the admission of California to the Union as a free state, and to the abolition of the slave trade in the District of Columbia. Presiding over the meeting were Nott's father-in-law, James Deas, the old South Carolina states' rightser, and Mobile lawyer Philip Phillips. Phillips had come to Mobile from Charleston, where his family had been prominent members of the Charleston Jewish community. Nott was Phillips' family physician and friend. One historian of American Jews has referred to Phillips as "perhaps the most accomplished and respected American Jew of the first half of the nineteenth century."[46]

In December Nott was invited to address the new association. He took the opportunity to commit himself to the southern cause and in doing so became one of the earliest southerners openly to espouse a southern nation and the futility of further efforts at compromise. On this occasion he did not delve into biblical or scientific problems, but as usual he took the opportunity to say that the Bible "was clearly intended, not as a book of science, but to teach mankind their duties towards each other, and towards their maker."[47] The bulk of Nott's address dealt with the political

46. Bertram W. Korn, "The Jews of Mobile, Alabama, Prior to the Organization of the First Congregation in 1841," in *Hebrew Union College Annual*, XL–XLI (Cincinnati, 1969–70), 490–91. The Philip Phillips Family Papers are in the Library of Congress. The meeting was described in the *Alabama Planter* (Mobile), October 14, 1850. For a discussion of states' rights politics in Mobile at this time, see Alan S. Thompson, "Southern Rights and Nativism as Issues in Mobile Politics, 1850–1861," *Alabama Review*, XXXV (1982), 127–41.

47. Nott, *An Essay on the Natural History of Mankind, Viewed in Connection with Negro Slavery: Delivered Before the Southern Rights Association, 14th December, 1850* (Mobile, 1851), 6.

situation in which the South found itself. It soon became obvious that in a town that was still predominantly Whig, Nott had thrown his support to the extreme states' rights wing of the Democratic party.

The theme of Nott's address was that the deep-seated intellectual and physical differences between the white, black, and red races bore directly on the political issues that were now dividing the nation. Nott argued that he had long been convinced that simply telling the North that emancipation would desolate the South, ruin the North, and destroy Negro happiness was not enough. Nor was it effective to point out to the North that the Constitution guaranteed the South its slaves and that the South simply wanted to manage its own domestic affairs. The North was treating slavery "as an *abstract* question," above any law or constitution; it had become a matter not of law but of conscience. Thus, Nott argued, he had attempted to show the North that it was acting on a false philanthropy, that the same God who had permitted slavery to exist had also "stamped the Negro Race with *permanent inferiority*." Yet, said Nott, the northern extremists were not listening; ignorance and fanaticism were immune to reason.[48]

Scientific exposition, argued Nott, was no longer enough: "There is a great convulsion before us, the end of which God alone can see, and it is time we should arouse from our lethargy and prepare for the crisis." The South now had three million slaves, bequeathed by England and the American colonies. Their liberation, argued Nott, would bring misery to them and the destruction of the prosperity and happiness of the southern states; no one had proposed a scheme of emancipation that would provide safety for the whites and benefit the blacks. Yet northerners attacked southerners as barbarians. "Such conduct is unjust—is insulting," said Nott, "and not to be tolerated by men worthy of liberty." Some restrictions on liberty were essential to good government—England had a church, a nobility, and a law of primogeniture that were wrong, but these institutions could not be eliminated without destroying the fabric that contained them, and to do so would produce anarchy. In the same way, slavery was part of the very being of southerners, and even if it were admitted to be an evil it could not be touched without destroying southern society.[49]

Nott stressed that his own belief in the original diversity of human be-

48. *Ibid.*, 4–5.
49. *Ibid.*, 4, 7–8.

ings was not essential to his present arguments. Everyone agreed that distinct races had existed for at least several thousand years and that distinct
racial types were permanent. If they were not separate species they were
"permanent varieties"; even Bachman, said Nott, argued that the Negro
was a permanent variety, incapable of self-government. God had created
blacks with original "*intellectual inferiority,*" and he had designed the
Caucasian races to be rulers of the world. Africa south of the Sahara was
"a perfect blank in the world's history." Philanthropists had mistakenly
assumed that defective brains could be expanded through cultivation over
a series of generations. This notion was demonstrably false as science, and
only "absurd religious opinions" could explain the adoption of the idea.
Blacks had been made inferior by "a fixed law of nature" that could not be
changed.[50]

Nott despaired of a solution to the abolitionist attack on slavery. The
South had watched the growth of evils "which ere long must inevitably
end in bloodshed." Slaves were doubling in numbers every thirty years. If
the South educated the slaves as far as possible for emancipation, what
would become of them? The free states were continually passing laws in
an attempt to exclude free blacks, and obviously, he said, three million
former slaves could not be turned loose within the southern states. In
Alabama alone, he argued, there would be three hundred thousand former slaves. The suggestion of some that blacks could be educated, freed,
and gradually intermarry with whites was not only "insulting and revolting to us," it was also impractical. Such interbreeding would drag down
the whites, not elevate the blacks. "A great aim of philanthropy," said
Nott, "should be, to keep the ruling Races of the world as pure and wise
as possible, for it is only through them that the others can be made prosperous and happy." Slavery might be an abstract wrong, argued Nott, but
in practice in the South it was a blessing to the Negro.[51]

Nott drew pessimistic conclusions. He saw little chance for a solution
within the Union. The facts that he had detailed in his talk, he said, were
"the strongest of all arguments for a severance of this Union, and for the
formation of a Southern Confederacy." The South had "no friends, no
sympathisers, no protectors on earth." If the North continued in her
course, the South would be compelled "to protect herself, and to carve
an outlet for her Negroes with the sword, from the territory which has

50. *Ibid.,* 9–16.
51. *Ibid.,* 17–19.

been plundered from her." The South should remember the law of self-preservation. Though the North denied the right of secession, the South was ready for resistance, and, said Nott, "my solemn conviction is, that events are fast ripening, which must end in blood." He urged those gathered to hear him to press the Alabama legislature to establish a military school, better organize the militia, and provide the munitions of war. The best way to maintain peace was to prepare for war, and the South should arouse from its slumber and remember the ghosts of the murdered whites of St. Domingo.[52]

In 1843 Nott had been a rising but nationally obscure southern physician who devoted most of his attention to medicine. By 1850 Nott still devoted most of his time to his practice, but he had become one of the best-known ethnologists in the country, a friend of Morton, and an ally of Agassiz. Now Nott had committed himself openly on the major issue of the day: the growing rift between North and South. His extremist position on the necessity for war and the creation of a southern nation stemmed logically from his scientific beliefs as well as from his natural desire for a continuation of the existing southern way of life. His analysis of racial history and human nature convinced him that black inferiority made black slavery the only feasible relationship between southern whites and the millions of blacks in their section, and he had been confirmed in this belief by the support of the best northern scientists. Yet he had no faith that what he believed was scientific truth would affect the growing feeling outside the South that slavery would have to come to an end. From 1850 Nott committed himself to the idea of a southern nation, a nation that would recognize the realities of human nature and the supposed innate differences between human races, but his writings were still concerned mostly with race and medicine, not slavery itself. Ultimately his dream of a southern nation was to bring disaster to his section, his family, and himself, but while the South ran with increasing speed down the slope to ruin, Nott's national and international reputation soared and he reached the height of the medical profession in Mobile and the Southwest.

52. *Ibid.*, 23–26.

Chapter 6
THE GOOD YEARS

By the middle years of the nineteenth century Mobile was a surging commercial town with a life and bustle that seemed far in excess of its population of some twenty thousand. Many of its residents left in summer, but in winter its population was augmented by a variety of visitors from upstate and elsewhere. It was a city of compelling charm for the elite that had the money and status to enjoy its best society. Visitors enjoyed being driven along Government Street with its prosperous houses amid their flower- and shrub-laden gardens and through the beautiful groves and winding paths on the outskirts of town. Along the streets near the river the atmosphere was very different. The streets in this area were dirty, often dangerous, and crowded in winter with a host of merchants, seamen, steamboat men, planters from the up-country, visitors from the North, and local stevedores and laborers: "Every corner has its *Exchange,* or great room, with its bar and immense display of bottles, where a swiss organ or hurdy-gurdy may be heard constantly grinding, and a crowd constantly drinking."[1]

Among the throngs were a great number of blacks—domestic servants from some of the larger houses and slaves who had been hired out as urban laborers. There was also a sizable minority of free blacks, nearly all mulattoes, who prided themselves on their French and Spanish heritage. The slaves in Mobile had a freedom of movement that was rare in the rural areas of the South. A Mobile newspaper commented in 1854 that hundreds of blacks were to be seen drunk every twenty-four hours. Later

1. J. W. Hengiston, "Mobile—Pensacola and the Floridas," *New Monthly Magazine* (London), XCIII (1853), 367.

in the decade the proportion of blacks in the streets was fewer because immigrant Irish and German laborers began to replace the expensive slaves in many tasks. From 1850 to 1860 the white population of Mobile increased almost 70 percent from thirteen thousand to nearly twenty-one thousand, and the black population increased under 12 percent from seventy-five hundred to eighty-four hundred.[2]

Critics of the city tended to be taken aback by its easygoing acceptance of drinking and gambling and by a general atmosphere of relaxed enjoyment, but most visitors praised it. Frederick Law Olmsted found the business district "dirty and noisy, with little elegance, or evidence of taste or public spirit, in its people," but visitors more often were impressed by the town's exotic qualities. One young woman from Maine, who was in the city early in 1854, was stunned by winter on the Gulf. "The air is like summer," she wrote, "the houses are all open and families sitting on their piazzas." Flowers were in bloom, trees had rich foliage, and she could not describe "the beauties that every where meet my eye." Another visitor thought the houses in Mobile were more southern in appearance than those of New Orleans. "Almost all," she wrote, "are surrounded by verandas and gardens filled with roses, orange and lemon trees, and magnificent magnolias."[3]

Nearly all the travelers who were admitted into the small Mobile elite wrote with warmth of their weeks in the city. Nott and his wife entertained visiting intellectuals and were usually invited to meet prominent visitors to the city, but the foremost hostess in Mobile society in these years was Octavia Le Vert, the wife of Nott's friend Dr. Henry Levert. She spelled their name *Le Vert*, her husband spelled it *Levert*. Mrs. Le Vert was a famous southern belle and a good friend of Henry Clay. Lady Emmeline Stuart-Wortley said she was "one of the most delightful people in the world." At the Leverts' one could meet not only the social elite of Mobile but also local writers, visiting politicians and dignitaries, and actors and actresses from the Mobile theater.[4]

2. *Alabama Planter* (Mobile), February 13, 1854; Peter Kolchin, *First Freedom: The Responses of Alabama's Blacks to Emancipation and Reconstruction* (Westport, Conn., 1972), 11.

3. Frederick L. Olmsted, *A Journey in the Seaboard Slave States in the Years 1853–1854, with Remarks on Their Economy* (2 vols.; 1856; rpr. New York, 1904), II, 210; Harriet Eaton, "Journal of a Voyage from Portland [Maine] to Mobile," SHC; Francis and Theresa Pulszky, *White, Red, and Black: Sketches of Society in the United States* (2 vols.; New York, 1853), II, 112.

4. Lady Emmeline Stuart-Wortley, *Travels in the United States, Etc, During 1849 and 1850* (New York, 1855), 135. See also Perceval Reniers, *The Springs of Virginia: Life, Love and Death at the Waters, 1775–1900* (Chapel Hill, 1941), 121–23.

Nott was Dr. Levert's own physician, and he mixed with great success in the Levert society and that of the general Mobile elite. All who knew Nott agreed that he was a scintillating conversationalist, rich in anecdotes and excelling in gay, lively dialogue. Nott was a man of great enthusiasms, and his reading went far beyond ethnological and medical works to include English and American literature. Literary allusions were common even in his letters on scientific matters. Much of Nott's social life in Mobile revolved around lively dinner tables. Though extremely moderate both in eating and drinking, he enjoyed the opportunity for animated discussions as a break from his intense schedule of medical visits and writing.

Even those visitors who disliked slavery were charmed by the relaxed society of the city and by the beauty of the surroundings in which the elite of Mobile lived. Swedish visitor Fredrika Bremer remembered with pleasure the "grandees" and "lovely young ladies" she met at Mrs. Le Vert's, and she thought that the elderly gentlemen, "men of office in the states," were "nice and clear on all questions, with the exception of slavery." Any expectation that slavery might dim her enjoyment of her stay on the Gulf vanished in her pleasure in the society and her surroundings. "I like Mobile," she wrote, "and the people of Mobile and everything in Mobile; I flourish in Mobile."[5]

Though Nott often complained of the lack of libraries and books in Mobile, he built himself a happy life there in the years before the tragic yellow fever epidemic of 1853. For the masters, Mobile provided a prosperous, comfortable life, and for Nott the city also provided an increasing personal satisfaction in his work. The national and local fame he had achieved as a racial theorist helped increase an already flourishing medical practice. Nott was one of a narrow elite of doctors in the first half of the nineteenth century in that he came from a good family, had attended two first-class American medical schools, and had studied for a year in Paris. He was also a man of the widest medical and general scientific interests who devoted himself energetically and carefully to his patients, and he continued to write on medical as well as racial matters.

His extensive and successful medical practice helped make Nott a very prosperous as well as a noted Mobile resident. By 1850 his household was substantial, and Nott needed the large income he was making from his

5. Fredrika Bremer, *The Homes of the New World*, trans. Mary Howitt (3 vols.; London, 1853), III, 17–24.

medical practice. Two sons, Edward Fisher and James Deas, had been born to the Notts before they left South Carolina, and other children were born regularly after their arrival in Mobile: Henry Junius in 1838; Emma in 1842; Josiah, Jr., in 1845; Sarah Alice in 1849; and Allen in 1852. In 1851, the eldest son, Edward, entered the University of Alabama in Tuscaloosa. James was soon to follow him there. By 1850 Nott also was the owner of sixteen slaves, eight of them aged fourteen or under. In the same year his real estate was worth $15,000 at a time when only twenty-five residents of the city, most of them merchants, had real estate worth more than $30,000. Nott's friend Dr. Henry Levert, husband of Mobile's famous hostess and one of the most prominent doctors in the city, owned four slaves.[6]

Nott's practice had expanded rapidly in the late 1840s. His regular duties were heaviest from November to June, but in years when yellow fever struck he also worked incessantly from late August to October. In June a great many of Mobile's white population left the city for the various summer springs and resorts, and Nott had a less hectic time through the early summer. By September, even if there was no severe yellow fever epidemic, Nott was often fully engaged in treating the various malarial fevers. Early in September, 1848, he commented in a letter to Squier that he was working "literally 18 hours a day" and that he was catching up on new magazines by taking "a *running read*" as he was "driven from one patient to another." In the following February he apologized to Squier that his latest pamphlet was hurriedly done "on account of my increasing professional avocations," and in March, 1851, he said that his practice had increased "almost beyond endurance." One of Nott's colleagues, Dr. William Anderson, said that when yellow fever epidemics came to Mobile Nott was riding day and night for two months at a time.[7]

Most of Nott's increasing professional duties came from his growing general reputation in Mobile and the surrounding areas, but Nott also added a new special medical responsibility in 1849. In partnership with

6. Mobile, Census of 1850, in RG 29, NA; Harriet E. Amos, "Social Life in an Antebellum Cotton Port: Mobile, Alabama, 1820–1860" (Ph.D. dissertation, Emory University, 1976), 109. For a brief discussion of the wide variation in the status of physicians in the nineteenth century see John Duffy, *The Healers: The Rise of the Medical Establishment* (New York, 1976), 180–81; gravestones, Magnolia Cemetery, Mobile, Alabama; *Alabama Genealogical Register*, VIII (1966), 226.

7. Nott to Squier, September 7, 1848, February 14, 1849, March 26, 1851, in Squier Papers, LC; William H. Anderson, *Biographical Sketch of Dr. J. C. Nott* (Mobile, 1877), 7.

Dr. William B. Crawford he opened a private infirmary for blacks. It was intended for the use of slaveowners in Mobile and the surrounding area and was located on Royal Street within a few blocks of the river, close to the railroad station and next to the cotton warehouse of Sarah Nott's brother-in-law Charles Auzé.

Many southern physicians had an extensive practice among the slaves; slaveowners were often anxious that good medical care should be provided for their expensive and valuable property. Clinics or infirmaries that devoted at least part of their space to blacks were common in the South in these years. Some physicians, most notably the famous J. Marion Sims, a South Carolinian who settled in Alabama before achieving his greatest fame in New York, used these clinics specifically to expand their surgical knowledge and develop new techniques, but it seems that Nott's clinic was more a pragmatic expansion of his practice than a means through which his medical knowledge was purposely expanded. His many published accounts of his cases do not include discussions of special cases from his infirmary.

Nott and Crawford bought the first land for their infirmary in 1849, erected buildings, and enlarged the establishment in the following years. Even though they had chosen an area in which much of the property was used for commercial purposes, at first they ran into resistance from some of the residents in the neighboring squares who feared contagion from such an establishment in their immediate neighborhood. The Mobile Marine Hospital had been built much farther out, on the edge of town. At first the protests were successful. In September, 1849, the Mobile Common Council passed an ordinance that no hospital or infirmary could be put into operation in the city without a petition with the signatures of the majority of the citizens living in the squares immediately adjoining the proposed establishment. Nott and Crawford's infirmary was temporarily closed, but they quickly obtained the necessary signatures. Their letter accompanying the petition stated that it had been voluntarily signed "by those interested in negro property in the upper part of the town to whom an Infirmary will be a great convenience."[8]

8. Land Records, in Mobile County Court House, Mobile, Alabama; Crawford and Nott to the Mayor, Aldermen, and Common Council of Mobile, October 3, 1849, in Mobile City Records, Box 18008, Envelope 6; *The Comprehensive Mobile Guide and Directory, Referring to the Business Locations for 1852* (Mobile, 1852). See also Todd L. Savitt, "The Use of Blacks for Medical Experimentation and Demonstration in the Old South," *Journal of Southern History*, XLVIII (1982), 331–48.

Nott's infirmary was a flourishing establishment in Mobile in the years before the Civil War; in that conflict it became an army hospital. In the 1850s it became "Nott's infirmary" because he played the dominant role in the hospital, and on several occasions he changed partners. Crawford was succeeded by Dr. Henry S. Levert, Levert by Dr. F. E. Gordon, and Gordon by Dr. D. D. Childs. The main purpose of the hospital was to treat male black laborers, particularly those who worked on the cotton presses and steamboats. In defending the establishment of the hospital in May, 1849, Nott pointed out that the black laborers working in the cotton presses of the city were in particular danger of disease because they were lodged in crowded, dirty, and badly ventilated apartments. In 1855 and 1856 male blacks were admitted to the infirmary at a rate of two dollars a day, with surgical operations and "cases requiring extraordinary attention" costing extra. For a time there was apparently a separate building for whites, but the establishment was always regarded primarily as a slave infirmary for male workers. It is possible that Nott was ready to change this arrangement somewhat in the late 1850s, when he took on as his partner Dr. F. E. Gordon, who specialized in obstetrics and the diseases of women and children. That the infirmary flourished is indicated by Nott's purchase, late in the decade, after Dr. William B. Crawford's death, of his old partner's share in the property for $4,375.[9]

Although Nott's was the main slave infirmary in Mobile in these years before the Civil War, there were a number of institutions that served both races. Drs. F. A. Ross, George A. Ketchum, and William H. Anderson opened a private infirmary on St. Anthony Street near the Marine Hospital in 1853. The first floor was devoted to male and female black patients and the second floor to white males. At the beginning of the Civil War, Dr. Henry Levert also had a private infirmary that served both white and black patients; he charged less for blacks than for whites. The Providence Infirmary, maintained by the Sisters of Charity, had accommodations for male and female slaves in a separate part of the building.[10]

The range of Nott's practice was extremely wide. Along with his extensive work among Mobile's slaves, he was the private physician of many of the elite of the city, was called into a Mobile brothel to treat cases of

9. Nott and Wm. B. Crawford to [Mayor and Aldermen], May 20, 1849, in Mobile City Records, Box 18008, Envelope 6; Mobile *Register*, November 25, 1855; *Directory of the City of Mobile, 1861* (Mobile, 1861); Land Records, in Mobile County Court House; Nott and George R. Gliddon, *Indigenous Races of the Earth; or, New Chapters of Ethnological Inquiry* (Philadelphia, 1857), 369.
10. Mobile *Register*, June 3, 1853, May 2, 1856, September 13, 1861.

yellow fever, traveled to Pascagoula to treat a United States Army colonel, and particularly prided himself on his practice among the Mobile clergy. He said in 1850, with some exaggeration, that he was "the family physician and confidential friend of every parson in town." Dr. William Anderson later wrote of Nott that "though he was claimed by no denomination, and even looked upon by some as a free thinker in religious matters, yet, strange to say, he was greatly loved by the clergy of all the Churches, and held the post of family physician and confidential friend to most of these holy men."[11]

Nott's reputation as a physician and his known integrity brought him tasks that were unusual for a man who frequently uttered anticlerical statements. An indication of the respect in which his skills were held came in 1850, when a well-known northern minister, the Reverend John Newland Maffitt, came to Mobile after a scandal had cast doubts on his moral character. In Mobile he preached to large crowds, but a local newspaper printed articles about him from a New York City journal, and the scandal became well-known in Mobile. When Maffitt suddenly died, there was suspicion that he had committed suicide. Some of his friends were anxious to clear his name of this accusation and asked Nott to perform a post-mortem. When Maffitt had been taken ill with a severe pain in his chest, a young friend of Nott's, Dr. E. P. Gaines, had been called and had not helped the heart-attack victim by giving him enemas and large doses of calomel and morphine. Nott's autopsy demonstrated that Reverend Maffitt's fatty, ulcerated heart had ruptured, causing his death. In his published report on the case, Nott commented that he could give no opinion regarding Maffitt's general guilt or innocence, but "the *post-mortem* examination has at least wiped from his memory the damning sin of suicide."[12]

Nott's early experience as a demonstrator of anatomy in Philadelphia and his year of work in France, where there was great emphasis on following the patient, if necessary, from symptoms through diagnosis and treatment to post-mortem, made him willing and even eager to undertake a variety of post-mortems to check the effectiveness of his diagnoses. He appears to have been remarkably effective in convincing relatives that such post-mortems would be of value. In 1847 it was said that he was "one of the most competent and careful pathologists in the South." In 1854 and

11. Nott, "Sketch of the Epidemic of Yellow Fever of 1847, in Mobile," *Charleston Medical Journal and Review*, III (1848), 20; Mobile *Register*, August 5, 1853; Nott to Squier, May 4, 1850, March 26, 1851, in Squier Papers, LC; Anderson, *Biographical Sketch of Nott*, 10.

12. "Post-Mortem Examination of the Rev. John Newland Maffitt," *New Orleans Medical and Surgical Journal*, VII (1850), 148–51.

1855, on the death of two young patients—a girl of two and a boy of nine—Nott obtained permission to perform post-mortems and published the results. In the boy's case, which Nott had diagnosed as yellow fever but which he now reported as a case of "phlebitis" (a vein was completely blocked), Nott stated simply in his published report that he had asked permission to make a post-mortem examination because he had been at fault in his diagnosis.[13]

The medical range of Nott's practice was as varied as his patients. He combined the treatment of all the diseases encountered by a general practitioner with obstetrics and practically all the surgical operations performed in his day. "I have today," he told Squier in 1849, "operated on a cataract, cut a stone out of a fellows bladder, bored a hole in a Womans belly & let out four gallons of water." In typical Nott vein, he added (quoting one of Tobias Smollett's characters), "I don't know how the hell it got into her, for she never drank anything but brandy." He also added in the same letter that another of his patients at that time was Dr. Henry Levert, who was on his back with pneumonia.[14] He closed one letter to Squier with the comment that "here I am 5 miles from home, at 2 oclock at night sitting up with a woman in labor!" In the spring of 1851 he told Morton that he was fully occupied with measles, whooping cough, and teething complaints and had no time for books. To add to his daily rounds, special cases, and his infirmary, Nott also acted as examining physician for several insurance companies. This job often involved slaves who worked in the hazardous occupation of deckhands on steamboats.[15]

Nott's medical training, his intelligence, his personality, and his family connections ensured him an extensive and profitable practice in Mobile, but it was two special interests—surgery and yellow fever—that gave him more than a local reputation in medical circles. At this time Nott had few equals as a surgeon in the South. It was later said that his reputation could only be compared to that of Dr. Warren E. Stone of New Orleans.[16]

Although the use of ether and chloroform spread rapidly in the late 1840s, and by 1848 a Mobile newspaper was able to write that chloroform

13. Dr. Paul H. Lewis, "Medical History of Mobile," *ibid.*, IV (1847), 161; *New Orleans Medical News and Hospital Gazette*, I (1854), 395–97, I (1855), 489–90.

14. Nott to Squier, March 8, 1849, in Squier Papers, LC. Nott's comment was adapted from Smollett's *The Adventures of Peregrine Pickle*.

15. Nott to Squier, August 18, 1848, in Squier Papers, LC; Nott to Morton, April 6, 1851, in Morton Papers, HSP; *American Journal of the Medical Sciences*, n.s., XXXII (1856), 329; *De Bow's Review*, IV (1847), 287.

16. Anderson, *Biographical Sketch of Nott*, 5.

"is now used in nearly all the important surgical operations of which mention is made in the papers," Nott had learned his surgery in the age before anesthetics, when strong nerves, decisiveness, and speed were all-important. Like all early nineteenth-century surgeons, Nott was severely limited in the work he could perform—fractures, abscesses, amputations, lithotomies (removal of stones), cataracts, and obvious tumors formed a large part of the work of the surgeons of this era, and Nott was no exception. His great strength as a surgeon was the calmness and confidence he brought to the scene of the operation.[17] Whatever went wrong, and much did in these years, Nott was usually equal to the occasion.

Nott frequently published his observations on surgical cases that came under his care, and he continued to show both the willingness to experiment and the practical streak that had marked his earlier medical career. One of Nott's earliest medical publications had been a description of a wooden splint that he had developed to deal with a complicated fracture of the leg, and he continued this interest in the problems posed by fractures and with the general area that was later to become the province of orthopedic surgeons. In 1855 Nott reported on a visit he had made to the Brooklyn Orthopaedic Institution, a pioneer institution in the field in the United States. Nott strongly favored the development of specialized treatment in diseases of the joints, clubfoot, and spinal problems. He emphasized that it was extremely difficult for a general practitioner to handle these problems requiring complicated mechanical apparatus. He had, he wrote, abandoned his efforts to treat clubfoot. Any success achieved was in no way in proportion to the trouble, expense, and annoyance involved. It had once been thought that clubfoot could be cured by "cutting a tendon or two" and using a special new shoe. This notion, wrote Nott, had been a delusion that was now dying away. Nott was hopeful, however, of the results that could be achieved by specialists in orthopedic problems. Chloroform, he said, as of great use in both the process of diagnosis and the actual operation on diseased joints. Though it had long been argued that joints could not be opened without serious danger to life, the Brooklyn Institution had demonstrated that suppurating joints could and should be opened and cleaned out. With specialization and the use of anesthetics, Nott argued, much more might be possible.[18]

Nott continued in the 1850s to treat large numbers of fracture cases and

17. Mobile *Register*, February 11, 1848; Anderson, *Biographical Sketch of Nott*, 6.
18. *American Journal of the Medical Sciences*, o.s., XXIII (1838), 21–29; *New Orleans Medical and Surgical Journal*, XI (1855), 460–63.

to experiment with different types of splints. In 1856 he suggested that wire splints be used in fractures of the extremities. Nott argued that the standard solid materials—wood, patchboard, gutta percha, and the rest—had the difficulty that they kept the inflamed parts too warm and did not permit the application of cold water. Woven wire splints, he wrote, had the advantage of coolness as well as easy availability from hardware stores. He said nothing about the possible problems of achieving sufficient rigidity with his wire splints.[19]

Although physicians in the mid-nineteenth century had a reasonable degree of success in setting simple fractures, they had much greater difficulty with compound fractures when the skin was broken. In these cases, because they had no efficient way of preventing or fighting infection, they frequently had to resort to amputation in an effort to save the patient. Amputation was a regular stock-in-trade of physicians in these years, and Nott was to gain extensive additional experience in this area in the years of the Civil War.

A problem with many of Nott's published reports on the different procedures he had used is that there is usually no follow-up report to indicate the degree of success. In 1855 he reported on the case of a young slave, aged about eight, who had been brought to him from Selma, Alabama, about six months after he had been kicked in the lower jaw by a horse. Nott noted that the jaw appeared to have been fractured, that there was enormous swelling, and that there were two openings with suppuration. Nott operated, taking out a large piece of dead bone. The operation was a success in the immediate sense, but Nott in his report on the case asked the question whether the remaining bone and teeth could stay healthy when so much had been removed.[20]

Even in the case of operations that had been shaped after centuries of experimentation, Nott was inclined toward further modifications, particularly of a mechanical nature. In 1852 he commented that he had performed the operation of lithotomy (cutting into the bladder to remove calculi or stones) ten times, "and there are very few Surgeons south of the Potomac who have performed it so often." The operation was usually done with three surgical cutting instruments—the scalpel, the bistoury, and the gorget. Nott suggested that the bistoury could be eliminated. He

19. Nott, "On Wire Splints," *American Journal of the Medical Sciences,* n.s., XXXII (1856), 125.
20. Nott, "Three Surgical Cases," *ibid.,* XXX (1855), 78–79.

thought that the gorget could take its place, particularly with a modest modification in shape that he suggested. He had had a modified gorget made to his specifications. Although there are no indications at this time that Nott's modification was accepted by other surgeons, it was typical of the man that he should change existing methods and instruments for his own purposes. His justification for publishing the account of his own technique was that he had "lost but one patient after this operation, and this one from pleurisy consequent to exposure three weeks after the operation."[21]

The mechanical problems of surgery continued to interest Nott, and in 1855 at the annual meeting of the Medical Association of the State of Alabama in Mobile he presented the association with an instrument he had invented for the removal of tonsils, along with some remarks on surgery. The *New Orleans Medical News and Hospital Gazette,* in commenting on this occasion, urged Nott to go into print more often on surgical topics. "Southern surgery," the editor wrote, "has not been awarded the position to which it is entitled, and it is simply because our surgeons are too sparing of their ink; we know of no one better calculated to place us aright than Dr. N., and we are sure that his silence is not because he loves surgery less, but that he loves other subjects more."[22] Nott, of course, had to fit his medical writing into the demands of his extensive practice and his copious writing on ethnological matters. All in all, it is surprising that in these years he wrote as much as he did on medicine.

In writing on medical matters Nott never demonstrated the arrogant certainty that he showed in writing on race. One obvious reason is that the fallibility of medical solutions was constantly thrust upon practicing physicians of any intelligence. Nott, as a physician of great experience, simply could not express on medical matters the confidence he showed when writing on the supposed irreversible distinctions between races. In his medical writings he was willing to point out his own errors of diagnosis and to acknowledge those areas in which he felt less confident.

One of the most common operations performed by Nott was for the removal of cataracts. In 1855 he wrote that in his twenty years in Mobile he had done this operation "very often." He admitted, however, that his original approach had been dictated by what he viewed as his own limita-

21. Nott, "Operation of Lithotomy—A Modification of Gorget Proposed," *New Orleans Medical and Surgical Journal,* VIII (1852), 549–55.
22. *New Orleans Medical News and Hospital Gazette,* II (1855), 272–74.

tions. When he first began operating for cataracts, he did not feel sufficient confidence in his skill to risk direct extraction. Instead, Nott chose
the couching procedure by which a needle was used to displace and break
up the cataract. It was then left for absorption. Finding that four-fifths of
the cataracts he encountered in Mobile were "soft or milky," he continued
to use this method of breaking up the cataracts with a needle. "I do not
claim any peculiar skill as an oculist," wrote Nott, "but my success in cataract has been remarkable." He advised operation by absorption rather
than extraction because extraction was more hazardous. The operation as
he performed it, Nott argued, if done with a very delicate needle, did
very little injury to the eye, caused little inflammation, and required only
moderate skill.[23]

Though not claiming expertise on problems of the eye, Nott also published on the subject of "rheumatic ophthalmia" (a form of conjunctivitis). Several years before, in dealing with a severe case, Nott said that he
had "cupped, leached, applied soothing poultices, anodyne applications,
constitutional remedies, etc.," without relief. Despairing of finding any
solution, Nott had put a mercury ointment on a rag and laid it over the
eye. The patient was cured, and Nott said that this had happened in repeated cases since. Nott had here apparently stumbled onto a treatment
that was effective in some forms of conjunctivitis; for many years other
doctors were to use a mercury ointment as one possible treatment for the
affliction.[24] In search of cures, Nott frequently experimented, and it is not
surprising that he should have turned to mercury, which in a variety of
forms was a staple of medicine in the first half of the nineteenth century.

There are many indications in Nott's published reports of his cases that
he read widely to keep abreast of the latest developments in medicine,
particularly surgery, and that this, combined with his own undoubted
skill, meant that increasing numbers of patients were referred to him by
doctors both in Mobile and in other parts of Alabama when it seemed
likely that surgery would be required. In spite of this added load, Nott
did not slacken in his work as a general practitioner. Surgery was merely
fitted into his daily routine, a routine that became ever more crowded in
the years leading to the Civil War.

Most of Nott's writing that was not concerned in one way or another
with surgery was on the topic of yellow fever. Living in Mobile, he had

23. *Ibid.*, 81.
24. *Ibid.*, 81–82.

ample opportunity to observe the disease that swept through many of America's coastal cities in the nineteenth century. In his writings on yellow fever he came much nearer to understanding the course of the disease than most of his contemporaries, although in treating it he was to suffer the greatest tragedies of his life.

Yellow fever had been a scourge in North America since the seventeenth century. There had been an epidemic in New York in the 1660s, the disease had beset America's ports from time to time in the eighteenth century, and it had wrought devastation in Philadelphia in 1793. In the nineteenth century the disease was generally centered in the southern port cities; there were only two years between 1800 and 1879 when it did not occur in the United States. New Orleans was swept by the disease on numerous occasions. Some twenty-five thousand people were estimated to have died from the disease in the city in the 1850s alone, eight to nine thousand of them in 1853. As late as 1878 more than four thousand deaths resulted from the disease in New Orleans, and more than four hundred people died in 1905.[25]

For the individual sufferer the onset of the disease was sudden, the effects devastating, and death frequently the result. In the first stage the sufferer has headache, chills, pain in the back and limbs, and a rapid rise in temperature. Often there is vomiting, constipation, and a decrease in urine. This stage lasts from a few hours to two or three days, when the patient often appears to be better. The calm stage often lasts for a day or two, when a crisis is reached, usually on about the fourth day. In this stage the patient appears to be in a state of collapse, often takes on a yellow tinge, and is beset by the characteristic "black vomit." In this last symptom the patient constantly brings up from the stomach a clear fluid containing black flakes (blood acted on by the gastric juices). Within two more days the patient is usually either dead or on the road to recovery. The disease is usually milder in children, those who have the disease as children gain immunity, and blacks are more resistant than whites.

The disease is caused by a virus, which is transmitted to humans by the bite of the *Aedes egypti* mosquito. The virus is in the blood of a yellow fever victim during the first three or four days of the disease. If the victim

25. William G. Rothstein, *American Physicians in the Nineteenth Century: From Sect to Science* (Baltimore, 1972), 59–60; John Duffy, "Pestilence in New Orleans," in Hodding Carter *et al.* (eds.), *The Past as Prelude: New Orleans, 1718–1968* (New Orleans, 1968), 88–114; John Duffy, *Sword of Pestilence: The New Orleans Yellow Fever Epidemic of 1853* (Baton Rouge, 1966).

is bitten by an *Aedes egypti* mosquito, the virus passes into the mosquito, which then injects it into everyone it bites until it dies. The mosquito feeds every three days. The *Aedes* mosquito was essentially a city mosquito in the United States, and the disease was predominantly a disease of urban areas.[26]

In the first half of the nineteenth century, the medical profession was in considerable confusion concerning the origin, nature, and treatment of yellow fever, and there was much argument as to whether the disease was contagious. Because of the lack of knowledge of the role of the mosquito in transmitting the disease, the confusion is understandable. It seemed clear that the disease was not necessarily spread by direct contact, yet at the same time it seemed frequently to occur in a city after the arrival of a ship with the disease on board.

The controversy surrounding the disease is revealed by the attitudes of two of the most prominent American physicians of the postrevolutionary generation. The most famous and influential, Benjamin Rush, argued that yellow fever was a locally produced, noncontagious disease that arose from the miasmas produced by decaying vegetable and animal matter. Rush also lumped all the fevers together, arguing that in essence all illness arose from vascular tension. New Yorker David Hosack agreed that decomposing animal and vegetable matter created atmospheric conditions suitable for the transmission of yellow fever, but he thought it was a tropical disease that could be brought by seamen and transmitted to others when the air was in a state of uncleanliness. Both agreed on the importance of clearing away from the city and its environs any decaying matter that might pollute the atmosphere.[27]

Rush and Hosack differed sharply on the treatment of the disease, and in this regard, unfortunately for yellow fever patients, Rush had the most influence on other physicians. After failing to effect cures in treating yellow fever with reasonably moderate remedies, Rush turned to massive dosing in an effort to defeat the disease. His conclusion was that the best remedy was a combination of violent purging and generous bloodletting. Although at times he achieved success, presumably mostly in cases that

---

26. Erwin H. Ackerknecht, *History and Geography of the Most Important Diseases* (New York, 1965), 50–58.

27. For Rush see Nathan G. Goodman, *Benjamin Rush: Physician and Citizen, 1746–1813* (Philadelphia, 1934); and Duffy, *Healers*, 91–97. For Hosack see Christine C. Robbins, *David Hosack: Citizen of New York* (Philadelphia, 1964).

were mistakenly diagnosed as yellow fever, his remedies were often disastrous for genuine yellow fever patients. The best approach would have been cautious care and supportive nursing, but Rush was prescribing three doses, each consisting of ten grains of calomel (mercurous chloride) and fifteen grains of jalap (a strong herbal purge) to be given every six hours, along with generous bloodletting and a cooling of the patient. Hosack advocated more moderate treatment in which a key element was to induce profuse sweating. Although this treatment was also of more harm than good, it was not nearly as harmful as Rush's violent purging and bloodletting. Hosack opposed the use of calomel in yellow fever cases.[28]

Rush's drastic measures were the most common treatment of yellow fever in the first three decades of the nineteenth century, but by the 1830s many were questioning the results of "heroic" medicine. Many of these doubts were raised by general practitioners and the public who used common sense to estimate the evident ill effects of the more drastic remedies. The disillusionment of the general public was such that many turned away from calomel and massive bleeding to the herbal medicine of the Thomsonians or the minute doses of the homeopathic physicians. In the same way some local physicians simply ignored prevailing medical theory and followed what seemed, on the basis of their practical experience, to be more reasonable treatments.

The impact of the French schools of medicine also began to moderate American medicine in the 1830s. After the bloodletting practices of Broussais were discredited, the French clinical school used statistics and the autopsy room to point out the ineffectiveness of a variety of treatments. By the 1830s the observations of the French school combined with the practical doubts of many American physicians to produce far less certainty about the massive purging, bleeding, and blistering of the early years of the century. Many were to continue violent treatments, but some now rejected drastic action. Along the Gulf coast, particularly in New Orleans, the French influence was strong, for in addition to the American physicians, like Nott, with some French training, there were many French-speaking physicians who tended to turn to France for their medical literature. For a time in the 1830s and 1840s, however, massive doses of calomel

28. Duffy, *Healers*, 94–95; Robbins, *Hosack*, 37–41. In 1844 Nott referred to Benjamin Rush as "the blood-thirsty Rush," in *American Journal of the Medical Sciences*, n.s., IX (1845), 293.

were succeeded by massive doses of a drug equally useless for yellow fever—quinine. Quinine was proving of great use for malarial infections, and because many still held to the theory of the unity of fevers, there seemed to be no reason why quinine should not be of equal use in yellow fever. Not until after the great epidemic of 1853 was quinine largely abandoned in New Orleans as a treatment for yellow fever.[29]

Nott's interest in yellow fever was natural for a man who had grown up in South Carolina, who had received his medical education in New York, Philadelphia, and Paris, and who practiced in Mobile. Charleston and Mobile both were often swept by yellow fever epidemics, and the doctors with whom Nott had studied were interested in the disease. Samuel Jackson, his mentor in Philadelphia, had written on the subject, and after his year as an anatomical demonstrator in Philadelphia and his period in the Paris hospitals, Nott was always interested in what could be learned of the disease in the autopsy room. He was a firm believer in careful observation and the rejection of preconceived theories. Nott's first publication on yellow fever, in 1845, was entitled "On the Pathology of Yellow Fever." It owed much to his French training and to his careful reading of the French authorities. "Rational practice," he wrote, "can only be based on sound Pathology." His intention in the article was to give "*facts* derived from bed-side and *post-mortem* observations."[30]

This first article was a cautious, sensible piece. He said that he had witnessed five epidemics of yellow fever during his residence in Mobile. During each epidemic, Nott and his medical friends made autopsies, but only in the last two—those of 1843 and 1844—had they kept detailed notes. After deleting doubtful cases, Nott based his observations on sixteen autopsies, which had been conducted by Nott and four other doctors. At the heart of Nott's argument in this article was that there was great variety in the different epidemics of yellow fever and in the symptoms of the disease. He showed a healthy disinclination to accept monolithic explanations of the nature of yellow fever. He stressed the importance of Louis' work on the Gibraltar epidemic of 1828 but emphasized that, as Louis had indicated and as sometimes had been forgotten, Louis' observations applied only to that particular epidemic. Each of the five epidemics

29. Duffy, *Sword of Pestilence*, 149–54.
30. Samuel Jackson, *An Account of the Yellow or Malignant Fever as It Occurred in the City of Philadelphia, 1820* (Philadelphia, 1821); Nott, "On the Pathology of Yellow Fever," *American Journal of the Medical Sciences*, n.s., IX (1845), 277.

that Nott had observed in Mobile had needed some modifications in treatment.

The core of Nott's article was a discussion of the post-mortem condition of the various body organs. The most important of his conclusions concerned the liver and the black vomit typical of yellow fever. The liver, he pointed out, did not consistently have the straw color that, based on his observations of the Gibraltar epidemic, Louis said was a constant sign of yellow fever. In regard to the black vomit, for which there had been a variety of explanations, Nott reached the correct one that it consisted of blood acted on by the stomach's secretions. In the epidemic of 1844 Nott, along with Dr. Paul H. Lewis, had tested this theory by mixing muriatic acid with blood from the heart of a corpse dead from yellow fever.

In the course of his argument, Nott once again demonstrated the depth of his reading and the extent to which he had tempered his youthful enthusiasm for the theories of Broussais. "Broussais," he wrote, "has done much towards the advancement of pathology, though, like most medical reformers, he has pushed his peculiar notions to extremes." Nearly all the best pathologists—Gabriel Andral, Auguste Chomel, Pierre Louis, William Alison, Alexander Tweedie, Thomas Watson—agreed, Nott argued, that distinctions had to be made between broad classes of disease, and all disease could not be viewed as stemming from inflammation.

The conclusion that Nott drew from his post-mortem examinations and his experience in Mobile was that yellow fever was a poison received through the atmosphere. This poison probably acted on the nervous system and the blood in a manner that greatly changed the blood from its normal state. These conclusions, said Nott, had implications for treatment. Because yellow fever was "a depressing morbid poison," rather than inflammatory in nature, bleeding should be used cautiously. "I would lay down as a *general rule*," wrote Nott, "that it is not a disease which demands *active* depletion, either by blood letting or purging." According to the established rules of practice, said Nott, bleeding was used to combat inflammation, plethora, and active congestion, and there were no indications of these in yellow fever. He was not prepared to rule out the use of bleeding in specific cases in which "excitement in the arterial system" produced an accelerated pulse. Physicians, however, should not expect to bleed the poison out of the system—"the *rule* is, beware of the lancet."[31]

31. Nott, "On the Pathology of Yellow Fever," 277–93.

Nott's most significant article on yellow fever was written in 1848; in it he discussed the possible origins of the disease. In this article Nott missed a breakthrough that would have given him a permanent, major place in medical history, but he showed a fine knowledge of the literature, effectively disposed of some of the myths and misconceptions surrounding yellow fever, argued correctly that it was a disease *sui generis*, and showed himself to be far closer than most of his contemporaries to an understanding of the nature of the disease. In the degree to which it described the contents of the article, Nott's title had an eighteenth-century ring to it: "Yellow Fever contrasted with Bilious Fever—Reasons for believing it a disease sui generis—Its mode of Propagation—Remote Cause—Probable insect or animalcular origin, &c."[32]

The main purpose of Nott's article was to argue that the prevailing theory regarding malaria—that it arose from an emanation produced from the earth's surface by decaying matter—was wholly inadequate to explain the propagation of yellow fever. He intended, he stated, to give "reasons for supposing its specific cause to exist in some form of Insect Life." All fevers, he argued, could not be lumped together as though they had a common origin, and they could not all be dealt with in a similar manner. Yellow fever was a distinct disease, and it was possible that among the various fevers others would also be found to be distinct.[33] It becomes clear in the course of Nott's article that in arguing that yellow fever was caused by "insects" he was using the term as a convenient way to describe the microorganisms, invisible to the naked eye, that had usually been described as "animalcules." He reasoned from what he knew about the breeding and distribution patterns of visible insects that invisible insects might act in the same way.

Observation of microscopic life forms had begun in the seventeenth century with the development of the microscope. A Dutchman, Anton Van Leeuwenhoek, had used a microscope to describe a large number of minute organisms. Although there had been suggestions as far back as

32. Nott, "Yellow Fever contrasted with Bilious Fever," *New Orleans Medical and Surgical Journal,* IV (1848), 563–601. The importance of this article has been recognized by several medical historians; see Paul F. Clark, *Pioneer Microbiologists of America* (Madison, 1961), 53–54; Robert Wilson, "Dr. Nott and the Transmission of Yellow Fever," *Annals of Medical History,* n.s., III (1931), 515–20; Wilbur G. Downs, "Yellow Fever and Josiah Clark Nott," *Bulletin of the New York Academy of Medicine,* 2d ser., L (1974), 499–508. For the failure of the article to influence later investigators see Eli Chernin, "Josiah Clark Nott, Insects, and Yellow Fever," *Bulletin of the New York Academy of Medicine,* 2d Ser., LIX (1983), 790–802.

33. Nott, "Yellow Fever," 563–64, 569.

classical times that disease was caused by particles, invisible to the naked eye, that were carried through the air, Van Leeuwenhoek's observations did not lead to any immediate suggestion that his animalcules had a direct connection with the causes of disease. It was not until the work of Louis Pasteur in the second half of the nineteenth century that it was discovered that among the minute organisms observed as long ago as the seventeenth century were bacteria capable of causing disease. It was even later when it was realized that there were even tinier viruses that had a direct relationship to specific diseases. These viruses were not made visible until the development of electronic microscopes.

Although the revealing of the direct relationships between microscopic organisms and disease had to await the work of Louis Pasteur, several physicians and others speculated in the eighteenth and early nineteenth centuries that infectious diseases could be caused by minute animalcules or "seeds" spread through the air. Such ideas were generally looked upon as farfetched, and at the time Nott obtained his medical education there were very few supporters of the animalcular theories.[34]

Nott acknowledged in his article that the theory of the animalcular origin of disease was not new, and he made reference to earlier arguments, but he contended that the subject had been given a new meaning by the publication of Christian Gottfried Ehrenberg's "great work" on "Insuforia" in 1838. Ehrenberg, a German naturalist, had been trained as a physician. In his work he stressed that the world was permeated by minute organisms. He showed that many rock formations were made up of minute forms of animals or plants and that the phosphorescence of the sea was caused by organisms. Nott argued that Ehrenberg's work had cast a new light on old arguments about the animalcular origins of disease. In a more specific sense, the most direct influence on Nott's ideas on yellow fever was an article by the English physician Sir Henry Holland, who had included an article on the subject of insect life as a cause of disease in his *Medical Notes, and Reflections,* published in 1839. This article had little general impact, but it helped Nott formulate the views he had been developing regarding the unusual patterns he had traced in the various epidemics of yellow fever in Mobile.[35]

Much of Nott's discussion in this article was devoted to the various

34. See Peter Baldry, *The Battle Against Bacteria: A Fresh Look* (Cambridge, England, 1976), 1, 7, 13–17; Wyndham E. B. Lloyd, *A Hundred Years of Medicine* (2d ed.; London, 1968), 90–102.
35. Nott, "Yellow Fever," 563.

ways in which the Mobile yellow fever epidemics had spread through the city. Their pattern led him to the conclusion that the "morbific cause of Yellow Fever . . . accords in many respects with the peculiar habits and instincts of Insects" and did not at all accord with the idea that the disease arose from emanations from decaying matter or from peculiar atmospheric conditions. The epidemics of 1842 and 1843 had been particularly influential in shaping Nott's ideas, for in both of those years the disease had advanced slowly, house by house, while breezes swept the town in every direction. Wind and weather had no impact on the manner in which the disease was spreading. Even the epidemics of 1837, 1839, and 1841, which had started in many places and had brought cases here and there in every direction, though different from the two other epidemics, argued Nott, fitted the insect theory and no other. Based on the evidence of these epidemics, Nott contended that there was a "perfect analogy between the habits of certain insects and Yellow Fever." [36]

To illustrate his argument, Nott used a subject with which he was well acquainted—the manner in which the different parasitic pests affected cotton fields in different years. There was no consistency in how the cotton fields were attacked; in some years there was massive infestation, in other years none; in some years certain fields were affected, in some years not; in some years one part of the plant, in others years some other part. Animal and vegetable decomposition occurred every year in a regular pattern in Mobile's climate, and some form of disease carried by insects, not general bad air, was the only explanation for the odd pattern of the various epidemics. In passing, Nott also suggested that various "Marsh Fevers" might consist of different diseases and might be caused by different insects.

To combat those who argued that yellow fever and the marsh fevers were the same, Nott specifically refuted point by point the arguments of Frenchman Nicolas Chervin, who Nott thought had made one of the fullest arguments in favor of the common nature of the different fevers. A key factor in Nott's argument was that yellow fever sprang up independent of any meteorological changes and spread regardless of wind or weather patterns. The only exception was that once started the disease progressed more rapidly in dry than in very wet weather. This could well be explained, wrote Nott, by rains impeding the march of insects. Moreover, only a killing frost stopped yellow fever. This again accorded with

36. *Ibid.*, 565–67.

an insect origin rather than some miasma in the air, for the decomposition of animal and vegetable matter resumed again if there was warm weather after a killing frost.[37]

In explaining why some fevers spread upward, and were prevalent out of low-lying areas, Nott came painfully close to understanding what was happening in yellow fever epidemics. "It would certainly be quite as philosophical (as the Malarial theory)," he argued, "to suppose that some insect or animalcule, hatched in the lowlands, like the musquito, after passing through its metamorphoses," takes flight from the lowlands to the higher ground. Nott, of course, had no way of knowing that there were two vital factors in the spreading of yellow fever, an invisible animalcule (the virus) and a visible mosquito (the vector). Had he understood this, he would have understood why sometimes the disease seemed to be contagious although it was clearly not contagious in any general sense. Nott was thinking of one minute animalcule, an insect invisible to the naked eye breeding and spreading in the same manner as visible insects, carrying the disease from victim to victim. A physician friend of Nott's, Dr. Stanford Chaillé of New Orleans, later told the story that at the autopsy of a patient who had died of yellow fever Nott had turned to him and said, "Chaillé, I'm damned if I don't believe its bugs."[38]

Yet, though Nott did not understand the role of the mosquito in spreading yellow fever, he cut through and dismissed misconceptions held by some of the most influential American and European physicians of his day. "Vegetable matter," he wrote, "is *certainly* not a cause of Yellow Fever." Nott consistently argued that miasmas had nothing to do with causing the disease. He was also confident at this time, though he was to waver a little after the epidemic of 1853, that yellow fever was not contagious, if by this it was meant that "a morbid poison" generated in one body could be passed on by contact. Yet, he suggested, it was possible that "the germ or *materies morbi*" might be transmitted or transported from one locality to another. Here again Nott was getting near to the truth, but lacking the knowledge of even the existence of pathogenic viruses and the role of the insect vector, he was unable to put the pieces together.[39]

Although Nott believed that yellow fever could be transmitted by ships,

37. *Ibid.*, 567–72.
38. *Ibid.*, 580; Nott file, School of Medicine, in University of Pennsylvania Archives, Philadelphia.
39. Nott, "Yellow Fever," 583, 589–90.

he also believed at this time that that was not a major danger. A ship with yellow fever on board should not be allowed near a town, he argued, but there was no need for strict quarantine laws against all shipping, which would only interfere with commerce. "Commerce," he wrote, "is one of the *great necessities* of society."[40] He wrote as a true resident of a city that made its living on the exports and imports through Mobile Bay.

Nott concluded this perceptive and sensible article with a general discussion of what had recently been learned about the "Infusoria, or Microscopic animalcules." He justified this discussion with the comment that few of his readers would have access to the original sources on the subject. In this discussion Nott demonstrated an ability to appreciate the significance and future possibilities of this still controversial subject. He said that though Ehrenberg had shown that five hundred million infusoria might exist in a single drop of water, there was "every reason to believe that countless species still exist, too small to be reached by our most powerful microscopes." Nott was convinced here, as in so many other subjects, that a fearless pursuit of reality through scientific investigation would overturn vague theories based on superstition and ignorance. He found the idea of yellow fever being spread by some microscopic-sized "insect" was, unlike the theories of atmospheric miasmas, "something tangible and comprehensible." Nott believed that yellow fever was spread by microscopic-sized animalcules or insects that, unable to fly themselves, were transported for long distances in a variety of ways, while at the same time slowly making their way from house to house. If he could have conceived of the animalcules as carried in the bodies of mosquitoes, he would have had the answer, but that possibility he never suggested or considered. He did, however, see the patterns and possible cause of yellow fever more clearly than any of his contemporaries, who in essence disregarded his acute observations on the likely role of animalcules in causing the disease. At the close of his article, he argued that it was "highly probable" that it would be found that animalcules (or germs) caused not only yellow fever but also smallpox, plague, cholera, and other diseases.[41]

That Nott had shown great imagination and a willingness to discard accepted but demonstrably false hypotheses was unfortunately of little

40. *Ibid.*, 592.
41. *Ibid.*, 592–95, 598.

use to him in combating yellow fever in Mobile. Even if the disease was caused by microscopic animalcules that followed the migratory patterns of visible insects, Nott had no way of either preventing such a spread or effectively treating the disease when it occurred. This inability was to bring him much frustration in his medical practice and great tragedy in his personal life.

Chapter 7
YELLOW FEVER

Yellow fever was the scourge of Mobile during the prosperous years from the 1830s to the Civil War. Nott commented in 1848 that from the time of his arrival in the city in 1836 there had been no year without sporadic cases, and five epidemics occurred, in 1837, 1839, 1842, 1843, and 1844. Of these epidemics, Nott characterized the 1844 outbreak as very mild, and most commentators omitted it from their lists.[1] Also, both Nott and other commentators at times thought of 1847 as an epidemic year, though not a severe one. In the 1850s there was a disastrous epidemic in 1853 and lesser outbreaks in 1855 and 1858. The threat of yellow fever, combined with the general heat and humidity of Mobile, caused a large-scale exodus from the city in the summer months. Many went to the Virginia Springs, or even north to Saratoga or Niagara, and others went to resorts and watering places around Mobile Bay or in the interior. Nott was often in Mobile during the most dangerous months—August to October—but his family moved to Spring Hill west of the city, and he spent nights there. In epidemic years all who could get away did, but physicians and ministers often regarded it as their duty to stay and tend to the population.

Because no one knew why yellow fever appeared in some years and not in others, there was very little that could be done to avoid the disease. The contagionists (and there were very few of them in Mobile) sometimes argued for a port quarantine to avoid the danger of infected ships, but the city depended so much on its commerce that there was no serious support for such a measure. More general were the demands that the city should be cleaned of all decaying matter. In spite of Nott's hypothesis of

---

1. Nott, "Yellow Fever contrasted with Bilious Fever," *New Orleans Medical and Surgical Journal,* IV (1848), 565.

an animalcular origin of yellow fever, the prevailing argument in these years was that the disease arose from the noxious emanations produced by the decay of vegetable and animal matter. When news came that yellow fever was striking New Orleans, or other ports, there was usually a flurry of activity to clean up Mobile. Clearly, when this involved clearing away low-lying wet areas, it helped reduce mosquito breeding grounds and thus inadvertently attacked a source of the disease, but there was of course no special attack on the mosquito problem because the mosquitoes were regarded as a major inconvenience but not as a threat to life.

A major problem with the mosquitoes was that they were nearly as much of a scourge indoors as outdoors. Houses in Mobile and throughout the South were generally not mosquito-proof. In the spring of 1853, the Mobile *Register* referred to the mosquitoes as these "pests and plagues of each man's home." Although mosquito netting was almost universally used around beds, it was not usual on windows or in the rest of the house. The *Register* suggested that more families should use bobbinet netting at the windows and doors to mosquito-proof their sitting rooms. A visitor to Mobile in the summer of 1857 later reminisced that "what impressed me most was the multitudinous swarm of mosquitoes that filled the air like the Egyptian plague of flies." Two years earlier, in the middle of July, a young man writing a letter from the city commented that the mosquitoes were swarming as he wrote. They "are dreadful," he said, "I have never known them to be half as bad both night and day." In the mosquito season in Mobile there was no way of avoiding bites.[2]

Year after year the residents of Mobile waited anxiously in midsummer for any sign of yellow fever. Although it was generally accepted that an epidemic of the disease would end with the first frost, there was far more variation in the time when epidemics began. August was the likeliest month for news that the disease was spreading, but outbreaks occurred as early as July and as late as September. Local newspapers tended to deny that yellow fever was present in the city until it was impossible to ignore it. The announcement of an epidemic caused a further flight of the population and a stagnation of trade.

In the first epidemic that Nott witnessed and practiced in—that of 1837—the Mobile *Register* announced as late as September 29 that the "city is, and has been, entirely free from epidemic or contagious disease. We are assured by the Physicians that this is the season of great health."

2. Mobile *Register,* May 14, 1853; John Massey, *Reminiscences* (Nashville, 1916), 87; W. A. Witherspoon to H. L. Reynolds, July 16, 1855, in Henry Lee Reynolds Papers, SHC.

Nott later commented on the epidemic of 1837 that there were four or five isolated cases in September but that the next cases did not occur until October 10, and it then spread "rapidly in all directions as an Epidemic." Although the epidemic ended with the coming of the first frost at the end of the month, it was responsible for the death of some 350 persons in the city. In 1837 Mobile's total population, even when they were all in residence, was only about 10,000.[3]

Two years later, in the summer of 1839, the city was hit by a more severe epidemic. It was made worse by widespread fires.[4] The epidemic began in the first days of August with a few cases near the corner of Government and Hamilton streets. Nott later pointed out that this was half a mile from the shipping, in a clean, well-ventilated, and fashionable part of town. The residents still hoped that these were the isolated cases that occurred in any year, and on August 12 the local Board of Health, which at this time consisted of three physicians, including Nott, responded to a request from the mayor and made a public announcement that there had been no more than three cases.[5]

Any hope that these were isolated cases disappeared rapidly in the following weeks. Yellow fever now, in Nott's words, "burst forth in every direction with extraordinary violence." Within a week of announcing that there had been only isolated cases, the Board of Health called on the mayor to take prompt action to clean the city. In 1839 Nott had not yet developed his theories of the insect origin of yellow fever, and the best available information was that decaying matter was the most likely cause of the disease. The board advised that twenty-five or thirty carts should at once be employed to spread lime twice a week on all the filthy gutters, privies, and yards within the city. Some had suggested that the weeds growing about the city were productive of disease. The board disagreed with this idea, unless offal and other refuse had been thrown among the weeds, but said that if it was decided to remove the weeds they should be taken beyond the limits of the city.[6]

By the second week in September the epidemic was raging. The editor

3. Nott, "Yellow Fever," 566; Mobile *Register,* September 29, October 30, 1837, November 4, 1839.
4. Caldwell Delaney (ed.), *Craighead's Mobile: Being the Fugitive Writings of Erwin S. Craighead and Frank Craighead* (Mobile, 1968), 81–83; G. Lewis, *Impressions of America and the American Churches: From Journal of the Rev. G. Lewis* (Edinburgh, 1845), 172.
5. Nott, "Yellow Fever," 566; Mobile *Register,* August 12, 1839.
6. Nott, "Yellow Fever," 566; Mobile *Register,* August 19, 1839.

of the Mobile *Register* reported that his junior editor was dangerously ill (he soon died) and that "our friends are falling around us like the leaves in autumn." Some four-fifths of the residents had now left the city, the streets were deserted, and most of the stores, except the druggists, were closed. Nott's family was outside the city at Spring Hill, and Nott slept there, but for long hours he rode through the city tending the yellow fever victims. On September 18 the *Register* asked subscribers to call at the newspaper office for their papers because nearly all the stores in the city were closed and several of the newspaper carriers were ill. On the next day the mayor declared "a day of fasting, humiliation, and prayer." Some of the prominent remaining residents formed a "Can't Get Away Club" as a relief society to provide food, medicine, physicians, and nursing care for the sick. This club was to operate during epidemics throughout the century. Near the end of the month, it was reported that nurses were unobtainable to help the sick, even though $40 a month was being offered.[7]

In October conditions worsened as large fires swept through the central parts of the city—Nott's office was among those burned—and burglars took advantage of the confusion and the lack of people to make off with a variety of goods. By the time the first killing frost made it safe to return to the city, yellow fever had been responsible for some five hundred deaths, even though at the height of the epidemic only about three thousand residents remained in the city.[8]

Although yellow fever periodically made its appearance in the 1840s, it was not as severe as it had been in 1837 and 1839, and residents were hopeful that the worst had passed. The pattern of the outbreaks in the early 1840s convinced Nott that decaying matter could not be the cause. In 1842, when few died, the outbreak began on August 29 in Spanish Alley, "a very filthy place near the docks," and spread slowly from house to house on one side of the town. In the following year the epidemic was far more severe. It began on August 19 on the opposite side of the town and again spread slowly, but this time with severer effect, killing about 240

7. Mobile *Register*, September 12, 18, 23, 1839; Harriet E. Amos, "Social Life in an Antebellum Cotton Port: Mobile, Alabama, 1820–1860" (Ph.D. dissertation, Emory University, 1976), 131, 263–64; Howard L. Holley, *The History of Medicine in Alabama* (Birmingham, 1982), 19–20.

8. Nott to Joseph W. Lesesne, October 9, 1839, in Joseph W. Lesesne Papers, SHC; Henry S. Levert to Francis Levert, December 30, 1839, in Levert Family Papers, *ibid.*; Charles Lyell, *A Second Visit to the United States of North America* (2 vols.; New York, 1849), II, 88; Nott, "Yellow Fever," 566.

out of an estimated 850 cases. Statistics were never exact because there were mild as well as severe cases of yellow fever, and many physicians had difficulty in separating the various fevers endemic in the area.[9]

By 1843 Mobile physicians were showing a good deal of common sense in treating yellow fever. In the 1830s bleeding, strong purges (calomel and jalap), antimony, and tartar emetics were often used, but by the mid-1840s much more moderation prevailed. One Mobile practitioner and medical historian, Dr. Paul H. Lewis, commented in 1846 that by that time no physician of any experience in Mobile expected to cut the disease short. Excessive dosing was avoided, and emetics and bleeding were generally viewed as "highly pernicious." Stimulants, including brandy, were given when the collapse stage was reached, and some followed the common New Orleans practice of giving quinine.[10]

After the 1843 epidemic, Mobile had good reason in the next ten years to believe that the worst scourges of yellow fever had passed from the city. In 1844 there were only some forty deaths from the disease, and in the following years a cautious optimism prevailed. There was still a general belief that the cleanliness of the city was of great importance in avoiding the disease, and in the spring of 1845 the incumbent president of the Mobile Medical Society, Nott's old colleague Dr. Richard Lee Fearn, wrote to the mayor on behalf of the society to suggest preventive measures that would, as far as possible, guard Mobile's citizens "from those causes usually recognized as producing or fostering malignant fever." It was suggested that after June 1 two citizens from each ward should be required to attend the weekly meetings of the Board of Health to facilitate carrying out the recommendations regarding the cleanliness of the city. The board had a long list of recommendations: garbage should be carefully removed from the market; ditches and gutters should be cleaned, pools and low places in streets filled in, and standing water and other nuisances dealt with before July 1; from July through October there should be no extensive turning of earth, filling of lots with rubbish, or depositing by city carts; lime should be freely and constantly used; scavenger carts should go through the streets daily rather than three times a week during the key four months; slips and wharves were to be inspected every fifteen days for nuisances; and laws relating to sweeping sidewalks and cleansing gutters

9. Nott, "Yellow Fever," 566–67.
10. P. H. Lewis, "Medical History of Alabama," *New Orleans Medical and Surgical Journal*, IV (1847), 167–75.

should be strictly enforced. Fearn pointed out that these recommendations had also been made in the summer of 1844, but many of them had been ignored.[11]

The nearest that Mobile came to a full-scale epidemic in the second half of the 1840s was in the summer of 1847. Nott estimated that in the months of August, September, and October of that year there were probably seven or eight hundred cases of yellow fever, but of these less than seventy people died; a few more were to die in November. The disease was so mild and manageable that Nott thought that it should perhaps be called "an ephemeral epidemic." Cases had begun as early as July 18, when a ship captain from New York came down with the disease, but it progressed very slowly through August. In September it spread rapidly but mildly; the disease was most prevalent, wrote Nott, among newcomers to the city. The epidemic, like those earlier in the decade, helped confirm Nott in his belief in an animalcular origin of the disease. The outbreak began early in the summer, ran its course, and ceased in the middle of warm weather, long before frost. Nott believed that this pattern showed "a strong analogy with the habits of insect life." Vegetable and animal decomposition went on well past the time when the epidemic stopped. In an article on the 1847 epidemic, Nott made several perceptive comments on the nature of yellow fever. He emphasized the great variation in symptoms. Some cases were mild, and not even fever and a fast pulse necessarily accompanied the disease. Again in this epidemic, Nott tested black vomit and, having read a rebuttal of his earlier arguments by another physician, he defended his contention that it consisted of blood.[12]

Nott argued that most Mobile practitioners were in general agreement on the treatment for yellow fever, but he also discussed his own experiments to find a specific remedy for the disease. The older Mobile practitioners, Nott wrote, because of their ample experience and frequent interchange of ideas, were in accord on methods of treatment, although treatments were modified for different patients and in different epidemics. Nott considered that the main medical areas of dispute in treating yellow fever were bleeding, purging, quinine, mercury, and stimulants. Mobile doctors had become cautious in the use of bleeding. They bled

11. Nott, "Yellow Fever," 566; Richard Lee Fearn to the mayor of Mobile, May 16, 1845, in transcripts, Mobile City Records, Local History Room, Mobile Public Library.

12. Nott, "Sketch of the Epidemic of Yellow Fever of 1847, in Mobile," *Charleston Medical Journal,* III (1848), 1–12.

not for a particular disease but because of the symptoms in an individual case, particularly for a rapid, agitated pulse. In the epidemics that Nott had seen, bleeding had been the exception, not the rule. Nott's own view was that in such diseases as yellow fever, which he said were really cases of poisoning, the strength of the patient had to be husbanded.[13]

Mobile doctors, wrote Nott, were also moderate in the use of purgatives; one reason was that in the Mobile epidemics there was not the severe constipation described by some writers on yellow fever. What Nott considered moderation is a good indication of the violent purging that had been the norm of American medicine. Nott argued that in the cases he had seen, ten grains of calomel and a dose of oil would suffice as a purge and that after the first stage of the disease mild purgatives such as oil or rhubarb were adequate. Mercury (in the form of calomel) was used, he said, because it was the least irritating.

Nott also confirmed the impression of Mobile physician Dr. Paul H. Lewis that quinine never achieved the popularity in treating yellow fever in Mobile that it had in New Orleans. Nott said that although no one doubted the value of quinine for intermittent fevers and some other diseases, he found it of no use for yellow fever. He had no doubt that it had injured as many as it had benefited. In speaking of quinine, Nott used the sarcasm that was more common in his racial than in his medical writings, saying that in the 1847 epidemic quinine had been used in New Orleans "*with immense success*," but that somehow or other about three thousand people had died. Nott had every reason to attack the New Orleans physicians for their use of quinine in cases of yellow fever.

In regard to stimulants Nott argued that all Mobile physicians (and he meant the trained elite with whom he consorted) were agreed on their use; they were given when the pulse began to flag. The usual stimulant in the collapse stage of yellow fever was brandy. "Nothing seems to hit a Mobile stomach like a mint julap," wrote Nott, "whether it be or not because we like this charming beverage so much in health I cannot say, but certain it is that the brandy julap is *the* thing for the collapse stage." Sometimes champagne or porter was given, but Nott totally disagreed with chlorate of ammonia at this stage—he had never seen it suit the patient.

Although Nott said that Mobile's physicians were generally agreed on

13. Nott's discussion of therapeutics here and in the following paragraphs is in *ibid.*, 14–18.

yellow fever treatment, he conceded that even in Mobile there was argument about the specific virtues of the universally used mercury. Nott himself had no doubts about its advantages as a mild and efficient purgative, but, he wrote, "as to its great *specific* virtues, *j'en doute*." He thought Louis had perhaps gone too far in saying that no dependence could be placed on mercurial preparations because in certain yellow fever cases, when the stomach was not disturbed by the medicine, it was of definite use. If it caused nausea, he said, it was worse than useless. All in all, he was inclined to doubt the effectiveness of mercury in treating yellow fever because there was so much dispute about it; in those cases in which there were no questions about the specific treatment for a disease—such as quinine in periodic fevers, iodine in scrofula, bleeding in phlegmasia, nitrate of silver in opthalmia—all practitioners accepted it without discussion.

In treating yellow fever Nott argued that he was a strong believer in the golden rules: (1) be sure you do no harm, and (2) do all the good you can. Chervin, he said, had demonstrated that mortality did not change much whatever the treatment, and Nott's own opinion was that the history of yellow fever in the last half century had convinced him that all known modes of treatment were insufficient to combat the disease in its malignant forms. With good sense that was still rare in such matters in the 1840s, Nott wrote that he was "thoroughly convinced of the great abuse made of all the heroic remedies used in this disease."

In discussing the 1847 epidemic, Nott also indicated that since 1843 he had been experimenting with his own possible specific for yellow fever. His justification was Louis' assertion that because physicians did not know the cause of what they were treating, they could reject no empirical treatment, however absurd it might seem. Nott had decided on his experiment in 1843 after discovering that the first fifteen patients to contract yellow fever in the city had all died, although he learned from their attending physicians that some of them had been freely bled, all had been purged, and all had been given greater or lesser doses of mercury. Because it was apparent that none of the approved methods was working, Nott decided to experiment "against this unknown cause."

His choice for the experiment was creosote. His reason was that creosote was a powerful antiseptic, and if an animal after taking it for a few days was killed and cut open the creosote pervaded every tissue and fluid of its body—the odor was present everywhere. Nott's theory was that if for a few days there was a morbid poison acting on the fluids or solids of the body, perhaps creosote could exert some influence on it, "either for good or evil." His formula called for a mixture of creosote, alcohol, and spiritus mindereri (a solution of ammonium acetate). A tablespoonful was to be taken every two hours in a glass of sweetened water.

Since its discovery in the 1830s, creosote, distilled from pine or beech wood, had been used in a variety of medicinal ways, usually externally, but other physicians before Nott had experimented with the use of this powerful antiseptic internally.

It was probably not accidental that Nott first tried his mixture not on the wife of a prominent Mobilian but on two prostitutes in a Mobile brothel. He was called to the two women, one of whom had been taking calomel every two hours by the prescription of another Mobile physician who had himself contracted yellow fever. She was vomiting incessantly, but after she was given the creosote mixture her vomiting ceased. This is not surprising because she had stopped taking the calomel and was taking creosote, which has been used as a remedy for seasickness, and the solution of ammonium acetate would also have had a soothing effect. The other woman, after first being given a dose of purgative pills (calomel, rhubarb, and aloes), also was put on creosote. Both patients survived, and for the next month Nott treated his yellow fever patients with creosote, losing not a patient.

But Nott rarely deceived himself on medical matters as he did on racial questions, and though he thought he had perhaps found a specific for yellow fever, he asked around and discovered that the disease was losing its virulence. Very few other doctors were losing patients either. Later that year Nott lost several patients who were on the creosote cure, but his experience that year and in two succeeding ones left him with the opinion that creosote was a valuable remedy but not a specific; at least, he wrote, it could safely be considered harmless. His general conclusion was that creosote quieted the stomach and did not cause the wear and tear on the system that bleeding, purging, and mercury did. This seems a fair assessment. At least, wrote Nott, "it does not interfere with other remedies; and, if it does good in no other way, might amuse the patient's mind, where some are physicing without rhyme or reason."[14]

By the time of the epidemic of 1847, Nott was acknowledged as the leading Mobile practitioner in the field of yellow fever, and when early in

14. *Ibid.*, 19–21.

November of that year much dispute and even panic arose in the city because of a fear that yellow fever was still spreading rapidly at a time when many were anxious to return for business reasons, Nott sought out the editor of the Mobile *Register* to allay the widespread fears. The editor reported that Nott assured him that there were now relatively few cases being treated in the city and that these cases were mild. The editor commented that this "should be sufficient to convince everyone that there is now no dangerous disease in the city." [15]

When Nott read the editor's assurance that no dangerous disease was present in the city, he thought he was being misinterpreted and immediately wrote to the paper to say that he would not go that far. By talking to other physicians he had decided that probably about a dozen cases of yellow fever were under treatment, though the sexton had informed him that during the week there had been no deaths from the disease. A key question was whether it was safe for Mobile's many absentees to return, and Nott said the physicians were not agreed on this point before going on to give his own opinion. "We have yet had no weather calculated to put an end to the disease," he wrote, "and there must be *some* risk until there is a decided frost, but my own opinion is that it is very small." The epidemic had started earlier than usual and thus, said Nott, was running its allotted time at an earlier date. "My opinion is," he wrote, "that those who are in a healthy locality and can conveniently delay had better do so, but I doubt whether there is more danger here from Yellow Fever than there is from Bilious fever in most parts of the interior." [16]

After the brief flare-up of yellow fever in 1847, there was again hope that it was disappearing from Mobile. There were epidemics of scarlet fever in 1848 and 1849, which resulted in some 125 deaths, and a fairly mild outbreak of cholera in 1849, but no epidemics of the dreaded yellow fever. [17] For Nott these years at the end of the 1840s and the beginning of the 1850s were among the best of his life. He was now generally regarded as one of the best physicians in the South, his reputation as an ethnologist was soaring, and his flourishing practice was providing the income he needed to live a comfortable life with his growing family.

When in the early summer of 1853 Nott heard of the rapidly spreading

15. Mobile *Register,* November 4, 1847.
16. *Ibid.,* November 5, 1847.
17. *Alabama Planter* (Mobile), March 24, 1853; Martha C. Mitchell, "Health and the Medical Profession in the Lower South, 1845–1860," *Journal of Southern History,* X (1944), 431.

yellow fever epidemic in New Orleans, he could have had no idea of the extent of the tragedy that was soon to befall both him and Mobile. He knew that it meant that in all likelihood Mobile would suffer a yellow fever epidemic, but he had lived through a few of them, and it seemed that the epidemics of the 1840s had been less virulent than those of earlier years.

Both in New Orleans and in Mobile there was the usual reluctance to believe that an epidemic was about to start. In early July a Mobile newspaper printed a letter from New Orleans, dated June 28, denying reports of a yellow fever epidemic. "The yellow fever has ceased to be a terror to the public here," the correspondent wrote, "and is rarely fatal when properly attended to." Three weeks later another Mobile newspaper reprinted a very different story from New Orleans. A New Orleans paper admitted that yellow fever prevailed in the city to an extent probably never before equaled. The editor of the Mobile *Register*, with misguided complacency, contrasted the health of Mobile with the sickness of New Orleans. Nott was less sanguine. He had regularly observed that when a widespread outbreak occurred in New Orleans, it was only a matter of time before Mobile was also affected.[18]

In the first two weeks of August, the Mobile newspapers continued to contrast the disastrous state of affairs in New Orleans with the health of Mobile. On the fifth, the *Register* referred to the "present unsurpassed healthiness of the city" and later said that the healthy state had been achieved by cleanliness and the use of lime. News from New Orleans continued to describe widespread suffering: on the eighth it was reported that victims were dying at the rate of more than one hundred a day. A few days earlier Nott had been sent for to go to Pascagoula to attend a friend, a colonel in the United States Army, who was in critical condition from "high Bilious fever." He died soon after Nott arrived. The Gulf was swept by disease in 1853, and Mobile could not hope to escape for much longer. By August 15 the *Alabama Planter* commented that the yellow fever epidemic prevailing in New Orleans was without parallel in the history of that city and argued that Mobile needed more than its usual sanitary measures. By that date the epidemic was beginning in Mobile.[19]

The first yellow fever cases Mobilians saw that summer came from New Orleans. In the mass exodus from that city some who were already sick

18. *Alabama Planter* (Mobile), July 4, 1853; Mobile *Register*, July 16, 1853.
19. *Mobile Register*, August 5, 9, 1853; *Alabama Planter* (Mobile), August 8, 15, 1853.

with yellow fever died in Mobile in July. Nott later confirmed that the first cases came from a ship that had sailed from Portland, Maine, to New Orleans, and then to Mobile. Several of the crew had already died of yellow fever before the ship anchored in Mobile Bay, some fifteen or twenty miles below the city, on July 11. Others from the crew died in Mobile in that month, and one of the stevedores who loaded the vessel with cotton also died of the disease.[20]

Mobile's epidemic began to get under way in the second week of August, but at first the newspapers still purveyed an empty optimism. The *Alabama Planter* commented on August 22 that though yellow fever was now in Mobile it seemed a much milder variety than that in New Orleans; but the same weekly reported increasing numbers of yellow fever victims. The fever increased with dramatic suddenness in the last week of August and the first weeks of September. City officials now took emergency measures to try to curb the disease. Beginning on Sunday night August 21, for a week the hot, humid city was ablaze with light and additional heat as the mayor arranged for barrels of tar, rosin, and pitch and bonfires of trash to be set alight at nearly every corner. The whole city was in a blaze, commented the *Register,* "and if there be any noxious quality in the evening air which flame and smoke can eradicate, it ought to be done now." It was no use. Thirty-seven victims of yellow fever died in the week ending August 26, 156 in the week following, and 194 in the week after that.[21]

Out at Spring Hill, in the little meeting house served by visiting ministers, the ministers preached of death. The church was well-attended, and diarist Eliza Clitherall commented that "some impressive discourses upon the necessity of a preparation for death were deliver'd by the different ministers who preach'd. As the fever & mortality encreased so did the wavering voices of the preachers, sound with redoubled zeal." The same diarist wrote on August 20 that "persons are Panic struck & leaving the city." The prominent local attorney Philip Phillips quickly decided to visit his wife's parents in Savannah. Nott, his family physician and friend, sent them off with a basket of drugs and a letter on how to use them. On the second day out, the family seamstress was taken ill with what was sup-

20. Nott, "The Epidemic Yellow Fever of Mobile in 1853," *New Orleans Medical and Surgical Journal,* X (1854), 572–73.

21. *Ibid.,* 574; *Alabama Planter* (Mobile), August 22, 1853; Mobile *Register,* August 19, 20, 23, 1853; John Duffy, *Sword of Pestilence: The New Orleans Yellow Fever Epidemic of 1853* (Baton Rouge, 1966), 125.

posed to be yellow fever, but Nott's drugs and the nursing of Mrs. Phillips brought her through the crisis. Near the end of the month, some citizens began to arrive home under the mistaken impression that Mobile had escaped yellow fever, and on the thirtieth the *Register* warned absentees to stay away until the late fall.[22]

In the first two weeks of September, the epidemic raged through the city and began to spread into the surrounding areas. At the beginning of the month, the *Alabama Planter* suggested that merchants should close their stores and offices by 3:00 P.M. to give young men not acclimated time to get into the country and those who were now healthy a chance to attend their sick friends. This request was hardly necessary, for many merchants were now opening for only a few hours daily; the insurance offices were open from 10:00 A.M. to 1:00 P.M. One of Mobile's main hotels, the Battle House, closed in the first week of September. Most of the visitors who had remained there after the start of the yellow fever epidemic had contracted the disease. In the same week the mayor declared Tuesday a day of humiliation and prayer and asked for a suspension of all business. Later in the 1850s, Mobile novelist Augusta Evans Wilson incorporated scenes from the 1853 epidemic in one of her novels. She wrote of streets powdered with lime, huge fires of tar, terrified citizens fleeing in all directions, stores closed, few people about, carts filled with coffins, and church bells tolling unceasingly. At noon, one September day, her heroine Beulah "stood at the open window of her room. The air was intensely hot; the drooping leaves of the China trees were motionless; there was not a breath of wind stirring; and the sable plumes of the hearses were still as their burdens." A minister who lived through the epidemic was struck by the haste with which the dead were buried—often within a few hours—and by the scant attendance at the funeral services.[23]

By the second week of September the *Planter* reported that the disease appeared to have shifted from the central parts of the city and was affecting the outskirts; it was reaching areas that had always been considered safe from the disease. For Nott this had ominous implications, for his family was established for the summer at Spring Hill. This small pine-hill settlement about six miles west of the Mobile waterfront had been Nott's

22. Eliza Carolina Clitherall Diary, August, 1853, in SHC; Philip Phillips, MSS Autobiography, in Philip Phillips Family Papers, LC; Mobile *Register,* August 30, 1853.

23. *Alabama Planter* (Mobile), September 5, 1853; Clitherall Diary, September, 1853; Augusta J. Evans [Wilson], *Beulah* (New York, 1859), 198–99; Robert Nall, *A Voice from Twenty Graves: A Sermon Preached December 4, 1853* (Mobile, 1854), 10–11.

home when he first came to Mobile. It was served by excellent springs, and even after Nott established his family home in the center of Mobile he often took his family to spend part of the summer with his father-in-law, James Deas. Deas had a large home there and other residences on his property, which in the summer months were filled by his various relatives and their families. The entire settlement of Spring Hill consisted of about thirty families scattered among the pine trees, and there was also a small college, St. Joseph's, with about two hundred resident students.[24]

The epidemic had filled Nott's days since early August. He had been driven through Mobile to visit a variety of patients. One of his actions, which was later to cause him tortured thoughts about the once discarded possibility of yellow fever being contagious, was to move a yellow fever patient from Mobile to a house in Spring Hill. He did this on August 14. The patient recovered. But on September 5 two of the children in the same house came down with yellow fever, and within a few days other cases occurred in the Spring Hill settlement. Although Nott could never be sure whether the patient he had moved to Spring Hill had brought the disease, in reality the disease was already spreading rapidly in the environs of Mobile. Even Citronelle, thirty-three miles from the city, shared in the epidemic. Nott commented that Spring Hill "heretofore has been considered exempt from Yellow Fever, or any form of malarious disease."[25]

By September 7 the disease reached the extended family of Nott's father-in-law. By this time Deas's family group, including slaves, consisted of sixty people in his own home and the adjoining houses. First, one of his slave women came down with the disease, on the next day his daughter-in-law, Mrs. John Deas, and on the next day one of his daughters, Mrs. N. Harleston Broun. Yellow fever then swept through the Deas households and reached with devastating effect into Nott's own family. Within fourteen days, fifty-four of the sixty people in the Deas households had contracted yellow fever. Of these, five whites, two mulattoes, and one black died "with black vomit," and at the end of the fourteen days all the rest were convalescent. Of the ten whites attacked, half were dead. Nott was helpless. He had no remedies; "I had never in twenty-five year's practice witnessed such a scene, among a class of people well lodged in clean, well ventilated apartments and surrounded by every possible

24. *Alabama Planter* (Mobile), September 12, 1853; Nott, "Epidemic Yellow Fever of Mobile in 1853," 573–74.
25. Nott, "Epidemic Yellow Fever of Mobile in 1853," 573–76. This article is also the source of the material and quotations in the next paragraph.

comfort, and this, too, on a high, barren sand hill, nearly six miles from the city."

In Nott's own family the disease had a horrifying effect. Four of his children were stricken—Sarah, Emma, Allen, and Edward. Much later in his life, when writing of the prevalence of insect pests in the South, Nott commented that "on rising from my own bed in the morning I have many times seen my little children lying in a trundle-bed covered by mosquitoes, after, as Mrs. Jackson said, 'kicking the kiver off.'"[26] It was difficult to keep mosquito nets intact around children's beds. Nott was never to know that the cause of yellow fever, which he sought with such tenacity and imagination, was in some of those mosquitoes.

Nott now worked around the clock, but one by one his children and some of the others who were close to him went through the rapid crises of yellow fever, culminating in the dreaded black vomit. The first to die (on the fifteenth) was Sarah, who was nearly four; the next day his wife's brother, James Deas, who was thirty; on the eighteenth Emma, who was ten; on the nineteenth Allen, the baby, who was nearly two; and finally, on the twentieth, Edward, the eldest son, who was nineteen. The obituary for Edward in the *Alabama Planter* said he was a boy in years "but a man in bearing." The obituary for James Deas described the great efforts made around his sickbed, efforts in which science and skill were "warmed and quickened by fraternal love and sympathy." But the skill and love of the Notts were equally ineffective.[27]

In less than a week, Nott and his wife watched and frantically worked while four of their children and a brother died of yellow fever. Even yet the tragedies were not over. At the beginning of November, little Charles Auzé, who was nine, the son of Sarah Nott's sister Margaret, was added to the long list of deaths. Later, after her husband's death in 1856, Margaret and her daughter came to live with Josiah Nott's family and stayed with them for the rest of their lives. Eventually the graves of Nott's children in the Mobile cemetery had, along with their headstones, a handsome cast-iron effigy of the dog that had been with them in their last sickness. It was a fine effigy and well over a hundred years later was still lying near the graves.[28]

26. *First Annual Report of the Board of Health of the City of New York* (New York, 1871), 363.

27. Clitherall Diary, September, 1853; gravestones, Magnolia Cemetery, Mobile; *Alabama Planter* (Mobile), September 26, October 3, 24, 1853; *Alabama Genealogical Register*, VIII (1966), 118.

28. Magnolia Cemetery, Mobile. An old newspaper clipping in the local history room of the Mobile Public Library indicates that the dog died shortly after the children and that

For a while in the fall of 1853 and into 1854 Nott's flow of ebullient letters to his friends was nearly stilled. He told his friend Gliddon that "I am driving away care by driving 3 horses (professionally) night and day." There was still ample work to be done in Mobile, and Nott flung himself into it with a passionate desire to forget. A year later he told Squier: "I had not the heart or physical force to raise a pen in reply to your kind letter of Condolence to my poor wife."[29] Nott's "poor wife" is a shadowy figure, but even in the nineteenth century few women had to bear the loss of four children and a brother within a week. Like Nott, she could never be fully happy again, and she had yet to face the sight of her sons marching off to the Civil War.

Far away in Europe, Sarah Crawford, the wife of Nott's partner and friend Dr. William Crawford, reflected in her journal on what these deaths would mean to the Notts. "This is an awful blow," she wrote, "& I do not see what on earth supports them under such an afflictive visitation." Religious consolation could be their only hope, and she thought that perhaps this bereavement might draw Dr. Nott—"a disbeliever in religion"— nearer to "the Great orderer of all things." The change in the Notts was bound to be great—they had both been "gay—remarkably so—their house always open to gay company." Sarah Crawford obviously liked Nott. She wrote that he was "always so sympathetic—So regardful for the feelings of others—to be thus sorely tried—oh! I am so sorry for him—He has been an unchanging friend! A brother could not have been more friend than he has always been to us in times of sickness, & trouble, and whenever the D^r [her husband] was the least sick Dr. Nott would come straight to see & advise without waiting to be sent for." Sarah Crawford was soon to need her own consolation, for her husband was dying of tuberculosis.[30]

For Nott there were no sharp changes in attitude after the cataclysmic events in the fall of 1853, but the cynicism and disgust with the world

---

Nott had a cast-iron effigy made and placed at the foot of their graves. In the late 1970s the effigy had been moved to an adjacent plot. Nott may have gotten the idea for a cast-iron dog from the one that was made for the front of Mesher's hat store in Mobile in 1851; see Mobile *Register*, November 8, 1851.

29. George R. Gliddon to John R. Bartlett, November 21, 1853, in John R. Bartlett Papers, John Carter Brown Library, Brown University, Providence, Rhode Island; Nott to Ephraim G. Squier, October 5, 1854, in Squier Papers, LC.

30. Sarah Gayle Crawford Journal, October 22, 1853, in Sarah Ann and William B. Crawford Papers, William Stanley Hoole Special Collections Library, University of Alabama, Tuscaloosa.

which had often been a pose now rang truer. The tragedy increased his feeling that the world and the people in it were largely irrational, but it did not drive him to religious consolation. His anticlericalism and free-thinking were still integral to his character. Unsurprisingly, his writing on the 1853 epidemic reflected, in indirect ways, the shock of the events he had lived through. In December he wrote an account of Mobile's experiences in the past four months. He began by discussing the first cases of yellow fever brought in July by ships from New Orleans, but he then ignored the spread of the disease through the main part of Mobile and jumped directly to a detailed discussion of the impact of the epidemic on Spring Hill, with the exception that he failed to mention that of the eight deaths in the family of Colonel Deas four were of his own children.[31]

Nott was puzzled by certain features of the 1853 epidemic, and even in his distress he tried to add to the general knowlege of yellow fever. Usually, Nott stressed, blacks had escaped yellow fever, but in 1853 they suffered, and though the disease was less severe among them than among whites there were at least fifty deaths among the blacks. Also, children, who previously had suffered less than adults, were in 1853 generally and violently attacked. The 1853 epidemic caused confusion in Nott's thinking about whether yellow fever was contagious. He had previously dismissed this idea and thought that the evidence of earlier Mobile epidemics was decidedly against contagion. After his experience in these terrible months, Nott now said that he leaned toward the hypothesis that the 1853 epidemic was contagious. There was no change, however, in Nott's view that yellow fever could not be caused by decaying matter. Gaseous decomposition, he argued, could be ruled out as a cause because the disease skipped about far too much for that to be possible.

The 1853 epidemic confirmed Nott in his animalcular hypothesis, even though his friend and correspondent, the well-known Professor Joseph Leidy of Philadelphia, had recently condemned the idea as "absurd." Nott's response to Leidy was that "microscopic observations are yet but in their infancy, and in reaching the causes of disease it is as far behind reality as we know chemistry to be."[32]

The 1853 epidemic had been Mobile's worst. Nott's own estimate of yellow fever deaths from the beginning of August to the middle of December was almost twelve hundred. These deaths were out of a total population of twenty-five thousand, but out of a summer population that

31. Nott, "Epidemic Yellow Fever of Mobile in 1853," 571–83.
32. *Ibid.*, 577–81; Clitherall Diary, December, 1853.

probably did not exceed half that. Not until October 27 did the Board of Health announce that yellow fever no longer existed as an epidemic in the city and that there was no further danger to returning residents or strangers; the first frost had been experienced a few days earlier. Some who had contracted the disease were still to die, but the epidemic was over.[33]

Mobile was never again to suffer as it had in 1853, nor was Nott, though he was to experience some tragic days. Yellow fever returned to Mobile again in 1855, without devastating effects, but in the next few years the most serious outbreak was in 1858. In that year there was an isolated case in the first half of August, but the main outbreak did not begin until the end of that month. About seventy died from the disease in September, and almost the same number in October, but, unlike 1853, the disease was generally confined to the central part of the town.[34]

Nott's scientific interest in yellow fever continued for the rest of his life, and for the remainder of the antebellum years he generally defended the analysis of the disease he had made in the 1840s. He remained convinced that yellow fever was a disease distinct from all other fevers and that it had an animalcular origin, and he retreated from his thoughts in 1853 that it might after all be contagious. In 1855 he took strong issue with the arguments of the well-known New Orleans physician Dr. E. D. Fenner, who had written an article arguing that yellow fever was only one of a number of endemic fevers common to the Gulf region. Nott vigorously defended his previous arguments in favor of the nonidentity of bilious and yellow fevers and pointed out that whether or not yellow fever was contagious, it was certainly transmissible over sizable distances. He thought quarantine was of use in northern ports but not in southern because in southern ports yellow fever was now endemic. Nott was perhaps not as certain as he once had been about the noncontagiousness of yellow fever, but his main emphasis in his writings was now on the manner in which the "germ" of yellow fever could be transmitted over distance by ship, baggage car, or other means.[35]

33. Nott, "Epidemic Yellow Fever of Mobile in 1853," 583 (the figures given by Duffy, *Sword of Pestilence*, 126, are somewhat lower); *Alabama Planter* (Mobile), October 31, 1853; Clitherall Diary, December 1, 1853.

34. Dr. C. H. Martin to Francis Levert, September 28, 1855, in Levert Family Papers, SHC; Clitherall Diary, September–October, 1855, September–November, 1858; Mobile *Register*, October 26, 1855; Nott, "Yellow Fever in Mobile, A.D., 1858," *New Orleans Medical and Surgical Journal*, XV (1858), 819–24.

35. Nott, "Non-identity of Bilious and Yellow Fevers," *New Orleans Medical News and Hospital Gazette*, II (1855), 339–46.

In the spring of 1856 Nott's spirits had revived enough for him to point out to the citizens of Mobile the futility of much that had been done in the past twenty years to avert attacks of yellow fever. Every year at this time, he wrote to the *Register,* the Board of Health had urged Mobilians and the city fathers to spend money on scattering lime through the streets and burning tar barrels at the corners "for the amusement of the children." Nott said he had watched these proceedings and had shared in them for twenty years and that he had long since reached the conclusion that the money might better be spent ministering to the wants of the poor and the victims of disease. The efforts had been useless. In 1853 the city had never been cleaner, but to no avail. He questioned whether there were sanitary regulations that would help banish yellow fever from Mobile. Yet there were other intermittent and remittent fevers and other forms of malarial disease that afflicted the city more or less every year. In these cases, Nott argued, moisture was a key factor in creating foul air through decomposition.

To help alleviate the various fevers that harassed Mobilians every year, Nott suggested that the money should be spent not on burning tar and the like but on a system of drainage and grading for both the city and suburbs. The city could be made much freer of the various malarial diseases (but not yellow fever) if the low, marshy lands were drained—"in our climate, without a thorough system of drainage, we can never have health." Nott here was accepting the older ideas of a bad atmospheric origin for certain fevers, but his pragmatic recommendations, by leading to the clearing out of large breeding areas for mosquitoes, would have had the effect of attacking the roots of yellow fever as well as the various malarial fevers he was suggesting that the city should concentrate on.[36]

By 1858 Nott had returned to his original belief that yellow fever was not contagious, but now he stated categorically that "the *germ* of yellow fever may be transported in a vessel, in the closed baggage cars of rail roads, or otherwise." In the southern seaports, including Mobile, yellow fever, he wrote, "has no particular connection with filth or even crowded population."[37] Both the contagionists and the noncontagionists erred in some of their arguments about yellow fever. Yellow fever was originally brought in, and still could be, but it could also be domesticated and lie dormant. The great epidemics, such as in 1853, which swept along with great malignity, could leave behind less malignant germs.

36. Mobile *Register,* April 16, 1856.
37. Nott, "Yellow Fever in Mobile, A.D., 1858," 821–22.

Nott thought as intelligently about yellow fever as any man of his generation and more intelligently than most. He swept aside many of the myths surrounding the disease, and much of what he wrote helped to remove misconceptions concerning its origin, nature, and progress. In treating the disease, he also moved away from the harmful therapeutics he had been taught in his youth and generally saw the value of moderation in dosing and supportive nursing. He said in 1855 that "more good is effected by good nursing and constant attention to varying symptoms than by violent remedies." This was eminently sound advice. In an age before the role of bacteria, viruses, and insect vectors had been revealed, there was little more Nott could do. The tragedy was that one of America's leading and most perceptive writers on yellow fever, a man who had a lifetime of experience in treating it, should have had to watch four of his children die of the disease. In October, 1854, Nott traveled to Toulminville, near Mobile, to deliver the first child of Josiah and Amelia Gorgas.[38] Nearly fifty years later, long after Nott's death, this William Crawford Gorgas was to do much to end the scourge of yellow fever when he went as a member of the yellow fever commission to Cuba.

38. Nott, "Facts upon Yellow Fever—Its Progress Northward," *De Bow's Review*, XIX (1855), 445; Mary Tabb Johnston and Elizabeth Johnston Lipscomb, *Amelia Gayle Gorgas* (University, Ala., 1978), 36.

Chapter 8
A MAJOR REPUTATION

In August, 1853, as yellow fever began to spread through Mobile, Nott was hurriedly finishing his introduction (written last) to a major work of ethnology that was to bring him fame throughout the United States and Europe. In later years, when a traveler met Nott or a diarist mentioned him, he was almost always identified as the famous Dr. Nott of Nott and Gliddon's *Types of Mankind*. The book was the major achievement of his ethnological career, and until the theories of the American school of ethnology were overthrown by Charles Darwin, it was the standard scientific explanation of racial origins and distinctiveness. In an obituary of Nott in the *Anthropological Review* of London it was said of *Types* that "its publication marks an era in the history of anthropology."[1]

The book had its origin in the happy, hectic months following the triumph of Nott's ideas regarding separate creations in 1850 and 1851. Agassiz' abandonment of monogenesis and Morton's open fight with Bachman made Nott feel fully vindicated. His bubbling confidence knew no bounds, and he constantly urged his ethnological friends to complete the rout of the clergymen. He believed that scientific proofs of separate creations and innate differences between races were now so soundly based and generally accepted that no reasonable defenses could be erected against the new theories.

In his desire to continue the attack on clerical attempts to block unfettered scientific inquiry into the history of human origins, Nott was now

1. *Anthropological Review*, VI (1868), lxxxi. This was a premature obituary stemming from a false report of Nott's death. In *The Mismeasure of Man* (New York, 1981), 36, Stephen J. Gould points out that *Types of Mankind* was not a fringe document but the leading American text on human racial differences.

prodded and abetted by George Gliddon. Gliddon was very much an in-tellectual entrepreneur. In the 1840s he had been careful not to endorse Nott's views in his public lectures on Egypt because he had no desire publicly to offend the clergymen and other pillars of the community who subscribed to his attractive, illustrated lectures. In his private letters to his friends, however, he lambasted the clergy and delighted in Nott's fearless attack on the scientific validity of Genesis.

In the early 1850s Gliddon sensed accurately that it was now safe to take a stronger stand. He told Squier in April, 1851, that, in spite of Mrs. Grundy, the time was fast approaching when a "man may speak the thing he will, and *I*, for one *will* speak." Gliddon reveled so thoroughly in his new freedom that Nott began to protest at the blatantly anticlerical tone of some of Gliddon's writings. "Gliddon . . . has published another dam'd book," he wrote to Squier in March, 1851, "& in spite of all sorts of pledges has pitched into the Bible and Parsons again, & I hope most devoutly I shall never hear the words Mono-& Polygenesis pronounced—I have no longer any doubts about his insanity on the subject."[2] To a great degree this was a pose on Nott's part, for he continued to be at least as out-spoken as Gliddon in attacking those clergymen whom he accused of at-tempting to block free scientific inquiry.

After suggesting that Gliddon was going too far in his anticlerical statements, Nott within a few weeks justified to Squier his own actions for the past seven years. "My experience has taught me," wrote Nott, "that if a man wants to get on fast he must kick up a dam'd fuss gener-ally—a decent, civil, competent meritorious man may rot in obscurity— a man must get *notoriety* in some way or the tide will run by him." Nott reflected on what had happened to him after he had stopped simply being a quiet, efficient doctor and achieved nationwide attention by de-fending human inequality and attacking the scientific authority of the Bible with rare candor. His friends, he said, were alarmed when he began his "theological disquisitions." They thought his attacks would ruin him. Instead the reverse had happened, and Nott's fame and fortune had ex-panded. Now, he wrote, "I am getting more out of this small world than I ever hoped for."[3]

Though Gliddon was nearly as much a traveling showman as an Egyp-tian scholar, and though Nott thought of himself as a southern gentle-

---

2. Gliddon to Squier, April 22, 1851, Nott to Squier, March 1, 1851, in Squier Papers, LC.
3. Nott to Squier, March 26, 1851, *ibid.*

man who fearlessly pursued scientific truth, they were kindred spirits. On racial questions both wanted to overwhelm their opponents. The balance and moderation that Nott brought to his medical arguments were totally lacking in his formal and informal writing on racial matters. "The Clergy have been licked on every point," he told Squier. In trying to maintain monogenesis, said Nott, Bachman had revealed his total inability to defend his point of view. Nott told Morton that he had read his last two pummelings of "the *Old Hyena*" (Bachman) with great gusto. He felt as though a viper had been killed in the fair garden of science. Science, wrote Nott, "should not be polluted by passion & controversy, & wherever I have fought back at these skunks, it has been solely with the view of keeping the ball of truth rolling."[4] Nott was always capable of referring to clerical opponents as "skunks" while complaining of those who polluted science with passion and controversy.

Both Nott and Gliddon hoped that Morton would write a book summarizing the new discoveries and arguments, and Nott urged him to do so, but Morton was a sick man; just how sick Nott did not realize, and he was shocked in May, 1851, to receive a letter from Gliddon containing the news of Morton's death. Morton had been one of the few men to whom Nott deferred. He was "our leader," he told Squier, and "I am really too distressed to write."[5]

For Gliddon, the death of Morton presented an opportunity. He was anxious to write, to become more famous as a scholar, and to make money. Morton could never have been a collaborator with Gliddon. He was far too much the Philadelphia scholar, even in his more daring later years, and Gliddon far too much the traveling showman. But Nott, though now regularly complaining about Gliddon, had the flair, the wit, and even the dramatic expression in his racial writings to appeal to the showman in Gliddon. He was also generous in an expansive, unpetty, southern way and, perhaps because he was always so busy, was ready to write quickly and not make any project a lifetime's work. From the time of the death of Morton, Gliddon began his efforts to get Nott and others involved in writing a book summing up the work of the new American racial theorists.

In the summer of 1851, soon after Morton's death, Nott traveled to the North. He had originally planned to spend time with Morton in Phila-

4. *Ibid.*, and Nott to Morton, April 6, 1851, in Morton Papers, HSP.
5. Nott to Squier, May 24, 1851, in Squier Papers, LC.

delphia, but now he had to be satisfied with a meeting with Squier in New York and a visit to Boston. Gliddon urged Squier to discuss future plans with Nott. "He, you, and I," he wrote, "are the only 3 men who can carry on the great cause, now that *Morton* is no more." If they could agree on some plan for future publication, he would "cooperate in giving their 'Reverence' a d——d deal of trouble!" Gliddon planned to be in Mobile the following winter on a lecture tour, and there he intended to confer with Nott, "whom I look upon as Morton's successor." Gliddon now seemed to be echoing some of Nott's language. He told Squier that he planned to "'come out' strong on *Ethnology &c*, so as to keep the ball in motion." Squier resisted Gliddon's blandishments, but Nott was far more susceptible to the idea of a large-scale defense of racial inequality and another jab at the parsons.[6]

Gliddon came to Mobile in April, 1852, after lecturing in New Orleans. He held long discussions with Nott about writing a book on the various human races and their origins. Nott did not need much persuasion to write on this subject, but the demands of his practice made him reluctant to commit himself to a major work. Gliddon used his ample powers of persuasion, and Nott first agreed to collaborate on articles based on the correspondence and printed papers of Morton that they had in their possession. They wrote to Mrs. Morton for her approval and asked if there were any other manuscripts that they could use. She immediately sent them a mass of Morton's unfinished and unpublished papers, along with other books and papers she thought might be useful. Gliddon was now able to persuade Nott that they should produce a major work. His later comment was that they agreed to erect a literary cenotaph *"To the* MEM-ORY OF MORTON," and there is no question that this argument carried weight with Nott; but there is also no reason to doubt Nott's later comments that Gliddon's usual financial problems played a large part in convincing Nott that it would be unfair to Gliddon if he did not agree to cooperate with him.[7]

When, late in 1857, Nott heard of Gliddon's death in Central America, he reminisced to Squier about the decision to write *Types* and his problems with Gliddon. Only with reluctance, wrote Nott, had he agreed to enter into such a large-scale project: "I did a vast deal of hard work for

6. Gliddon to Squier, June 24, October 23, 1851, *ibid.*
7. Nott and Gliddon, *Types of Mankind* (Philadelphia, 1854), ix–x, 626. Also see notes in Morton Papers, HSP; Nott to Squier, September 26, 1852, in Squier Papers, LC.

him much against my inclination simply because he required my labour to feed his wife & child." Moreover, said Nott, he supported Gliddon for a year while he was working on the book, to the amount of at least $500 (Nott had not kept an exact accounting). From the summer of 1852 to the summer of 1853 Gliddon spent much of his time in a cabin in the woods near Baldwin on the eastern shore of Mobile Bay; his only absence was for a few months of lecturing in the winter of 1852–1853. There is no reason to doubt Nott's assertion that he supported Gliddon for much of this period; it accords with what is known of both Nott's and Gliddon's financial arrangements. In 1857, with Gliddon dead and his wife needing help, Nott, already permanently out of pocket for the support he had given Gliddon, told Squier to put him down for $100 for the subscription that was being raised for the family. Nott often complained about Gliddon, but he liked him. "With all his faults and follies," he told Squier, "I had a kind feeling for him & am grieved at his death."[8]

Nott also continued to insist after Gliddon's death that the question of attacks on religion and the clergy had been a major point of contention between the two authors in the preparation of their work. Nott said that he was not surprised that Gliddon had died in an overwrought condition because he had previously reached the conclusion that Gliddon's mind was unhinged on at least one subject—that of religion. In the years after *Types* was published, Nott consistently attacked Gliddon's section because of its continual emphasis on the errors of the Bible. Whatever Nott said in private about clerics and religion, he believed that in his published writings he challenged the biblical account of creation in a scientific manner whereas Gliddon threw out gratuitous insults. Nott contended that he had agreed to collaborate with Gliddon on the condition "that he should never *allude* to the Bible, or to Parsons, & I really believe he had no control over tongue or pen on these subjects."[9] Yet for all Nott's fine distinctions between gentlemanly and ungentlemanly attacks, scientific and nonscientific positions, Nott was fully as capable as Gliddon of offending the religious by the nature of his writing.

Neither Nott nor Gliddon feared to take chances in print, and once they had decided in April, 1852, to collaborate, they moved with great rapidity. In about fifteen months they produced a book of more than 700

8. Nott to Squier, September 26, 1852, December 7, 15, 1857, in Squier Papers, LC; Nott to Joseph Leidy, October 4, 1854, in Leidy Papers, ANSP; Nott and Gliddon, *Types of Mankind*, xi, 626.
9. Nott to Squier, December 15, 1857, in Squier Papers, LC.

pages. Some of it was written by other contributors, but more than 600 pages came from Nott and Gliddon, more than 350 by Nott himself. The two authors agreed that Nott would undertake the physical and anatomical portions of the work (those pertaining to the natural sciences) and that Gliddon was to be responsible for the archaeological and biblical parts. In the course of the following year, they were to acquire other contributors, and they also gained the vital services of Mrs. Gliddon, who did more than 300 drawings for the work.[10]

When in the early fall of 1852 Nott told Squier that he was at work with Gliddon on a major project, his letter confirms the accuracy of his later memories of how the book came about. Nott said that he had got into it because of his good feelings for Gliddon, even though he was reluctant to attempt anything beyond article length because of the demands of his profession. Gliddon needed money, wrote Nott, and thought that he could make the book pay. "I shall do a good deal of work," he told Squier, "& as I want no pay, I shall be delighted to see him make something out of it." Nott and Gliddon were still disagreeing about what Nott perceived as Gliddon's obsession with attacking the clergy. Like Mercure in Molière's *Amphitryon,* said Nott, Gliddon had not hit anybody for so long he felt immensely strong in the arm. As usual, however, Nott's own lack of moderation bubbled through. "The Skunks (parsons) have been hitting at him so long," Nott wrote, and he had been quiet so long from policy, that Gliddon was now ready for a major fight. Nott argued that the best policy was to ignore the opposition and simply "put science up to date." This may have been Nott's ideal, and he repeatedly told himself and others that this was what he should do, but in reality he never achieved the scientific detachment he professed to admire. After regretting Gliddon's probable lack of moderation, Nott suggested to Squier that "an immense point is gained in the admission, which is now general among the well informed Skunks, that time and climate cannot change one Race into another." With Nott perceiving himself as the moderating influence in the partnership, it was clear that clerical hackles would rise to new heights.[11]

Nott was hard at work on his sections of the book by the winter of 1852–1853; he was finished by the following August. As usual, he took from what he read, and from his friends, any arguments and evidence that would support his preconceived ideas. Nott was constantly looking

10. Nott and Gliddon, *Types of Mankind,* xii–xiii, 626.
11. Nott to Squier, September 26, 1852, in Squier Papers, LC.

for quick ways of acquiring racial information that would serve his cause, and Gliddon had always proved extremely useful to him in this respect, filling letters with references to new works on the races and antiquities of ancient Egypt. Nott later said to Squier that "our poor friend Gliddon was an invaluable caterer to me." Nott also turned to Squier for help on subjects about which he felt he had insufficient time to complete the necessary general reading. He asked Squier for anything he could give him on the antiquity of the American Indians; he was so pressed for time, he said, that he wanted all the shortcuts he could find. He was clear on what he wanted from Squier: "The great point with me is to carry them back as far as possible."[12]

By late 1852 the pressure on Nott to complete his sections was increased when Gliddon arranged for the issuing of an ambitious prospectus announcing the book to the world and asking for subscribers.[13] The authors tried to enlarge the work's appeal by including chapters by other naturalists. They had already decided to include a section consisting of Morton's unpublished manuscripts which had been provided by Mrs. Morton, and they also obtained for the volume a sketch of the life of Morton by Dr. Henry S. Patterson; an essay on geology and paleontology in connection with human origins by Dr. William Usher; and, best of all, a sketch of the natural provinces of the animal world and their relationship to the different types of man by Louis Agassiz.

This last coup stemmed from a visit that Agassiz made to Mobile in the spring of 1853. Agassiz, who had been in Charleston, returned north by way of Mobile, New Orleans, and St. Louis, giving lectures in each place. In the early months of 1853 the Mobile Franklin Society had an ambitious program of lectures, which included a number of lectures by both Nott and Agassiz. In his lectures in February and March, Nott made use of the material on the antiquity and indigenous origin of the aboriginal population of North America that he was working on for the book, and in July he published an article on the subject in the *Southern Quarterly Review*. He argued for the separate creation of the American Indians, maintained that the available evidence carried them back to the remotest period of man's existence on earth, and suggested that they would eventually disappear.[14]

12. Nott to Squier, August 22, 1860, January 6, 1853, *ibid.*
13. Nott to Squier, January 6, 1853, *ibid.;* Nott and Gliddon, *Types of Mankind,* x.
14. Elizabeth Cary Agassiz (ed.), *Louis Agassiz: His Life and Correspondence* (2 vols.;

Agassiz arrived in Mobile late in March and by the middle of April had delivered a course of six lectures on the geographical distribution of animals and their relationship to man, in connection with his theory of distinct zoological provinces. While in Mobile he agreed to contribute a chapter to Nott and Gliddon's book. Nott attended Agassiz' lectures, and in private the two men discussed racial matters. Agassiz told Nott that a peculiar conformation characterized the brain of an adult Negro—it never matured beyond that of the brain of a Caucasian boy. He offered to demonstrate this to Nott, but Nott was unable to procure a Negro's brain during Agassiz' stay in the town. Agassiz did, however, examine two native Africans produced by Nott and went with him to look at the heads of some one hundred Choctaws in and around the city. He confirmed Nott's assertion that all the heads were of the same distinct type.[15]

The ease with which Nott charmed and impressed the scientists who met him was demonstrated by Agassiz' reaction. Two years later, when a friend questioned Agassiz' decision to allow his paper to be published as part of Nott and Gliddon's book, Agassiz wrote of Nott with warmth and admiration. He said that he did not regret contributing the paper: "Nott is a man after my heart, for whose private character I have the highest regard. He is a true man." Anyone who knew how Nott suffered in Mobile from the recriminations of bigots, wrote Agassiz, would not wonder at his enmity to such men. Agassiz admitted, however, that Nott had no sympathy for the church, though "I know him to be a man of truth and faith." Agassiz was less complimentary about Gliddon. "Gliddon is coarse," he wrote, "especially in his utterances and has allowed his resentment to mislead him to personalities which all his friends blame." But even in regard to Gliddon, Agassiz argued that "he would rather meet a man like him, who knows as much as he does about antiquity and who cares to investigate it, than any of those who shut their eyes against evidence."[16]

Nott was able to make use of Agassiz' lectures and conversation in pre-

Boston, 1885), II, 512; Mobile *Register,* February 2, March 1, 1853; *Alabama Planter* (Mobile), March 7, 1853; Nott, "Aboriginal Races of America," *Southern Quarterly Review,* XXIV (1853), 59–92.

15. Mobile *Register,* March 18, 19, 23, 24, 25, 28, 1853; *Alabama Planter* (Mobile), April 18, 1853; Nott and Gliddon, *Types of Mankind,* 175, 351–52, 414, 415, 444.

16. Agassiz to James D. Dana, July 18, 1856, in Louis Agassiz Papers, Houghton Library, Harvard University, Cambridge, Massachusetts.

paring his material for the new book, and in the spring and early summer of 1853 he quickly completed his chapters. As well as sending off his article on Indians to the *Southern Quarterly Review*, he also sent off what was to be the first chapter of the book to the *New Orleans Medical and Surgical Journal*; this article on the geographical distribution of animals and the races of man came out in May. By that time it was becoming obvious that the forthcoming book would be a success. In June the Mobile *Register* announced that the work had already obtained 565 subscribers at the extremely high price for 1853 of $5 a copy. The newspaper thought the number would soon exceed 600, but even that estimate was low. Apart from single subscriptions, booksellers in the North as well as the South subscribed for multiple copies, and Nott's Mobile friends and relatives also rallied round. His wife's brother-in-law Charles Auzé subscribed for twenty-two copies for himself and his friends. Some interest also appeared in the nation's capital: Secretary of State Edward Everett subscribed for one copy for himself and one for the State Department; the Treasury Department ordered a copy; and Secretary of the Navy John Kennedy subscribed for one for himself and one for the library of the Navy Department. For a book on ethnology, *Types of Mankind* was a best-seller before publication.[17]

Gliddon finished his sections in July, 1853, while still living on Mobile Bay, and in the following month Nott wrote the introduction. Gliddon then left for Philadelphia to see the book through the press.[18] It had a first-class publisher in J. B. Lippincott. Although Nott had prepared some 350 pages for the press in twelve months—much of it new writing and some of it based on new research—he had no time to rest. While Gliddon dealt with the publishers, Nott tried unsuccessfully to cope with the yellow fever that swept through Mobile and Spring Hill. He was to have little immediate joy in his new book.

Overseeing the production of *Types* in Philadelphia, Gliddon expressed his sorrow at Nott's afflictions, but he could not restrain his glee at the likely success of the new book. "'Types' flourishes!" he wrote to John R. Bartlett in Providence, "we have stereotyped already 494 pages!" Subscribers, he said, were coming in at the rate of six a day, even though "we have not begun to 'get up' an excitement!" By March, 1854, the book was

17. Mobile *Register*, June 14, 1853; Gliddon to Squier, March 7, 1854, in Squier Papers, LC; Nott and Gliddon, *Types of Mankind*, 733–38 (list of subscribers).
18. Nott and Gliddon, *Types of Mankind*, xi, 61, 626, 716.

ready for distribution. Gliddon was bubbling with excitement at the interest the book had created and the revenue it was generating. He was also busily trying to puff a book that hardly needed puffing. The first printing of a thousand copies was exhausted on publication. Nearly all of the copies were subscribed for, and reviewers and some of the prominent men in the field had to be sent the second printing (called a second edition). Gliddon even told Squier to stop getting names but to urge everybody to buy the second edition because every copy was putting fifty cents in Gliddon's pocket. He was also to think of reviewers he could influence, and Gliddon would send copies for them; it was in Squier's interest, said Gliddon, because his name appeared throughout the book.[19]

Gliddon thought it essential that notices appear in the New York *Herald* and *Tribune,* and he urged Squier to use any influence he had to make sure the book was reviewed in these two newspapers. They would receive copies of the first edition; the rest of the press would have to make do with the second, which was already coming off the presses. Squier exceeded Gliddon's fondest hopes by arranging to review the book for the *Herald* and asking Gliddon to supply the draft of the review. Gliddon quickly provided it, saying that it was written "widely" so that Squier could alter the style before presentation. "You give me a most difficult job," wrote Gliddon, "—to write my own puff, and not betray *my* style! I have endeavored to imitate the 'Herald's' here & there, but you can touch it up." On hearing that the book was likely to be attacked in *Putnam's,* Gliddon said that Squier was to tell Putnam, "I'll lay him out stiff, as I owe him for 12 years of *back-biting.*"[20]

In the following months the success of the book became obvious. Early in June Gliddon told Squier that orders were flowing in at the rate of six hundred a month. By the middle of July the book had sold thirty-five hundred copies in four months, a volume that was little short of remarkable for a tome on ethnography.[21] The success continued in the following years, and even the arrival on the scene of Darwin's *Origin of Species,* which effectively destroyed the book's arguments, did not stop its sales. By 1871 it had gone through ten editions.

19. Gliddon to John R. Bartlett, November 21, 1853, in John R. Bartlett Papers, John Carter Brown Library, Brown University, Providence, Rhode Island; Gliddon to Squier, March 7, 1854, in Squier Papers, LC.
20. Gliddon to Squier, April 6 (2 letters), 9, 10, 23, 1854, in *ibid.*
21. Gliddon to Squier, June 4, July 14, 1854, *ibid.*

By the spring Nott was beginning to renew his regular correspondence. The tone of his letters and his attitude toward the new book differed greatly from Gliddon's. The tragedies of the previous fall had temporarily dulled his usual pleasure and excitement at the prospect of an intellectual fight. As usual, he said much in his private letters that he did not mean. He expressed pleasure at the mercantile opportunities that were coming Squier's way with the tongue-in-cheek comment that it "has always been my creed that intellectual enjoyments are all very well in their way but they are secondary to the physique." On the publication of *Types*, Nott commented, "I probably feel as little personal interest, or excitement about it as any man in the United States—I don't care a curse what people say about it or think about it—the devil was in me & as soon as he got out the excitement passed away." Nott was still worried about Gliddon's section of the book. He thought his coauthor had assumed "a very impolitic & undignified tone—I tried my best to keep him down and finding I could not do it I insisted upon his assuming his own sins as far as possible—I am as bold in my opinions as any body, but I have my own ideas about what a *gentleman* should do." [22]

But even while deprecating Gliddon's approach, Nott wished him no ill. He thought the book would have excellent sales in the South because "the parsons are making ready for an onslaught & this will do it immense good," and he hoped that Gliddon would make money from the book. Although Nott had given the profits to Gliddon—"I get nothing substantial but abuse"—even in this letter complaining about Gliddon's approach Nott encouraged Squier to find paying employment for his coauthor: "You may rely upon the most indomitable energy & industry—I have never seen his equal." Nott did not know that Squier's review of the book in the New York *Herald* had actually been written by Gliddon, and he commented to Squier on reading it: "You have been a little fulsome in your flattery, but that will not be *disagreeable* to friend Gliddon who finds more pleasure in it than I do." Gliddon, he said, had for years injured his reputation by puffing his own writings and lectures in the newspapers for everyone recognized his peculiar style (which in this case he had managed to disguise). It was a misfortune, said Nott, for Gliddon had the ability and knowledge to survive without puffing and to have "made a most enviable reputation had he preserved the dignity of Morton or Agassiz." [23]

22. Nott to Squier, April 10, 1854, *ibid.*
23. Nott to Squier, April 30, 1854, *ibid.*

It is difficult after the passing of more than a century to imagine that the disjointed and ponderous *Types of Mankind*, which in Gliddon's sections is often practically unreadable, should have caused such a stir, made the authors famous or notorious throughout the United States, and given them a major reputation across the Atlantic. Nott's is by far the most readable part of the book. He stated vigorously and in more detail what he had been saying for ten years and added new generalizations on the role of race in world history. Gliddon chose to devote much of his material to a detailed examination of aspects of the tenth chapter of Genesis. His was not a connected narrative, but rather a series of glosses on words, expressions, geographic locations, and peoples. The problem was not that Gliddon made outlandish statements—there is none of the sharp mockery of which Nott was capable—but rather than writing of Egyptian chronology and races, leaving what this did to Genesis unsaid, he discussed the tenth chapter of Genesis as a historical document that could be examined and questioned like any other. In his tedious commentary he argued that only the white races were descended from Noah, that biblical ethnography could not be taken literally, and that there were definite problems with the various biblical translations.[24] Gliddon's fault in Nott's eyes, and his crime in clerical eyes, was that he did more to challenge the Bible than to advance the discussion of racial types. He did this in a pedantic, nonsensational way, but it still roused the fury of the orthodox.

The book betrayed the haste with which it was written and put together, and the pagination of the long introductory section does not jibe with the pagination of the rest of the book. This introductory section contains a memoir of Morton written by Dr. Henry S. Patterson, Agassiz' sketch of the natural provinces of the world, and Nott's introduction to the entire work. Agassiz' sketch had to be put into the introductory material rather than in the book proper because he did not send it until December, 1853. Its addition threw off the pagination. The main importance of Agassiz' sketch was that he clearly and forthrightly defended the idea that human races consisted of distinct species and argued that there was no evidence that they descended from a common stock. "I maintain distinctly," wrote Agassiz, "that the differences observed among the races of men are of the same kind and even greater than those upon which the anthropoid monkeys are considered as distinct species." His contribution also helped to

---

24. Nott and Gliddon, *Types of Mankind*, 466–716.

give the work scientific authority. In particular, it was a coup for the peripatetic Gliddon to be associated in a book with Agassiz.[25]

The essay by the Mobile physician Dr. William Usher, which discussed geology and paleontology in connection with human origins, was incorporated by Nott as one of the chapters in Part I, which was mostly written by Nott. Usher's essay used the evidence provided by fossil and other remains to push human origins into the ever more distant past. He let others deduce what this did to accepted biblical chronology. Nott also incorporated as a chapter in Part I two unpublished and unfinished essays by Morton on the different sizes of the brain in different human races and on the origin of the human species. In the latter, Morton suggested that scientific evidence supported the idea of many human creations.[26]

Even with the additions that Nott incorporated in Part I, he alone was responsible for some 350 pages of text and notes. In his prefatory and introductory remarks, Nott clearly delineated the authors' responsibility for different parts of the text. In a postscript that he added to the preface in January, 1854, he stated that Parts II and III were "almost exclusively" the work of Gliddon. This disclaimer was in reaction to Gliddon's effort to give Nott equal responsibility for the latter part of the book. Gliddon had written in his text that not only did Nott take responsibility for Part I, but he had also revised Gliddon's studies as presented in Part II.[27] Internal evidence of approach and style, together with Nott's reputation as a stickler for the truth in such matters, makes it clear that Nott's version is the correct one. Nott did not have the opportunity to make changes in the proof sheets as they came from the press, for at the time Gliddon was working on the proofs in Philadelphia, Nott was immersed in and recovering from Mobile's disastrous yellow fever epidemic.

Nott's chapters for *Types* were a series of independent essays, but all the evidence he used was directed toward specific ends, some of which he summarized at the end of his section of the book. Nott was far less interested in combating the account of human origins given in Genesis than in his previous writings. At times in the 1840s it had appeared that Nott was more interested in proving that the account of human origins given in Genesis was wrong and that the Bible could not be used as a scientific document than he was in delineating the existing differences between

25. *Ibid.*, xvii–lxxvi, lxxv (Agassiz quotation).
26. *Ibid.*, 298–372.
27. *Ibid.*, xiii, 626.

races. By the early 1850s, however, with nearly all of America's prominent ethnographers defending the idea of separate creations, and with Nott himself deeply committed to the necessity of the South's maintenance of slavery, he devoted much of the space in his chapters to proving that there were broad, unbridgeable gaps between races and that white supremacy and racial purity were the keys to civilization and future world progress. "Whether an original diversity of races be admitted or not," Nott wrote in his introduction, "the *permanence* of existing physical types will not be questioned by any Archaeologist or Naturalist of the present day," and the same experts could not deny "the consequent permanence of moral and intellectual peculiarities of types."[28]

Using an argument that Agassiz had published in the *Christian Examiner* in 1850 and that Nott had previously suggested in addressing the Mobile Southern Rights Association, Nott attacked the evils of "false philanthropy." Even though no race had the right to enslave or oppress the weaker, any change in institutions had to be tempered by experience. Only the whites had ever created a true civilization. The blacks had created none at all, China and Japan only "semi-civilizations," and Peru and Mexico not even that. Even the Indo-European and Semitic group had to be divided into a variety of races with different capabilities. "Looking back over the world's history," Nott wrote, "it will be seen that human progress has arisen mainly from the war of races. All the great impulses which have been given to it from time to time have been the results of conquest and colonizations." The false dreams of philanthropy had to be tempered by the realities of science.[29]

After praising English ethnographer and monogenesist James Prichard for producing one of the "noblest monuments of learning and labour" in his *Researches into the Physical History of Man*, Nott proceeded to attack him for his defense of "false theory." Prichard knew that the Pentateuch was inaccurate as science, argued Nott, but defended it anyway. Nott quoted from a penciled note written by his old mentor Thomas Cooper in a copy of Prichard's first volume: "No man *can* be a good reasoner who is marked by clerical prejudices." Nott had lived by that creed, and he believed that if all scientists were honest to their research they would admit that the account of human origins given in Genesis was false, that races had separate origins, and that they were innately different. How

28. *Ibid.*, 50.
29. *Ibid.*, 52–54.

much more becoming to science and religion it would have been, Nott suggested, if Prichard had acknowledged "that the Bible really gives no history of all the races of Men, and but a meagre account of one?"[30]

After this brief return to attacking the Old Testament, Nott remembered the constant warnings he had given to Gliddon and argued that he was done with trying to reconcile science with theological prejudice. He was simply going to concentrate on showing what science knew about race, and one of his main objects was to demonstrate that "the diversity of races must be accepted by Science as a *fact*." Theology had nothing useful to say on this subject; to try to reconcile science with the general outline of events as given in Genesis simply confused the issue: "It is now generally conceded that there exist no data by which we can approximate the date of man's first appearance upon earth; and, for aught we yet know, it may be thousands or millions of years beyond our reach."[31]

Although Nott incorporated previous work, such as his article on the physical history of the Jews, the sheer bulk of the work he completed in one year is remarkable. Apart from his introduction, Nott contributed eleven chapters, each of them the length of one of his usual racial articles. The first two chapters, which dealt with the distribution of races and original racial types, were basic to his entire argument.

In the first chapter he argued that the human races had been created as separate species in numerous centers of creation throughout the world. These races had vastly different attributes. To the highest castes of the Caucasian races had been given "the largest brains and the most powerful intellect." They had also been given the mission of extending and perfecting civilization. The Caucasians were a mixture of an infinite number of primitive stocks. Other races were not such a mixture and had a greater love of home. All races were fixed in type, but any mixture of the blood of another race brought changes. All evidences of civilization among the American Indians came from an admixture of white blood. Full-blooded Indians could never be civilized and were doomed to extinction. By "gradually supplanting inferior types," the Caucasian races were "fulfilling a law of nature." In all ages Caucasians had been the rulers, and they were destined to conquer any area in the world where climate did not make it impossible. "Nations and races, like individuals," he wrote, "have each an especial destiny: some are born to rule, and others to be ruled.

30. *Ibid.*, 54–55.
31. *Ibid.*, 56, 59.

Dr. Philip Syng Physick
Courtesy National Library of Medicine

Samuel George Morton
From the *Dictionary of American Portraits* (New York, 1967)

Louis Agassiz, portrait by Daniel Huntington, 1857
Courtesy American Philosophical Society

Ephraim George Squier, portrait by Jacob H. Lazarus, 1873
Courtesy of the New-York Historical Society, New York City

William Gilmore Simms
From the *Dictionary of American Portraits* (New York, 1967)

James Marion Sims
Courtesy National Library of Medicine

Josiah C. Nott
Courtesy Library of Congress

Dr. Warren Stone
Rudolph Matas Medical Library, Tulane
University Medical Center, New Orleans, Louisiana

Point Clear Hotel, Mobile Bay
Courtesy Museum of the City of Mobile

Dr. Stanford E. Chaillé
Rudolph Matas Medical Library, Tulane
University Medical Center, New Orleans, Louisiana

Dr. Joseph Leidy
From the *Dictionary of American Portraits* (New York, 1967)

Braxton Bragg
Chicago Historical Society

Citizen volunteers assisting the wounded on the battlefield
Courtesy National Library of Medicine

City Hospital on St. Anthony Street, Mobile

From the Annual Announcement of the Medical College, 1883–1884,
University of South Alabama Photographic Archives

Mobile waterfront, late 1860s

From Alexander Stephens, *History of the United States,* University of South Alabama Photographic Archives

And such has ever been the history of mankind. No two distinctly marked races can dwell together on equal terms. Some races, moreover, appear destined to live and prosper for a time, until the destroying race comes, which is to exterminate and supplant them." When the inferior race had died out, and the superior had intermingled and spread over the world, then perhaps man would eventually die out, for nature often forbade the intermingling of species.[32]

After asserting that races were created in distinct regions and had distinct characteristics, Nott further developed his general concept of distinct types. These types were independent of climate or external physical influences, and no external causes could transform one type into another. Nott suggested that *"types"* and *"species"* were not substantially different. The Jew, the Teuton, the Sclavonian, the Mongol, the Australian, the coast Negro, and the Hottentot were all distinct species and distinct types. To Nott there were many races, many species, many types even within the white and black races.[33]

After establishing his basic premises, Nott devoted separate chapters to the Caucasians, Africans, Negroes, Jews, and American Indians. He also had special chapters on the Egyptians and on the manner in which Caucasian types were depicted on Egyptian monuments. He finished with chapters on the ways in which the hybridity of animals cast light on human history and on the comparative anatomy of races.

Most writers, Nott believed, included far too many races in the Caucasian category. In reality, he argued, it consisted of many different races. Even for the Caucasian races there must have been many centers of creation. Although Nott wandered in discussing the Caucasians, mentioning in passing that there was no chance of a brighter future for the "organically-inferior" Negroes, his conclusion was that the world was now advancing more rapidly in civilization because the higher types of mankind had advanced so much in power that they could not be molested by the inferior. Ultimately the latter would disappear. In discussing Caucasian types in relation to the Egyptian monuments, Nott emphasized that the first available evidence showed diversity even among the Caucasians. He used extensive illustrations to demonstrate that some thirty varieties of the Caucasian type were depicted on the Egyptian monuments. Such varieties, which Nott regarded as races, were permanent. If there was no

32. *Ibid.,* 62–80.
33. *Ibid.,* 80–87.

admixture of blood from another race, the type remained the same. External factors could not change it.[34]

In discussing the history of the Jews, Nott was most interested in showing the permanence of type through all vicissitudes and in all climates, but, in spite of his admonitions to Gliddon, he could not resist discussing the Old Testament in a manner obviously designed to annoy the orthodox. After indicating that because of the inadequacy and inaccuracy of the King James version of the Bible he was using the twenty-two-volume Bible published by the director of the Israelite School of Paris, Nott proceeded to discuss the delinquencies of Old Testament figures. "The history of the connubial life of the patriarchs, Abraham and Jacob," he said, "presents a picture quite revolting to the standard of our day." David, "the man after God's own heart," kept concubines and committed adultery with Bathsheba. King Solomon opened his career "with murder" and closed it "in Paganism." Some comentators, he wrote, "have imputed scandal even to the 'Queen of Sheba,' the sombre belle of Southern Arabia." Ministers fumed when confronted with such a total lack of respect for the Scriptures.

Nott's main point in discussing the Jews, however, was to advance all possible evidence to show permanence of type. He printed a reproduction of a twenty-five-hundred-year-old Chaldean head, which he said every Mobile resident would recognize as a "facsimile portrait of one of their city's most prominent citizens, who is honored alike by the affections of his co-religionists, and the confidence of the community which has just elevated him to a seat in the National Councils." This was Nott's friend, the Mobile Jewish lawyer Philip Phillips. Jews scattered throughout the earth, said Nott, had preserved unchanged the same features stamped by the Almighty on the first Hebrew pairs created. In discussing the Jews, as in discussing the Caucasians, Nott again let his preoccupation with abolitionism and southern slavery show through his supposedly disinterested scientific discussions. "The illiterate advocates of a pseudo-negrophilism," he wrote, "more ruinous to the Africans of the United States than the condition of servitude in which they thrive, multiply, and are happy, have actually claimed St. Augustine, Eratosthenes, Juba, Hannibal, and other great men, as historical vouchers for the perfectibility of the *Negro* race, because born in Africa! It might hence be argued that 'birth in a stable makes a man a horse.'"[35]

34. *Ibid.*, 88–110, 141–79.
35. *Ibid.*, III–41.

As Nott pressed on through his chapters on Africans, Negroes, and American Indians and on the distinct types shown on Egyptian monuments, his comments became increasingly repetitious. There was never any doubt as to where his extensive reading was leading him: there were numerous permanent types, races, or species; white supremacy was essential to world civilization and progress; nonwhite races were permanently inferior; and many inferior races were doomed to extinction. "The whole of Africa, south of 10 N. lat.," he wrote, "shows a succession of human beings with intellects as dark as their skins, and with a cephalic conformation that renders all expectance of their future melioration an Utopian dream, philanthropical, but somewhat senile." Philanthropists were baying at the moon, for every anatomist now admitted that the brain could not be expanded or altered in form, and Negroes had less brain than whites. The American Indians were of great antiquity on these continents and had come into being by separate creations—unable to become civilized, they were doomed to extinction.[36]

Nott wrote with more vigor in the chapter on his old subject of hybridity. Here, and in his last chapter on the comparative anatomy of races, he said he was writing generally in the first person because the subject related to his own research. After affirming that he still was convinced of the general truth of his previous arguments that mulattoes were less prolific and weaker than the parent stocks, he advanced certain modifications of his original views. Although he said that these arguments still held for crosses between Anglo-Saxons or Teutons and blacks it was not the same for the French, Italians, Spanish, or Portuguese. These "*dark-skinned*" races, Nott argued, mixed more readily with blacks and produced mulattoes who were more prolific and longer-lived than Teutonic-black crosses. Nott argued that in his recent thoughts on hybridity he was adapting Morton's writing on animals to the study of human beings, but he advanced a modification of Morton's definition of a species. Nott suggested that a species was "*a type, or organic form, that is permanent; or which has remained unchanged under opposite climatic influences for ages.*" Examples were an Arab, an Egyptian, a Negro, a greyhound, or a wild common dog, all of which had been represented in Egypt four thousand years before, exactly as they were in the nineteenth century.[37]

When widely separated species, such as Anglo-Saxons and Negroes, crossed, they tended to die out if they were not strengthened by breeding

36. *Ibid.*, 184–85, 280.
37. *Ibid.*, 372–75.

with the parent stocks. Nott said he had not been able to gather statistics to support this hypothesis because of "the want of chastity among mulatto women, which is so notorious as to be proverbial. Although often married to hybrid males of their own color, their children are begotten as frequently by white or other men, as by their husbands." Nott in this way sidestepped the problem that, in spite of his assertions, mulattoes continued to be prolific. Racial purity was essential, he argued, for even a small admixture of different blood had profound effects. If the superior races were not kept from adulteration, the world would regress, not advance, in civilization. Already southern Europe was dragging behind the Anglo-Saxons because its people had suffered too much adulteration. Only the "strictly-white" races were "bearing onward the flambeau of civilization, as displayed in the Germanic families alone." If there was a thorough amalgamation of the various types of mankind now existing on earth, the human family, through the laws of hybridity, might become extinct.[38]

In his last chapter, on the comparative anatomy of races, Nott indicated that he disagreed even with some of Morton's racial groupings because Morton had placed some dark Egyptians and Hindus in with the Caucasian white races. To secure fuller information on the head size of white Americans, Nott had contacted three hat dealers in Mobile and a manufacturer in New Jersey. Based on their figures for thousands of hats, he had decided that the average size ("Horizontal periphery") of the crania of the white races in the United States was about twenty-two and a half inches, less hair and scalp, leaving about twenty-one inches. Morton had found that the mean for aboriginal Indian races was but nineteen and a half inches. Nott suggested that pure Teutons in the north of Europe would have an even larger head size than white Americans, and the general run of southern Europeans would be smaller. Gliddon, he wrote, had told him of watching hundreds of regular Greek soldiers obliged to tie handkerchiefs around their heads to keep their hats from falling over their noses; the hats had been made for English soldiers. The conclusion from all this, and many of Nott's conclusions were based not on comic Greek soldiers but on Morton's supposedly scientific cranial comparison, was of course that the whiter the race the bigger the brain. Blacks were deficient in anything pertaining to thought, painting, or sculpture, but "every Negro is gifted with an ear for music."[39]

38. *Ibid.*, 376–410.
39. *Ibid.*, 417–65.

In summarizing his contribution, Nott stressed that the globe consisted of different zoological provinces, each with its own human creations; that mankind consisted of several groups of races; that a race was a type permanent in time; that races of men most separated in physical organization, such as blacks and whites, amalgamated imperfectly because they created hybrids; and that all this led to the conclusion that "there exists a GENUS HOMO, embracing many primordial Types or 'Species.'"[40]

The great attention paid to *Types* before publication, its very rapid sale, and the help given by Agassiz' contribution meant that those who held a traditional view of the literal meaning of the Bible were eager to point out its weaknesses. The book offended not because it emphasized the deep and unchangeable differences between races that was now a generally accepted idea both in North and South but because it rejected the account of human origins given in Genesis and because it went out of its way to treat the Bible as just another text rather than a holy document. In the South commentators were often anxious to distinguish between what they thought of the book as an explanation of racial difference and what they thought of its religious attitudes. Even at home in Mobile, where the *Alabama Planter* referred to *Types* as one of "the most notable books of the times," there was an air of caution. "Whether the conclusions of the book be demonstrated or not," commented the *Planter*, "no one can doubt that it possesses a vast and universal interest." The same paper was somewhat puzzled that the Boston *Atlas* had published a complimentary review of *Types*, even though one of the editors had taken orders in the Episcopal church. The *Planter* suggested that perhaps he had backslidden.[41] Even among those inclined to be friendly, there was an air of waiting for a religious storm to break. When it did, and it did with speed, it was all that Gliddon could have hoped for. The book was discussed throughout the length and breadth of America, the sales climbed, and the fame and notoriety of the authors increased.

The initial responses from the two most important southern journals—*De Bow's Review* and the *Southern Quarterly Review*—were generally favorable, though even there were some caveats and a later reversal. De Bow's journal treated the authors well. A prompt review article on the unity of the human race praised the book for containing all that ethnological science had to offer in refutation of the theory of the unity of the human race and as a work of great learning and research. The initial

40. *Ibid.*, 465.
41. *Alabama Planter* (Mobile), May 8, June 5, 1854.

review article in the *Southern Quarterly Review,* in October, 1854, was also favorable. After a long discussion of both sides of the argument on original unity, the reviewer concluded that either "there were separate creations of different types of mankind, or man must have existed on earth for Chiliads of years. Both of these propositions may be true—one of them must be true." The reviewer did, however, find that Nott and Gliddon were too flippant in their comments about the Bible, and early in the following year the *Review* printed another article on the racial question that took *Types* to task. This reviewer was particularly disturbed by the antibiblical tone of the writing, which he construed as antireligious, and he suggested that there were serious blemishes in the book, together with "improprieties of tone and purpose, so marked and so extensive, as unavoidably to weaken, if not actually to neutralize its claims to scientific authority." The author was particularly perturbed by Gliddon's attitudes.[42]

The *Southern Literary Messenger,* a magazine far less involved than *De Bow's* or the *Southern Quarterly Review* with the main lines of the unity controversy, published two articles by William Archer Cocke attacking the infidelity of *Types.* After arguing that in a religious sense no scientific subject had the same interest or importance as that of this book, the author concisely summed up the dilemma of the orthodox. "If there are distinct species of Man," he wrote, "then the Bible is untrue; if there are other races than the descendants of Adam, they are free from the penalty 'of man's first disobedience' and the tragic scene of Calvary but a mockery and a delusion." Cocke, who referred to Nott as "the able and learned contributor," was more worried about the religious than the racial implications of the book and accused the authors of trying to destroy the Bible, of "trying to repair the old and rotten ship of infidelity, to seek to bring to their aid the force and misapplied light of science." Cocke also, more unusually in the mid-1850s, defended the idea of common humanity.[43]

Gliddon's fear that *Putnam's Monthly Magazine* was preparing to attack the book initially proved false. After pointing out that *Types* was original, elaborate, and revolutionary, the reviewer in that journal concluded that "the preponderance of evidence is on the side of fixed and primordial dis-

42. *De Bow's Review,* XVII (1854), 25–39; *Southern Quarterly Review,* XXVI (1854), 274–304, 304 (quotation), XXVII (1855), 116–74, 121 (quotation).
43. *Southern Literary Messenger,* XX (1854), 660–86, 661, 668 (quotations), XXI (1855), 23–30, 30 (quotation).

tinctions among the races, and of a multiple or national, rather than an individual or dual origination in history." As in the case of the *Southern Quarterly Review*, an initially favorable review produced an adverse reaction, and early in 1855 *Putnam's* published an article defending "the moral, religious, and physical unity of the human race." Most reviewers of *Types* accepted a high degree of contemporary racial inequality but could not accept the denial of biblical truth.[44]

The Reverend John Bachman, one of the few prominent naturalists still defending the doctrine of original unity, needed an entire pamphlet to express his anger at *Types*. He came into print quickly, arguing that he was gratified that the distinguished original contributors had aided Nott little scientifically and had not aided Gliddon in "his grand design of discrediting the christian religion, and heaping on the Holy Scripture all manner of epithets of derision and contempt." For once Bachman cast off his usually detached style to respond to "the vile aspersions of Dr. Nott and his associates." Morton, said Bachman, "was a man of integrity and great moral worth," but Nott was a bad naturalist who was "heedless in his quotations and personal in his attacks." Bachman's view of Nott's writing was that because of the institution of slavery Nott "had long been labouring, not to prove that the negro was a variety of man, inferior in intellect to the white man, although physically his equal, which all of the South, who were believers in unity admitted; but that he was of a different species and not of the same blood." Nott was readily admitted into southern journals, wrote Bachman, because this "doctrine was acceptable to the politicians of the South."[45]

Bachman had maintained a relatively scholarly and moderate stance in the growing controversies of the past ten years. He had conducted his differences with Morton on hybridity and racial history with courtesy and respect, for Morton's scholarly style appealed to him even when he disagreed with the conclusions, but Nott's vigorous, controversial style had finally gotten under his skin. Nott, as Bachman realized, conducted no basic research on racial difference; he simply snatched arguments from anything he read to bolster his preconceived views. For years Bachman

44. *Putnam's Monthly Magazine*, IV (1854), 1–14, 14 (quotation), V (1855), 79–88, 88 (quotation).

45. John Bachman, *A Notice of the "Types of Mankind," with an Examination of the Charges Contained in the Biography of Dr. Morton, Published by Nott and Gliddon* (Charleston, 1854), 3, 21, 22–23, 28.

had dodged direct confrontation with Nott, but *Types* was too much for him. It is also possible that he had heard that Nott usually referred to him in private correspondence as "the old hyena." In response to the new work, Bachman released pent-up frustration at Nott and lashed out at his old adversary more than he reviewed the book. Yet even at this stage of their conflict, his depiction of Nott was reasonably fair. "The abilities of Dr. Nott as a physician, or a politician, we have not called into question," Bachman wrote. "His private character we have no right to assail and know nothing on the subject. His writings, however, savour too much of the wrangler, and too little of the close research of the naturalist and the calm and dignified temper of the philosopher. He delights to live in the atmosphere of controversy." This assessment was fairer to Nott than Nott usually was to Bachman.[46]

Bachman was an excellent naturalist, who abandoned science for religious belief when he entered the unity controversy and defended the account of human origins given in Genesis. Nott was right to challenge the scientific accuracy of Genesis, but Bachman correctly assessed him as a controversialist who used the research of others to defend a personal point of view that had nothing to do with scientific research.

Types of Mankind was a famous book in the 1850s, and it was constantly on the lips of naturalists, ethnologists, and general racial theorists. Its conclusions about racial diversity and inequality were not seriously challenged, but its cavalier dismissal of the Bible as the source of truth concerning human origins caused great offense. Although Nott came in for a share of abuse, it was Gliddon who was looked upon as an arch-enemy of religion. As a traveling lecturer, he did not have to be respected as a gentleman. Nott, praised on all sides as a southern gentleman of the best type, did not provoke the same enmity as Gliddon, even though at times he was far more mocking about religious matters. Nott, living in a society that felt increasingly beleaguered and vehemently anxious to defend slavery, experienced no ill effects from his publication of *Types*. His passionate defenses of racial inequality and slavery, his personal charm, his family connections, and his medical skills made him not only the most famous but also one of the most admired citizens of Mobile.

46. *Ibid.*, 29.

Chapter 9
RACE IS ALL

By the time *Types of Mankind* came from the presses in the spring of 1854, Nott had spent nearly two years in unremitting labor. During that same time, he had endured the deaths of most of his children. The prospect of the appearance of his big new book did not stir him from his depression, but along with his book spring brought a scandal in Mobile that helped dispel some of the gloom.

In the ten years since Nott had taken up the cause of separate creations, his most prominent local opponent had been the Reverend William T. Hamilton. The English-born Hamilton had become the best-known Mobile clergyman since he had assumed the pastorate of the Government Street Presbyterian Church in 1834. Hamilton had adversely reviewed some of Nott's writings and had engaged in a public controversy with him in the Mobile press in 1850. In 1852 he had taken up the challenge to the Bible in a more comprehensive manner by the publication in New York of *The "Friend of Moses,"* a book that was very well received in religious circles. The book was an all-out defense of the Pentateuch. Hamilton was willing to accept the evidence that there were distinct races in ancient times, but he argued that they had come about by divine intervention at the time of the Tower of Babel and the creation of the variety of human languages. Although Hamilton differed with Nott, he treated him with great respect. The dedication of *The "Friend of Moses,"* which was a general one, included the statement "To Dr. J. C. Nott of Mobile, whom, widely though we differ in our views of the subject here discussed, I yet respect as a scholar and a writer, esteem as a man, and value as a friend."[1]

1. *The "Friend of Moses": or, a Defence of the Pentateuch as the Production of Moses and an Inspired Document, against the Objections of Modern Skepticism* (New York, 1852). See also

In the summer of 1852 the Reverend Hamilton had obtained a leave of absence from his church and had left on an extended visit to Egypt, Nubia, and Palestine to expand his knowledge of biblical times. On the way he had visited the libraries and museums of London, Paris, and other European centers. Writing to the Mobile *Register* in February, 1853, he commented, after three months on a boat on the Nile, that the monuments were overpraised and that Karl Richard Lepsius (on whom Nott had depended for much of his information) and others were laboring under a delusion as to the immeasurable antiquity of the Egyptian remains. When Hamilton returned to Mobile just before the beginning of the great epidemic of 1853, his church was filled to hear his first account of his visit to the Holy Land.[2] He now thought that he was well-armed to continue his intellectual struggle with Nott, but concern for such matters temporarily vanished as yellow fever swept through Mobile.

In the spring of 1854, with the publication of *Types,* Hamilton could be expected to take up the struggle again, but in April Nott's friends heard astounding news. Gliddon reported that Nott had written from Mobile that " 'the *Friend* of *Moses*'—His Reverence the great-gun of the Presbiterians—our mortal foe—His Eminence the 'Revd. Dr. W. T. Hamilton, Pastor of 1st Congregional [*sic*] Church at Mobile'—has— — — — what do ye think? In Nott's own words—'The Friend of Moses has buggered a boy and has fled'!!! 'he attempted to thrust the Christian Religion in *per ano.*'" Nott also had reported that Hamilton had confessed the crime before fleeing to Tennessee.[3]

The unadorned truth of these sensational charges is hard to find. The subject is not one that was discussed in public in Mobile in 1854. Hamilton did end his twenty-year pastorate of the Government Street Church in 1854, although he lived for many more years. He died in Mobile in 1884. Whatever the truth of this private tragedy of 1854, it helped to bring Nott out of a long winter of depression. Nott commented, reported Gliddon, that "so dies the last enemy here of note, to Types; and it would seem that

Nott to Squier, September 26, 1852, in Squier Papers, LC. Nott said that the book was leveled mainly at him but was "very respectful."

2. See William Hamilton to John Bragg, June 4, 1852, Peter Hamilton to John Bragg, July 5, 1852, in John Bragg Papers, SHC; *Alabama Planter* (Mobile), July 3, November 22, 1852; Mobile *Register,* July 18, 1853; letter from W. T. Hamilton, February 14, 1853; in Mobile *Register,* April 1, 1853.

3. Gliddon to Squier, April 24, 1854, in Squier Papers, LC.

Providence has taken us under his especial wing." Gliddon expressed it more simply—"the Lord is with us!"[4]

Nott had decided to take a much needed break and go north in the summer of 1854. A journey to Philadelphia, Boston, and New York, returning through South Carolina, would help to take his mind off the events in Mobile. There are indications that Nott perhaps relaxed a little more than usual this year in meeting with Gliddon in Philadelphia and Squier in New York. At his last session with Gliddon in Philadelphia, Nott, who was known as an extremely careful drinker and eater, talked and drank with a group from the Academy of Natural Sciences until 2:00 in the morning. Gliddon reported that Nott was "highly delighted" with his month at the North. Nott particularly enjoyed his time with Squier in New York, and they became good friends during this visit. Writing to Squier in October, after his return to Mobile, Nott commented in his postscript, "You are right my young friend. I do not do my rogering as fast as I used to, but I cant say that I begrudge the time." When a few weeks later he heard that Squier was going to Paris, he said, "I feel a painful anxiety about your proposed visit to Paris, for your moral character seems to me weak at least, & I fear a 40 parson power can't keep you from working your Arse on the Sabbath & violating other of the holy commandments."[5]

Nott to some degree had thrown off the malaise brought on by the death of his children, and in private he reacted in his old, inimitable style to Bachman's attack on him following the publication of *Types*. He said that he admired "the rage & villainy of the Old Hyena" and indicated that he had written a brief note to the *Charleston Medical Journal* defending Dr. Patterson, who had died since writing the memoir of Morton for the book. But otherwise, Nott said, for the time being he was keeping quiet—"How I'll skin the old Skunk in due time!" Once again in the fall of 1854 the demands of Nott's practice were great, but he was relieved that there was no epidemic of yellow fever and was ready to continue his writing on the disease. He asked Squier if he could initiate inquiries to Rio de

4. *Ibid.;* also gravestone, Magnolia Cemetery, Mobile; Charles D. Bates, *The Archives Tell a Story of the Government Street Presbyterian Church, Mobile, Alabama* (Mobile, 1959), 188. The sessional records of the church and the records of the trustees and the board of deacons are lost for the years 1842 to 1854 (*ibid.*, 23). See also Erwin Craighead, "The Hamiltons," in *Mobile: Fact and Tradition* (Mobile, 1930), 246–52.

5. Gliddon to Squier, July 14, 21, August 20, 1854, Nott to Squier, October 5, 24, 1854, in Squier Papers, LC.

Janeiro about the first appearance of the disease there and about its subsequent history. Nott was interested because he thought that yellow fever had apparently started there years before and had been traveling north ever since.[6]

Week after week through the winter of 1854–1855 Nott had news of the stir caused by the publication of *Types of Mankind*. It was reviewed, included in general articles, damned, praised, but continually noticed. A visitor to Mobile at this time mentioned that he had had the pleasure of seeing "the celebrated Dr. Nott" but thought that his book, "bigger than the Bible," would never be read because of its bulk and cost. Yet even those who never read it knew about it. This visitor, like most who met Nott, was charmed by him. He blamed Gliddon for the infidel portions of the work—Nott is "by no means an infidel"—and it is clear that Nott was now stressing to all who would listen that Gliddon had inserted offending portions without Nott's approval. For all of Nott's sarcastic attacks on the Bible, on clerics, and even on religion itself, those who met him were usually ready to make excuses for him. "Dr. Nott," wrote this visitor, "like all persons found in suspicious company, unfortunately has to suffer for his companionship. He is at the head of the medical profession here; a South Carolinian, a man of fine intellect, agreeable manners, and with the finished air of a thoroughbred and born gentleman. I liked him very much the few moments I was in his company."[7]

By the early months of 1855 Nott was again in full swing. He was working on several articles, sponsoring and contributing to a major translation, and flirting with the possibility of writing another book with Gliddon. For the moment, his major interest was a translation and abridgment of Count Joseph Arthur de Gobineau's *Essai sur l'inégalité des races humaines*. Nott had arranged for this translation and was planning to add his own appendix. It is not surprising that Nott should have been attracted to Gobineau's four-volume work, which was published in 1853 and 1855. Gobineau was to have a far more permanent impact on racist thought than Nott, but many of his arguments were similar. Gobineau divided mankind into three races—the white, the yellow, and the black—and argued that all civilization stemmed from the white race. Those peoples who were savage in the nineteenth century, argued Gobineau, had always

6. Nott to Squier, October 5, 1854; September 18, 1854, *ibid.*
7. J. H. Ingraham (ed.), *The Sunny South; or The Southerner at Home, Embracing Five Years' Experience of a Northern Governess in the Land of the Sugar and the Cotton* (Philadelphia, 1860), 513–14.

been so, and always would be, regardless of the civilization with which they were brought into contact. The races of mankind were innately unequal, and racial mingling ruined civilizations. Gobineau differed from Nott most sharply in finding no need to argue for a multiplicity of creations or of species; he thought that the obvious presence of fertile half-breeds as well as religious doctrine made it difficult to make such a case.[8]

Highly impressed by Gobineau's conclusions, Nott decided to arrange for the translation of much of the theoretical section of his work. The translation was to include those parts that best suited Nott's own views and those of the South. It omitted Gobineau's suggestion that the United States had no great future and his conclusion that slaveholding presented a major problem. The translation was so selective that Gobineau complained about it. The way Nott treated Gobineau's volumes—stripping from them the parts he agreed with and using them to support the southern point of view—was typical of Nott's "research" on racial matters.[9]

To undertake the translation, Nott secured the services of the Swiss-born Henry Hotze, who became a naturalized American citizen in Mobile in 1856. Hotze was a young man—only twenty-one at the time he undertook the translation for Nott—but Nott was extremely impressed by his intellect. Later Hotze was to work for the Mobile *Register,* serve for a time in the Mobile cadets at the beginning of the war, and be sent to London as a commercial agent for the Confederacy. While there he established a Confederate newspaper, the *Index,* that was published until after the end of the war.[10]

Nott had decided that he would use the opportunity presented by the publication of the Gobineau translation to add an essay that would counteract Gobineau's unwillingness to accept the idea of multiple creations and separate species. He would also have the chance to take on Bachman again. Nott was still bedeviled by the problem that had beset him since he first entered the racial argument with his essay on hybridity in 1843. In spite of all Nott's statements to the contrary, mulattoes were obviously

8. Joseph Arthur, Comte de Gobineau, *Essai sur l'inégalité des races humaines* (4 vols.; Paris, 1853–55). For a discussion of Gobineau's life and work see Michael D. Biddis, *Father of Racist Ideology: The Social and Political Thought of Count Gobineau* (New York, 1970).

9. Biddis, *Father of Racist Ideology,* 146–47. See also John R. Baker, *Race* (New York, 1974), 55. See Nott to Gobineau, March 7, 1855, in Ludwig Scheman, *Gobineaus Rassenwerk: Aktenstücke und Betrachtungen zur Geschichte und Kritik des Essai sur l'inégalité des races humaines* (Stuggart, 1910), 192–93, also 190–91 and 193–207.

10. Henry Hotze, *Three Months in the Confederate Army,* ed. Richard B. Harwell (1862; rpr. University, Ala., 1952), 3–10.

fertile and there was no evidence that they became less so over time. But Nott was still searching, in desultory manner, for such evidence. He wrote to the *New Orleans Medical and Surgical Journal* in June, 1855, saying that he had been told that there were settlements of mulattoes of Louisiana in which there had been intermarriage for several generations. Nott wanted to know if this was the case, and if so what was known about their prolificacy; he hoped to use any information he could obtain in the Gobineau work. Though Nott's comments on hybridity had always been unscientific—this area of his writings had particularly shocked Bachman—Nott never gave up hope that he would find positive evidence to back up his contention that mulattoes were less fertile than either whites or blacks because they represented the interbreeding of separate species. Two years earlier he had asked a friend in Columbia to find out if Colonel Wade Hampton, as he had promised, had experimented with his Angora goats on the subject of hybridity. This might have practical results, Nott had written, "to say nothing of the bearing on the 'vexed question.'"[11]

Nott thought he was in a position to set Gobineau right on some points because Gobineau wrote as a historian, not as a scientist. Gobineau appealed to him because he stressed, in the same manner as Nott, the vital importance of race on the course of human history and the permanence of racial distinctions. "I have seldom perused a work which has afforded me so much pleasure and instruction," Nott said of Gobineau's book, "and regard most of his conclusions as incontrovertible." He told Dr. Joseph Leidy of Philadelphia that Gobineau's work was "done with great boldness, talent, originality & learning—it will create a sensation."[12]

In spite of his scientific pretensions on racial matters, Nott made extensive use of historical and cultural materials to shape his views. Most of his conclusions were based not on misguided science or flawed scientific research, which could be said of Morton, but on supposed evidence drawn from the historical records of peoples, nations, and races. He was constantly trying to remedy the lack of current scientific data—he told Leidy in April, 1855, that he had begun a series of measurements of the crania of living Negroes—but such research was never systematic.[13] He

11. *New Orleans Medical and Surgical Journal,* XII (1855), 143; Nott to Robert W. Gibbes, January 14, 1853, in Dreer Collection, HSP.

12. Count A. de Gobineau, *The Moral and Intellectual Diversity of Races,* trans. H. Hotz. *To Which is added an Appendix Containing a Summary of the Latest Scientific Facts Bearing upon the Question of the Unity or Plurality of Species.* By J. C. Nott (Philadelphia, 1856), Appendix, 463; Nott to Leidy, March 18, 1855, in Leidy Papers, ANSP.

13. Nott to Leidy, April 6, 1855, in Leidy Papers, ANSP.

wrote to hat companies for lists of the sizes of hats they sold, wandered around Mobile with Agassiz looking at the heads of Choctaws, or took a few measurements of Negro heads. But he did not undertake scientific research.

The Gobineau translation was finished by August, 1855, and Hotze carried it personally to Philadelphia. Nott sent a letter introducing Hotze to Leidy with the comment that he was "the greatest intellectual prodigy You ever met . . . & though but 21 Knows everything." Nott had not finished his appendix on species when Hotze left but sent it on after him. As usual, Nott was frantically trying to write in the time left from his practice. The book was out by the fall, and the Mobile *Register* commented that though it had created a sensation in Philadelphia it was destined "to take a much deeper hold upon readers of the South." The *Register* was particularly gratified that as the book was coming "from a French Savan, it will not be charged with sectional prejudice as many of our Southern books are."[14] Nott had realized the same thing when he had arranged for it to be published.

In his main appendix to the translation Nott tried to demonstrate that Gobineau should have accepted original diversity. Gobineau experienced difficulty with this question, wrote Nott, because he had been taught to believe that two distinct species could not produce perfectly prolific offspring; he had concluded that all races of men must have had one origin because they were prolific when interbreeding. Nott tried to counter this idea by arguing that there was no abrupt line of demarcation on hybridity, but rather a gradation "from perfect sterility to perfect prolificacy." Between closely related species there was prolificacy, which would diminish depending on how far the species were apart. Again Nott suggested that mulattoes from strictly white and strictly black species were less prolific than the parent stocks. The animal kingdom, he argued, showed similar examples of gradations of fertility. Most of Nott's argument was by now familiar to readers of his abundant writings. Again, as in *Types*, he emphasized that there were more distinct races than Morton had realized and that cranial and other physical and moral comparisons demonstrated that even under the name "Caucasian" there was a variety of different races.[15]

In discussing what constituted a species, Nott again took issue with

14. Nott to Leidy, August 22, 24, 1855, *ibid.;* Mobile *Register,* December 19, 1855.
15. Nott, Appendix to Gobineau, *Moral and Intellectual Diversity of Races,* 464–72, 489–504.

Bachman, though in a moderate and nonpolemic manner. Nott actually seemed to respect Bachman more since his adversary had lashed back at him. Nott argued that though different genera were for the most part well-defined by anatomical features, species could be differentiated only by permanence of type. Dogs and wolves, he wrote, had been ranked as distinct species not because of specific anatomical differences but simply from their permanence of type as derived from their history. The same applied to the races of men that could be distinguished on the Egyptian monuments. They had maintained their type through all times and climates since that period and were distinct species. As usual, Nott called on his latest friend for support—Dr. Leidy. He had once differed with Nott, but Nott now regarded him as a supporter. Nott quoted a private letter from Leidy to the effect that *species* was an arbitrary term, which did not depend on establishing specific anatomical differences. The core of Nott's argument was that species could not be separated by anatomical characteristics "and that it is from their history alone naturalists have arrived at those minute divisions now generally received." [16]

Gobineau had also stated that he had not challenged the idea of the unity of human races because the acceptance of original diversity would impugn a religious interpretation sanctioned by the church. To Nott this statement was a further challenge, and after arguing in his main appendix that the supposed prolificacy of half-breeds was irrelevant to the definition of species, he decided to take a few extra pages to answer Gobineau's second doubt. In doing so, he went against all his warnings to Gliddon and all his avowed intentions in his private letters by commenting directly on the ways in which religion stifled scientific investigation and on the scientific fallibility of the Bible. The state of toleration, Nott wrote, was much improved, but "the day has not come when science can be severed from theology, and the student of nature can calmly follow her truths no matter whither they may lead." Other areas of science, such as geology, had struggled for independence and won, and the Bible stood as firmly as before. What was left, Nott argued, was the last great struggle between science and theology over the natural history of man. [17]

The main part of Nott's argument on this point was sound, but it was also irritating and blasphemous to the orthodox. The Bible, he said, "should not be regarded as a text-book of natural history." The writers of

16. *Ibid.*, 474–87.
17. *Ibid.*, 504–506.

the Old and New Testaments showed no knowledge of science beyond that of their profane contemporaries. What the world needed for guidance, wrote Nott, was truth, and science had long "been stifled by bigotry and error." In spite of all orthodox resistance, it was now known that the earth revolved around the sun, that it had existed for countless ages, and that the stars were millions of light years away. No living naturalist, he said, believed the story of Noah's Ark. To this point Nott could hope for support from most scientists and many others, but he then went on to a more detailed criticism of the Old Testament that was bound to cause offense. The Pentateuch, he wrote, nowhere referred to a future existence; this idea only clearly appeared in Jewish writings after the return from the Babylonian captivity. The ethnology of Genesis was "incomplete, contradictory, and unsatisfactory"; Cain took a wife in a foreign land before any women had been born of his parent stock.[18]

Nott risked even greater clerical wrath by gratuitously commenting on the New Testament. Like the Old Testament writers, Nott wrote, those of the New Testament gave no evidence of additional or special knowledge on secular matters of relevance to scientists. If the common origin of man was so all-important to the Almighty, he wrote, it was strange that the subject was left in such confusion by the inspired writers. On diligently searching the New Testament, he had found only one text that directly bore on the question: "And hath made of *one blood* all nations of men" (Acts 17:26). Nott said he had then wondered if there could be some error, and he had asked a friend in Philadelphia to examine all the Greek texts. He discovered that the word "blood" was not in the original texts; it was a later interpolation rejected by the Catholic church from the time of St. Jerome. The verse, wrote Nott, should read "And hath made of *one* all races (genus) of man." His object, he said, was simply to show that the Bible left the field open: "The sermon from the Mount comes like a light from Heaven," but the New Testament "is mute on all that pertains to the physical laws of the universe."[19]

In adding his gloss to Gobineau, Nott had begun by discussing species and hybridity and had ended by engaging in biblical criticism. That he was right in arguing that undue respect for the Bible should not be used to stifle scientific investigation in no way deflected clerical anger that this physician and amateur ethnologist should lecture them on problems in

18. *Ibid.*, 506–10.
19. *Ibid.*, 511–12.

the biblical text. Nott had two powerful beliefs—one was a conviction of racial inequality and the necessity of white supremacy, the other was opposition to religious interference with the course of scientific inquiry. The first stemmed naturally from his environment and self-interest, the second was unusual in that it would have been easier for him to have pursued his racial interests without challenging the clergy at every possible turn. But whether it was faith in the new science and technology of the nineteenth century, resentment at the manner in which his father and brother had suffered from the attacks of the orthodox, or the more positive impact of the ideas of Thomas Cooper, Nott carried into the mid-nineteenth century an attitude toward religion and the clergy that smacked of the eighteenth century. He did not need to fight passionately to free science from religious orthodoxy in order to defend white supremacy and the South and its institutions.

More ambitious than the Gobineau edition was a plan for a sequel to the *Types of Mankind*. Gliddon was thinking of a new book; Nott was thinking more of a revised and improved edition of *Types*. The main impetus for the new work was Gliddon's desire to make money, but Nott was interested because of the possibility of bringing Squier, Agassiz, and Leidy more fully into the project and because of his desire to continue the pressure on those who opposed the new ethnology. Gliddon first wrote of this proposal to Squier only a few months after *Types* was published. He said that there was a plan for a "paying work on Anthropology." With Nott's cooperation, Gliddon argued, it would be easy to get six hundred subscribers at $5 each. Four hundred more would not be hard to find. Gliddon's suggestion and his bait to Lippincott (to whom he had also used Nott's name) was a work of universal ethnology, encompassing every variety of man. He tempted Squier with the idea of "Squier & Gliddon," or vice versa. If *Types* had sold thirty-five hundred copies in six months in dull times, he argued, together they could do better.[20]

Gliddon had decided to go to Europe to earn some money and collect material for the book. His letter to Squier had simply been a feeler to see if he could interest Squier in contributing. Nott, who found it hard to resist Gliddon or the prospect of publication, was his main hope, and within a few weeks Gliddon was again writing to Squier saying that when he came back from Europe he would be ready to produce a new "Nott &

20. Gliddon to Squier, August 31, 1854, in Squier Papers, LC.

Gliddon" with contributions from others. In spite of his protestations, Nott was easily caught, and in the fall of 1854 Nott was trying to interest Leidy, Squier, and Agassiz in joining in such a work as Gliddon proposed. Nott insisted that he would not allow his name to go before the public again "in any but a purely scientific book, entirely free from all personalities & religious controversy." Because Nott rarely went before the public with anything else, Leidy presumably took this statement with a pinch of salt. Gliddon had told Nott, with a liberal use of his imagination, that Leidy was "heartily" ready to cooperate on the book, and Nott insisted to Leidy that this weighed heavily with him. Nott was also extremely hopeful of getting Agassiz to cooperate. The object, wrote Nott, was to take *Types* as the basis, work the material over, and bring in more authoritative statements. Such a volume, he argued, would finally free science and would combat "Bachman & his clan." With a remarkable degree of self-deception, Nott commented that "while I am averse to controversy, I am desirous of seeing Science triumph."[21]

To Squier, Nott told essentially the same story, insisting that he would not come before the public again in book form "unless I can fully control the tone & do the thing as a *gentleman*." He wanted Squier to write the section on American Indians. In suggesting to Squier, as he had to Leidy, that a revised *Types* could be a basis for a new book, he emphasized that his own sections could be much improved and that Gliddon's sections on chapter 10 of Genesis "should be kicked to hell." Squier, who showed no desire to be involved as joint author with Gliddon and Nott, suggested a book in which all the contributors would simply be responsible for their own chapters. Nott's objections were that "1st it does not put all the money in Gliddon's pocket, & 2d such fellows as Agassiz are too busy or too lazy to quit fish for niggers or other small game." Moreover, he said, "the idea is to make a great *populous* book that everybody will read & thus spread infidelity as rapidly as possible."[22] A year after his tragedies in Mobile, Nott was back in his old irreverent form.

Gliddon was in Europe longer than expected. He finally returned in May, 1856. Preparations for his proposed book were not well advanced, but he had Lippincott issue a prospectus with Nott's name on the title page. Nott protested to Leidy that he had done so in spite of all his re-

21. Gliddon to Squier, September 9, 1854, *ibid.*; Nott to Leidy, October 4, 1854, in Leidy Papers, ANSP; Nott to Squier, October 5, 1854, in Squier Papers, LC.
22. Nott to Squier, October 5, 24, 1854, in Squier Papers, LC.

fusals and remonstrances, but in reality he had never said no. He knew that Gliddon had told Lippincott that Nott was to be a coauthor of the new book, but he had not written to Lippincott to withdraw his name. He might better have done so, for he did not have the material to take any large part in any new book on race. He was written out. He admitted to Leidy that he had said all of importance that he had to say in *Types*.[23]

Nott would have thrown himself with more vigor into a new book if Agassiz, Leidy, and Squier had come in, but they all avoided committing themselves to contributing chapters. Nott enjoyed good relations with all three—he corresponded with them all, was a close friend of Squier, and regularly arranged for specimens to be collected along the Gulf for Agassiz and Leidy[24]—but they were wary of being involved with the flamboyant Gliddon, and it may well be that Nott was becoming too much an outspoken proslavery southerner for them to wish a close association in print.

With Agassiz, Squier, and Leidy unwilling to participate, and Nott willing to have his name used but having neither the inclination nor the material to provide half of a new book, Gliddon was in some difficulty. Eventually the book became largely Gliddon's, together with a collection of essays by different authors, including Nott. This was somewhat the form suggested by Squier, except that Gliddon wrote far too much and the most important American names, except for Nott, were missing. The book was given the title *Indigenous Races of the Earth;* Gliddon said that this title was suggested by Nott. Although Nott contributed only one chapter, Gliddon listed him as joint author. He also managed to get the names of Agassiz and Leidy onto the title page. They did not contribute articles, but Gliddon printed a letter from each of them in the volume.

When Gliddon arrived back from Europe in May, 1856, only one chapter was written, that of the Frenchman Alfred Maury, who contributed what became the first chapter, "Distribution and Classification of Tongues." This philological contribution gave little help to the pluralist cause because Maury was chiefly interested in tracing the origin of languages back to Asia. The second chapter had also been solicited by Gliddon in Europe. It was an essay titled "Iconographic Researches on Human Races and Their Art" by the Hungarian Francis Pulszky. Pulszky had earlier ac-

23. Gliddon to Squier, January 10, March 21, 1856, *ibid.;* Nott to Leidy, April 6, 1856, in Leidy Papers, ANSP.
24. Nott to Leidy, March 15, May 15, November 30, 1856, in Leidy Papers, ANSP.

companied Lajos Kossuth to the United States and had visited Mobile. His essay found another way of dividing human beings—into artistic and nonartistic races.[25] The third chapter, "The Cranial Characteristics of the Races of Men," by Dr. J. Aiken Meigs, a young Philadelphian, was a very long one of 150 pages. It was based on the Morton collection of crania, which had been deposited in the Philadelphia Academy of the Natural Sciences. The essay was careful and scientific, and though he pointed out cranial differences he avoided conclusions regarding human origins.[26] The rest of the book belonged to Nott and Gliddon, primarily Gliddon. In the summer and fall of 1856 Gliddon managed to produce some 250 pages of confused detail on Egypt and related subjects. If anything, this long section was even more unreadable than his contributions to *Types of Mankind*.

After discussions that went on for two years, Nott finally agreed that he would supply a chapter on acclimation. Nott had published so often in the previous ten years that he was struggling for a new way of approaching his subject. He had kept up to date on his reading, but the pluralists had made most of the points they had to make by the mid-1850s. In this situation Nott temporarily allowed his racial views to become entwined with his medical writing. The impetus that eventually produced not only a chapter for Gliddon but also an article for the *American Journal of the Medical Sciences* was his reading of Dr. René La Roche's standard book on yellow fever. La Roche's assertion that human beings could be acclimated in a great variety of climates stirred Nott's opposition and gave him a new theme to work on in the summer and fall of 1856. He had touched on this subject previously, but this was the first time he had tackled it in a sustained way. The first result of his work was the article for the medical journal, which he modified for *Indigenous Races*.

In his article Nott first praised La Roche's book as the standard work on the subject but indicated that there were aspects of it with which he differed and regarding which he could help in developing the "true history of southern diseases." Generally, Nott had been too good a doctor to allow his professional views to be permeated by his public and private

25. Alfred Maury to Squier, August 24, 1854, in Squier Papers, LC; Nott to Leidy, April 6, 1856, in Leidy Papers, ANSP; Nott and Gliddon, *Indigenous Races of the Earth; or, New Chapters of Ethnological Inquiry* (Philadelphia, 1857), vii and chapters 1 and 2.

26. See J. Aiken Meigs to Squier, February 10, 1860 (with enclosure), in Squier Papers, LC; Nott and Gliddon, *Indigenous Races,* chapter 3.

stance on race. But increasing discussion throughout the South in the 1850s of the "southern practice" of medicine had gone beyond simply acknowledging that there were special disease problems in the region. Some physicians were even beginning to argue that southern physicians should be trained in the South because of the lack of understanding of the South outside the region.[27]

Nott's extensive connections in the North and in Europe and his respect for the best theorists wherever they lived to a large extent enabled him to resist this trend, but as his obsession with the racial question grew there were signs that it was permeating larger areas of his thinking. Nott was led to disagree with La Roche's assertion that human beings became acclimated in a great variety of climates and eventually reacted as though they had always lived in the place in which they had settled. La Roche was prompted to make this assertion by the acknowledged vulnerability of newcomers to yellow fever and the far greater resistance of old residents. Nott differed not in the specific case of yellow fever but regarding La Roche's generalizations about acclimation.

Part of Nott's criticism was sound. He argued, with reason, that La Roche needed to distinguish between the endemic, malarial fevers prevalent in southern rural districts and the yellow fever that was essentially an urban disease. Although there was acclimation against the yellow fever of the cities, there was none against the endemic rural fevers. As usual, Nott included letters from friends and colleagues, in this case from those living in the South, to support his statements.[28]

An article that could have been a useful refinement and correction of La Roche's standard work was spoiled by being permeated with Nott's general racial arguments. The question of acclimation, he argued, had to be considered in connection both with the permanency of human type that went back five thousand years and with Agassiz' division of the world into eight zoological provinces, with animals and plants peculiar to each zone. Groups of human beings in each zone, Nott posited, were adapted by nature to the surrounding climatic influences. Races removing to other zones did violence to their natures, although those from the temperate zones, the world's conquerors and civilizers, were most effec-

27. Nott, "Thoughts on Acclimation and the Adaptation of Races to Climates," *American Journal of the Medical Sciences*, n.s., XXXII (1856), 320. See also John Duffy, "A Note on Ante-Bellum Southern Nationalism and Medical Practice," *Journal of Southern History*, XXXIV (1968), 266–76.
28. Nott, "Thoughts on Acclimation," 320–22, 326, 333–34.

tive in moving between zones. In the Gulf region, the indigenous American Indians were the healthiest for they were in harmony with the climate. They were even healthier than the blacks, although blacks were much less susceptible to yellow fever than whites, and even the smallest drop of Negro blood diminished the susceptibility of whites to the disease. Based on his experience in Mobile, Nott argued, there was reason to believe "that the susceptibility of races to yellow fever is in direct ratio to the fairness of complexion."[29]

Races, according to Nott's argument, were originally made to suit the climates in which they were placed. The Anglo-Saxon race deteriorated in hot climates, although he agreed that new immigrants suffered more. As usual Nott drew on his reading of European authorities to support his general position, commenting on the nature of endemic fevers in countries such as Italy. He also used the evidence of Frenchmen who had written on Algeria. There, he wrote, the mortality among Frenchmen was greater than among Jews. The statistics in this case suited his argument, but even when they were unsuitable he quickly shifted ground and found reasons to explain the discrepancy. The statistics showed that the "Moorish" population of Algeria was also decreasing, which should not have been occurring according to Nott's theory of the placing of races in climates that suited them. In this case, however, he asked whether the Moorish decline could not be "explained by that mysterious law in virtue of which inferior races seem destined to disappear through contact with superior races?"[30]

A medical article pointing out the problems of acclimation in regard to different diseases and giving some indication of the different susceptibility of different population groups would have been useful, but in this case Nott had allowed his general racial theories, some based on the wildest speculations, to meld with his accumulated knowledge of yellow and malarial fevers, based on more than twenty years of observation and reading. The result was a hodgepodge of an article, in which his usual careful medical observations were swamped by a tide of general racial theory.

While working on his new subject of acclimation, Nott had little direct contact with Gliddon regarding the new book on the indigenous races of the earth. Gliddon spent much of his time in Philadelphia on this visit, and although he corresponded with Nott and visited him in Mobile in

29. *Ibid.*, 322–25.
30. *Ibid.*, 327, 330–32.

November, 1856, Nott never saw the chapters of the book, except his own, until they were in proof. Gliddon was still hoping that Nott would write the preface to the book when the proofs were sent to him, but Nott claimed that delays in the mails, caused by the bad state of the winter roads, had made this impossible. Nott told Leidy that Gliddon had "provoked me so by his vulgar theology that I have not read ten pages of his proofs, & I do not know that I shall ever read any more of his articles."[31]

Gliddon wrote his own preface but claimed, regarding Nott, that this book "owes far more to his personal science and propulsion than appears on its face."[32] Gliddon was here engaged in his common occupation of slightly bending the truth, for he had been the great driving force behind *Indigenous Races*. He wrote most of it, and he edited it into its final shape. Although it was known as another book by Nott and Gliddon and was advertised as such, only *Types* was truly a joint production of the two authors.

Nott's chapter on acclimation in *Indigenous Races* had much material from his earlier article on that subject, but it was reshaped and more forcefully expressed for the book, and some new sections were added. His basic argument was that each type of mankind, like a species of animals or plants, had its appropriate climate or "milieu" and that even over generations it could not become habituated to another milieu. This, argued Nott, was yet another confirmation that distinct racial types were as ancient and permanent as the fauna and flora that surrounded them. Nott also introduced in this chapter yet another variant of his idea of the disappearance of races. He had already suggested that many inferior races were doomed to extinction in their contact with superior peoples, he had suggested that mulattoes if left to breed among themselves would eventually die out, and he had even envisioned a situation when full racial amalgamation in the world would lead to the disappearance of all human beings; he now suggested that the fair races of northern Europe would eventually become extinct in the tropics if not strengthened by fresh settlers from home.[33] The young man who had plied his trade in the autopsy and dissection rooms of Philadelphia, Paris, and Mobile and who had watched yellow fever reap so many victims in his maturer years was fascinated by the idea of racial extinction.

31. Nott to Leidy, March 30, 1857, in Leidy Papers, ANSP; Nott and Gliddon, *Indigenous Races*, vii–viii.
32. Nott and Gliddon, *Indigenous Races*, viii.
33. *Ibid.*, 353–56.

As in most of his writings, Nott made use of mulattoes, about whom
he had constantly admitted that it was impossible to secure any accurate
statistics, to support his general points. In regard to acclimation, he argued, mulattoes had characteristics intermediate between those of the
white and black races. Blacks were comparatively immune from yellow
fever, and whites gained this comparative immunity by the admixture of
black blood. "I hazard nothing in the assertion," he wrote, "that one-
fourth negro blood is a more perfect protection against yellow fever, than
is vaccine against small-pox."[34] Here Nott seemed to be denying his own
assertion that mulattoes fell midway between blacks and whites in degree
of acclimation.

An area that Nott emphasized more strongly in the book than in his
article was the difference between races in their response to disease, a difference he thought stemmed not merely from their original adaption to
one zoological province and climate but from marked physiological differences. Here again, as in his article, Nott began to show signs of accepting the extreme views of those southern physicians, such as Dr. Samuel
Cartwright of Louisiana, who emphasized the supposedly basic physiological differences between whites and blacks. Nott quoted with approval
the remarks of a University of Pennsylvania physician to the effect that
Negroes were much less subject to inflammatory diseases, with high vascular action, than whites, and rarely bore bloodletting or depletion in any
form. Even in pleurisy and pneumonia, he wrote, Negroes often required
stimulants instead of depletants. Nott commented that these observations were "unquestionably true" and that they had been borne out over
the years in his private infirmary in Mobile. Black laborers when seized in
winter with pleurisy or pneumonia almost invariably showed a feeble
pulse, cool skin, and unstrung muscles, and they needed to be treated
mainly with "revulsives," quinine, and stimulants. Here Nott was going
farther down the path of corrupting his medical theories racially. This
had not been his custom during the 1840s and early 1850s, when southern
physicians of less ability found a wide range of ways, many of them imag-
inary, in which blacks were physiologically different from whites. Nott
also argued in this chapter that the Negro always suffered more than
whites from cholera, typhoid, plague, smallpox, and all the diseases arising from "morbid poisons," except marsh and yellow fevers, "to which he
is infinitely less liable." Nott also suggested that though yellow fever,

34. *Ibid.*, 367.

with perhaps a few exceptions, had a preference for the races of men in proportion to the lightness of complexion (with the greatest danger to the pure white), plague preferred the reverse course.[35]

That whites and blacks had somewhat different susceptibilities to certain diseases was a help to southern racists in their effort to show that the two races were entirely distinct. Blacks were more resistant to yellow fever than whites, those suffering from sickle-cell anemia had immunity from the worst form of malaria, and blacks generally were more susceptible to respiratory diseases. But these differences were minor compared to the broad areas in which the problems of disease and injury were identical for black and white alike. Some southern physicians grossly exaggerated racial differences in response to disease in the same way that they grossly exaggerated detailed anatomical differences. Nott generally resisted bringing his extreme racial views into his medical observations, but in this latest book with Gliddon he was struggling to find material and allowed his usual good sense on medical matters to be corrupted.[36]

Toward the end of his chapter in *Indigenous Races*, Nott drifted away from his concern with racial and medical questions to express his disillusionment with human beings and mankind in general. This became a more marked feature of Nott's writing in the last twenty years of his life. It was revealed in his predictions of extinction for so many races, in his belief that the philanthropists could not be deflected from what he viewed as their hopelessly misguided desire to end slavery, and in his lack of faith in man's reason or in the power of civilization to achieve worthwhile progress.

Nott now increasingly characterized human beings as unreasoning, greedy, and shortsighted. In *Indigenous Races* he commented that anatomically and zoologically man was "but an animal; and governed by the same organic laws as other animals." He had more intelligence than other animals and combined a moral with a physical nature, but though boasting of reason as his distinguishing feature, he was "in many respects, the most unreasonable of all animals." Civilization, he argued, "represses the gross vices of barbarism, and brings the refinements of music, poetry, the fine arts, together with the precepts of a purer religion," but "it al-

35. *Ibid.*, 368–69, 393.
36. There are good discussions of the actual differences between whites and blacks in regard to disease in Todd L. Savitt, *Medicine and Slavery: The Diseases and Health Care of Blacks in Antebellum Virginia* (Urbana, Ill., 1978), and Kenneth F. Kiple and Virginia H. King, *Another Dimension to the Black Diaspora* (Cambridge, England, 1981).

most balances the account by luxury, insincerity, political, and trading vices, which follow its march everywhere." In a decade in which the prevailing doctrine in America was that the gloriously ameliorating effects of Western commerce and Christianity were to transform an unenlightened world, Nott was unconvinced. He thought that the only real civilization lay with the white races, but he had grave doubts about the ability of any human beings to achieve a sane, rational life. "Fashion, in our day, has substituted moral for physical cruelty. The ancient barbarians plundered and cut each other's throats. Civilized man now passes his life in scandal and tricks of trade." For the last half century, Nott argued, so-called civilized nations had been warring, fighting, destroying body and soul by vice and luxury. Colonizers went out and died in climates never intended for their settlement.[37]

After wandering away from the point of his chapter and suddenly remembering what he was writing about, Nott finally returned to his usual confident conclusions on racial matters: the earth was naturally divided into geographical realms; each realm possessed a group of human races closely allied with one another and disconnected from all others, the types of men belonging to each realm antedated all human records, and in each they were as ancient as the fauna, were separated by specific characters, and were affected by both the physical and medical climates of a realm. No race of man was cosmopolite, no race could be assimilated to all physical or medical climates, but the races in the temperate zones came nearer to cosmopolitanism than any others.[38]

Indigenous Races came out in the spring of 1857. In no way did it match the success of *Types*. For the most part it was an extremely tedious, ill-written work. *Types* had been too long and diffuse, and Gliddon's sections were opaque, but the first part of the book was written in Nott's often vigorous, striking style. Also, it effectively summed up the results of the previous fifteen years in which the American school of ethnology had taken an entirely new look at the origin of human beings and the nature of human races. *Indigenous Races* was an uneasy addenda. Writing to Squier in the spring of 1857, Nott referred to the book as the "Indignant Races" and said that they had "the right to be indignant, for Gliddon has surpassed himself in folly & confusion." Gliddon's chapters, he wrote, were hopelessly jumbled, and he had tried in vain to read them. He

37. Nott and Gliddon, *Indigenous Races,* 399–400.
38. *Ibid.,* 401.

hoped Squier could "find some *physical* employment for him, for he is not fit for book making."[39]

The new book did not cause the stir or provoke the reaction of *Types*. It was a much tamer piece, and *Types* had blunted the opposition's slashing edges of criticism. One commentator, Abraham Coles, however, was moved enough by what he viewed as this new attempt of Nott and Gliddon to subvert true religion that he published a pamphlet attacking both books and both men. Nott and Gliddon, he wrote, made "no secret of their devotion to Slavery and Infidelity." An attack on the common origin of man was a challenge to Christianity itself. The advocacy of the doctrine of many origins "inclines, if it does not necessarily tend to infidelity; otherwise how shall we explain the notorious fact that the majority of its supporters are open, and, in some cases, passionate rejecters of Revelation." Like most of the earlier critics, Coles believed that Gliddon "outrages decency the most," but both Nott and Gliddon were out to disprove the Scriptures. The Bible, argued Coles, "clearly and unmistakably affirms the unity of the species." Even if Negroes existed three or four thousand years ago, this was no proof of diversity of origin. The law of variety began to operate at a very early period, either by natural causes or by divine intervention. "A large part of both volumes," wrote Coles, "particularly that contributed by Mr. Gliddon, has no other object than to vilify Revelation." The attack on Nott and Gliddon as subverters of religious truth continued strongly in the late 1850s. Attending a religious convention in May, 1857, Nott's old adversary the Reverend Moses Ashley Curtis wrote home to his wife that as he left church that morning a fellow worshiper had commenced an attack on "my old friend Dr. Nott of Mobile whom he had talked with, & whom he abused with fierce contempt." Apparently one man had met Nott without being charmed out of opposition to his views.[40]

Indigenous Races was to be Gliddon's last effort at money and fame by cooperating with Nott or other American racial writers. He had begun the year in high spirits, seeing *Indigenous Races* through the press and telling Squier that with his wife and son in Memphis he was "a perfect ex-

<hr/>

39. Nott to Squier, April 26, 1857, in Squier Papers, LC.
40. Abraham Coles, *A Critique on Nott and Gliddon's Ethnological Works* (Burlington, N.J., 1857), 5–9, 30–34. This piece was originally published in the *Medical and Surgical Reporter*. Coles was a physician. Moses A. Curtis to his wife, May 24, 1857, in Moses Ashley Curtis Papers, SHC.

ample of celibacy . . . a dam'd sight too busy . . . to go a whoring!" Within twelve months he was dead, and Nott was given another reason to reflect on the ephemeral nature of human existence. As Nott had repeatedly urged, Squier found Gliddon a paying post—with the Honduras Interoceanic Railway Company. Off he went to Central America, and there on November 16, 1857, he died.[41] Nott missed him. He was always complaining about him, but Gliddon had a bit of Mr. Micawber in him and was good company, both in person and through his letters. Nott could have benefited from his optimism and exuberance in the years after 1861.

41. Gliddon to Squier, January 1, 1857, in Squier Papers, LC; William Stanton, *The Leopard's Spots: Scientific Attitudes Toward Race in America, 1815–59* (Chicago, 1960), 180–81.

Chapter 10
MEDICAL EDUCATION

Within three years, from 1854 to 1857, Nott had his name on three books—
Types of Mankind, the Gobineau translation, and *Indigenous Races of the
Earth*—as well as publishing a variety of articles on both racial and medical matters. He had always been a man of great energy, but there is a frenetic quality to the amount of work he produced in the years after the
deaths of his children. In the months immediately following their deaths
he had told Gliddon that he was working night and day to blunt his feelings, and this pattern continued in the years leading up to the Civil War.
Even for a full-time writer, Nott's production would have been substantial, but he was working in the time he could snatch from an extremely
successful medical practice.

Beyond the desire to forget private cares by throwing himself into his
work, Nott was also spurred in these years of the mid- and late 1850s
by increasing tensions between North and South. From the time of the
Kansas-Nebraska Act in 1854 the normal business of government was
swallowed up by increasingly bitter sectional harangues that made Nott
and the South as a whole feel threatened not only by the minority abolitionists but also by the rapidly growing Republican party. The Republicans' insistence that slavery should expand no further confirmed all Nott's
worst fears that those who wished to abolish slavery would not be deflected from their course. Nott and many others in the South feared, with
good reason, that a victory for those who wanted slavery to be confined
to its present limits would ultimately become a victory for the ideas of the
hated abolitionists.

In spite of his commitment to southern slavery, Nott largely avoided
involvement in formal southern politics. He preferred the role of a scien-

tist informing the country of supposed realities about race. When he did take a public stance, it was to support those candidates who were perceived as posing least danger to the South. In July, 1856, he let his name be used in Mobile in the movement to secure the election of James Buchanan to the presidency. With the Republicans now replacing the Whigs as the second major political party, it was essential to the South that a friendly Democratic candidate should win the presidency. At a large meeting held in the hall of the Franklin Society in Mobile it was asserted that the election of Buchanan would be of vast importance to the South, and officers were nominated to form an organization to promote his election. There were to be a president and twenty-five vice-presidents; among the latter were Nott and his father-in-law, James Deas. Nott was obviously there not to work but for the strength of his name.[1]

The heightened fear and the siege mentality that were now sweeping the South became apparent in Mobile in the election summer of 1856. Since the development of radical abolitionism in the 1830s, southerners had made every effort to stop abolitionist doctrines from being spread in the South. Year by year it became increasingly unsafe for those who opposed slavery to make their views known in the region, and every effort was made to exclude abolitionist works. In the summer of 1856, the prominent Mobile booksellers Strickland and Upson learned how dangerous it was to stock abolitionist literature. In August, 1856, the Mobile *Register* reported that there was "considerable excitement" in the community because of the discovery that Strickland and Upson were selling publications of "an incendiary and insurrectionary character." It had been discovered that the bookstore had stocked titles by Frederick Douglass and that William Strickland had given copies of *Uncle Tom's Cabin* to his up-country customers who were interested in the book.

Following the discovery that the bookstore had stocked and distributed abolitionist works, a meeting of those referred to as some of Mobile's "best, calmest, and most influential citizens" was called to consider what action to take. There were twenty-nine men present at the meeting, including Drs. Nott, Levert, Ketchum, Ross, and J. C. Woodcock. It was decided that a committee would investigate the matter and report back to the main body. The committee consisted of three of the doctors (Nott,

---

1. Mobile *Register,* July 18, 26, 1856. James S. Deas was elected to the Alabama Senate in 1857 and served for one term. He carried the Spring Hill precinct by a vote of 32 to 2 (*ibid.,* August 9, 1857).

Levert, and Woodcock), John Bragg (politician and brother of Confederate General Braxton Bragg), and one other. Strickland and Upson were given a chance to speak in their own behalf, but it did no good. The committee quickly condemned the booksellers in its resolutions to the main body. Its comment regarding the literature was that "the character of the evidence and of the books brought before the Committee, is such that it would be unsafe and dangerous to make them public."[2]

The commitee went on to report a set of resolutions which read as though Nott had drafted them. It was decided that Strickland and Upson had willfully deceived the meeting regarding the procurement and sale of the books in question; that the two were either abolitionists anxious to propagate their faith among slaves and slaveowners or they were unscrupulous and unprincipled speculators ready to make money by the sale of any books to anybody; and that in either case they were dangerous persons in a slaveholding community and should be ejected from it. It was stressed that such an ejection should be peaceful, and it was suggested that a committee of three, including Nott and Levert, should visit the booksellers and tell them what had been decided. At a second meeting the main body accepted the recommendations and asked the committee of three to warn Strickland and Upson that unless they left within five days their personal safety could not be guaranteed. When Nott and the others went to the bookstore, they discovered that Strickland and Upson had already left the city. The *Register* praised the firm and moderate course followed by the committee. A few days later it was reported that a painter was already at work "erasing the very name of the abolitionist agents from the sign-boards hanging over their late elegant store." Strickland tried to return early in 1858 but again was forced to leave the city. It was estimated that the loss of his business had cost him more than $40,000. When he next returned, in April, 1865, it was in the wake of an occupying Union army.[3]

Nott had long vigorously defended the freedom of science against religion, but he obviously had no more interest in the abstract defense of the right of free expression in the South than he had in the abstract right of freedom. Nott had long argued that certain rights had to be qualified for

2. Mobile *Register,* August 17, 1856.

3. *Ibid.,* August 17, 22, 1856; Caldwell Delaney, "The Banishment of Strickland," in *A Mobile Sextet: Papers Read Before the Alabama Historical Association, 1952–1971* (Mobile, 1981), 151–79; Mobile *Daily News,* April 20, 1865.

the good of stable government. By 1856 many southerners, including Nott, feared that they were sitting on a powder keg and that the abolitionists were deliberately throwing matches in their direction. The attitude of both the Mobile *Register* and the citizens who dealt with the problem was that they had done well to remove Strickland and Upson from the town without violence. Nott undoubtedly believed that no "gentleman" would either write or sell books that might stir slave unrest and bring danger to the community. He therefore felt fully justified in taking a leading role in quietly but decisively expelling Strickland and Upson from Mobile.

Although Nott was fully committed to the defense of the South and its institutions, he never, even in these last years before the Civil War, became completely parochial in his outlook. Many of his most regular and close correspondents continued to be in the North, he continued to correspond with Europeans interested in ethnology, and he continued to visit Philadelphia and New York. He also saw that his eldest surviving son, James Deas Nott, was given a northern and European medical education. There was much talk in the South about the southern practice of medicine, but Nott knew full well that the South could not offer as good an education as was available in Philadelphia and Paris.

James had attended the University of Alabama for a year before transferring to his father's old institution, South Carolina College in Columbia. While there, in February, 1856, he was involved in a student riot that resulted in his suspension. Following the arrest of a drunken student, most of the students at the college went to the guardhouse, and two of them attacked the marshal. The student was quietly released later in the day, but the next day it seemed that the affair might prove serious because more than one hundred students, armed with guns from the college arsenal, went back into town and were confronted by some two hundred citizens as well as by the police. Open fighting was avoided when a former president of the college persuaded the students to return to the campus.[4]

James Nott was one of the students suspended as a result of his part in this affair, and his father agreed that rather than returning to South Carolina College he could go the University of Pennsylvania in the fall of 1856 to study medicine. Nott explained to Joseph Leidy that his son had been "in a boyish rebellion" with three-quarters of the other students. James,

4. *Alabama Genealogical Register,* VIII (1966), 118; Daniel W. Hollis, *University of South Carolina,* I, *South Carolina College* (Columbia, 1951), 197–99, 201.

he wrote, "has decided talent, is a high toned, & rather self willed fellow, with considerable fondness for general reading, & is not to be driven." He was not yet fully committed to medicine, said Nott, but he thought he would like it. Nott's only worry was that his son might not tackle his studies with the necessary earnestness. If he did become fully interested, Nott wanted to send him to Europe after his graduation "& give him the best advantages the world affords." He asked Leidy to try to interest James in medicine, particularly anatomy. The young man was apparently not unlike his father, for Nott said that he had "a great deal of physical & mental energy." Nott greatly admired Philadelphia medical training, and he sent other young Mobilians to study there.[5]

James Nott spent two years in Philadelphia and served a medical apprenticeship with Dr. Leidy. Nott was happy with his progress. He told Leidy in March, 1857, that James "seems to be gradually sowing his oats & becoming more studious—He is a manly, self willed fellow, with a quick mind, & I think he will come out all right in the long run—He is one of those that would have been ruined by a tight rein." Nott was a tolerant, understanding father. He showed little impatience with either the follies or the uncertainties of youth.[6]

James graduated from the University of Pennsylvania Medical School in 1858. For the following year he applied for a residency at Blockley, the successor to the "Old Blockley," where his father had spent a year thirty years before. Thinking that the competition would be very stiff, his father made alternate plans to send his son to Paris to complete his medical education and "to let him run his race & be done with it." The Blockley residency did not come through in time, and early in October, 1858, James left for France. Nott supported two sons in Paris in these years directly preceding the Civil War, for Henry Junius Nott, who was going into business, was also given the chance to go abroad. There was less reason for Henry than for James to go to Paris, but the excuse was the completion of his education; Henry was twenty when the brothers left for Paris, James twenty-two. Later, in writing about one of them to Squier, Nott commented that his son was "improving his morals in Paris."[7]

Nott was very pleased in 1856 when his eldest son decided to follow a

5. Nott to Leidy, September 14, 1856, in Leidy Papers, ANSP; Nott to Leidy, September 29, 1856, September 12, 1859, in Leidy Papers, CPP.
6. Nott to Leidy, March 30, 1857, in Leidy Papers, ANSP.
7. Nott to Leidy, August 15, September 2, 1858, *ibid.*; Nott to Squier, August 22, 1860, in Squier Papers, LC.

medical career. Whatever the other disillusionments in his life, Nott had remained convinced that medicine was a profession whose value went far beyond the healing of the sick. He thought it developed the scientific, rational mind that was essential for dealing with a variety of other problems. Since those early days in Columbia, South Carolina, when he had taught medical college preparatory courses, Nott had continued to have a strong interest in medical education. In Mobile, as his reputation grew, he took in private pupils and in the 1850s usually sent them on to his friend Dr. Leidy in Philadelphia. In the four years before the Civil War, Nott was to devote much of his time to medical education—first in teaching medicine in New Orleans and then in the formation of a medical school in Mobile.

In the spring of 1857, Nott was offered and accepted the professorship of anatomy in the medical school of the University of Louisiana in New Orleans (later the Tulane School of Medicine). He said, probably not very seriously, that the position would give him "more money & less work."[8] The school had been founded in the 1830s as the Medical College of Louisiana. A leading figure in its establishment had been a Charlestonian, Dr. Thomas Hunt, who had graduated from the University of Pennsylvania in 1829 and had studied in Paris. In the mid-1840s it had become the medical department of the new University of Louisiana in New Orleans, and it prospered in the following years. By 1858 it had more than 250 students. Among its faculty members were Nott's brother Adolphus and Dr. Warren Stone, one of the most prominent of southwestern surgeons. Adolphus, who had been given financial support by Nott in his early years in New Orleans, had later done well and was professor of materia medica. Nott had kept in touch with his brother over the years, and they had traveled north to Philadelphia together in the summer after Nott's family tragedies in Mobile.[9] For several years Nott had tried to interest the Alabama legislature in establishing a medical school in Mobile, but his efforts had not yet been successful. Nott was frustrated at the delay, and the New Orleans offer gave him the chance to satisfy his love for medical education while staying in the Gulf area.

8. Nott to Squier, April 26, 1857, in Squier Papers, LC.
9. See William Frederick Norwood, *Medical Education in the United States Before the Civil War* (Philadelphia, 1944), 363–68; Francis R. Packard, *History of Medicine in the United States* (2 vols.; 1931; rpr. New York, 1963), II, 787–89; John P. Dyer, *Tulane: The Biography of a University, 1834–1965* (New York, 1966), 19–23; George R. Gliddon to Squier, July 14, 1854, in Squier Papers, LC.

Although Nott accepted the position, he was not convinced that either he or his family would want to leave a city in which they had lived for more than twenty years. He decided that he would leave his house, office, and possessions essentially intact in Mobile while he and his family moved to New Orleans for the four months of the school year. Nott was happy in Mobile, and he was happy on the Gulf coast. He told Leidy that after four months in New Orleans he would settle down either there or in Mobile "for the balance of my life." [10]

Nott also decided that in 1857 he would practice in Mobile until August and then go north. After a brief rest at the Virginia Springs, he would visit Philadelphia to work up his lectures on anatomy and to practice dissection. He also hoped to see Squier in New York and "get a peep at" his "licker." Nott could relax with Squier in a way he had never been able to do with Morton or could do with Leidy. Nott thought he needed two months in Philadelphia because he was afraid that he was a little rusty in anatomy. He had dissected extensively when demonstrator to Dr. Horner thirty years before and had dissected a good deal for the ten years after that, but since coming to Mobile his experience had been limited to his autopsies. He felt that he needed to freshen his knowledge of instructional dissection. He had stated his intention of concentrating his lectures on practical "special and surgical anatomy," for the most part leaving aside histology. Although the medical museum he could use in New Orleans was generally good, Nott thought it had deficiencies, and because the school had not provided him with funds for additional teaching materials he decided to supply the deficiency out of his own pocket. He immediately asked Leidy to find out if he could have a large-scale model of the brain made, which could be used in front of the class. He also arranged for a series of drawings of the bones and the circulatory system. He decided not to acquire more items because of the expense but suggested to Leidy, with a comment such as he usually saved for Squier, that the drawings "will give *brilliancy* to my debut." [11]

The only major medical scare in Mobile in the spring and summer of 1857 was the rumor that a smallpox epidemic was breaking out. In June, Nott, who that year was president of the Mobile Board of Health, allayed

10. Nott to Squier, April 26, 1857, in Squier Papers, LC; Nott to Leidy, May 3, 1857, in Leidy Papers, CPP.
11. Nott to Squier, April 26, July 1, 1857, in Squier Papers, LC; Nott to Leidy, May 3, July 8, 1857, in Leidy Papers, ANSP.

fears with a statement in the Mobile *Register*. There was no smallpox epidemic, he announced, for there had only been six or seven cases in the
past month, but he thought such an occasional panic had its uses, for it
served to remind Mobile citizens "of the necessity of vaccination." It was
a relatively trouble-free early summer, although Nott had enough cases at
this time of the year to make it extremely difficult for him to prepare the
one hundred lectures he wanted to get ready for New Orleans. His intention was to write them on his trip to the North.[12]

As soon as possible, Nott left for the Virginia Springs with his wife
and her sister, Margaret Auzé. Her husband had recently died, and she
and her daughter had moved in with the Notts. She was to stay with
them for the rest of their lives. Nott enjoyed visiting the various springs
and spas frequented by antebellum southerners, and he praised their re-
cuperative powers. The Virginia Springs were always among his favorites,
although before his mother died in the late 1840s he liked to travel to the
up-country springs on the borders of his home state of South Carolina,
and he also visited some of the springs and resorts scattered around Alabama. A particular favorite was Point Clear on Mobile Bay. In the 1850s
the proprietors of the Battle House in Mobile had a summer hotel at
Point Clear, which was open from June to October. The hotel fronted
directly on the sea, there were pine hills behind it and drinking water
from fresh springs, and patrons crowded it in summer to enjoy the sea
breezes and bathe in the salt water. During the summer months it was
connected to Mobile by a daily steamer. Nott allowed his name and a
letter to be used in advertisements for the hotel. He not only said that he
preferred it to any other watering place on the Gulf, he also gave it the
major accolade that it had escaped the yellow fever epidemic of 1853. In
the Civil War it was to be used for wounded Confederate soldiers. Nott
managed to get there, if only for a brief time, in most summers, but he
was happy when he could go to more cosmopolitan spots such as the
Virginia Springs. There he could meet the social elite of the South and a
variety of national politicians and leaders.[13]

After several weeks in the mountains of Virginia, Nott went to Phila-

12. Mobile *Register*, June 10, 1857; Nott to Squier, July 1, 1857, in Squier Papers, LC.
13. Advertisement for Point Clear, 1858, in Parham-Winston Papers, Alabama Department of Archives, Montgomery; see also William P. Browne Papers, *ibid*; *Daily Picayune*
(New Orleans), October 10, 1857; Mobile *Register*, June 17, 1857; James F. Sulzby, *Historic
Alabama Hotels and Resorts* (University, Ala., 1960), 135–44.

delphia and spent September there working on his anatomy course for New Orleans and practicing dissection. He returned to the Gulf early in October after a quick visit to New Haven, where he had been called to treat the sick child of a friend. By the middle of the month he was in New Orleans to get ready for the beginning of the academic year.[14]

New Orleans was not unlike Mobile in character, with an even stronger French and Spanish influence, but it was much larger and more cosmopolitan. It was also much richer culturally with its French opera, theater, and libraries. In the winter months strangers flocked there on business and pleasure; one commented that "all who love society, pleasure and comfort never fail in winter to pass a few weeks in New Orleans." Nott had ample opportunities to make racial observations, for the mixture of nationalities and races on the streets of New Orleans was one of the city's most commented-upon characteristics. The main complaint of visitors was that the city was crowded, dirty, ill-paved, ill-drained, and dreadfully unhealthy in summer. Respectable visitors were also shocked by its frivolity and its open immorality. One who was there over the Christmas season of 1857–1858 remarked that it was "the dirtiest town without any exception that I ever saw."[15]

New Orleans began to fill up with summer exiles and visitors about the time that Nott arrived in October, 1857, and the various winter amusements commenced.[16] Within twenty-four hours of his arrival, Nott sat down to write an article. The editors of the *New Orleans Medical and Surgical Journal* had asked him for a few of his ideas on medical education, and he dashed off his first thoughts before the journal went to press. It was a slight piece but fresher than his last few writings on race. He obviously needed something new to think about, and he temporarily ignored the race question in developing his ideas on southern medical schools.

The basic point of his article was that there had long been a strong belief, which he himself had held, that the southern climate presented a

14. Nott to Leidy, September 28, October 4, 1857, in Leidy Papers, ANSP; *Daily Picayune* (New Orleans), October 15, 1857.

15. Lillian Foster, *Way-Side Glimpses, North and South* (1860; rpr. New York, 1969), 165, 150–52; Barbara L. S. Bodichon, *An American Diary, 1857–8,* ed. Joseph W. Reed (London, 1972), 111, 67–77; [Aleksandr Borisovich Lakier], *A Russian Looks at America: The Journal of Aleksandr Borisovich Lakier in 1857,* trans. and ed. Arnold Schrier and Joyce Story (Chicago, 1979), 232–40; [William Kingsford], *Impressions of the West and South During a Six Weeks' Holiday* (Toronto, 1958), 54.

16. *Daily Picayune* (New Orleans), October 11, November 15, 1857.

barrier to successful medical schools, even though from the earliest times to the sixteenth century medical education had centered successively in the warm countries of Egypt, Arabia, Greece, Rome, and Italy. Nott wrote that he had begun to think that the "sceptre of science" as well as political power had passed to the northern peoples. He had decided, however, that the decline of the ancient schools in the hot climates had stemmed from much more than climatic conditions—the main early centers of medical education had been crushed by the "beastly Turk" and "the despotic Austrian." In a statement that, for Nott, was remarkably lacking in racial bias, he suggested that the genius in these early centers was simply pressed down by despotism.

In more practical terms, Nott had decided that the great problem in developing southern medical schools in the United States was keeping bodies fresh for dissection in the warm climate. This was vital, argued Nott, because anatomy was at the center of the best medical instruction; "other things being equal, the student should always seek that school where anatomy is best taught." His experience in Philadelphia within the past few months had convinced him that it was now possible by means of "antiseptics" to keep bodies fresh in the warmest weather. He was therefore optimistic about the prospects for further development of medical education in New Orleans, for no city in the United States had so great an abundance of bodies for dissection. They could be obtained simply for the price of transportation to the dissection rooms. One suspects that this was because of the large numbers of poor free blacks in New Orleans. Moreover, Nott argued, New Orleans, in its large Charity Hospital, had better facilities for clinical instruction than any other place in the United States, and the University of Louisiana had a medical museum of similar quality.

Even in suggesting that southern students had a reason for studying at southern schools, Nott kept to medical not racial reasons. The advantage of such study for those who were going to practice in malarial districts was that they would work with professors who for twenty or thirty years had treated such diseases. Northern physicians knew much less about them. Similarly, a northern lecturer "would laugh at the idea of a New Orleans physician attempting to teach him anything about pneumonia." Nott concluded that with fine instructors New Orleans could become one of the leading medical schools in the United States, although he still insisted that the medical student should go where he could learn the most anatomy, physiology, and pathology. He finished his article by praising his alma mater, the University of Pennsylvania, as "the mother of medical science in America."[17]

Although Nott's article was refreshingly free from the racial obsessions that had dominated his work in the past few years, it probably ruffled a few feathers in the medical school he had just joined. Without much subtlety, he had suggested that all this medical school needed to become one of the leading schools in the United States was enough good teachers, and he had argued that anatomy, the chair he had just accepted, was the key to medical education.

Having dashed off his quick thoughts to meet the printer's deadline, Nott sat down and wrote a fuller, more pretentious, and less spontaneous piece on the somewhat unlikely topic of the influence of anatomy on the march of civilization. His main theme was that legislatures and the public did not realize the valuable impact that medical colleges and medical education had on civilization in general. All branches of medical education elevated other areas of knowledge, but he proposed to confine his remarks to the vital area of anatomy. All knowledge, argued Nott, was derived from the study and observation of nature; the mind of man "can *invent* nothing, but *falsehood*." Man did not invent, he discovered. Man's mind was a blank until he received perceptions through his five senses.[18]

Anatomy, said Nott, did not simply pertain to medicine, for it was the "*Science of Organization*" considered in all living beings from the simplest zoophyte up to man. Here again, Nott showed the power of his imagination, when he suggested that "even the animalculae, so infinitely small to our senses, may in turn become gigantic, compared to others yet to be discovered with more perfect instruments." Nott went on to discuss the connection between anatomy and philosophy, fine arts, zoology, geology, jurisprudence, political economy, ethnology, natural and revealed religion, and even physics. None of his comments was particularly profound, but they did reveal that Nott had one of the essential characteristics of the

17. Nott, "Medical Schools," *New Orleans Medical and Surgical Journal*, XIV (1857), 353–57. At the request of correspondents, Nott later printed a formula for keeping bodies fresh for dissection: a mixture of two parts of muriatic acid to one of water and as much metallic zinc as could be dissolved, to be injected through the arch of the aorta (*ibid.*, XV [1858], 65). When the Yale scientist Benjamin Silliman visited the South in 1845, he noticed that the subjects on the dissection tables of the Medical College of Charleston were black (Benjamin Silliman Diary, in Silliman Family Papers, Sterling Memorial Library, Yale University, New Haven).

18. Nott, "Influence of Anatomy on the March of Civilization," *New Orleans Medical and Surgical Journal*, XV (1858), 65.

successful teacher—he believed in the all-pervading importance of what he was teaching and thought that the world would be a better place if everyone knew much more about his subject.[19]

In this longer, much less spontaneous piece, Nott also brought in his racial obsessions and gradually moved his theme from anatomy and civilization to race and religion. He pointed out that it was impossible to explain the differences between certain species from the anatomical structure, and he emphasized that fossil evidence showed that a variety of life forms had existed through thousands, tens of thousands, and probably millions of years. Anatomy had traced "the foot-prints of the Almighty" into the most distant past. Ussher's chronology, he said, had now generally been abandoned. Distinct races existed into the distant past, and these were permanent types, differing widely in anatomical structure. The African, the Negro, and the Anglo-Saxon differed as much as the polar and tropical bears, the horse and the ass, the dog and the jackal, the lion and the tiger. This difference was particularly apparent in the size of the brain. Civilization had existed only in the large-headed, fair-skinned races. Education could not enlarge the brain. Anatomical peculiarities were stamped on the Negro by his maker. At the very end of his essay, Nott suddenly remembered what he had started to write about and stated that medical colleges had been the foci around which had clustered the whole circle of the natural sciences, but most of his peroration had been not on that major theme but on the unchangeable differences between races.[20]

The intensive lecture courses that constituted the four-month medical school year began in mid-November, 1857. During the year the faculty also acted as visiting physicians to the Charity Hospital, which treated thousands of cases yearly, and the students accompanied the faculty on their rounds of the hospital. Nott enjoyed his teaching, although to Squier he referred to it "as poking anatomy down boys throats 6 times a week" and said that he was "working like a horse all the time. He said he intended to give a little ethnology when he talked about the brain, but generally he hoped to avoid chapter 10 of Genesis.[21] Nott also managed to find time during the year for writing on both medical and racial matters.

19. *Ibid.*, 66–74.
20. *Ibid.*, 74–77.
21. *Daily Picayune* (New Orleans), October 13, November 15, 1857; Nott to Squier, December 4, 1857, in Squier Papers, LC.

The former writing was much the fresher of the two. There were still definite signs that Nott had exhausted what he had to say on racial matters.
When in January, 1858, he delivered a paper before the New Orleans
Academy of Sciences, he chose his well-worn and familiar topic, the permanency of human types. He emphasized that religious interpretation of
the Scriptures had been changed in the past to accommodate changes in
astronomy and geology and that the same would happen in regard to
multiple creations. The content of the lecture was very familiar to those
who had read Nott's works. Human races, he emphasized, had permanent and unalterable characteristics, and the efforts of philanthropists
would always prove ineffectual; the colored races could not be educated
to a level of equality with whites unless a physiological law was discovered by which the size of their brains could be materially increased.
His remarks that as long as Negroes were Negroes they would be inferior
to whites and in their present position were punctuated by cries of
"Hear! Hear!"[22]

Nott's effort to write on a new racial theme—the history of dogs in its
relation to human races—was weak, and in this case one could well believe his apology that owing to his other duties the article had been written in the "small hours" of the morning to fulfill a promise to the editors
of the *New Orleans Medical and Surgical Journal*. The main problem, however, was less his tiredness than the exhaustion of his vein of invention on
the subject, the lack of recent relevant writings by others, and the lack of
any real research by Nott. His main argument was that the distinct species of dogs had separate origins and had remained unchanged since depicted on the walls of Egyptian tombs; and he advanced the generaliza-
tion that any animal form that had been permanent for five thousand
years had to be regarded as a species. He also took from Agassiz the idea
that the flora and fauna for particular zoological provinces had perhaps
been created en masse and extended it to suggest that it was not necessary
for there to have been a single pair of anything, including individual human races. In a private letter he suggested that he did not think that "a
Race can be perpetuated from a single pair."[23]

22. *Daily Picayune* (New Orleans), January 13, 1858; Bodichon, *An American Diary,* 84.
23. Nott, "A Natural History of Dogs," *New Orleans Medical and Surgical Journal,* XV
(1858), 484–500; Nott to Dr. William S. Forward, February 27, 1858, in William Stump Forward Papers, Trent Collection, Medical School Library, Duke University, Durham, North
Carolina.

In contrast to his writing on racial matters, Nott's medical writing was stimulated by his presence at a medical school, and he wrote and published reports on several cases that had arisen in his Mobile practice. These cases confirm the impression that Nott's surgical practice was heavily involved with cataract and bladder operations and with amputations, all procedures that fell within the province of successful mid-nineteenth-century surgeons.

In a follow-up to his earlier article on cataract operations, Nott stated that he had continued to use a needle to displace or break up the cataract and leave it for absorption rather than using a knife and extracting the cataract through an opening in the cornea. This method, he argued, had continued to be successful. He acknowledged that opthalmic surgeons now regarded the surgeon who used the needle as an "old fogey," but he defended himself by calling attention to an article in an English journal which gave statistics from the Liverpool Eye and Ear Infirmary supporting the use of the needle procedure. Nott's conclusion was that until statistics as satisfactory in regard to extraction were produced, "I must believe that the needle properly used, as a general instrument, is more reliable than the knife, although neither should be exclusively used." In this article Nott was apparently falling into the trap of supporting the method he had grown used to rather than the best practice.[24]

The bladder case which Nott reported on was not the usual lithotomy operation but an odd case concerning a young man who had inserted a long piece of wax through his urethra into his bladder. About four inches of the wax had broken off, and Nott said that the patient was in a bad physical and mental condition when he came to him. Nott operated to remove the wax, and the patient hemorrhaged, collapsed, and died. After a post-mortem Nott was still not sure what had happened and, with his usual willingness to publicize his medical failures, admitted that the case "was altogether an embarrassing one." His conclusion about the patient reflected a typical mid-nineteenth-century medical attitude. From the circumstances of the case, combined with the man's debilitated mental and physical condition, Nott determined that the man was "a broken down onanist," a self-abuser, particularly because the bladder was in a thickened and diseased condition. In this case, because of the peculiar manner in which the man had injured himself, Nott had perhaps more reason for

24. Nott, "Remarks on Operations for Cataract," *New Orleans Medical and Surgical Journal*, XVI (1859), 1–8.

his conclusions than most mid-nineteenth-century physicians who used self-abuse as the reason for a variety of ailments.[25]

The amputation case Nott reported concerned a black male suffering from syphilis who was brought to Nott only when the disease was far advanced. The doctor who was treating him sent him to Nott when the toes on one of his feet became gangrenous. Nott put him on a "generous diet, porter, etc." for two weeks and then amputated the left leg below the knee. He was surprised to find that no arterial blood came out of the stump when he relaxed the tourniquet. On examining both legs, he found that there was no pulsation in either leg below Poupart's ligament. In a short time the remaining foot appeared to be becoming gangrenous, and Nott amputated part of that leg by cutting through the line of demarcation between sound and gangrenous parts; he thought the patient could not stand a regular amputation through live tissue. In any event, the patient died two days after the second amputation.

Nott conducted a post-mortem and discovered fibrinous material blocking the two external iliacs. This condition, he argued, had resulted in the mortification of the two lower extremities. Nott examined the heart and found signs of endocarditis. In raising the question of what caused the coagula and subsequent mortification, Nott said that he was entering a wide and debatable field. Some contended that a coagulum formed "*in the heart*," was then detached, and finally settled in an artery too small for its passage; others suggested that the coagula might be formed in the arteries themselves because of a diseased state of the blood or local effects of diseases producing endocarditis. Nott had no answers—he simply said that he was recording a few facts, "which may be used by those who have made pathology more a speciality than I have."[26]

Nott's teaching and his work at the Charity Hospital undoubtedly stimulated his interest in medical research and writing, but he was not satisfied in New Orleans. He was in good humor, with an exuberance he had not had for several years, but he missed Mobile. As early as December, 1857, only three weeks after he had begun lecturing and less than two months after he had arrived in New Orleans, he told Squier that though life in New Orleans was in most respects agreeable and would pay

25. Nott, "Remarkable Case of Vesical Calculus formed on Wax," *ibid.*, XV (1858), 183–86.

26. Nott, "Mortification of both Lower Extremities, caused by Coagula in the Common Iliacs—Amputation of both Limbs. Post-mortem examination," *ibid.*, XV (1858), 577–80.

well, he had "no home feeling" in the town. He said that he had "broken up old associations in Mobile which had been long & firmly entwined around me." It was more probable, he said, that he would return to Mobile in the spring. There was no suggestion of depression in this letter to Squier. He joshed Squier with great glee about his impending marriage—"the most extraordinary occurrence since the fall of the friend of Moses." If "she is a decent respectable woman," wrote Nott, "please give her my kind sympathies." He hoped she would have a better time than she had any hope to expect, but men "sometimes reform on the gallows." In fact, Squier's marriage was to end in a sensational divorce in the year of Nott's death.[27]

Nott did not take long to make up his mind. On February 2, 1858, he announced publicly that he had resigned his chair of anatomy in the University of Louisiana and would return to Mobile in late March to resume his practice. Nott said that his friends and relations in Mobile had helped sway him in this course. The editor of the *New Orleans Medical and Surgical Journal* suggested that perhaps some sad as well as pleasant memories tied him to Mobile—"gravestones as well as hearth-stones."[28] Even in an age in which the death of children was commonplace, Nott's contemporaries recognized that he and his wife had suffered an overwhelming affliction in the death of four children in less than a week.

Nott's brief stay in New Orleans had revealed to him the extent to which he liked his life in Mobile, but it had also reminded him of how much satisfaction he found in teaching. Since the 1840s there had been serious talk of establishing a medical college in Alabama, and in December, 1855, a committee of the Alabama Senate had reported favorably on a bill to establish such a college in Mobile. The state medical association had approved this location, and the Mobile Medical Society, very much inspired by Nott's efforts, had offered to raise $40,000 for a museum and teaching equipment if the state legislature would provide $50,000 for buildings. Nott had long urged the establishment of a medical college in Mobile and in late November, 1855, had spent a week in the state capital in an effort to win legislative support. His arguments had obviously carried great weight with the senate committee, for many of his ideas were woven through its report. A medical college, said the com-

27. Nott to Squier, December 4, 1857, in Squier Papers, LC.
28. *New Orleans Medical and Surgical Journal*, XV (1858), 160.

mitee, would be a center for the study of all the natural sciences, and southern students would be better served by southern professors. Financially, the state would be helped because some $200,000 a year that was now carried out of the state by medical students would stay at home. Also, the creation of a medical college in Mobile would stimulate the development of bookstores, druggists, and instrument makers and thus enable the city better to serve the needs of Alabama's twelve hundred physicians.[29]

Nott's efforts and the favorable senate committee report helped in passing the bill to incorporate the college over the governor's veto, but this was a Pyrrhic victory because in the following month a bill making an appropriation for the medical college was killed in the senate. The governor had convinced the legislature that the state could not afford to spend the money. Nott continued his efforts in behalf of the college and, to rally more support, took a larger role in the Alabama Medical Association, a body that had been organized in 1846. Nott was first vice-president in 1856 and president in 1857 and again in 1859, a year in which all the officers of the association were from Mobile. In the late 1850s Dr. William Anderson of Mobile served as treasurer. Anderson, a Virginian, who had earned his first medical degree at his state university, had settled in Alabama and traveled extensively to further his medical education—to Baltimore, Philadelphia, and New York, and, in the late 1840s, to Europe for four years of study. He was associated with Nott in pressing for a medical college and became a firm friend and colleague.[30]

Nott used his influential Mobile friends, the Alabama Medical Association, and the Mobile Medical Society to lobby for the new college. At its annual meeting in February, 1857, the Alabama Medical Association met in Mobile and agreed to continue to urge the legislature to found a medical college in the city. In addition to a committee that was already working on the subject, two members from each county were appointed

29. *Alabama Senate Journal, 1855–56* (Montgomery, 1856), 80–84; Mobile *Register,* November 27, 1855; Jack D. Holmes, *A History of the University of Alabama Hospitals* (Birmingham, 1974), 57; Minnie C. Boyd, *Alabama in the Fifties: A Social Study* (1931; rpr. New York, 1966), 185; Emmet B. Carmichael, "Josiah Clark Nott," *Bulletin of the History of Medicine,* XXII (1948), 252.

30. *Alabama Senate Journal, 1855–1856,* 256–57; Mobile *Register,* January 27, February 2, March 8, 1856; *Daily Picayune* (New Orleans), March 7, 1857; Alabama Medical Association Records, Alabama Department of Archives and History, Montgomery; obituary of William H. Anderson, in Emma H. Mettee Scrapbook, Alabama Department of Archives and History, Montgomery.

to use their influence with the respective members of the state legislature. It was at this meeting that Nott became the president of the association for the following year (part of which he spent in New Orleans).[31]

On his return from New Orleans in the spring of 1858, Nott flung himself into the effort to establish a medical school in Mobile and secured the help of some of his medical friends. In later years everyone connected with the school and medical education in the state agreed that it was Nott's energy, vision, and popularity, and sheer persuasiveness that brought the school into existence. When the state still balked at providing the necessary money, Nott persuaded his rich merchant friends in Mobile to subscribe $25,000 to begin the college without state aid. The faculty, as in other American medical schools, would be paid by the number of students enrolled in their classes, but the money was needed to furnish the medical museum, to obtain the teaching equipment that Nott thought essential, and to rent a building. It was decided that the college would open in November, 1859, without state help, and that in the summer of 1859 Nott, who had been planning a trip to Europe, would use his visit to buy medical models and apparatus for what he said would be the best medical teaching museum in the United States. Never had his fellow citizens better shown their faith in Nott's judgment and integrity.[32]

Nott left Mobile in May for Philadelphia, accompanied by his family. He was in Liverpool by mid-June and immediately went to London. He was in Europe until the beginning of October.[33] During that time he traveled extensively. His main object was to visit all the centers where he might obtain the variety of medical models and other teaching aids that he required, but he also visited important hospitals, talked to doctors about the latest surgical techniques, and saw at least as many European sights as the typical tourist. He also wrote long letters (of practically article length) to Alabama newspapers to tell the citizens of Mobile and the state how he was spending the money that had been given to him. As

31. Typescript copy of account from *Daily Messenger* (Montgomery), March 10, 1857, in Alabama Medical Association Records.

32. Carmichael, "Josiah Clark Nott," 252–53; Howard L. Holley, *The History of Medicine in Alabama* (Birmingham, 1982), 81–85; Nott to Joseph Leidy, March 17, April 12, May 3, 12, 1859, in Leidy Papers, ANSP.

33. See Nott, "Medical Museums and Schools, with remarks on the Radical cure of Hernia," *New Orleans Medical and Surgical Journal*, XVII (1860), 74–82. In this letter, dated London, September 27, 1859, Nott gives an account of his European visit. A variety of other details appear in the letters cited below.

usual with Nott, it is difficult to imagine how he managed to do all he did do in the next three and a half months. Both the public and private aspects of his trip were a complete success.

Nott's medical purchases exceeded his best hopes; he threw himself into the task with unquenchable enthusiasm. On his first stop, in London, he spent most of his time arranging for the purchase of wax models of skin diseases made by Joseph Town at Guy's Hospital. This collection was extensive, and the maker also supplied a series of models of the brain, some models of pathological specimens, and a few others of normal anatomy. Nott paid $4,500 for about one hundred models, mostly of skin diseases. From London he traveled to Edinburgh but finding nothing that he wanted went on to Paris. Paris, Nott considered, had the best and cheapest range of articles of all types, with the exception of wax models. One wonders if Nott played down the Paris wax models because he had already bought a great many in London.[34]

In Paris Nott bought a wide range of articles, including a series of skeletons, in every stage of development from the fetus to old age, a collection of diseased bones, and a collection illustrative of comparative anatomy, including animals. He also bought preserved preparations of parts of the human body (the main ones being a set illustrating the vascular and lymphatic systems); a series of models in *papier mâché* of normal, human, comparative, and pathological anatomy; a series of larger-than-life-size models made of a composition material, demonstrating human and comparative anatomy; and a set of materials to illustrate a course on materia medica. This last, in attractive bottles also suitable for a museum display, cost $800. In Paris alone Nott apparently spent more than $5,000. By mid-July he was bubbling with excitement at what he was accomplishing. "I shall have such a Museum in Mobile next winter," he wrote, "as never has been brought from Europe before." While in Paris, Nott also found time each morning to visit the clinics of some of the great French surgeons, including Alfred A. L. M. Velpeau and Jean Civiale. Nott's Paris purchases and visits were made easier because his physician son James, who was studying there, had obtained as much information as possible before Nott arrived.[35]

From Paris, after a pleasure trip to Switzerland, Nott went to Munich.

34. *Ibid.*, 75–76.
35. *Ibid.*, 76–79; letter from Dr. Nott, Paris, July 15, 1859, in Dallas (Ala.) *Gazette*, August 19, 1859.

There, for about $1,000, he secured a series of ten models of normal anatomy. These were made of a composition of wax, cotton, and lime, which made them extremely solid. Nott was delighted with them. He considered them "one of the most valuable parts of my collection." By the time Nott went through Switzerland and Munich, he was becoming caught up in the delights of sightseeing, but he pressed on in his search for medical materials. Vienna and the main German cities were a disappointment; there was nothing he wanted for sale. In Italy he had great hopes for Florence, which was famous for its wax models, but he decided on close examination that the models available contained far too many errors. He advised others going to Italy that Bologna would probably be better for filling an order than Florence.[36]

Nott believed that his European shopping expedition had resulted in the nucleus for one of the best teaching museums in the world. Along with his European purchases, he had also brought a good many models from a young man in Philadelphia who had done much work for Dr. Leidy. In general, Nott's conclusion was that the best models and teaching apparatus could be obtained in Europe. The one exception that he mentioned was surgical instruments; if he had his work to do over again, he said, he would purchase the college's instruments in the United States. Surgical instruments made in America were as good as those made in Europe, there was no material difference in price, and makers in New York and Philadelphia were more punctual and reliable than those in Paris.[37]

Nott's delight in supplying his medical college and in visiting the medical centers of Europe was matched by his pleasure in simple sightseeing. On his first trip to Europe in the 1830s, his reactions had tended to be unemotional and utilitarian, simply listing the important public buildings to be seen in each city. On this visit his emotions were far more involved. What started out as a practical medical visit took on some of the aspects of a sentimental journey.

Nott was all business through England, Scotland, and Paris. In Paris in the middle of July he could still say that he had seen little outside of the medical departments except the exteriors of palaces, churches, gardens, and the rest. His wife, Sarah, and her sister had been "delivered" to his

36. Nott, "Medical Museums," 79–81; letter from Dr. Nott, Munich, July 30, 1859, in Mobile *Register,* September 2, 1859.
37. Nott, "Medical Museums," 79; Nott to Leidy, April 12, May 12, October 26, 1859, in Leidy Papers, ANSP; Nott, letter of July 15, 1859, in Dallas (Ala.) *Gazette,* August 19, 1859.

sons for sightseeing. For Sarah, who had lived through the horrors of yellow fever in Mobile and had not seen her two eldest surviving sons for nearly a year, Paris was a delight. She was to buy so many pictures in Europe that Nott later tried to get out of taking one that he had promised to buy from Leidy because he no longer had room on his walls.[38]

On leaving Paris, Nott had decided that he would take his family to Switzerland and let them amuse themselves there and on the Rhine while he dared the summer heat of Florence. His plans changed when he reached Switzerland because he was overwhelmed by the scenery. From the time he was in Switzerland, Nott became more a tourist than the founder of the Medical College of Alabama. He was in Switzerland for less than two weeks, but it put him in a quite different mood. With his family he went from Paris to Geneva, back into France to visit Mont Blanc, then on a quick tour of the Swiss lakes, visiting Vevey, Lausanne, Yverdon, Bern, Thun, and Interlaken before going on to Zurich and Munich. At Geneva, Nott wrote, "I struck the point of scenery which had haunted my imagination from childhood on through life." They had reached Geneva on a cloudy day after a hot fifteen-hour journey from Paris. When Nott awoke at 5:00 the next morning he looked out of his window and saw the Alps against a cloudless sky. "The sight," he wrote, "brought up such a crowd of mingled emotions that I cannot trust myself to speak of them without the fear of making my gray hairs ridiculous."[39]

For the rest of his journey, Nott was to let down his intense professional and public guard in a way that was rare for him. When he went with his family to Chamonix at the foot of Mont Blanc, they rode mules up to overlook the Mer de Glace and other spots previously known to Nott only through his reading. Writing home to America, he said that he would have to refer his readers to Byron or other poets for a description—"I had never imagined anything like it, and have no language to express what I felt." Nott was overwhelmed by the Alps, and thoughts of dashing off to Florence were banished. He stayed with his family as they traveled through Switzerland and then went with them to Munich, deciding to see Munich and Vienna and then to go to Berlin and other German cities before making his Italian trip.[40]

38. Nott, letter of July 15, 1859, in Dallas (Ala.) *Gazette,* August 19, 1859; Nott to Leidy, November 23, 1859, in Leidy Papers, ANSP.

39. Nott, letter of July 15, 1859, in Dallas (Ala.) *Gazette,* August 19, 1859; Nott, letter of July 30, 1859, in Mobile *Register,* September 2, 1859.

40. Nott, letter of July 30, 1859, in Mobile *Register,* September 2, 1859.

In Munich he completed his purchases and set about sightseeing with his usual vigor, tempered by a new emotion. In typical Nott fashion he took his wife and Mrs. Auzé to four churches and an art gallery but then went to a large Catholic cemetery with elaborate tombs and frescoes. He said he saw "a young virgin" carried off to her final resting place on a bier of green velvet strewn with wreaths of white flowers. He seemed surprised that though he knew no one he "dropped a tear." More typical of Nott was a visit to the king's stables, where he saw more than two hundred horses of which, he said, he would have been glad to have had six of the meanest. Nott thoroughly enjoyed Munich. Switzerland had relaxed him, and his emotions had come nearer to the surface, temporarily piercing the cynical front he usualy put on before the world. In Munich he even bought a porcelain Madonna.[41]

After a quick swing through Vienna and the principal cities of Germany, the Notts returned to Paris, traveled to Marseilles, and took ship to Genoa. Even in an age of indefatigable travelers, Nott's itinery was formidable. From Genoa the party went through Livorno, Pisa, Florence, Bologna, Parma, Venice, Padua, Verona, Milan, and Turin, before crossing Mt. Cenis to return to Paris. In Italy Nott was most interested in the chances for progress and revolution. As in Europe as a young man, he expressed his hatred of tyranny. The best hope of Italy, he thought, was Victor Emmanuel; in his province of Sardinia there were signs of progress everywhere. But in the old states of Tuscany, Modena, and Parma, teeming with art and antiquities, there was a struggle to prevent decay; and in Venetia, ruled by Austria, one saw "at every step the withering influence of Austrian despotism." Venice was now "a mass of foul and rotten ruins." Even the gondolas were painted black by order of the government, and they looked like hearses.[42]

His travels in Italy, wrote Nott, had blighted his hopes of Italian independence and regeneration. The Austrians were too powerful, the Italians crushed by misrule. "The power of the Church," he wrote, "is a stumbling block which makes all patriots and reformists shudder." Religion and politics should each be restrained within their proper sphere. When Nott was in Europe, writing of both northern and southern countries, he did not slip into the racial arguments that dominated so much of his

41. Nott, letter of July 30, 1859, in Mobile *Register,* September 2, 1859.
42. Nott to John Forsyth (editor of the Mobile *Register*), September 8, 1859, in the *Independent* (Gainesville, Ala.), October 8, 1859.

American writing. He did not, for example, suggest that the Italians were under the control of the Austrians because they were an inferior, less-white people. Yet when he wrote of white and black in America, he often supported his arguments by maintaining that the southern Europeans had more affinity with the blacks. The position of the blacks in America and the continuation of slavery in the South were at the heart of his racial theories, and in America he used every possible argument he could think of to justify the continuation of the existing southern system. In Europe he could abandon this obsession.

Nott was full of sympathy for the Italians in their struggle with the "despotic" Austrians, but even in Italy the sentimental streak that had been touched in Switzerland and revived in Munich emerged once more. In Verona this determinedly cynical scientist went to the supposed tomb of Juliet, and he believed all he saw. In a letter he described his visit to Juliet's grave in an old convent that had become a stable. A poor Italian family who lived in an adjoining shanty unlocked the stable and showed the visitors around. The remains of Juliet lay under a dilapidated sarcophagus across from a donkey. On the wall were frescoes of the Virgin and the cruxifixion. Nott thought the scene pointed a moral, but it was not the moral but buried emotion that surged to the surface as Nott reflected on his own youth and dreams. "There still linger with me," he wrote, "a few 'green spots on memory's waste,' to which my mind wanders from time to time in solitary moments with much pleasure; death alone can crush out human nature; it *will* rise up and have its say in spite of philosophy and even religion. No man who has anything noble, generous and good in his composition can look up at the little window not far off, from which Juliet told her tale of love, and then gaze upon the tomb as I have seen it, without experiencing emotions which even Shakespeare himself could not portray."[43] Nott's extensive reading in English literature obviously helped give him an emotional release that was not always present in his life, and his visits to places he had read and dreamed about brought to the surface the streak of romantic melancholia that had been fed by the tragic deaths of many near to him.

Nott was back in Mobile by late October, 1859, with only a few weeks to complete the arrangements for the opening of the new medical school. He had arranged for a faculty of seven. He was to be the professor of

43. *Ibid.*

surgery, and his friend Dr. William H. Anderson was to be dean and professor of physiology. There were chairs of the theory and practice of medicine; materia medica, therapeutics, and clinical medicine; chemistry; obstetrics and the diseases of women and children; and anatomy. There were also two demonstrators of anatomy, both of them qualified M.D.'s [44]

The college was an immediate success, even though it opened in rented quarters. It enrolled more than a hundred students in the first session of 1859–1860. Its prospects improved dramatically during the first winter, for the state legislature at last provided money—$50,000 for a building. Mobile money had already been used to buy a plot of land, and Nott and two trustees had traveled to Montgomery to state the school's needs to the governor and legislature. Their lobbying was helped by the increasing tension between North and South that was causing southern medical students to leave northern schools. The college became a department of the University of Alabama, but it was given its own board of trustees composed of Mobile businessmen. Nott had an extremely busy winter, combining daily lectures with the demands of his practice, and in February his difficulties increased when he contracted an eye infection that produced severe inflammation. He managed to complete his lectures in March, but for four months beginning in April he was unable to read, a severe blow to him. [45]

In March, 1860, Nott was still well enough to give the first commencement address of the Medical College of Alabama. There were fifteen graduates, for some of the students had already completed work elsewhere. This first commencement was well attended by Mobile's citizens, and Nott took the opportunity to appeal for more financial support. Now that he had his museum, he wanted a library. To the citizens he stressed Mobile's lack of a public library and pointed out that to carry out his own work in natural history he had been forced to spend several thousand dollars to import books. The college could have a sound scientific library if $20,000 or $30,000 of the "superfluous wealth" of the community were given to the college. His justification was one he had used before. Medical colleges were not simply places where young men were

44. Nott to Leidy, October 26, 1859, in Leidy Papers, ANSP; Willis G. Clark, *History of Education in Alabama, 1702–1889* (Washington, 1889), 148–49; Norwood, *Medical Education,* 376.

45. Clark, *History of Education in Alabama,* 147–49; Nott to Leidy, November 23, 1859, in Leidy Papers, ANSP; Mobile *Register,* December 9, 1859.

taught how to treat their fellow creatures, they were "the very fountains from which have flowed the whole chain of natural sciences." Aristotle himself was a member of a hereditary family of physicians. He told the citizens of the rapid progress that had been made and of some of his future plans for the school. His appeal, combined with the efforts of the trustees, was successful—the state grant was matched by another $50,000 from private subscriptions.[46]

Turning from the citizens to the students, Nott told them, "we do not profess to have made you accomplished physicians, we have taught you *how to learn,*" and then proceeded to paint a vivid image of a better society along the Gulf of Mexico, "the finest country on the face of the globe." Though the resources of the region were limitless, it was not money but knowledge and virtue that made a nation great. Nott said that he would like Mobile to have a law school and a university. Ancient Memphis, Thebes, Athens, and Rome were admired not for their wealth but for the wisdom of their philosophers and the excellence of their poets, historians, orators, and artists—for their progress "in all those things which give evidence of intellectual development, and which ennoble man and elevate him above the baser tendencies of his nature." This enhancement of existence, he said, was the channel in which his patriotism and ambition ran—he wanted to found institutions and libraries. Nott did not speak specifically of a separate southern nation, but he clearly seemed to be thinking of one.

Finally, he told the students how to conduct themselves as physicians. No profession, he said, demanded a higher moral tone; a physician "sees and hears much that should go down with him in silence to the grave." Above all, he told the students, their mission was one "of charity." They should see those without money as well as those with it, and they should help the poor and helpless: "I can honestly say, gentlemen, and it is the proudest boast of my life, that for the first ten years of my professional career I never refused to see a human being, night or day, far or near, or in any weather, because he could not pay me." This was a proud day for Nott, and his address reflected the best aspects of his character.

Both while he was planning his medical school and later, after the dis-

46. Mobile *Register,* March 8, 1860 (typescript in Lister Hill Library, University of Alabama Medical School, Birmingham); Nott to Leidy, September 23, 1860, in Leidy Papers, CPP. The material in the next two paragraphs is taken from the article in the Mobile *Register.*

asters of the war, Nott revealed how much he had thought about the problem of better medical education in America. He did not agree that America was establishing medical schools too fast and was creating too many. The existing system of medical education was imperfect, he believed, and for the present competition could only improve it. "You cannot have a good hotel, livery stable, or even bar-room, without competition, and the professors of our schools are always made to do their work more faithfully by neighboring opposition." Ultimately, however, Nott hoped for much more. Existing medical schools, he thought, were too much the product of private speculation and interest. Great improvements in medical education would come only when state governments supported it, treated it like other areas of education, and made it as near free as possible. The pay of professors should not depend on the size of classes, they should be paid out of public funds, and they should be required to devote more time to instruction. Courses should be seven not four months in length and should last three or four years not two. They should begin with elementary branches such as anatomy and chemistry, and there should be frequent examinations to keep the students at work. His hope, if the South had continued to prosper, was to gain a large enough endowment for the college in Mobile so the professors could be independent of revenue from classes. He thought medical education in America, as in Europe, should be conducted on the same general principles as other areas of education and not made an excuse for "quackery."[47] Nott was always at his best when dealing with his own specialty—medicine. He was a first-class physician, who combined skill as a practitioner with marked organizational ability and the personality to inspire respect and enthusiasm.

47. Mobile *Register,* March 8, 1860; also letter of Nott, August 14, 1870, typescript in Lister Hill Library; letter of Nott, September 27, 1859, in *New Orleans Medical and Surgical Journal,* XVII (1860), 82.

Chapter 11
SECESSION

In the spring and summer of 1860 the South simmered and seethed as the sectional conflict reached a crisis. Nott was completely committed to the southern cause, but he played no overt role in the political events that eventually led to secession. He did of course continue to be an ardent defender of the southern position, and in the spring of 1860 he joined with a group of his fellow prominent Mobilians in urging the selection of prosouthern delegates to the state Democratic convention, which was to appoint delegates to the national Democratic convention in Baltimore. The announcement said that it was of vital importance to nominate a president and a vice-president who might be able to save the government from the hands of those who would violate the South's constitutional rights and who could be the means of securing the perpetuity of the Constitution and the Union.[1] All now knew that the idea of a southern nation was no longer a distant dream, and some thought that secession was inevitable.

Nott's main personal concern in the early summer of 1860 was the acute irritation of his eyes. For about six weeks in May and early June he spent much of his time in a darkened room with his eyes bandaged against the light. He then left for a rest at the Virginia Springs. But Nott never really rested. His mind was still occupied with the development of his medical college, and even while ill he was busily dictating a syllabus for his course of lectures on surgery. The syllabus was to be substantial, and he arranged for its publication with Lippincott in Philadelphia. He wished it to be a student aid that could be used at the Medical College of Alabama and

1. Mobile *Register*, May 25, 1860.

elsewhere. He admitted in his preface to the work that he had been so restricted in his reading and writing that he had leaned heavily on Professor Samuel D. Gross's well-known *System of Surgery,* a basic textbook much used in the mid-nineteenth century. Even some of Gross's language had been included because Nott had used a scribe unfamiliar with medical terms to take his dictation. The syllabus, which exceeded 180 pages in length, summarized a variety of medical conditions and their treatments but was incomplete at the time of its publication. Nott indicated his intention to complete it, but he never did so. He was unable to examine the manuscript and printed sheets as they went through the press, but this did not particularly disturb him. His object, he said, had not been to write an original book but simply "to make something which would be useful to the class."[2]

As Nott recovered his sight in August, 1860, he felt well enough to skim through Charles Darwin's *Origin of Species,* which had been published in the previous year. Darwin stated categorically that "species are not immutable." Species had changed and were still in the process of slowly changing by the preservation and accumulation of favorable variations. Not only were species always gradually changing, they all had a common origin. "Probably all the organic beings which have ever lived on this earth," wrote Darwin, "have descended from some one primordial form, into which life was first breathed." The only consolation for Nott was that Darwin made it clear that he believed that this process of gradual change had taken place over a hundred million years through "an almost infinite number of generations." Darwin said nothing to support Nott's view that blacks and whites had separate origins, but at least he ignored accepted biblical chronology and pushed human origins back into an even more distant past. Nott had no idea on first glancing through Darwin's book that it was to bring about a revolution in natural history. He told Squier that "the man is Clearly crazy, but it is a capital dig into the parsons— it stirs up Creation." Much good, he commented, came out of such discussions.[3]

At a later date Nott was to take a measured view of Darwin's work and

2. Nott, *Syllabus of a Course of Lectures Delivered in the Alabama Medical College, Mobile* (Philadelphia, 1861); Nott to Leidy, August 3, 1860, in Leidy Papers, CPP; Nott to Squier, August 22, 1860, in Squier Papers, LC.

3. Charles Darwin, *On the Origin of Species,* intro. Ernst Mayr (1859; rpr. Cambridge, Mass., 1964), 6, 480, 481, 484; Nott to Squier, August 22, 1860, in Squier Papers, LC.

accept it, although he was more in sympathy with the writings of Alfred Russell Wallace, who, independently of Darwin, had in the 1850s developed his own theory of the crucial importance of natural selection.[4] Darwin's theories of evolution were in reality alien to Nott's modes of thought. Although Nott had maddened the clergy by saying that the Bible was wrong scientifically and chronologically, he had always imagined some time in the far distant past when a variety of peoples of different races had come into being by acts of creation. What he had disagreed with was the idea that God had created just one couple less than six thousand years before.

The rapid deterioration of relations between North and South in the late summer and fall of 1860 at first did not deflect Nott from his absorption with his new medical college—"my own Creation & hobby." The prospects of the college now seemed excellent, particularly because at the opening of the second school year it was to move into the new building paid for by the state.[5] Although a later generation thought the building was cramped and inconvenient, Nott and the citizens of Mobile were proud of its large auditorium, lecture rooms, laboratories, and medical museum. Nott's main difficulty as he prepared for a new academic year was an embarrassing staffing problem, which was exacerbated by the growing sectional tension between the North and South.

In these last years preceding the war, Nott was on excellent terms with Dr. Joseph Leidy of Philadelphia, but this relationship experienced some strains as a result of Nott's problems with the faculty of the college. On the recommendation of Leidy and others, Nott, in the previous year, had arranged for the appointment of a Mr. Taylor to the chair of chemistry. Taylor had not worked out and had been let go to be replaced by John W. Mallet of the University of Alabama in Tuscaloosa. Taylor had apparently suggested to Leidy that his removal had been the result of antinorthern feeling. In a letter to Leidy, Nott denied this interpretation, commenting that though he had not wanted to make it public, Taylor "is utterly incompetent to discharge the duties which devolved upon him—he does not know Chemistry, was unable to arrange a course, failed signally in his

4. Mayr, intro., Darwin, *Origin of Species*, xiv; William M. Polk, "Josiah C. Nott," *American Journal of Obstetrics*, LXVI (1913), 957–58.
5. Nott to Squier, August 22, 1860, in Squier Papers, LC. In his commencement address in March, 1860, Nott had indicated that the medical college building was in the course of rapid construction (Mobile *Register*, March 8, 1860).

experiments, & is totally wanting in lecturing talent." There had also been numerous complaints from students. Because the school was succeeding so rapidly, it was essential to have an efficient professor of chemistry. The sectional argument, said Nott, was false—he had heard it only on arriving in Philadelphia.[6]

Leidy was disturbed, particularly because a problem had arisen with another proposed staff addition from Philadelphia. Nott had persuaded the man who made medical models for Leidy, and from whom Nott had bought, to come to Mobile to give a class on the use of microscopes, to deliver a course of lectures on minor surgery, and to start an orthopedic department. When the new man also talked of the possibilities of general practice, Nott expressed doubts whether he had "the tact necessary to get along with the mass of mankind, as a general practitioner." At this, the new appointee took offense and decided to go to New Orleans rather than Mobile, proving to Nott that his assessment had been correct. The fate of the two northern appointees disturbed Leidy, and he was reluctant to accept Nott's explanations. Nott took the trouble to provide a more careful explanation, but when Leidy still showed a reluctance to agree that Nott had acted for the best, Nott lashed back. He told Leidy that he had acted from a sense of duty to the college and to the state of Alabama: "If you look at Your own School You must see and feel the incubus that weighs You down—You ought to have the largest Class in the U.S. & You must make great changes before you can attain the success I most heartily wish You."[7] As a physician Nott was extremely hardworking and conscientious. He had little patience with incompetents or fools and certainly put the cause of medicine and education before individual sensibilities. There are no indications that Nott had prejudice against northern scientists and physicians; just the contrary. The affair had strained his relations with Leidy but was not to have the effect it might have had because the growing sectional crisis was soon to sever all Nott's contacts with the North.

Through the summer Nott was unwilling to take seriously the likelihood of war if Lincoln were elected. He still hoped against hope that all would end well. In August he told Squier that his syllabus would be out "about the time of 'Lincoln's election,' after which My mind & body will

6. Nott to Leidy, September 23, 1860, in Leidy Papers, CPP.
7. Nott to Leidy, August 3, September 30, 1860, *ibid.*; Nott commencement address, March, 1860, Mobile *Register,* March 8, 1860.

be somewhat at ease—By the by I am a Lincoln man—I want this thing to Come to a fight—kill all the damd fools north and south, & take a fresh start."[8] He did not mean it. Nott had long suggested that the South would probably have to secede, but he always hoped that somehow, against all rational expectations, the North would leave the South alone.

Writing to Squier at the end of November, after Lincoln's election, Nott began and ended the letter in his usual joking manner—commenting at the beginning that he was replying immediately to Squier's "villainous Black Republican Communication"—but in between he wrote seriously about his own and the South's confidence and determination. Squier had downplayed the seriousness of the South's threats, and Nott corrected him. "I see no reason to doubt," he wrote, "that all the States, at least from South Carolina to Texas will *go out*." Once this had happened, he thought the Union could not be mended. With commercial relations between the two sections disrupted, both North and South would see hard times. "It is no childs play, & I tell You there is a spirit afloat that will meet any emergency—the South like the North has its mouthy, blustering fools, but better fighting stuff never walked the earth than we have." Nott always took pride in a high-spirited, dashing southern youth. In 1858 he had tried to intervene with James Hammond on behalf of his father-in-law's ward, who had been cashiered from the army for slapping a superior officer in the face. He commented that he understood the provocation was such "as could not be borne by a high spirited Southern Boy."[9] Nott thought the South was undergoing provocation that could and should not be borne.

Nott told Squier in November, 1861, that he was now what he had never been before, "a rank secessionist—the irrepressible conflict has gone to a point (& increasing all the time) which renders it absolutely necessary that we should split & then begin to treat as Separate powers." Though there would be difficulties, he thought, the South could bid defiance to the world by withholding her cotton. Nott said that he would volunteer for the fight when the time came, and he meant it, but he lightened the seriousness of his beliefs by saying that "I hope I may have the good luck to confine my fighting to some one about Your size." In Alabama, he asserted, there was no division to speak of, "& she goes out certainly."[10]

8. Nott to Squier, August 22, 1860, in Squier Papers, LC.
9. Nott to Squier, November 28, 1860; *ibid.*; Nott to Hammond, November 17, 1858, in Hammond Papers, LC.
10. Nott to Squier, November 28, 1860, in Squier Papers, LC.

Nott was right about the determination of many southern states to secede, but like so many other southerners he misjudged the value of economic sanctions. He also had the feeling that pervaded so many in the
South that young southern manhood had the fighting qualities to defeat
any enemy, however strong. In January, 1861, Alabama followed South
Carolina, Mississippi, and Florida out of the Union. Georgia, Louisiana,
and Texas were to follow in the coming weeks, and Nott's prophecy was
proved true. In February delegates from these states met upriver from
Mobile in Montgomery, Alabama, to form a new government—the Confederate States of America.

In Alabama not all looked upon these events with joy. Nott's friend
Judge John Campbell of the United States Supreme Court reluctantly resigned and served in minor posts in the Confederacy. Regular army and
navy officers had painful decisions to make, and many gave up their hard-
earned commissions and came home. In Montgomery, in January, when
Alabama seceded, politician William Russell Smith wrote to his wife that
"I am trembling under the scenes around me—I mean the frantic character of the rejoicing." The same politician said a few months later that
though southerners thought the "War is to be child's play," he feared the
worst. "I have no fears for the courage of the South," he wrote, "but I am
oppressed with the idea of our poor preparations."[11] Nott was too caught
up in his dreams of a southern nation and his pride in southern manhood
to take a calm, rational look at the dangers that faced the South. He believed with all his heart that the South was right in fighting to resist
northern efforts to dictate internal southern policies. He thought that
the freeing of the slaves would be disastrous to Alabama and the South
and that southern whites were fighting to prevent a tyrannical, unconstitutional use of federal power.

Yet though Nott's belief in secession had originally been inspired by his
fears that the North would not leave existing white-black relations in the
South intact, he justified the South as acting for freedom and self-
government, not racial necessity. Although he had frequently suggested
that slavery was a moral evil but a practical necessity, he refused to admit
that the South was fighting to preserve slavery. Nott believed the fight
was over the South's constitutional right to have the internal institutions
it desired. This conviction that the South was engaged in a just cause was

11. See Henry G. Connor, *John Archibald Campbell* (New York, 1920); William R. Smith
to his wife, January 11, May 7, 1861, in Easby Smith Family Papers, LC.

common throughout Alabama and the South, and it was to persist through the trials of war. Northerner James Williams, who settled in Alabama before the war and served in the Confederate army, wrote to his father in the North in August, 1862, "My whole soul is in the sucess [sic] of our struggle for independence, which *sooner or later we will win*—If I should not survive the war to see you again be assured that I feel my life has been devoted to a good cause."[12]

In May, 1861, Nott gave Squier his last prewar explanation of southern actions. In April the South Carolinians had fired on Fort Sumter, Lincoln had called on the northern states to furnish seventy-five thousand militia, and several states of the upper South, including vital Virginia, prepared to leave the Union. To Squier, Nott revealed, through the guise of humor, that his intense southern patriotism was still struggling with a deeper feeling that human beings were unable to deal rationally with their lives. He said that two such philosophers as themselves, "who regard mankind as a miserable abortion," a pack of apes unable to rise above barbarism, could talk about the questions dividing North and South without disturbing their appetites or their digestions, but he quickly revealed his deep commitment to the southern cause.

When Nott had last seen Squier in New York, Squier had joked over dinner about southern blustering and bravado, and Nott remembered that even then he had thought that the South had serious intent: "I believed that by unjust tariffs—by denying us an equal right in the territories—& more than all by, a denial of the right of secession," northern politicians were forcing the South into a major upheaval. He said he knew that "when there was . . . a *formal denial of the right of* self government, the Southern people would rise up as one man & resist it with the old spirit of '76." The Anglo-Saxon race, wrote Nott, sailed by the chart of the Declaration of Independence; the doctrine was repeated in all the state constitutions. Rather than yielding on the question of self-government, "the Southern people will see all the whites & blacks on the globe slaughtered." He admitted that he had underestimated "the *animus* of the North"; he had not believed it would plunge into a war of immense cost in blood and money "without the remotest prospect of any good result." When all the states from Virginia to Texas had risen up to

12. James Williams to his father, August 18, 1862, in John Kent Folmar (ed.), *From That Terrible Field: The Civil War Letters of James M. Williams, Twenty-First Alabama Infantry Volunteers* (University, Ala., 1981), 102.

assert the rights for which the colonies had fought England, how could the North expect to gain anything from a long and bloody war? Did the North expect to conquer the South and make its inhabitants vassals? The South would fight for thirty years to avoid such a disaster. The region had abundant provisions, cotton vital to Europe, and "more courage, more unanimity, more determination did not exist at Thermopyle." Every southerner was brought up as a horseman and a marksman and to resist aggression. The South had officers equal to any in the world and a determination not to stop fighting until it was "*free—even the women are mad for Contest.*" [13]

Nott believed the South could not lose the war. He was truly mystified as to why the northerners were prepared to fight, for he thought they could not win. Nott liked to think of himself as a scientific realist, but he was a romantic in everything but his medicine. He even fought for scientific truth against religious control with all the enthusiasm of St. George tilting at the dragon. He had now convinced himself that high-spirited, chivalrous southern gentlemen would fight to the death before submitting to northern tyranny, and he could not believe that such self-sacrifice would not prevail. He gave no careful thought to blockades, armaments, medical supplies, hospitals, or money. Nott believed that cotton could be used as an economic tool, and because the South grew ample provisions, the men were brave, and the cause was just, what more was needed? He also was completely unwilling to admit the possibility that the southern way of life and the existing relations between whites and blacks could change. He suppressed his fleeting fears that men were irrational and that they often conducted their affairs for the worst rather than the best. Happily situated in a city he enjoyed and a region he loved, Nott could not believe that this life might change. The very prosperity that surrounded him and the vision that had produced ample private gifts to his medical college convinced him that the North could not impose its will on the South.

In these last years before the antebellum way of life was to disappear forever, Mobile was a prosperous, bustling, lively city of some thirty thousand inhabitants. On the eve of war, more than ever cotton was king. Visitors in the late 1850s could not escape its pervasive influence. One said the merchants "talk of cotton by day, and dream of it by night." Another

13. Nott to Squier, May 3, 1861, in Squier Papers, LC.

said "the people live in cotton houses and ride in cotton carriages. They buy cotton, sell cotton, think cotton, eat cotton, drink cotton, and dream cotton. They marry cotton wives, and unto them are born cotton children."[14] Perhaps it was understandable that Nott thought Europe could not do without this cotton and that support for the South was assured.

The substantial wealth that cotton brought to Mobile was reflected in the lives of the cotton merchants. "The superb villas, the palatial mansions lining its noble streets, the elegant country seats that adorn the suburbs," wrote one visitor, "are occupied almost exclusively by merchants." As a successful physician and noted southern author, Nott mixed comfortably with this merchant elite. Although it was taken for granted that the merchants dominated the wealth of the city, visitors to Mobile agreed that the bar, the doctors, and the ministers also exercised decisive leadership. James De Bow wrote of the city with affection, commenting that the "merchants are active and enterprising; the lawyers eloquent and able; the physicians—but who are the superiors anywhere of Nott and Levert?"[15] Levert's glory depended more on his wife than on his own medical skill, but Nott's fame was his alone.

Although slavery was of vital importance for the plantations that supplied the cotton on which Mobile thrived and the slave population of Alabama was some 435,000 by 1860, the institution was becoming of less significance in Mobile itself in the years directly preceding the war. Immigrants were entering Mobile in increasing numbers and displacing slave labor in many occupations. In 1860 foreign-born whites constituted 62 percent of the free labor force in Mobile. It was generally agreed in the years immediately preceding the war that immigrant Irish women were more numerous as servants than blacks. The hotels were staffed almost entirely with Irish servants; one visitor commented that the "price of the hire of colored servants here is so great that, probably, white servants are employed from motives of economy." Another visitor in December, 1859,

---

14. Charles Mackay, *Life and Liberty in America: Or, Sketches of a Tour in the United States and Canada, in 1857–8* (2 vols.; London, 1859), I, 282; [Hiram Fuller], *Belle Brittan on a Tour at Newport, and Here and There* (New York, 1858), 112.

15. J. H. Ingraham (ed.), *The Sunny South; or, The Southerner at Home, Embracing Five Years' Experience of a Northern Governess in the Land of the Sugar and Cotton* (Philadelphia, 1860), 506–507; John Oldmixon, *Transatlantic Wanderings* (London, 1855), 155–56; James De Bow, "Editorial Misc.," in Eugene L. Schwaab and Jacqueline Bull (eds.), *Travels in the Old South: Selected from the Periodicals of the Times* (2 vols.; Lexington, 1973), II, 479.

commented that he was surprised how effectively free labor appeared to have driven slave labor from the wharves and public places; the Irish and Germans seemed to do the work of the streets, and white girls were increasingly employed in domestic service.[16]

Black slaves, of course, were still being employed as domestic servants and were being hired out as laborers both on the docks and in the town. In 1860 blacks made up a little over a quarter of Mobile's population, and of this black population of 8,404 more than 800 were free. Some northern visitors were impressed by what they perceived as a free and easy atmosphere in racial relations in the city. One northern visitor, who thought there were "many more mulattoes and quadroons here than negroes," was impressed by the well-dressed "yellow girls and boys" he met on the streets on Sunday. "By what I have seen of slavery," he wrote in his diary, "I think it is *not* morally or politically wrong. The darkies live well and are protected by state law." He concluded that "there is more equality of the races in the South than in the North. There are few Southern boys who would not sleep with Negresses. These girls of mixed or African blood preserve the virtue of the white girls here, as women of loose character do in the North. Here I see White men and negroes shaking hands and conversing freely."[17] The bleaker side of black-white relations in Mobile was seldom easily visible to the casual visitor, and in general slavery and white-black relations appeared less degrading in southern towns, particularly in Mobile or New Orleans with a visible population of free blacks, than in rural plantation areas.

When in May, 1861, the London *Times* correspondent William Russell arrived in Mobile by steamboat from Montgomery, Nott showed him around the city. Russell dined with the acting British consul and with Nott, whom he described as "well known to ethnologists for his work on *Types of Mankind*," and after dinner walked with them through the city, which he described as abounding in "oyster saloons, drinking-houses,

16. Peter Kolchin, *First Freedom: The Responses of Alabama's Blacks to Emancipation and Reconstruction* (Westport, Conn., 1972), II, 149; Harriet E. Amos, "Social Life in an Antebellum Cotton Port: Mobile, Alabama, 1820–1860" (Ph.D. dissertation, Emory University, 1976), II, 100–101; John S. C. Abbot, *South and North; or, Impressions Received During a Trip to Cuba and the South* (New York, 1860), 112; Ingraham (ed.), *Sunny South*, 504 (economy quotation).
17. *The Population of the United States in 1860: Compiled from the Original Returns of the Eighth Census* (Washington, 1864), 9; Horace Howard Justis Diary, in William R. Perkins Library, Duke University, Durham, North Carolina.

lager-beer and wine-shops, and gambling and dancing places." His hosts told him that the people in Mobile were ultrasecessionist and that the wealth and manhood of the city would, to the last, be devoted to repelling Lincoln's measures. A week later, Russell dined at Nott's home. Among the guests was Judge Campbell, late of the United States Supreme Court. Nott, Russell commented, had been led by his studies to take "a purely materialistic view of the question of slavery, and, according to him, questions of morals and ethics, pertaining to its consideration, might be referred to the cubic capacity of the human cranium." Nott said that he detested slavery but that he did not see what could be done with the slaves if the institution came to an end. Russell's view of the Mobilians was that "a fierce Marseillaise are they—living in the most foreign-looking city I have yet seen in the States."[18]

The home that Russell visited was a very comfortable one. Nott was not rich by the standards of the great cotton merchants, but he lived in fine style. In the 1860 census he gave the value of his real estate as $40,000, his personal estate as $10,000. He owned ten slaves, a large number for a professional man in the city, and was still to own them in 1865. In the Mobile tax records for 1860 Nott gave his annual income as $10,000, and it seems likely that this was a conservative figure. It testified to his success as a physician, for the prominent Dr. Levert, who was married to the most active hostess in the city, had real estate worth $19,000, a personal estate of $5,000, and an annual income of $6,000. Nott was well-off on the eve of war and was able to support his family in considerable comfort. Most of this comfort was based on the yearly income from his practice, and this source was to cause him some difficulties in the following years. The hardships of war meant that Nott could not always earn as much money as he had grown used to in the late 1850s. His stated income on Mobile tax assessments was given as $7,000 in 1861 and $5,000 in both 1862 and 1863. It was back to $8,000 in 1864, but that was a year of massive inflation. Nott was never to endure any real financial difficulties, although until the end of his life he had to continue to practice medicine to support his family in a comfortable style.[19]

18. William Howard Russell, *My Diary North and South,* ed. Fletcher Pratt (New York, 1954), 106–108, 126–27.

19. Mobile, Census of 1860, in RG 29; NA; Mobile City Records, Tax Assessments, 1860–65. See also Alan Smith Thompson, "Mobile, Alabama, 1850–1861: Economic, Political, Physical, and Population Characteristics" (Ph.D. dissertation, University of Alabama, 1979).

When the news of war reached Mobile, the young men of the city flocked to the colors. By the middle of June, Mobile had provided and equipped fifteen companies of one hundred men each for the Confederate army. The enlistment of fifteen hundred volunteers in two months from a city with a free white population of some twenty-one thousand illustrates the enthusiasm that was sweeping the South. Nott's son James, like many other young physicians, shunned serving as a doctor in favor of fighting in the war. On April 23 he enlisted as a private in the elite Mobile Cadets, a company that included the sons of the most prominent Mobile families. Another private in James's company was Henry Hotze, the translator of Gobineau. A great crowd gathered in front of the city arsenal as the first two volunteer companies, one of them the Mobile Cadets, dressed in gray, marched to the wharf to take a steamer up the Alabama River to Montgomery. There the Mobile Cadets became company A of the 3rd Alabama Infantry. Near the end of the month, nearly a thousand strong, they left for Norfolk, Virginia, accompanied by several hundred black servants.[20]

The excitement continued in Mobile as company after company marched off to war. When the Emerald Guards, who were mostly of Irish descent and had been a fire company in peaceful days, marched to the railway depot, they were dressed in dark green, and they carried a banner which on one side had the flag of the Confederacy with a full-length figure of George Washington in the center and on the other a harp, encircled by a wreath of shamrocks, the motto "Erin-go-Bragh," and the war cry "Faugh-a-ballagh!" When William Russell visited the city in May, he found that the "citizens were busy in drilling, marching, and drum beating, and the Confederate flag flew from every spire and steeple."[21]

With Alabama troops, including his son, in Virginia, and the first major fighting of the war soon to take place there, Josiah Nott could not restrain himself. Also, his family was used to spending the summer at the

20. Letter to Dr. A. J. Foard, Mobile, June 3, 1861, in Samuel H. Stout Papers, Confederate Museum, Richmond, Virginia; Mobile *Register*, June 16, 1861; material regarding James D. Nott in Military Records, Alabama Department of Archives and History, Montgomery; Military Service Record of James D. Nott, in RG 109, NA; Henry Hotze, *Three Months in the Confederate Army*, ed. Richard B. Harwell (1862; rpr. University, Ala., 1952), 13, 15–22, 37–38; Walter L. Fleming, *Civil War and Reconstruction in Alabama* (1905; rpr. New York, 1949), 207; W. O. Smith to S. D. Denison, May 14, 1861, in W. O. Smith Papers, William Stanley Hoole Special Collections Library, University of Alabama, Tuscaloosa.

21. Kate Cumming, *Kate: The Journal of a Confederate Nurse*, ed. Richard B. Harwell (Baton Rouge, 1959), 52–53; Russell, *Diary*, 107.

Virginia Springs and other resorts, and there seemed no reason to change their usual pattern. Nott wanted to visit the 3rd Alabama in Norfolk; his object, he wrote, was to look after the comforts and, if need be, "bind up the wounds" of "those dear to my friends and myself" in the regiment. If not needed by the 3rd, he said he was ready to make himself useful among other southern troops. In reality, he wanted above all else to be near the scene of action. Arriving in Norfolk, he quickly toured the camp of the 3rd Alabama and visited other camps at Lynchberg, Richmond, Manassas Junction, and elsewhere, as well as defensive positions at the navy yard, Craney Island, Fort Norfolk, and other places in the Norfolk vicinity.

Nott, who acknowledged that sickness and distress were inseparable from camp life, was pleased with the camp of the 3rd Alabama. The tents were pitched in a pine grove on sandy, dry soil, with good drainage. The troops had "pretty good water and excellent provisions," and although there had been some deaths and sickness and some of the sick had been sent to the hospital of the Sisters of Charity in Norfolk, the main complaint was that they were condemned to inaction "when our country has so many wrongs to be avenged." Nott was full of conventional patriotic southern rhetoric at the beginning of the war, and his almost naive, optimistic patriotism lasted into much darker days. When he wrote home to report on the state of the Mobile troops, he told of the "dear boys" who had come, if need be, "to sacrifice their lives at the altar of liberty." [22]

An odd feature of these very early days of the war, before the widespread bloodshed and suffering, was that it was difficult for many to realize that the northern and southern parts of the country were now decisively separated as enemies and that normal travel between the sections was ending. Early in May a number of southern men in the North who had remained loyal to the United States petitioned the government to arrange for their families to leave Norfolk and Portsmouth, Virginia, to join them. Norfolk was now blockaded, but the commander of the blockading squadron arranged for a steamer to leave Portsmouth under a flag of truce with more than one hundred women and children on board. They were to be taken to the federal fleet off Old Point Comfort to be transported to the North. Oddly, among the refugees were Sarah Nott, her sister, and

22. Letter from Nott, July 7, 1861, in Mobile *Register*, July 14, 1861. Trips to be near sons or brothers were common in these early days of the war. Mobile novelist Augusta Evans (Wilson) and her mother also traveled to Norfolk at this time to be near Augusta's two brothers, who were in the 3rd Alabama; see William P. Fidler, *Augusta Evans Wilson, 1835–1909: A Biography* (University, Ala., 1951), 97–98.

their two children. Most of the women and children were sent by steamer to New York, but about a third of them, including the Nott party, chose to be transferred to a steamer bound for Baltimore and Philadelphia. One of the summer resorts frequented by the Notts was Cape May in southern New Jersey, and it seems possible that Mrs. Nott had decided to visit her usual haunts and meet her friends, war or no war. To do so she had to spend several days with the federal fleet waiting out a gale. The war was soon to be taken far more seriously, and by early July Nott's family was back in Norfolk—presumably returning as genuine refugees going south.[23]

By early July, Nott was becoming impatient. He wanted to see more action. Because Norfolk was getting too hot and the mosquitoes were becoming troublesome, he decided to settle his family at the Montgomery White Sulphur Springs. From there he could run down to Norfolk by train in a few hours if he needed to, and he could also travel to the new seat of the Confederate government at Richmond or to any other place in the region when he heard of the disposition of the northern armies. In these early months of the war, there was a curiously amateur gentlemanly quality to the southern military preparations, which was never entirely to disappear, and the civilian Nott had influential friends who would let him go pretty well where he wanted to go. In the middle of July he was in Richmond. Mary Boykin Chestnut, a relative of his wife, noted his presence and, like many others, coupled him with Gliddon in the phrase "Nott and Gliddon, known to fame."[24] Richmond was crowded with southerners from all over the Confederacy, en route to join the army or assembling for the meeting of the Confederate Congress.

When Nott heard at Richmond that the Confederate army at Manassas was likely to be in the path of the first major northern advance of the war, he quickly left for the front. The regiment in which his son James and the sons of many of his friends were serving was safely encamped at Norfolk, complaining bitterly of its lack of action, but the 4th, 5th, and 6th Alabama were at Manassas. Nott was well acquainted with both of the commanding Confederate generals—Pierre G. T. Beauregard and Joseph E. Johnston—and with many of their staff officers. Among the latter was Zachariah (Zach) Deas, one of his wife's brothers, who was aide-de-camp

23. *Official Records of the Union and Confederate Navies in the War of the Rebellion* (30 vols.; Washington, 1894–1927), Series I, vol. V (Washington, 1897), 627–28, 634, 660, 684–85.
24. Letter of Nott, July 7, 1861, in Mobile *Register,* July 14, 1861; C. Vann Woodward (ed.), *Mrs. Chestnut's Civil War* (New Haven, 1981), 99.

to General Johnston. Zach Deas had moved to Mobile with his parents in 1835 and had become a Mobile commission merchant after service in the war with Mexico. Nott was thrilled by the idea of being at the center of mighty military events. When in Italy, he had toured the battlefields of Magenta and Solferino and had shown an interest in such details as the positioning of the cannons. At Manassas he was to exhibit more excitement at the dramatic pattern of events than horror at the great bloodshed.[25]

The battle at Manassas (First Bull Run) was precipitated by a Union army some thirty thousand strong advancing from Washington toward Beauregard's position. At that time Johnston was in the Shenandoah Valley ready to meet the advance of another Union force, but he was able to move his troops to join Beauregard in time to take a decisive part in the fighting. Nott arrived at Manassas on July 20, the day before the battle. Immediately he went to headquarters and spent the night in camp with his brother-in-law Zach Deas. The next morning they were up at daybreak, "took a cup of coffee and remained quietly laughing and talking at head-quarters." After several hours, Beauregard and his staff, Nott with them, rode about three miles to the center of the Confederate line, which was under cannon fire. Nott wrote that he felt very keenly the remark of Cuddy to his mother Mause that "a straggling bullet has nae discretion." Realizing that the main attack was being launched against the Confederate left, the headquarters group then rode another three miles to the main seat of the battle.

The fighting was very fierce on the Confederate left. From the top of a hill, Nott could glimpse the battle swirling back and forth through the woods; the musketry sounding "like a large bundle of fire crackers." At first, the Confederates feared the day was lost because their troops fell back, suffering heavy losses. Nott and one of Johnston's staff surgeons set to work in a ravine operating on Confederate wounded. For the first time, Nott experienced the reality of battle as he saw "load after load of our

25. Nott's trip to Manassas and his part in the battle discussed in this and the following paragraphs are described in Nott to Harleston, July 23, 1861, in Mobile *Register,* July 30, 1861. The letter is printed in Frank Moore (ed.), *The Rebellion Record* (11 vols.; New York, 1861–68), II, 93–94. For Zach Deas see Thomas J. Kirkland and Robert M. Kennedy, *Historic Camden,* Pt. 2, *The Nineteenth Century* (Columbia, 1926), 179; Willis Brewer, *Alabama: Her History, Resources, War Record, and Public Men: From 1540 to 1872* (Montgomery, 1872), 424–25. For Nott in Italy see Nott to John Forsyth, September 5, 1859, in the *Independent* (Gainesville, Ala.), October 8, 1859.

poor wounded and dying soldiers brought and strewed on the ground." One Confederate officer who was at Manassas later recalled seeing a shady little valley, where "the surgeons had been plying their vocation all morning upon the wounded. Tables about breast high had been erected upon which screaming victims were having legs and arms cut off. The surgeons and their assistants, stripped to the waist, and all bespattered with blood, stood around, some holding the poor fellows while others, armed with long bloody knives and saws, cut and sawed away with a frightful rapidity, throwing the mangled limbs on a pile near by as soon as removed."[26] Amputation was tragically common because the doctors could not stop wound infection, but in any case the amputee often died from shock or later infections.

The Union forces were still advancing, and Nott and other medical personnel had to fall back, taking the wounded with them in field ambulances. Finding that the wounded could now be taken to hospitals in the rear at Manassas, Nott returned to the scene of the battle. He was in time to view the arrival of more of Johnston's troops. These men stiffened the Confederate line and finally turned an apparent defeat into a striking victory. In the aftermath of that victory, Nott was still caught up in his romantic vision of mighty armies wheeling and charging in battle array through the woods, and he was able to forget the piles of dead and wounded. "No one can imagine such a grand, glorious picture," he wrote, "as these patriots presented, rushing to the field through the masses of wounded bodies which strewed the roadside as they passed along." "As I looked back," wrote Nott, "I could see a regiment of infantry coming in a trot, with their bright muskets glittering in the sun, then would come a battery of artillery, each gun carriage crowded with men and drawn by four horses in full gallop. Next came troops of cavalry, dashing with the speed of Murat." Nott took a naive delight in the events of the day. Beauregard and Johnston, he said, "played it like a game of chess without seeing the board," moving their men to check the enemy's moves.

Nott celebrated the victory with the rhetoric that came easily to his lips in the summer of 1861. "The victory was dearly bought," he said, "but still blood is the price of freedom; and we can at least . . . feel the proud con-

26. Quoted in Horace H. Cunningham, *Field Medical Services at the Battle of Manassas (Bull Run)* (Athens, Ga., 1968), 30–31.

solation that they have died like heroes, and given liberty to unborn millions." He saw nothing incongruous in arguing that the defense of slavery would give liberty to future generations. The North, he believed, would now have to sue for terms. Nott, caught up in the romance rather than the horror of war, was painfully overconfident after the victory, along with most other southerners.[27]

Nott returned to Richmond the day after the battle. There were enough army surgeons at Manassas, and Nott concerned himself with arranging for sending supplies needed by the patients. At Richmond he was in the happy position of bringing personal news of a great victory, and he was able to indulge in a little harmless boasting. He told Mrs. Chestnut that he "had slept under the same tree with Joe Johnston" and that Jefferson Davis had arrived too late to see the actual battle. It was even rumored that Nott might replace Camden DeLeon as the surgeon general of the Confederacy; Mrs. Chestnut commented that he was "looked upon by many as a fit person for it."[28]

In the weeks following the battle of Manassas, Nott had ample opportunity to see the human costs of the Confederacy's struggle. One Alabama regiment of infantry, the 4th, which had been in the thick of the battle, had suffered 38 killed and 208 wounded out of 750, and soon after returning to Richmond Nott received a telegram asking him to attend the wounded colonel of that regiment at Orange Courthouse. The colonel had a severe flesh wound in his thing but was much better off than many members of his regiment. Confederate wounded were scattered in buildings all around, in hurriedly created hospitals, or in private houses; among them were some of the wounded from the northern army. "The *science* of war," Nott commented, "has been so greatly improved, that we are now enabled to murder our fellow creatures much more successfully than in former times. The *Minnie* balls make such terrible wounds, that almost half of those placed on the list of wounded will die." The conical minié ball was fired from a rifled musket and had a greater velocity than the old round ball. It caused greater splintering of bone and increased the chances of infection. It was generally agreed that immediate amputation was the best treatment for minié ball wounds in the limbs. Grave problems still remained, of course, because amputation was followed by infection of the stump. Nott's martial enthusiasm had cooled a little after

27. Nott to Harleston, July 23, 1861, in Mobile *Register,* July 30, 1861, printed in Moore (ed.), *Rebellion Record,* II, 93–94.
28. Woodward (ed.), *Mrs. Chestnut's Civil War,* 107, 114.

touring the hospitals. He said that the wounded "present a horrible picture."[29]

Along with the general Confederate hospitals in Virginia there were hospitals established for their own troops by individual states. In Richmond two of the best-known hospitals devoted to Alabama troops were those looked after by Julie Opie Hopkins of Mobile. She helped raise much of the necessary money, personally directed their organization, and was officially appointed by the Alabama governor to the position of superintendent of Alabama hospitals in Virginia. At the beginning of August, her two Richmond hospitals were located in three-story houses, with a surgeon, a matron, and ten servants in attendance. Nott worked with the wounded here as well as at Orange Courthouse, and it was said that for his invaluable service to Alabama wounded "his praise is on every tongue."[30] The Hopkins hospitals were praised for their efficiency, but already the Confederate medical facilities were severely taxed by the wounded and by the patients suffering from the widespread camp diseases that were to plague both sides in the Civil War. With inadequate sanitation and a lack of knowledge of the causes of disease and epidemics, both armies were to lose great numbers to typhoid and dysentery and to have large numbers of soldiers dangerously weakened by malaria. By mid-August nearly five thousand of the eighteen thousand Confederate troops at Manassas were sick. With the pressure of the ever-increasing sick and wounded, medical and hospital conditions were to deteriorate badly throughout the Confederacy as the Civil War progressed. Although there were always some efficiently run hospitals, others failed to cope even in these first months of the war. After visiting one Richmond hospital Mrs. Chestnut commented: "Horrors upon horrors again—want of organization. Long rows of them dead, dying. Awful smells, awful sights."[31]

29. Nott to Dr. William H. Anderson, July 31, 1861, Mobile *Register,* August 8, 1861; Malcolm C. McMillan (ed.), *The Alabama Confederate Reader* (University, Ala., 1963), 113–14; Cunningham, *Field Medical Services,* 35–36; Paul E. Steiner, *Disease in the Civil War: Natural Biological Warfare in 1861–1865* (Springfield, Ill., 1968), 11. The most useful general account of Confederate medical problems is H. H. Cunningham, *Doctors in Gray: The Confederate Medical Service* (2d ed.; Baton Rouge, 1960).

30. See Lucille Griffith, "Mrs. Juliet Opie Hopkins and Alabama Military Hospitals," *Alabama Review,* VI (1953), 99–120; letter of Joseph Nicholson, August 8, 1861, in Caldwell Delaney (ed.), *Confederate Mobile: A Pictorial History* (Mobile, 1971), 19 (quotation); McMillan (ed.), *Alabama Confederate Reader,* 367; Fannie A. Beers, *Memories: A Record of Personal Experience and Adventure During Four Years of War* (Philadelphia, 1888), 43–44.

31. Cunningham, *Field Medical Services,* 25; Steiner, *Disease in the Civil War,* 14, 22, 24; Woodward (ed.), *Mrs. Chestnut's Civil War,* 158 (quotation).

But even with thousands sick and the hospitals crowded, the summer of 1861 was a joyful, optimistic time for many in the Confederacy. Volunteers were still flocking to the colors. The 3rd Alabama, which was still at Norfolk, had missed the battle of Manassas, and Nott's son James was determined to see action. Late in August, 1861, he obtained his discharge from the 3rd Alabama; he had decided to return with his family to Mobile, seek appointment as an officer, and find a battle to fight in.[32]

In August, Nott had rejoined his family at the Virginia Springs, and in early September they all returned to Mobile. Nott had experienced much excitement, hobnobbed with the great, and tended the Alabama wounded. He viewed it as a successful summer in every way, for the Confederacy seemed well on the way to establishing independence. The family carried back to Mobile news of the great events in Virginia. Soon after returning, Nott appeared at the Odd Fellows' Hall in Mobile to lecture on the battle of Manassas. Admission was a rather steep one dollar, but it was for a good cause—the soldiers' relief organization.[33]

With the Confederacy calling for volunteers, neither Nott nor his eldest sons could stay content in civilian life. In the middle of October, Nott enlisted as a surgeon in the medical department of the Confederate army. A few days earlier the Confederacy had established the Department of Alabama and West Florida. Its first commander was Major-General Braxton Bragg, who since the spring had been in command of the Confederate forces in the vicinity of Pensacola, Florida. Bragg was yet another of Nott's influential friends. A North Carolinian who had served in the army in the Mexican War and after, Bragg had resigned in the 1850s to live on a Louisiana sugar plantation. His brother John had settled in Mobile in 1835 and was a well-known lawyer and politician. Braxton visited him in Mobile and after the war was to make his home there. Braxton Bragg's prominence gave Nott another chance to be at the heart of events.[34]

The headquarters of Bragg's enlarged command remained at Pensacola,

32. Military Service Record of James D. Nott, in RG 109, NA; Military Records, Alabama Department of Archives and History, Montgomery.

33. Mobile *Register,* September 20, 25, 1861.

34. Military Service Record of Josiah C. Nott, in RG 109, NA. For Braxton Bragg see Grady McWhiney, *Braxton Bragg and Confederate Defeat,* I, *Field Command* (New York, 1969). For John Bragg see Brewer, *Alabama,* 409–10; Caldwell Delaney (ed.), *Craighead's Mobile: Being the Fugitive Writings of Ervin S. Craighead and Frank Craighead* (Mobile, 1968), 171–72.

but for the time being Nott stayed in Mobile. On joining the Confederate medical department, Nott had expected to become medical director to Brigadier General Jones M. Withers, who commanded the District of Alabama within Bragg's larger command. Withers, former mayor of Mobile, had been colonel of the 3rd Alabama, the regiment in which Nott's son James had first served, before his promotion. Withers had recommended Nott for appointment as his medical director, and Nott was friendly not only with Withers' commander, General Bragg, but also with Bragg's medical director, Dr. A. J. Foard. Foard, a Georgian, had been an assistant surgeon in the United States Army before secession.

Within a few days of receiving his commission, Nott was surprised to learn that a Mobile friend, Dr. F. A. Ross, had received from Richmond the appointment as medical director to General Withers. Nott took the loss well and wrote to congratulate Dr. Ross, but in a letter to Dr. Foard he revealed some resentment. He said that he did not know through "what influences" Ross had received the appointment, but that General Withers was "much offended," having assumed that this was a staff appointment which he could make personally. Nott also indicated that in congratulating Ross he had offered to take charge of the surgical wards because Ross had no taste for surgery. Nott believed that some special influence more powerful than his own had secured Ross the appointment as medical director to Withers, but in reality it seems likely that Ross was appointed because of his previous military experience. At the beginning of the war, the Confederacy tried to staff its medical department with surgeons who had served in some capacity in the United States Army, and Dr. Ross had served as a surgeon with the South Carolina Palmetto Regiment during the Mexican War.[35]

Nott's special experience was not wasted, for he became the medical director of the Confederate General Army Hospital in Mobile. He apparently did a good job of setting the tone of the establishment, for in July, 1862, after Nott had moved on to another appointment, a nurse who visited the hospital contrasted it favorably with those in Mississippi: "Every thing was in perfect order, and as cleanly as any private house."[36]

35. Nott to [Dr. A. J. Foard], October 20, 1861, in Samuel H. Stout Papers, Special Collections, Robert W. Woodruff Library, Emory University, Atlanta, Georgia. For Foard see the sketch by Samuel H. Stout in *Southern Practitioner*, XXIV (1902), 106–108. See also Norman V. Cooper, "How They Went to War: An Alabama Brigade in 1861–62," *Alabama Review*, XXIV (1971), 26–27, 37.
36. Military Service Record of Josiah C. Nott, in RG 109, NA; Cumming, *Kate*, 54.

The need for efficient hospitals for the Confederate forces scattered along the Gulf from Pensacola to Mobile was becoming acute in the fall of 1861. In the three months ending on September 30 of that year, there had been fewer than seven thousand Confederate troops in the Pensacola region, but in the same period Medical Director Foard reported the treatment of almost ten thousand cases. More than a thousand men had been sent into hospital, and 115 men had died, 74 of typhoid. A similar pattern prevailed in the Mobile area, and Nott was kept extremely busy attempting to provide the necessary hospital beds for the numerous sick. By late November some nine to ten thousand Confederate troops were encamped in the region around Mobile. It was reported to Dr. Foard that Nott was "getting things a little straighter by degrees," but that he was "still kept much worried." There was typhoid in the Mobile region as well as at Pensacola, and by the end of December Nott was considerably distressed at the difficulties of providing medical care for the numerous sick. "The whole affair now is horrible," Nott wrote to Foard. He thought the entire officer corps, including surgeons, was "utterly worthless" to the medical department. There was a great deal of "*bad* sickness" around, he reported, and if there was not a marked change, "the whole command will be rendered worthless." Nott was having difficulty diagnosing the sickness; he found it to be a strange mixture of typhoid and malarial fevers, "aided by the stupidity of Doctors or rather quacks."[37]

By the end of December, Nott had been obliged to open two branches of his main army hospital in Mobile.[38] Both armies quickly discovered at the beginning of the Civil War that crowded army camps in an age before the causes of disease were understood were even more dangerous than the bloody battlefields of the Civil War. With inadequate sanitation and a lack of cleanliness, typhoid was to prove a particular problem, but dysentery and malarial fevers were also to harass the forces of the lower South.

While Nott attempted to organize the Confederate hospitals and continued to treat individual cases, he also served on the Confederate Medical Examining Board in Mobile. The examining boards had the task of scrutinizing the moral and professional credentials of those proposing to be medical officers in the Confederate army. Given the pressure of events,

---

37. "Deaths in the Department of Alabama and West Florida," *Atlanta Medical and Surgical Journal*, n.s., VII (1866), 381–84; Dr. W. H. Anderson to Dr. A. J. Foard, November 28, December 3, 1861, Nott to Dr. A. J. Foard, December 27, 1861, in Stout Papers, Woodruff Library, Emory University.
38. Nott to Dr. A. J. Foard, December 27, 1861, in Stout Papers.

regimental surgeons often served for several months before appearing before an examining board. The boards were instructed to make favorable reports in all cases in which it seemed that there was a reasonable belief that the officer would be able to meet the professional requirements; and examinations of those of high reputation, medical school professors, and others of known merit were supposed to be *pro forma*.[39]

There are indications that Nott was loath to bend his professional standards to the exigencies of war. When one doctor, who was already attached to a regiment, appeared before the Mobile board in January, 1862, Nott indicated in his report that this man should not be given an appointment higher than that of assistant surgeon, even though it seemed from an earlier statement by the applicant that he would not accept an appointment at that level. Nott reported that the applicant was presumably a "pretty fair" practitioner in the ordinary, acute diseases of the country, "but is entirely ignorant of anatomy, Surgery, Physiology, Pathology & Chemistry, & is not in reality entitled to the place of *Ast*. Surgeon, but in consideration of services rendered, we have strained the point, to recommend him even for this grade."[40]

While serving in the Confederate forces, Nott also continued to advise the citizens of Mobile on a variety of medical and related matters. Through the press he told the citizens to avoid shortages of lint by the use of cotton, which he said was an excellent substitute and would answer every purpose in the dressing of wounds. Another, much different substitution that Nott recommended was that of vegetables for cotton on southern plantations. It was essential, he said, that the troops' diets include vegetables as well as meat and bread. Many of the gardeners around Mobile were in the army, and the immediate region could not grow enough vegetables for the townspeople and the many troops in the area. Nott recommended that planters in the interior grow potatoes, peas, cabbage, and turnips on their unneeded cotton lands. Some scattered cases of scurvy and other diseases were already occurring in the camps from too exclusive a dependence on meat. The history of war showed, wrote Nott, that most soldiers did not die "on the fields of glory" but "ignoble deaths from camp diseases." Much of their illness was caused by improper food.

39. See Confidential Instructions to the Medical Board of Examiners to Convene at Nashville, Tennessee, December 30, 1861, Dr. A. J. Foard Letter Book, Virginia State Library, Richmond.

40. Nott to Colonel Beck, January 7, 1862, in Samuel H. Stout Papers, William L. Perkins Library, Duke University, Durham, North Carolina.

The Confederacy needed all the troops it could muster. The young men should be kept healthy, Nott argued, and they would do their duty and fight. "A father," he wrote, "should rather see his son, like the Spartan, brought back dead on his shield, than to remain at home dishonored."[41]

Nott also tried to care for the troops by encouraging the establishment, in early 1862, of the Society of Ladies "for providing the sick and convalescent soldiers with such nourishment as is not provided by military usages." The society provided delicacies for more than 6,000 Confederate soldiers who passed through the Mobile Marine Hospital in 1862 (371 of these soldiers died). Nott's wife, Sarah, had been involved in such work since the beginning of the war. In the spring of 1861 the women (always called "ladies") of Mobile organized the Military Aid Society to provide bandages, lint, and other supplies (including brandy) to Confederate hospitals. In the fall they had worked toward providing money for the founding of a hospital for the Confederate maimed and disabled; Sarah Nott became treasurer of the organization.[42]

The Notts' commitment to the Confederacy was given additional meaning in the fall of 1861, when their two eldest sons entered the Confederate army, James for the second time. Their enlistment was a family affair typical of the higher reaches of the Confederacy. Zach Deas, the boys' uncle, had been authorized to raise a regiment of Alabama infantry, which became the 22d Alabama. He recruited it in the fall of 1861. Because the Confederate government had difficulty providing the arms to equip the new regiment, Deas provided $28,000 in gold out of his own pocket to buy eight hundred Enfield rifles. A year later he was given in reimbursement the same sum in Confederate bonds. In October, 1861, James Nott became a captain in command of company B of the new regiment. His brother Henry became a sergeant-major in the same regiment.[43]

41. Mobile *Register,* October 26, 1861; Delaney (ed.), *Confederate Mobile,* 44.
42. Selma *Daily Reporter,* February 24, 1863; Nellie Butler Scrapbook, William Stanley Hoole Special Collections Library, University of Alabama, Tuscaloosa; letter of Dr. C. H. Martin, May 28, 1861, in Braxton Bragg Papers, Western Reserve Historical Society, Cleveland, Ohio; Dr. G. A. Ketchum to Dr. A. J. Foard, May 30, 1861, in Stout Papers, Woodruff Library, Emory University; letter to Dr. A. J. Foard, June 3, 1861, in Samuel H. Stout Papers, Confederate Museum, Richmond, Virginia; Sidney A. Smith and C. Carter Smith (eds.), *Mobile: 1861–1865; Notes and a Bibliography* (Chicago, 1964), 7. Sarah Nott had been president of the Protestant [Episcopal] Church Employment Society in 1860. This organization employed women as seamstresses and sold the goods they made (Mobile *Register,* June 28, 1860; Amos, "Social Life in an Antebellum Cotton Port," 281).
43. Military Service Records of James D. and Henry J. Nott, in RG 109, NA; Mobile *Register,* September 24, 1861; Kirkland and Kennedy, *Historic Camden,* Pt. 2, p. 179; Brewer,

During the winter of 1861–1862 all members of the Nott family were in the vicinity of Mobile because the 22d Alabama went into camp there. This was still a reasonably happy time for Mobile and for the Notts. The Confederacy had won the only big battle of the war, and there seemed ample reason to be confident of ultimate victory. There were, however, some ominous signs. The North, surprisingly to many in the South, including Nott, was making preparations for a long and, if necessary, bloody conflict, and foreign nations were showing no signs of leaping to the support of the Confederacy. Even more ominously, the Confederacy was showing some signs of weakness in the Mississippi Valley. Fierce fighting near the Kentucky-Tennessee border resulted in February, 1862, in a major Confederate defeat. With the fall of Forts Henry and Donelson, control of Kentucky had been lost, some two thousand Confederate troops killed, and about fourteen thousand captured or missing. Before the end of the month, Nashville, Tennessee, had been occupied by Union forces.[44] It was obvious that when the major campaigns of the spring began, the Confederacy would be under considerable pressure, and the forces around Mobile would be needed to meet the dangerous thrust into Tennessee. The romantic euphoria of July, 1861, had gone forever.

Alabama, 424–25; Thomas M. Owen, *History of Alabama and Dictionary of Alabama Biography* (4 vols.; Chicago, 1921), III, 475.

44. See Thomas Connelly, *Army of the Heartland: The Army of Tennessee, 1861–1862* (Baton Rouge, 1967), 68–139.

Chapter 12
DEFEAT

In the late winter of 1861–1862 Confederate General Albert Sidney Johnston decided that the Confederate forces that were retreating in Tennessee should unite and gather their strength at the railroad junction of Corinth, just across the Tennessee line in northern Mississippi. From there he hoped to turn to the attack against the advancing forces of General Ulysses S. Grant. Johnston reached Corinth in the latter part of March; General Beauregard and his forces were to join him there. It was also decided that General Braxton Bragg would go to Corinth with some 10,000 troops from Pensacola and Mobile and that Brigadier-General Daniel Ruggles would join Beauregard's command with 5,000 men from New Orleans. In late March the force that was gathering in the vicinity of Corinth was designated the Army of Mississippi. It consisted of three main corps of some 30,000 men and a reserve corps of about 6,500. Johnston was in overall command, aided by Beauregard. Bragg commanded the large 2d Corps of more than 13,500 men and was named as Johnston's chief of staff.[1]

The decision to move reinforcements from the Gulf to help check Grant gave Nott and his sons the opportunity for action they had been seeking. In March, 1862, Nott obtained an appointment as medical director on the staff of Brigadier-General Daniel Ruggles. Late in February, Ruggles was ordered to move his troops from New Orleans and was assigned the command of the District of North Alabama. In the next month, for the coming battle, his force became the 1st Division of Bragg's 2d Corps. Although Nott's appointment was to Ruggles' staff, he actually

1. Thomas L. Connelly, *Army of the Heartland: The Army of Tennessee, 1861–1862* (Baton Rouge, 1967), 139–51.

served in the coming battle on the staff of his friend General Bragg; and in May, after the battle, this appointment was formalized.[2]

The massing of Confederate forces to resist Grant also gave Nott's sons the opportunity they had sought for direct action. The 22d Alabama was assigned to the 2d Division of Bragg's Corps, under the command of General Jones M. Withers. The meaning of secession was now to be fully brought home to the people of Alabama, for more than six thousand troops from the state were to be in the coming battle, one of the most fiercely fought and bloodiest of the war.

Early in April, General Johnston was ready to move. Grant's army was encamped on the banks of the Tennessee River near Shiloh Meeting House, and Johnston hoped to strike before it could be reinforced. His troops attacked the Union force on Sunday, April 6. The battle lasted for two days. Nott found it far more intense and wearing than the battle of Manassas. The 22d Alabama, in which two of his sons served, was engaged in some of the fiercest fighting of the battle. On April 6 it appeared that the Confederates were about to win a hard-fought and bloody victory as the Union lines were broken, but the fighting was extremely heavy and the battlefield swept by confusion. At the heart of the Confederate attack was the first brigade of Bragg's 2d Division, which was composed mostly of Alabama troops, including the 22d. It immediately suffered very heavy casualties. The general in command was killed, his second-in-command severely wounded, and Zach Deas left his 22d Regiment to assume overall command. Deas had two horses shot from under him and was wounded on the second day of the battle. He was later treated by Nott and recovered.

The 22d Alabama began the battle with more than 700 fighting men and when it was over pulled back with 123 effectives. Both of Nott's sons escaped wounds, although both were in the heavy fighting. Captain James Nott was commended by the acting commander of his regiment for his part in the engagement—with another officer he had led troops who had "gallantly charged the enemy" and driven them from the houses in which they were entrenched. James's brother, Sergeant Major Henry Nott, was also commended for bravery, both by the acting commander of the regiment and by his uncle Colonel Deas.[3]

2. Military Service Record of Josiah C. Nott, in RG 109, NA; Military Records, Alabama Department of Archives and History, Montgomery; *List of Staff Officers of the Confederate States Army, 1861–1865* (Washington, 1891), 122.

3. Connelly, *Army of the Heartland,* 151–69; Report of Lt. Col. J. C. Marrast, 22d Ala-

On the first day of the battle Nott spent most of his time alongside General Bragg. At times, with all other members of Bragg's staff absent on duty, Nott carried messages to different parts of the battlefield. By the end of the day the field was a chaotic sight. The Union troops had been forced to withdraw to the banks of the river, but the firing was still intense and the Union gunboats were keeping up a furious shelling. Even though the Confederates were claiming a victory, Nott later wrote that "our men, immediately in front of where we were standing, were much demoralized, and indisposed to advance in the face of the shells which were bursting over us in every direction." Nott was later called upon to comment on the situation, for a dispute arose over the decision to withdraw Confederate troops, particularly as to whether this was done by General Bragg on his own authority or whether it was ordered by General Beauregard, who assumed overall command after General Johnston bled to death from a wound in his leg. Nott believed that Bragg ordered the withdrawal because the troops in front of their position were in considerable confusion and demoralized by the shelling and intense Union resistance.[4]

On the second day of the battle the Confederate advantage of the first day was lost. The Union troops, who had been reinforced, successfully held their positions, and Beauregard withdrew his forces to Corinth. The Confederates had lost more than seventeen hundred dead, nearly a thousand missing, and more than eight thousand wounded; the Union had suffered comparable losses. The casualty figures were horrendous, and though there had been great bravery, there was little romance left in what had become a struggle to the death.[5]

As the Confederates pulled back into Corinth with their thousands of wounded, heavy rains turned the roads into a quagmire. When Mobile nurse Kate Cumming arrived in Corinth on April 11, she commented that the rain "had been pouring for days" and that mud and slush were every-

bama, April 12, 1862, Col. Z. C. Deas to Capt. D. E. Huger, April 25, 1862, *The War of the Rebellion: A Compilation of the Official Records of the Union and Confederate Armies* (130 vols.; Washington, 1880–1901), Ser. I, Vol. X, Part 1, 538–39, 542–43 (hereinafter cited as *OR*); Malcolm C. McMillan (ed.), *The Alabama Confederate Reader* (University, Ala., 1963), 126–27.

4. Nott to Gen. P. G. T. Beauregard, November 6, 1869 (extract), in Alfred Roman, *The Military Operations of General Beauregard in the War Between the States, 1861 to 1865* (2 vols.; New York, 1884), I, 535; Bragg to Brig.-Gen. Thomas Jordan, April 30, 1862, *OR*, Ser. I, vol. X, Part I, 469.

5. Connelly, *Army of the Heartland*, 169–75; Wiley Sword, *Shiloh: Bloody April* (New York, 1974); James L. McDonough, *Shiloh—In Hell Before Night* (Knoxville, 1977).

where. Amid "the slop and mud," stretching as far as the eye could see, were the tents of the Confederate army. On the eighth, as she was traveling toward Corinth, a train had passed filled with wounded on their way to Mobile and other points to the south.[6]

Most of the attendants in Confederate hospitals were men, often older or partially disabled soldiers detached for hospital duty, but some were female volunteers. In Mobile a local minister organized a group of women, including the Scots-born Kate Cumming, to serve as nurses, and they traveled north as the battle was being fought. When they reached Corinth in the mud and rain, they found that all the hotels and large buildings had been commandeered as hospitals. Kate Cumming was overwhelmed by the scene in Corinth—"nothing that I had ever heard or read had given me the faintest idea of the horrors witnessed here." If "uncomplaining endurance" is glory and heroism, she wrote, we saw plenty of it. "Gray-haired men—men in the pride of manhood—beardless boys—Federals and all, mutilated in every imaginable way, lying on the floor, just as they were taken from the battle-field; so close together that it was almost impossible to walk without stepping on them." Kate Cumming sat up all the first night at Corinth, bathing the men's wounds and giving them water. The next day she found that men were lying all over what was little more than a large house, "on their blankets, just as they were brought from the battle-field. They are in the hall, on the gallery, and crowded into very small rooms. The foul air from this mass of human beings at first made me giddy and sick, but I soon got over it. We have to walk, and when we give the men any thing kneel, in blood and water."[7]

Before she reached Corinth, Cumming had heard the "the surgeons entertain great prejudice against admitting ladies into the hospital in the capacity of nurses." One surgeon had even forbidden young ladies to visit his patients with gifts. "The doctors, one and all, are getting terrible characters from the ladies; even good Dr. Nott of Mobile is not spared." When Cumming reached Corinth, she found that the situation of the wounded was so desperate that any and all help was needed, and the feeling that respectable women could not deal intimately with strange men was by necessity abandoned. But prejudice against female nurses continued throughout the war.[8]

6. Kate Cumming, *Gleanings from Southland* (Birmingham, 1895), 44–45.
7. Kate Cumming, *Kate: The Journal of a Confederate Nurse*, ed. Richard B. Harwell (Baton Rouge, 1959), 14–15; McMillan (ed.), *Alabama Confederate Reader*, 132.
8. Cumming, *Kate*, xii, 12.

Nott's sons had come out of the battle unscathed, but on the day after it ended Henry, the less robust of the two, began to show symptoms of typhoid fever. To add to the horrors around Corinth an epidemic of typhoid began to spread through the camps in the days after the battle. Henry was taken back to Mobile, where he lingered for nearly a month before dying on May 8. He was twenty-five and had received an appointment as second lieutenant in company "C" of the 22d Alabama the week before he died. His gravestone in the Mobile cemetery read that he had "died from exposure and fatigue on the battlefield of Shiloh," a description that perhaps indicated Nott's desire to emphasize that his sacrifice had been made in battle.[9]

In Richmond, Mrs. Chestnut first heard that the Nott boys had safely survived Shiloh, but by June she had received a despairing letter from Henry's aunt, Margaret Auzé, who knew the Nott boys nearly as well as her own daughter. "She had no hope," commented Mrs. Chestnut. "To be conquered and ruined was always her fate, strive as she might—and now she knew it would be her country through which she would be made to feel. She had had more than most women to endure, and the battle of life she had tried to fight with courage, endurance, faith. . . . Long years ago, when she was young, her lover died. She was to have been married, but fever came instead. Afterward she married. Then her husband died, then her only son. When New Orleans fell, her only daughter was there, and Mrs. Auzé went for her—Butler to the contrary notwithstanding—and brought her back with her. Well may she say she has bravely borne her burden till now."[10] Mrs. Auzé was obviously doing little to cheer the Nott household in the weeks after the death of Henry Nott. With James still away with his regiment, the war had lost its early glamour.

The dangers and horrors of war reached southern Alabama with painful intensity in April, 1862, for after the tragic losses at Shiloh, New Orleans fell to David Farragut and the Union navy late in the month. While Mobile's citizens worried about soon being under attack, the city's hospitals filled with wounded and sick soldiers from northern Mississippi. Confederate hospitals were scattered in the cities and along the railroad lines of the South.[11]

9. Henry Nott's obituary is in the Mobile *Register,* May 10, 1862. See also Paul E. Steiner, *Disease in the Civil War: Natural Biological Warfare in 1861–1865* (Springfield, Ill., 1968), 156–85.
10. C. Vann Woodward (ed.), *Mrs. Chestnut's Civil War* (New Haven, 1981), 371.
11. Gerald M. Capers, *Occupied City: New Orleans Under the Federals, 1862–1865* (Lexington, Ky., 1965), 44–51.

Through the early spring the Confederate forces that had fought at Shiloh stayed in Corinth, and Nott helped with the wounded and inspected the hospitals. In the middle of May he was given an official appointment as medical director on Bragg's staff. When a few days later he examined a hospital, it was said that he "looked well," though he "has lost a son in the war." At the end of May, as the Union forces advanced slowly from Shiloh, Beauregard abandoned Corinth and retreated along the Mobile and Ohio Railroad to Tupelo, Mississippi. There, in June, he was succeeded in overall command by General Bragg, and Nott was again at the center of affairs.[12]

The many wounded at Shiloh and the extensive sickness among the troops since that battle had placed great strains on the medical resources of the Confederacy in the Mississippi Valley. There was a severe shortage of hospitals, medical supplies, and personnel. A woman who arrived in Corinth as it was being evacuated later wrote that "one of the most heart-sickening sights my eyes ever beheld was witnessed there and then. Everything seemed to be in perfect confusion. Thousands of sick and dying were scattered, far and near, around the depot for the purpose of being sent off, with the hot broiling sun beaming upon them." She said that most of them were "suffering much for want of food and water." Dr. A. J. Foard, medical director of the western army, did not have the resources to meet the many demands upon him. In the middle of July it was reported to Jefferson Davis that the medical department of the western army was "in a state of great confusion and disorganization." Many of the regiments had acting surgeons who had never been regularly appointed, medical stores were insufficient, hospitals were inadequate, and regular returns were not being made. Davis' investigator recommended that in view of "the almost utter helplessness of adequate hospital arrangements," sick soldiers should be distributed among the plantations in the region. To some extent this had already been done, and the people of Mississippi had given good care to the sick.[13]

In view of the critical state of medical care in the western army, it was decided to conduct a thorough investigation of conditions in the many

12. Military Service Record of Josiah C. Nott, in RG 109, NA; Cumming, *Kate*, 39; Connelly, *Army of the Heartland*, 176–81.

13. Mrs. S. E. D. Smith, *The Soldier's Friend; Being a Thrilling Narrative of Grandma Smith's Four Years' Experience and Observation, as Matron, in the Hospitals of the South, During the Late Disastrous Conflict in America*, rev. by Rev. John Little (Memphis, 1867), 58; Col. W. Preston Johnston to Jefferson Davis, July 15, 1862, in Letter Book of Dr. Andrew J. Foard, Virginia State Library, Richmond.

hospitals. Foard, who was of course under criticism, recommended to Bragg that Nott be appointed chief medical inspector for the army in the West with three other surgeons to assist him and that all these inspectors, including Nott, should report to him. This was a way to improve hospital conditions, but from Foard's point of view it was also a way to reduce possible competition from Nott. In the medical department of the Confederacy the lines of command were hazily drawn, and Foard had asked for clarification from Richmond as to the use of the term "medical director." The title was given not only to Foard, who was in general charge of medical affairs for Bragg's command, but also to surgeons such as Nott who were on Bragg's staff and to surgeons who were "medical directors" of the different corps within the army. Foard received confirmation from Richmond that he had supreme control of the medical department of Bragg's command, and he averted a potentially embarrassing situation by arranging for Nott to be given the major responsibility of inspecting all hospitals, with the understanding that he report to Foard.[14]

On July 16 Nott was ordered to inspect the entire medical department, particularly those hospitals along the lines of the Mobile and Ohio Railroad that were under the special instructions of Medical Director Foard (there were also a variety of private hospitals). This was an arduous task, which involved traveling the length of the Mobile and Ohio Railroad from Tupelo to Mobile, visiting numerous hospitals in Jackson, Clinton, Edwards Depot, Vicksburg, Canton, Granada, and other places, including Mobile itself. Nott was not only to tour the hospitals to inspect the physical facilities and personnel, he was also to examine the books of prescriptions, registers of admission, financial arrangements with private physicians, and culinary facilities.[15]

While Nott toured the hospitals and reported on their inadequacies, Foard tried to take steps to alleviate the critical personnel shortage. It had proved necessary to transfer able-bodied troops to hospital duty, and in August Foard recommended that all men now on extra duty in the hospitals be kept there as long as they were needed. In July he had given orders for blacks to be employed as nurses and cooks in hospitals, but he admit-

14. Surgeon A. J. Foard to Brig.-Gen. Thomas Jordan, July 9, 1862; A. J. Foard to Surgeon General S. P. Moore, June 27, 1862, Moore to Foard, July 8, 1862, all in Letter Book of Dr. Andrew J. Foard.

15. Foard to Brig.-Gen. Thomas Jordan, July 16, 1862, Special Order to Nott, July 16, 1862, Foard to Nott, July 17, 1862 (enclosing instructions), *ibid.*

ted that it was "impossible to hire Negroes in sufficient numbers to supply the demand for nurses" and that there were simply not enough
soldiers who were unfit for field duty but suitable for hospital service
available to supply the demand. Foard also defended himself to the surgeon general against the adverse reports on medical conditions in the
western army. His difficulties of supply and personnel had been increased
because the troops were badly clothed and miserably sheltered. There was
no solution to Foard's problems. All over the Confederacy tens of thousands of sick and wounded troops were overtaxing its medical resources.
Peacetime hospital facilities in the South had been extremely limited. In
wartime conditions and with limited southern resources it was impossible to create an efficient hospital and medical system for southern
armies.[16]

As Foard and Nott tried to cope with the medical problems of Bragg's
army, Bragg was beginning to respond to the threat that federal forces in
the Mississippi Valley were beginning to present to the major railroad
junction of Chattanooga, Tennessee. Late in July Bragg decided to move
a large part of his force—some thirty-four thousand men—from Tupelo
to Chattanooga to meet this threat and to take the offensive. The artillery,
cavalry, and wagons marched and rolled across the country while the infantry, some twenty-five thousand strong, was sent on a long, circuitous
rail journey from Tupelo to Chattanooga.[17]

After finishing his tour of hospitals, Nott joined the forces in Chattanooga. Bragg's move pointed up the huge difficulties facing the medical
services. The hospital system that Nott had just inspected and Foard had
tried to shore up was too distant to be of any use to Bragg's main force in
Chattanooga, although many of the medical personnel were still needed
in Mississippi to take care of the numerous sick left behind in the hospitals, as well as the new sick from the force stationed there. The medical
department had to find the facilities and personnel to meet the vastly increased demand for medical services in east Tennessee.[18]

The medical department centered under Surgeon Foard in Chattanooga now began to establish a series of new hospitals along the rail-

16. Foard to Surgeon J. A. Bowers, July 13, 1862, Foard to Asst. Ad.-Gen., August 4, 6,
1862, Foard to Surgeon General, August 5, 1862, *ibid.*
17. Connelly, *Army of the Heartland*, 196–204; Grady McWhiney, *Braxton Bragg and
Confederate Defeat*, vol. I, *Field Command* (New York, 1969), 266–71; Robert C. Black, *The
Railroads of the Confederacy* (Chapel Hill, 1952).
18. Foard to the Surgeon General, August 10, 1862, in Letter Book of A. J. Foard.

way line between Chattanooga and Atlanta. To achieve better direction of these hospitals, Surgeon S. H. Stout was given direct responsibility for all of them under the general orders of Foard. Nott was now again on Bragg's staff and late in August accompanied Bragg when he left Chattanooga to lead the new Army of Tennessee on an invasion of Kentucky. At first, the invasion went well. There was little resistance, and Bragg was able to "liberate" much of Kentucky. On October 8, at Perryville (Chaplin's Hill), the invasion soured. Bragg was soundly defeated by a force under Union General Philip Sheridan and was forced to retreat. By the end of the month his army was back in Tennessee. Nott had gained a great deal of experience in field surgery. The medical department, however, was now in further difficulties, for while it was trying to set up hospitals for thousands of new sick and wounded, Bragg recalled all the able-bodied men from hospital duty. Foard told his post surgeons to replace these troops with blacks and white persons not subject to conscription. If blacks could not be hired, they were to be pressed into service—free as well as slave.[19]

Nott had been on active service for a long time for a man who was nearing sixty, and though he frequently treated the wounded, his time was also taken up by inspections, administrative duties, and giving advice. As Bragg retreated and prepared to meet the Union attacks that were sure to come, Nott's romantic excitement of the early months of the war had long passed. Nott was wearying of military service in the field, and after Bragg's retreat from Kentucky he took an appointment as medical inspector in the Department of the Gulf, based in Mobile. He still inspected camps and hospitals, but he also carried out extensive surgery in the various military hospitals in Mobile. Nott's reputation was so high that many former soldiers suffering from the aftereffects of their wounds were sent to him from the interior of Alabama and from the adjoining states. Nott was hardly running away from danger in taking a position in Mobile because after the fall of New Orleans, Mobile was considered to be in great danger of attack. The Confederacy also faced military problems both in northern Alabama and in Mississippi. When in January,

19. Foard to Brig.-Gen. Jordan, August 3, 1862, *ibid.;* Order of General Braxton Bragg, August 22, 1862, in Samuel H. Stout Papers, Confederate Museum, Richmond, Virginia. For the invasion of Kentucky see Connelly, *Army of the Heartland,* 221–80; McWhiney, *Bragg,* 272–325; Foard to various post surgeons, November 8, 1862, in Letter Book of A. J. Foard.

1863, Nott recommended that Demopolis, Alabama, not be made the site of a military hospital, he commented that there were convenient hospitals at a number of places, including Jackson, but he added the priviso, "If Jackson is not taken by the enemy."[20]

By the beginning of 1863, Nott's friend General Bragg was a very controversial figure in the Confederacy, and there are indications that Bragg had asked Nott for a show of support. Nott did give some encouragement in private letters to Bragg, but he avoided any general public defense. Much of Bragg's unpopularity stemmed from a reputation for harshness, a dour personality, and his failure to achieve any striking victories. Nurse Kate Cumming had commented in June, 1862, that the soldiers called Bragg a "strict disciplinarian," and if half of the stories they told about him were true, he was "a perfect monster of cruelty," who made a pastime of shooting his men. Bragg had shot men for desertion, and this became a cause of major controversy. A letter to the Mobile *Register* in September, 1862, defended Bragg against the charge of unjust shootings, saying that "there seems to be an impression throughout the country that Gen. Bragg is in the habit of shooting men merely for the pleasure it gives him." The English diarist and army officer James Fremantle commented that Bragg was "in appearance the least prepossessing of Confederate generals" and that he "has the reputation of being a rigid disciplinarian, and of shooting freely for insubordination."[21]

Nott was clearly unwilling to be involved in an elaborate public defense of Bragg. At the end of January, 1863, he told him that he had written two labored defenses for the newspapers but had thrown them in the fire. What was the use of a medical officer speaking, asked Nott, when Bragg's own generals remained silent? Nott said that he had sought "to do even handed justice to a brave soldier who has sacrificed every thing in our cause" and that Zach Deas and Nott's son James "sustain you fully & wish no other Commander," but Nott took away much of the pleasure that Bragg could feel in this expression of support by pointing out a few of

20. Military Service Record of Josiah C. Nott, in RG 109, NA; Nott to Surgeon F. A. Ross, January 27, 1863, in Samuel H. Stout Papers, William R. Perkins Library, Duke University, Durham, North Carolina; Josiah C. Nott, *Contributions to Bone and Nerve Surgery* (Philadelphia, 1866), 50.

21. Cumming, *Kate*, 47–48; Mobile *Register*, September 9, 1862; James A. L. Fremantle, *The Fremantle Diary*, ed. Walter Lord (London, 1956), 115; McWhiney, *Bragg*, 254–55; Thomas L. Connelly, *Autumn of Glory: The Army of Tennessee, 1862–1865* (Baton Rouge, 1971), 73.

Bragg's faults. "Your best friends admit that Your Temper is irritable," he wrote, "—that under excitement you are sometimes harsh when there is no necessity for it & sometimes even wound an innocent man." Nott softened his criticisms a little by commenting that it was general knowledge that the army was "a lawless mob" when Bragg had taken charge of it the year before.[22]

A month later Nott again tried to pacify Bragg in a private letter while avoiding public commitment. He told Bragg that he had no general under him who was competent to command anything larger than a brigade, and he also explained, in behalf of John Forsyth, the editor of the Mobile *Register,* that letters attacking Bragg had crept into the newspaper without Forsyth reading them. The writer, said Nott, "is a coarse, drunken blackguard, & what St. Paul calls a 'pestilent fellow.'" Nott added that he assumed Bragg would have another fight and that if he knew when it was to be he would come up and give assistance. This promise was almost certainly not meant, for two days later Nott resigned his position as surgeon in the Confederate army. He had decided to return to private practice, although he would still give extensive help in Mobile's military hospitals. Mobile was now being prepared to resist a probable Union attack.[23]

For Mobilians, as for the troops at the front, the war had become a matter of endurance by the spring of 1863, although some were living much better than others. Of the very high proportion of the town's young men who had enlisted in the Confederate forces, many had died, some in battle but more of the complications of wounds or of camp diseases. The town itself had not suffered directly from the war, but the presence of Confederate troops was a constant reminder of danger. Northern blockades had led to shortages throughout the South, and fun-loving Mobile had to be content without many of its luxuries and some of what had seemed to be necessities.[24]

When Confederate nurse Kate Cumming visited Mobile in February, 1863, she noticed that there were a good number of troops about and that the city was being placed in a state of defense. Prices of provisions were

22. Nott to Bragg, January 31, 1863, in Braxton Bragg Papers, Western Reserve Historical Society, Cleveland, Ohio.
23. Nott to Bragg, March 1, 1863, *ibid.;* Military Service Record of Josiah C. Nott, in RG 109, NA. See also Nott to Bragg, December 10, 1863, in Braxton Bragg Papers, Special Collections, Robert W. Woodruff Library, Emory University, Atlanta, Georgia.
24. Cumming, *Kate,* 57–58; Mary D. Waring Journal, July 29, 1863, in SHC.

rising sharply, and there was a critical shortage of oil and candles.[25] One continuing sign of the danger from Union forces was the steady stream of New Orleans exiles still finding their way to Mobile and the refugees from Jackson, Mississippi, which, as Nott had feared, had fallen to Union forces. In May a meeting of the ladies of Mobile in the St. Francis Street Methodist Church took steps to receive the additional New Orleans exiles who were expected shortly; Nott's wife, Sarah, was on the executive committee of the ladies' organization. Mobile hardly seemed to be an ideal refuge, for after the fall of Vicksburg in July it was assumed that Mobile would soon be attacked. A twenty-five-man committee of safety, which included Nott, was established, and it met every Tuesday. The committee was responsible for all questions that pertained to good order and morale in the city, and it investigated cases such as that of a man who was accused of refusing to accept depreciated Confederate money. This particular man was cleared of the charges, but canny merchants were becoming increasingly reluctant to accept money that was dropping sharply in value.[26]

Defense preparations were now proceeding rapidly around the city. The forts in the bay were being strengthened, the channels were being mined with "torpedoes", and access to the city was generally being made more difficult. Much of the labor was carried out by a large force of slaves, many of whom had been sent from plantations in the interior. In August the Mobile *Register* assured their owners that careful medical inspections were being carried out, but the conditions under which they worked worsened in the coming months. Mobile's privileged free blacks were eager in these years to show their support for the Confederacy, and in November, 1862, the Alabama legislature had given them permission to enlist, with the proviso that they could serve only in Mobile. This restriction was later removed by the Confederate secretary of war.[27]

25. Cumming, *Kate*, 88, 101. See also John Kent Folmar (ed.), *From That Terrible Field: The Civil War Letters of James M. Williams, Twenty-First Alabama Infantry Volunteers* (University, Ala., 1981), 146, 147.

26. Maggie Graves to Charles Graves, May 28, 1863, in Charles Iverson Graves Papers, SHC; Mobile *Register*, May 24, June 10, July 12, and July and August, 1863, *passim;* Solomon Mordecai to Ellen Mordecai, June 21, 1863, in Mordecai Family Papers, SHC; William H. Semple to G. W. Bagby, June 7, 24, 1863, in Bagby Family Papers, Virginia Historical Society, Richmond; Capers, *Occupied City*, 93–94.

27. Walter L. Fleming, *Civil War and Reconstruction in Alabama* (1905; rpr. New York, 1949), 84–86; Mobile *Register*, August 19, 1863; Melton McLaurin and Michael Thomason, *Mobile: The Life and Times of a Great Southern City* (Woodland Hills, Calif., 1981), 60; *OR,* Ser. IV, vol. I, 1088, vol. II, 941.

The shortages that beset even the wealthy in Mobile were particularly hard felt by the poorer families of the city, especially those whose men were at the front. In September some of the women of Mobile staged a bread riot. They marched down Dauphin Street breaking into food and clothing stores and carrying banners inscribed "Bread or Blood" and "Bread and Peace." The rioters were aggrieved not only by their own hardships but also by the obvious signs in the city that not all were suffering for the Confederacy. At the beginning of the month, the Mobile *Register* attacked the signs of vice and corruption. On Royal Street, wrote the editor, there were no less than twelve gambling houses, "where Epicurean tables are spread and rich wines sparkle and flow." The owner of one of these gambling houses was estimated to have made more than $1 million in two years.[28]

To relieve the sufferings of the poor, prominent citizens of Mobile met to form the Confederate Society. There had already been efforts to feed the destitute by obtaining donations from the wealthy. The new society was to strive to reduce exorbitant prices, proceed against those who refused to accept Confederate money, and aid the wives and children of Confederate soldiers.[29]

The strain of life in Mobile was compounded for Nott by the knowledge that one of his two remaining sons was in the thick of the fighting with the Army of Tennessee. Nott's son James had fought with Bragg's army and the Twenty-second Alabama since Shiloh. He had participated in the invasion of Kentucky and was in the engagements that forced Bragg to pull back in Tennessee. He was a dedicated southern patriot who kept his enthusiasm as the South's hopes diminished. In the spring of 1863 he assigned two months' pay for the benefit of the state of Alabama.[30]

In September, 1863, Bragg's army and the 22d Alabama were in the fiercest fight since Shiloh. At Chickamauga, Bragg attempted to destroy the advancing Union forces in a two-day battle and failed. Confederate losses were heavy, particularly among the 22d Alabama, which formed the left wing of Bragg's attack. By this time, James Nott was the ranking captain in the regiment. He moved forward with the 22d Alabama on Sunday

28. McMillan (ed.), *Alabama Confederate Reader,* 335; Mobile *Register,* September 1, 1863; [John O'Connor], *Wanderings of a Vagabond: An Autobiography,* by John Morris (New York, [1873]), 253.

29. McMillan (ed.), *Alabama Confederate Reader,* 335–37; Mobile *Evening Telegraph,* September 15, 23, 1863; Mobile *Evening News,* October 9, November 21, 1863.

30. Military Service Record of James D. Nott, in RG 109, NA.

morning, September 20. As the Alabamans reached the main Union line they were met with heavy volleys of musketry coming from behind a log breastwork about three feet high. The regiment charged the breastwork. As James Nott led his company forward he fell, mortally wounded. He lived for a short time but never spoke. A few minutes later, Lieutenant Colonel John Weedon, the commander of the regiment, was killed. James's uncle, Zach Deas, who now commanded the brigade in which the 22d fought, said of James Nott that "no braver or better officer ever poured out his life's blood in his country's cause. He died where the brave and good should die—in the front rank, leading his men on to victory."[31]

James Nott's body was taken back to Mobile for burial. He was twenty-seven. On September 27 he was buried alongside his brother Henry and the four Nott children who had died in the yellow fever epidemic of 1853. The inscription on his gravestone said that he died "while leading a charge at the battle of Chickamauga." Nott also had another monument placed on the graves of his sons. The language was his: "It is a consolation to those who mourn their loss and erect this monument, to know that they died in defense of Liberty and left behind untarnished names."[32]

The obituary in the Mobile *Register* was not written by Nott. It was less an obituary than a cry of pain. It must have come from one of the two women in the Nott household—probably from James's aunt Margaret Auzé, who had poured out her despair in a letter to Mrs. Chestnut after Shiloh. In little more than ten years, Sarah Nott had lost five sons and a daughter; her sister Margaret had lost her husband and her only son. The latest blow was overwhelming. Sarah Nott now had one surviving child—a son; Margaret Auzé had one surviving child—a daughter. Most obituaries in the *Register* were prosaic accounts of careers combined with conventional rhetoric of patriotism and innate worth. James Nott's obituary had no details of his career. It simply anguished over his loss: "Wounded for life is the spirit of domestic love and affection, that brooded over the infancy—nurtured the youth, and rejoiced in the manhood of a man so lovely and attractive that all hearts were wooed by its beauty, and every tongue proclaimed its goodness." The shadow of "unspeakable grief rests on the household hitherto illumined and made

31. Report of Capt. Harry T. Toulmin, October 5, 1863, Report of Brig.-Gen. Zach C. Deas, October 9, 1863, *OR*, Ser. I, vol. XXX, Part 2, 331, 335–37; file on the 22d Alabama, in Alabama Department of Archives and History, Montgomery.
32. Gravestones, Magnolia Cemetery, Mobile, and Mobile County burial records.

joyous by his presence." The consolation for those who remained, said the obituarist, was that James Nott had died the hallowed death of a true patriot—God had given him a triumphant death: "And thus passed away one of the noblest spirits and most unselfish beings that ever dwelt on earth!"[33]

For the remaining years of the Civil War Nott could do only what he had done in the 1850s—throw himself into his work with frenetic vigor. Soldiers with unhealed, suppurating wounds continued to be sent to Nott from the interior of the Gulf region, and he continued to operate in the many military hospitals in Mobile. By January, 1864, there were five general military hospitals in Mobile with some six hundred beds. There were also hospitals at Spring Hill and at Point Clear; at Point Clear part of the resort hotel was converted for the use of wounded troops. One of the Mobile hospitals was Nott's old Royal Street Infirmary. Nott's brother Adolphus Nott, an exile from New Orleans, became the surgeon in charge of this hospital in 1864. The Nott hospital was described as "cleanly, well administered and well appointed in all respects." In the course of 1864, three more military hospitals were opened in Mobile, the bed capacity was increased, and a black hospital, housed in a warehouse and headed by an acting assistant surgeon, was opened for the slaves who became ill or were injured while working on the Mobile fortifications. The slaves suffered badly, and they had the worst of the medical facilities. Nott expressed concern at their condition.[34]

In spite of the blockade runners and an illegal trade with occupied New Orleans, most articles were in very short supply in Mobile, and the efforts of prominent, public-spirited citizens to keep down prices and bolster Confederate money had failed. In December, 1863, coffee was $15 a pound, tea $16. The very poor and the destitute were helped by the various voluntary groups that canvassed the streets of the city to discover where help was needed. Contrasting with this underlying distress was the desperate gaiety of many of Mobile's elite and the officers they entertained. In the late winter of 1863–1864 there was an almost partylike at-

33. Mobile *Register,* October 2, 1863.
34. Nott, *Contributions to Bone and Nerve Surgery,* 50; Mobile *Daily Tribune,* April 10, 1864; List of General Hospitals in the Department of the Gulf, January 17, 1864, in Letter Book of A. J. Foard; *OR,* Ser. I, vol. XLV, Part 2, 718 (quotation regarding Nott hospital); Fleming, *Civil War and Reconstruction,* 206; McLaurin and Thomason, *Mobile,* 60; W. J. Donald, "Alabama Confederate Hospitals," *Alabama Review,* XV (1962), 271–81, XVI (1963), 64–78.

mosphere in the city. An unexpressed feeling prevailed that there was still time for enjoyment before disaster and death overwhelmed the South. When Kate Cumming returned to Mobile in January and February, 1864, she found it "gayer than ever." At one party the "luxuries" were "coffee mixed with rye, with sugar and milk, wheat-bread and butter." Lights burned late as Mobilians strove to forget the war.[35]

Two visitors who arrived at about the same time as Cumming confirmed her impressions of a lively, still cheerful town. On the day they arrived to stay at the Battle House, British soldier Fitzgerald Ross and his American companion had "a capital breakfast" at a French restaurant in the city, visited the "Manassas Club" and drank "a cocktail," and in the evening went to "a grand wedding-party and ball," where they were impressed by the beauty of Mobile's women. Ross's companion left Mobile to return to Richmond, and he confirmed his fellow traveler's impression of the city, for Mrs. Chestnut commented about him in her diary that he was fresh from Mobile, "where he left peace and plenty. He went to sixteen weddings and twenty-seven tea parties. For breakfast he had everything nice."[36]

With the South losing the war, speculators and profiteers carousing in the Mobile gambling rooms and brothels, polite Mobile society attempting to ignore what was coming in a round of parties, and poor Mobilians trying to get enough to eat, Nott was still trying to forget his pain and bitter disappointment in a constant round of work. There were now no pleasant summer trips to the North, no stimulating correspondence with northern scientists, and little opportunity for writing and publication. His college was closed and his home filled with empty rooms and memories.

In August, 1864, the first phase of the Union attack on Mobile began. Union ships took command of Mobile Bay. The city itself was still intact, but now the maritime blockade was complete, and Forts Gaines and Morgan were in Union hands. While the assault in the bay was in its final stages, Nott took the time to write directly to General Bragg with a request that the son of a Mobile family Nott had served as family physician for twenty-five years be "detailed for some light duty." He said that there "has been no truer or braver young man in the Confederacy," but he was now "unfit for the field." As the Confederacy sank into defeat, perhaps Nott was hoping to help some young men survive the wreckage.[37]

After all the deaths of young people in the Nott family, there were at last two in the fall of 1864 that came in proper time. Nott's oldest brother, William Blackstone Nott, had for many years practiced medicine at Limestone Springs in South Carolina. Nott had been able to see him on his summer trips, particularly in his earlier years when his mother was still alive and spending much time in the South Carolina up-country. William died in September, 1864, at the age of sixty-nine. It was said of him that he had "a mind of depth, grasp, and compass of wide range; a disposition, enthusiastic, impulsive—even passionate, yet cheerful and amiable; manners easy and engaging." Though he was described as tottering and gray, he practiced medicine until a few days before he died. He was recognizably a Nott.[38]

A death that was far more disruptive to a pattern of life that Nott had developed over nearly thirty years was that of James Deas, his father-in-law, who died in November, 1864. Deas had been the center of a large clan since the family had moved from South Carolina in the mid-1830s, and the entire family had benefited greatly from his wealth and influence. He was eighty when he died, still a very wealthy man. A fellow resident of Spring Hill later called him a "most agreeable neighbor and cultivated gentleman of the old South Carolina English stock." When complimented on his vigor at an advanced age, he was likely to comment that "the disastrous results of the war to his property compelled him to move about so lively from place to place, and so often, that the Lord did not know where to put his finger on him."[39]

Deas had more than seven hundred acres of plantation property in Alabama and Mississippi, the acreage at Spring Hill, where he usually spent his summers, and a house in Mobile. At his death in excess of $200,000 was owed to him. He left all his real and personal property, including his slaves, to his wife. He also left $100,000 of the money owed to him for her to dispose of as she thought fit. The rest of the money owed to him was to be divided among seven of his eight children (the eighth, he said,

37. McMillan (ed.), *Alabama Confederate Reader,* 309–11; Fleming, *Civil War and Reconstruction,* 69–70; Nott to Bragg, August 18, 1864, in Bragg Papers, Western Reserve Historical Society.

38. MSS obituary of William B. Nott, in Joseph Banks Lyle Papers, SCL.

39. Sub Rosa [Paul Ravesies], *Scenes and Settlers of Alabama* (Mobile, 1885), 34.

had already had more than the others). Six of the seven to whom he left money (four women and two men) made their homes in Mobile County. They included Sarah Nott and Margaret Auzé. His son Zach was with the Army of Tennessee. In his wife's petition for probate, it was commented that this army was "supposed to be in Tennessee." As was well known, the Army of Tennessee had been driven back into Georgia.[40]

The war was now drawing to a close. All that Nott had hoped for was disappearing, but the Mobilians waiting for attack maintained their brittle gaiety. The city was filled with Confederate troops, and in the early weeks of 1865 there were constant parties and balls, given, it was said, for the benefit of the troops. The Mobile theater continued to operate while the city was in the process of being captured and was producing Shakespeare in January and February. Food and provisions were very scarce. Flour, tea, coffee, and sugar were obtainable only at famine prices, even the famous oysters had disappeared with the capture of the bay, and the staples were now peas, corn, meal, and bacon.[41]

The Union forces, some forty-six thousand strong, began their move against the city shortly after the middle of March. Only ten thousand Confederates were available to man the remaining forts and the entrenchments thrown up by the slaves to protect the city. The military authorities now searched all the houses in the city to assemble the remaining cotton for destruction should the city fall.[42] Fighting continued through the latter part of March and into April, but life in the city went on. One young woman, Mary Waring, noted in her diary at the end of March that very heavy firing could be heard. She had gone for her voice lesson, but her teacher had to send her home because she felt so bad about her son, who had just left for one of the forts. Later in the day Waring went to a private house for a meeting of the Soldiers' Hope Society; there the women picked lint for wounded Confederate soldiers.[43]

Throughout the first week of April the heavy firing continued and be-

40. Will and inventory of property of James S. Deas, in Probate Records, Mobile County Court House, Mobile. Sarah Nott eventually received some $12,000 from her father's estate; see Sarah Nott to C. H. Harney, May 2, 1882, in Nott Papers, William Stanley Hoole Special Collections Library, University of Alabama, Tuscaloosa.
41. Cumming, *Kate*, 248–49, 255–56, 261; Mobile *Register*, January–April, 1865.
42. Fleming, *Civil War and Reconstruction*, 71; Folmar (ed.), *From That Terrible Field*, 155. Much cotton still remained intact when Union forces took the city (*OR*, Ser. I, vol. XLIX, Part 2, 348–49).
43. Mary Waring Journal, March 31, 1865, in SHC.

came heavier. Mary Waring continued to pick lint and roll bandages. On April 8 she heard "terrible" musketry. "The firing is still rapid and heavy while I write. It is growing late so I must stop." Next morning she heard that the Spanish Fort had fallen, and "our soldiers were passing by in squads, from an early hour, dirty, wet and completely worn out." Two days later an alarm bell rang to call the troops together for evacuation. The great majority left on the night of April 11–12. In the morning only a few scouts were left, ready to decamp on the entrance of the Union forces. Some of the military stores were turned over to Mobile's needy, and there was scuffling and fighting in the streets as they divided the spoils.[44]

Toward noon the mayor went in a carriage with a white flag to meet the Yankees approaching the city, and in the early afternoon Yankee officers were to be seen riding through the city streets. A Yankee gunboat arrived at the wharf at the end of Government Street, and to the shock of Mobilians loyal to the Confederacy was greeted with cheers by a crowd that included some whites as well as many blacks. Late in the afternoon Yankee troops marched into Mobile to the tune of "Yankee Doodle." The city had surrendered unconditionally. On the following day, the thirteenth, Mary Waring commented that the "city is filled with the hated Yanks, who differ in the greatest degree from our poor dear soldiers—the commonest, dirtiest-looking set I ever saw." She admitted, however, that they were quiet and orderly. At church on Sunday, the sixteenth, the pews were filled with "blue coats."[45]

Even before the federal troops marched into Mobile, the Confederacy had collapsed. On April 9 Robert E. Lee had surrendered the shattered remnants of his army to Grant at Appomattox. The past few months had seen many parts of the South ravaged and destroyed by the invading Union armies. In February, when William T. Sherman took Columbia, South Carolina, Nott's home town, it was burned; the southerners blamed Sherman and Sherman the retreating Confederates. Early in April, a Union raiding party that reached Tuscaloosa, Alabama, burned most of the University of Alabama to the ground because it had been a military college during the war. Of the 825 University of Alabama students who had served in the war, 172 never returned.[46]

44. *Ibid.*, April 1–12, 1865.
45. *Ibid.*, April 1–6; Mobile *Daily News*, April 13, 1865; Sidney Adair Smith and C. Carter Smith (eds), *Mobile: 1861–1865: Notes and a Bibliography* (Chicago, 1964), 42–46. See also *OR*, Ser. I, vol. XLIX, 340, 348–49, 363.
46. Mobile had definite news of Lee's surrender by April 17 (Mobile *Daily News*, April 17,

At the end of May, Mobile "had the quietness of the grave. Scarcely a soul was to be seen on the streets, excepting negroes." A Union army band played in the public square, but the blinds of houses were all closed and the whites stayed home, though "the Federal soldiers have behaved very well to the citizens."[47] What Nott had feared and fought against had come to pass. The South was a conquered section, occupied by northern troops, and in Alabama more than 430,000 slaves had been freed. Two of his sons were dead in a war that Nott had supported as a sacred duty in the defense of liberty. Mobile was an occupied city; Columbia had been burned to the ground. Nott had to pick up the pieces of his life. For him there was little left but to practice medicine, always his first love, and to rail against human idiocy.

1865). For the burning of Columbia see *When the World Ended: The Diary of Emma LeConte*, ed. Earl S. Miers (New York, 1957), 42–64. For the University of Alabama see James B. Sellers, *History of the University of Alabama*, I, *1818–1902* (University, Ala., 1953), 281–88.
   47. Cumming, *Kate*, 306–307.

Chapter 13
OCCUPIED MOBILE

In the first months of 1865, the people of Mobile had held on to some forlorn hope that somehow all would turn out for the best. But with dramatic suddenness, Confederate troops marched away, Union troops marched in, slavery was ended, and the news came that Lee had surrendered and the Confederacy had lost. The world was turned upside down. Hundreds, and then thousands, of black freedmen were to be seen in the streets, and among the occupying forces were two regiments of black troops. A northern visitor who watched a review of the northern occupying force said that the "negro troops marched very handsomely, and made, perhaps, the best appearance of any regiment in the column; but every citizen seemed to consider their appearance as a personal insult to himself."[1]

Mobile's citizens did all they could to express their resentment at the Union troops and their disgust at the sight of freed slaves filling their streets. The Union general who commanded in the city in June later said that the large majority of the population did not attempt to disguise their disloyal sentiments and regarded the abolition of slavery as unconstitutional. His successor said that there was "always a smothered hatred of the uniform and the flag." As the summer advanced, the atmosphere in the city became uglier. The turning point was on July 4. On that day the general in command agreed to a request of the freedmen to celebrate Independence Day. "Six thousand well-dressed and orderly colored people, escorted by two regiments of colored troops, paraded the streets, assembled in the public squares, and were addressed in patriotic speeches

1. Whitelaw Reid, *After the War: A Southern Tour, May 1, 1865, to May 1, 1866* (New York, 1866), 213.

by orators of their own race and color." Kate Cumming remembered it as the day on which the public square (Bienville) was, by order, given up to the blacks.[2] From his house and office on the northeast corner of the square, Nott had a clear view of the celebration.

After the fourth, racial incidents swept the area. The military com-mander accused the mayor, the common council, the police, and the newspapers of inciting hatred against the freedmen. "The enormities committed by the police were fearful," he wrote. "Within my knowledge colored girls seized upon the streets had to take their choice between sub-mitting to outrage on the part of the policemen or incarceration in the guard-house." There were threats to destroy all buildings in which blacks were taught (two schools were set on fire) or worshiped (a church was burned down). In an attempt to stem the tide of freedmen coming into the city, the mayor ordered the police to arrest all persons found under suspicious circumstances or who had no homes or visible means of sup-port. Threats of assassination against colored ministers were ignored by Mayor R. H. Hough, and he was removed from office. By the end of July, nearly one thousand pupils were attending the colored schools daily, and a Union general said that the blacks generally were "orderly, quiet, indus-trious, and well dressed, with an earnest desire to learn and fit themselves for their new status," but white resentment increased. "Without the aid of the bayonets of the United States," General Thomas Smith wrote, "Ala-bama is an anarchy."[3]

Although the white officers and troops were shunned by many of the residents, the sharpest hatred and the violence were directed against the black troops and the freedmen. The black troops were pushed from the pavements by local residents and had to be armed while going to and from their fatigue duty. Black residents could not obtain justice in the local courts and were forced to appeal to the Freedmen's Bureau for pro-tection. The local police continued to harass blacks on the streets. "All

2. Statement of Maj.-Gen. Christopher D. Andrews, March 13, 1866, *Report of the Joint Committee on Reconstruction at the First Session Thirty-Ninth Congress* (1866; rpr. Freeport, N.Y., 1971), Part III, 148; statement of Brig.-Gen. Thomas K. Smith, September 14, 1865, in Carl Schurz, *Report on the Condition of the South*, 39th Cong., 1st Sess., Exec. Doc. No. 2 (1866; rpr. New York, 1969), 57–58; Kate Cumming, *Gleanings from Southland* (Birming-ham, 1895), 266.
3. Statement of Brig.-Gen. Thomas K. Smith, September 14, 1865, in Schurz, *Report on the Condition of the South*, 58–59; Mobile *Daily Tribune*, July 23, 1865. See also John B. Myers, "The Freedmen and the Law in Post-Bellum Alabama, 1865–1867," *Alabama Review*, XXIII (1970), 56–69.

hopes of equity and justice through the civil organization of this city is barred," wrote the assistant superintendent of the Freedmen's Bureau in the city at the end of July. "Prejudice and a vindictive hatred to color is universal here; it increases intensely, and the only capacity in which the negro will be tolerated is that of slave." In the rural counties around Mobile the situation was much worse. In these areas there was a reign of terror. The brutal murder of blacks became common. An area of particular violence and brutality was that around Bladon Springs, a resort popular with the elite of Mobile in the years before the war.[4]

Resentment of Union troops, and the lack of feelings of loyalty toward the United States were not surprising in the immediate aftermath of war, but ominous for the future was the outbreak of hatred, harassment, and outright violence toward blacks that swept across southern Alabama. For the white elite of Mobile a comfortable way of life had gone forever. The existing social fabric had been destroyed, and many could not conceive of life in this new, unbelievable society in which their slaves of a few months before now thronged the streets by the thousands, crowded the public square to hear their own orators, and were represented by rows of black faces in the regiments of the occupying power. The whites were fearful for their own position in this new black world, and in their fear and rage the worst elements in the white population lashed out in rage and violence.

In the spring and summer of 1865 it was difficult for Nott to accept life in Mobile, but he did not allow his horror at what had happened in the South to deflect him from his duties as a physician. On May 25 the main ordnance depot of the United States forces in Mobile blew up. The explosion destroyed several downtown blocks and killed more than two hundred people. The following month, a visitor described eight or ten city squares as a waste of broken brick and mortar. Among those killed and hurt were black troops in a hospital above the Mobile and Ohio Railroad Depot and freedmen in the Garner House hospital. The front walls of both these hospitals were destroyed, and the survivors were moved into the Kennedy Hospital, which was under the direction of Surgeon J. C. Richards of the United States Army. In the chaos following the explosion, Nott and two other Mobile doctors gave all the help they could to Dr. Richards, and Richards asked the Mobile *Daily News* to print his

4. Statement of Brig.-Gen. Thomas K. Smith, September 14, 1865, W. A. Poillon to Carl Schurz, July 29, 1865, in Schurz, *Report on the Condition of the South,* 58–59, 72–74.

thanks to them for their work among the colored troops and freedmen at the Kennedy Hospital. The editor commented that Surgeon Richards spoke "in high terms" of the work of the Mobile physicians.[5]

With the collapse of all his hopes, Nott gave much thought to leaving the city. When he resumed his correspondence with Squier, he wrote that he "felt so badly whipped after the Confederacy Caved in, & so desponding of the future prospects of the South" that he toyed with the idea of moving to New York. Northerners, he wrote, "are perfectly fair, in not *pretending* to have any honesty." Although he thought he was still likely to live and die in Mobile, he suggested that he might settle in Baltimore, New York, or Paris if he could raise enough money.[6] Like many other southerners, Nott believed that a fresh start in a new area might be preferable to living in a crushed and totally changed South.

Nott had always been cynical regarding human rationality and prospects, and in these years his bitterness increased. He told Squier that "God Almighty made the Nigger, & no dam'd Yankee on top of the earth can bleach him." For Nott the South would become a land he would enjoy living in only when the blacks had left or died out. With all other hope gone, Nott was now to develop an earlier suggestion that in freedom blacks could not survive with whites and that the "inferior" blacks like the "inferior" Indians were doomed to eventual extinction. He believed that though the South had lost the war, the United States itself had been fatally injured by the events of the 1860s. The federal government was compounding its mistakes by its "suicidal" policies toward the South and was driving southerners into the same feelings toward the government as the Poles had toward Russia. The breach might have been healed at the end of the war, argued Nott, if the North had given a general amnesty and simply invited the southern states back into the Union. But by treating southerners as traitors, forcing them to ask for pardons, and confiscating property, the North had ensured southern enmity. Nott told Leidy that "the old form of Government is gone & must terminate in One Man Power, or explode into fragments like a bomb—I go for an Empire & Nobility, & am in for one of the Nobles."[7]

5. Mobile *Morning News,* May 26, 27, 1865; Mobile *Daily News,* May 28, 1865; Mobile *Daily Tribune,* July 23, 1865; *OR,* Ser. I, vol. XLIV, Part 2, 907, 912–13; Reid, *After the War,* 214–15. See also Mrs. Hugh C. Bailey, "Mobile's Tragedy: The Great Magazine Explosion of 1865," *Alabama Review,* XXI (1968), 40–52.

6. Nott to Squier, December 5, 1865, in Squier Papers, LC.

7. *Ibid.;* and Nott to Leidy, December 12, 1865, in Leidy Papers, ANSP.

Above all else, Nott could not accept the freeing of millions of black slaves into southern society. The problem was not that they were poverty-stricken and unprepared, but that he believed with all his heart that they were a permanently inferior race, which no education or help could transform. "The negroes are going to give a great deal of trouble—they are lazy—improvident, & vicious, & must go to the wall—while the transition is taking place a residence at the South will not be desirable."[8] In reality, of course, no generous policy by the North would have persuaded Nott to accept the changed conditions of the South. If the North had given the South a free hand after the Civil War, Nott, like many other southerners, would have directed his efforts to placing the blacks in a controlled, subordinate status that he believed was their natural condition. He was absolutely unwilling to say, "slavery has ended, let's make the best of it," because he had raised his innate prejudices to the level of scientific truth. Nott believed that natural law dictated that free blacks in the presence of whites were destined to permanent inferiority and eventual extinction.

The desperation and frustration that Nott felt in the summer of 1865 turned into anger at the fate of the Medical College of Alabama in Mobile. "My pet," the medical college, he told Squier, has been taken by the Freedmen's Bureau for a "*negro school.*" All petitions for restoring it to its original use had been refused. Nott complained, "I confess it does not increase my love for the Government when I pass by every day or two & see two or three hundred negroes racing through it & tearing every thing to pieces—the Chemical Laboratory is occupied by negro Cobblers."[9]

The medical college building had been appropriated by the Freedmen's Bureau soon after the end of the war, and white northern teachers taught their black pupils in a building Nott considered his own. In September, in a letter to the Mobile *Register,* Nott said he was taking the opportunity to answer prospective students with the news that the medical college would not be open in the fall because the Freedmen's Bureau had taken it. "Moreover," he wrote, "a great number of the most beautiful and costly models, anatomical preparations, &c, have been taken off by those now in possession, and the chemical department, which is unequalled in any school in our country, is occupied by a negro cobbler." He hoped his explanation "would be perfectly satisfactory to those who feel any interest

8. Nott to Squier, December 5, 1865, in Squier Papers, LC.
9. *Ibid.*

in a scientific institution which has cost the state more than $100,000, and which, in completeness, is not surpassed by any one of the kind on the continent." There was obviously bitter resentment in Mobile that the freedmen's school was being held in the building that had been furnished with such pride in the years immediately preceding the war, and fear was expressed that the building and its contents were being ruined. Just before Nott had his announcement printed, the newspaper had reported that after a meeting of Negroes at the medical college on the previous night, a number of them, accompanied by a white teacher, had gone to one of the fire houses and attempted to break the doors open.[10]

When in the fall of 1865 the superintendent of the Freedmen's Bureau, Major-General O. O. Howard, visited Mobile, he called on Nott to discuss the use of the medical college as a Negro school. The meeting could hardly have been less productive. Nott told him that he would rather have seen the building burned to the ground than used for its present purpose. Efforts to discuss the general condition of the South were equally unproductive. Nott told Howard that the North had forcibly liberated more than four million slaves and had left the South to care for them. Howard replied that emancipation was the "work of God." Nott told Howard that the Freedmen's Bureau demoralized the blacks and produced antagonism between races. Howard told Nott that he had never seen a people more anxious for education than the "people of Alabama." Again Nott was riled, and he pressed Howard on the point that by the "people of Alabama" he meant the freedmen.[11]

The medical college did not return to its original use until the fall of 1868, and by that time Nott had left Mobile. In the spring of that year the Alabama Medical Association was attempting to revive interest in the Medical College of Alabama, and at the same meeting the absent Nott was elected an honorary member of the association "by acclamation."[12]

The freeing of the slaves, the taking over of the medical college, and the general tension in Mobile in the summer of 1865 temporarily revived

10. Willis G. Clark, *History of Education in Alabama, 1702–1889* (Washington, 1889), 149; Mobile *Register,* September 8, 19, 1865. For black schools in Mobile see Horace Mann Bond, *Negro Education in Alabama: A Study in Cotton and Steel* (1939; rpr. New York, 1969), 81–85; Peter Kolchin, *First Freedom: The Responses of Alabama's Blacks to Emancipation and Reconstruction* (Westport, Conn., 1972), 87–88.

11. *Report of the Joint Commission on Reconstruction,* 39th Cong., 1st Sess., Part III, 115; Nott, "The Negro Race," *Popular Magazine of Anthropology,* I (1866), 103–105.

12. Alabama Medical Association Meeting, March, 1868, in Alabama Medical Association Records, Alabama Department of Archives and History, Montgomery.

Nott's desire to express himself in print on the racial question. His first effort was directly inspired by his disgust at the activities of the Freedmen's Bureau. Soon after his encounter with General O. O. Howard, he wrote an article in the form of a letter to him. It was subsequently published in the short-lived London *Popular Magazine of Anthropology*. It was a hodgepodge of Nott's old arguments, freshened by a determination to avoid the old religious controversies and to concentrate on the inability of the free Negroes to survive and prosper in a white society. He suggested to General Howard that his problems were probably beyond solution but that he was unable to perceive this because he was the representative of a party that was educated to hate slavery. Howard, Nott argued, thus viewed slavery as an abstract question and was blind to the practical difficulties that confronted him. It was not, wrote Nott "a mere abstract question of liberty or slavery" but one of race.[13]

The main purpose of Nott's letter was to show that the problem involved more than dealing with "a simple-minded, uneducated class, ignorant of their wants"; it was a question of permanent deficiencies resulting from race. A large proportion of the "ignorant, improvident, and vicious" population that had been turned loose on the South was destined for pauperism, and education could do nothing to avert this fate. The Freedmen's Bureau, Nott wrote, was "the most mischievous institution ever established in this country." If the North had promptly withdrawn the bureau and its black troops, relations between the races "would have been much sooner and better regulated." There would have been some "insubordination" among the blacks, "and a few would have been shot and hung," but not a tenth part of those who would be sacrificed under the northern regime in the South. In Mobile, the Negroes were "huddled together in shanties around the town, stealing, burning fences for fuel, dying of disease and want," wrote Nott, "and yet you cannot get a cook or washerwoman at twenty dollars a month." Although the bureau had done some good, it had been more an instrument for evil. "No one," wrote Nott, "has more kindly feeling for the blacks than I have, or is more disposed to use every effort to benefit their condition," but to force them into a false position or elevate them above whites would only hurt them and anger whites. Emancipation was a right that belonged only to those who could benefit from it. History proved that superior and in-

13. Nott, "Negro Race," 102–103. In introducing this article, the editor wrote of Nott as "the greatest living anthropologist of America" (102n).

ferior races could live together only as master and slave; otherwise the inferior race was expelled or exterminated.[14]

At heart, said Nott, he was an emancipationist, but he had opposed the emancipation of blacks in the United States on the grounds that all the experiments of the abolitionists had failed to improve the condition of the blacks and freedom simply resulted in their gradual extermination. Nott said that he was opposed to the slave trade and to the coolie system (Chinese labor) because he desired to see America "a nation of white men." Slavery, though useful in developing agricultural resources, had become a great and growing evil. "The four millions of negroes in this country have had no more to do with the intellectual development of the country than mules or ploughs, and we shall advance in real power with tenfold speed when you substitute four millions of progressive population in their stead."[15]

After his impassioned comments on the contemporary scene, Nott proceeded to the historical and scientific part of his article. He suggested to General Howard that the Freedmen's Bureau had set itself an impossible task in trying to give the Negroes full equality with whites. Even among the white race a great many people were unable to vote with understanding on the affairs of the nation, but it was necessary to disseminate education widely because there was no way to determine in advance the grade of intelligence of different whites. With blacks, however, there was no room for dispute, for "not a single full-blooded negro has ever made a name worthy of being remembered," and in the South the best educated had been the most vicious.[16]

Nott's comments based on history were familiar to those who had read his earlier works. The Negro, he argued, had always been inferior and had never attained civilization: "His intellect for four thousand years has been as dark as his skin." The Egyptian monuments gave testimony to the permanence of physical types, and "intellectual peculiarities" were just as permanent. Africans had enjoyed every chance to grasp aspects of Egypt's civilization, but they had gained nothing. At a later date, trade and missionaries had failed to foster civilization among Africans, North American Indians, or "the dark-skinned races of Oceania." All the efforts of New England philanthropy had not enabled any among the five hundred

14. *Ibid.,* 103–105.
15. *Ibid.,* 105.
16. *Ibid.,* 106.

thousand free Negroes in the United States to write a page worth remembering. The disastrous condition of the Haitians, on one of the finest islands in the world, was proof of the inability of the Negro race to govern itself and achieve civilization. Russia 150 years ago had been a nation of uneducated barbarians with ignorant, cruel nobles domineering over hordes of serfs, but these barbarians had responded to the efforts of Peter the Great—himself "a coarse, illiterate brute"—and markedly improved themselves. They could do so because they were of the white race.[17]

Mulattoes, as usual, came in for Nott's scorn. With human races, as with dogs, it was vital to keep blood lines pure—otherwise the result was "curs." Whites were weakened by every drop of black blood as surely as the blood of a cart horse destroyed the speed and beauty of an Arabian racer, or a cur destroyed that of a greyhound or pointer. The difference in intellectual caliber between the different races was plainly shown by the difference in cranial capacities. Nott explained away the figures that showed that the Negro had a brain about the size of that of a Chinese and larger than that of a Hindu by arguing that in the Negro the posterior or animal part of the brain greatly predominated over the anterior or intellectual lobes. As usual, Nott made the "scientific" facts fit what he wanted to say. It was false science and false philanthropy, he argued, to maintain that the brain of a race could be enlarged by education. Although the North had produced philanthropists who argued for Negro progress, in practice the region admitted the inferiority of Negroes by consigning them to an inferior social position. Whites in the northern states would not associate with blacks or intermarry with them, and some states had passed laws against black immigration.[18]

In his conclusion, Nott conjured up a different and odd idea to explain why blacks were doomed to eventual extermination. For years he had contended that colored races living in proximity to whites were destined for extermination unless enslaved, but now in the case of America's blacks he used the argument that this was made inevitable because of the blacks' "instinctive and unconquerable antipathy to steady agricultural labor." Nott obviously had no proof for this remarkable assertion; he apparently based it on the number of blacks wandering in Mobile and other southern cities in the aftermath of the abolition of slavery. Nott ignored both African village life and more than two hundred years of plantation slavery in the South. None but an agricultural population, he argued, could

17. *Ibid.*, 106–109, 111–12.
18. *Ibid.*, 110–11.

flourish in numbers when unsupported by foreign commerce. Moreover, the gradual extermination of blacks in America would be aided by their want of care for each other in sickness and by infant mortality produced by parental neglect. Blacks, argued Nott, would care for their white masters but not for their own families. "Slavery," he wrote, "is the normal condition of the Negro, the most advantageous to him, and the most ruinous, in the end, to a white nation."[19]

Nott's remedy for the existing crisis was for the Freedmen's Bureau and northern troops (particularly blacks) to be withdrawn from the South so that relations between the races could regulate themselves. The planters of the South needed labor, and the Negroes had to work or starve—the law of necessity would produce an accommodation. After removing the bureau and the troops, the only duty remaining for the North would be to assist the South in feeding and clothing colored paupers. The old, the infirm, the women and children, had been fed by slaveowners when they were property, but southern capital could no longer provide such an enormous charity. Nott obviously envisaged a return to white dominance over a serflike black rural population.[20]

Nott's companion piece to his letter to General Howard was an article in the *New Orleans Medical and Surgical Journal*, "Instincts of Races." This article was also issued separately as a pamphlet. Its main purpose was to develop Nott's suggestions in his letter to Howard that races had instinctive likes and dislikes that went beyond rationality and that the Negro race had an instinctive dislike of agricultural labor. Nott made extensive use of a pamphlet by John Van Evrie, which had first been issued in the 1850s and was reissued in an enlarged edition during the Civil War. Nott was intent on showing that the ending of slavery in the United States would be a disaster, as it had been in the West Indies and other areas. He wanted to demonstrate in his article that "the practical results of Emancipation are nothing more nor less than the fulfillment of natural laws, long since demonstrated by the science of Ethnology."[21] To support his case, Nott extended his earlier comparisons between human beings and dogs. Also, as in his letter to General Howard, he avoided emphasizing multiple creations so as to concentrate more fully on the contemporary racial problem.

In reiterating his argument for the permanence of types, Nott now ac-

19. *Ibid.*, 115–17.
20. *Ibid.*, 117–18.
21. Nott, *The Instincts of Races* (New Orleans, 1866), 1.

knowledged that there was a school of naturalists, which included La-marck, Geoffroy St. Hilaire, and Darwin, which advocated "the *development* theory." These men, he wrote, not only contended that one type could be changed into another "but that man himself is nothing more than a developed worm." But this school, he argued, also maintained that such changes took "*millions of years*" by infinitesimal steps of progression. Because the Freedmen's Bureau would not have the vitality to see the "negro experiment" through many hundreds of generations, Nott con-tended that the Darwinian theories were irrelevant to his arguments about blacks in the South.[22]

In this article Nott laid great stress on his new idea that every perma-nent animal form or race along with its distinct physical type had a dis-tinct "*moral*" or instinct. The instincts of bulldogs or greyhounds were inseparable from their physical structure, and breeders laid great empha-sis on purity of blood in maintaining the peculiar physique and instinct of each breed of dog. Man, Nott said, was governed by the same laws that applied to the rest of the animal kingdom. The "*moral*" or instinct of each race was as permanent as the physical type, and these instincts "drive rea-son aside or override it in the great majority of mankind." Self-love and self-preservation, he argued, were the ruling instincts of every animal. These instincts drove even the most untutored races to desire immortality and to seek to propitiate good and evil spirits. It was not the love of the Lord, nor of virtue, that kept men on the straight and narrow path, but the fear of the devil and annihilation. Against his stated intentions, Nott, as usual, had slipped into religious comment.[23]

Instincts that were grounded in self-preservation showed themselves "in the forms of ambition and dishonesty" and held most people from the cradle to the grave; this was why honest figures such as Washington, Lee, or Stonewall Jackson were so highly esteemed. These men were moral giants, "particularly defective in the organs of self-esteem and ac-quisitiveness." They were not intellects of the first rank. Instinctive ac-quisitiveness was seldom rooted out—the love of money, the tricks of the trade, the corruption of politics, the animal passions were constant: "There are few men who would not prefer a good endorser to the fair promises of most pious neighbors."[24] The events of the past five years had confirmed Nott's earlier belief that most human beings were incapable of

22. *Ibid.*, 4.
23. *Ibid.*, 5–7.
24. *Ibid.*, 7–8.

calm rationality; they had also moved him further to the idea that the great majority were also dishonest and hopelessly self-seeking.

After his asides on human depravity, Nott returned to his major argument that each race had its own permanent instinct. A hundred children of each race placed on separate islands and reared, without instruction, by deaf mutes would still work out a social organization characteristic of the particular race. The Almighty gave races their peculiar instincts, argued Nott, which all the powers of the Freedmen's Bureau could not change. The Caucasian races were the only truly progressive races of history, but even among them it had to be remembered that reason was to a great extent subservient to instinct. The only real progress made by mankind was in the exact sciences; there was comparatively little progress in morals, and vice simply changed its forms. In the progress in the exact sciences "the Negro, Indian, and other inferior races, *take no part whatever*." [25]

Having argued that racial instincts were always dominant over education or even reason, Nott went on to develop the idea that he had suggested in his letter to General Howard—that the Negro by instinct was opposed to agricultural labor and would not till the soil for wages. This accounted for the comparatively sparse population of Africa compared to India or China, countries inhabited by races that were intensely agricultural. The same inertness, said Nott, characterized the Negro intellectually—Africa was barren of attainment. In other lands blacks had the same characteristics as in their original homeland. Blacks under slavery in the South had been made more useful than any of their race anywhere at any time. The free Negroes had achieved nothing of substance. [26]

The rest of Nott's article wandered badly. As usual, it included a section on the permanence of types, as proved by the Egyptian monuments, but it also made extensive use of Van Evrie's pamphlet to demonstrate that blacks in Haiti, Jamaica, Trinidad, and Barbados had ruined those regions and had shown a marked disinclination for agricultural labor. He concluded that "the Negro must fail as an agriculturalist, that the race will be gradually exterminated in this country, that they will deteriorate morally and intellectually, and that we must look to other sources of labor to produce the great staples of the Gulf States." He had, said Nott, "none but the kindest feeling toward the Freedmen" and had done them as many kindnesses as any member of the Freedmen's Bureau, but he would

25. *Ibid.*, 8–9.
26. *Ibid.*, 10–12.

continue to oppose utopian schemes that would end in disaster for blacks.[27]

Nott was unable to accept the social revolution wrought in the South by emancipation. He was obviously not alone, but as in the years before the Civil War he expressed the prejudices of his region far more overtly than most. He felt confident in expressing his racial views because he knew that many of them were endorsed by scientists throughout America and Europe. After 1876, when the South was left to manage its own affairs, southerners were to impose the social, political, and economic system that Nott thought was essential for white-black relations. In the direct aftermath of the Civil War, the Freedmen's Bureau and the northern armies were attempting to create an equality in the South that northern scientists said was impossible and that their own northern state governments and people would not permit. Nott believed that the ethnologists of the 1840s and 1850s, in the North and Europe as well as in the South, had proved that blacks were permanently and unchangeably inferior. Science had confirmed his deepest prejudices. The situation in Mobile and the rest of the South under northern occupation was a nightmare to him.

In the early fall of 1865, Nott had his first opportunity to travel to the North since before the Civil War. He was summoned to Washington, D.C., to give evidence at the trial of Henry Wirz, the Confederate commander of Andersonville, the southern prison where so many Union troops died. Nott was not called to the stand at the long Wirz trial; it seems likely that the only evidence he could give was not needed because it could be better given by other southern physicians. One accusation that had to be defended against was that impure vaccine had been given to Andersonville prisoners. Confederate physicians from other areas appeared to testify that such vaccine was used elsewhere in the Confederacy, and presumably it was decided that Nott's evidence was superfluous or too indirect to be of use. It is also possible that Wirz's counsel, who had summoned some 150 witnesses, decided that Nott's outspokenness combined with his care in medical matters might produce a negative impression for Wirz if Nott were questioned too closely. A man as outspoken as Nott could present problems as a defense witness; there was no way of forecasting exactly what he would say.[28]

27. *Ibid.*, 12–15, 16 (quotation), 17–27, 28 (quotation).

28. Nott to Squier, December 5, 1865, in Squier Papers, LC; Mobile *Register*, September 8, 1865; Henry Wirz, defendant, *Trial of Henry Wirz* (Washington, 1868).

While in the North for the trial, Nott went to Philadelphia and renewed his friendship with Joseph Leidy, but he did not have the opportunity to visit Squier in New York. As yet, Nott had difficulty in throwing off the despondency produced by the war and its tragedies, and on returning to Mobile he involved himself ardently in medical matters. The racial writings stimulated by his anger at the Freedmen's Bureau were his last hurrah on the subject. From this time until the end of his life, he was to devote himself more exclusively to his practice and to writing on medical matters than at any time since the mid-1840s.

Nott's first medical contribution after the end of the war was a direct result of his experiences in that conflict. He decided to make known what he had learned about the treatment of damaged bones by publishing a short book on the subject. The primary purpose of *Contributions to Bone and Nerve Surgery* was to provide information on a neglected area of surgery—"the sequelae of gunshot and other injuries of bones." The existing literature concentrated on the treatment of freshly inflicted wounds. Nott wanted to deal with the problems that ensued following the initial surgery and continued for years. After his resignation from Bragg's staff, Nott had had extensive opportunities to see the classes of cases he wanted to discuss, both in the surgical wards of Mobile's army hospitals and as a consultant for doctors in Alabama and neighboring states who referred former soldiers to him. His patients, he said, all came with suppurating wounds, and by far the greater part of them had some injury to the bones. In spite of his dreams of southern nationhood, Nott still looked to Philadelphia as the center of American medicine, and his brief work was published by J. B. Lippincott of that city. It was in proof by the late fall of 1865 and was out by January of the following year.

In the first part of his book, Nott simply summarized accepted practice, as discussed in the standard works, for dealing with traumatic injuries to bones and their consequences. In Part II, through the discussion of individual cases, he developed his own views, concentrating on treatment for necrosis (dead bone) and chronic osteitis (inflammation). Although all surgeons agreed that detached bone splinters should be immediately removed from a wound, there was disagreement as to what should be done with splinters still partially attached to muscles and tendons and with those still attached to the bone. Nott's conclusion was that surgeons could achieve some success by leaving the nondetached splinters for nature to weld together. At the beginning of the war, he said, his practice had been very different from that he had followed when he had gained more experience. As the war went on, he had been far more inclined to leave partially detached splinters in place, and he had also amputated less often. Nott expressed disagreement with surgeons who insisted that it was essential to remove all splinters from the site of the wound. He believed that his tendency toward less surgical interference as the war progressed had produced better results. In this age before antisepsis, it is possible that in some cases surgical interference had indeed produced worse effects than the original infection resulting from the contamination by the bullet and clothing. Nott also argued that the climate of the southern states was particularly favorable to recovery from gunshot wounds.

Along with his main material on injury to bones, Nott also commented on the applicability of his principles to traumatic injuries suffered in civilian life, and he described side issues of his basic subject, including complications resulting from "neuralgia" of the stump after amputation. In one case a soldier who had had a leg amputated after a railroad accident consulted Nott about the "neuralgia" in the stump. On several occasions Nott operated to remove more of the stump but then discovered that his patient had an opium addiction; he had been taking as much as twenty grains of morphia daily.[29]

The publication of this book on surgery confirmed southerners in their opinion that Nott was one of the most eminent physicians in the region if not in the country. When the Mobile Medical Society was reorganized in the fall of 1865, Nott was elected to the office of president. He was now recognized by both his fellow physicians and the elite of Mobile as one of their most eminent citizens, as well as their most famous physician. Another physician, who had served in the northern army and who was in Mobile in 1866, commented that one had to live for five to ten years in Mobile and keep up a good appearance before gaining any practice. "You must have rich and powerful friends at court to succeed," he wrote. His comments were accurate, but he must have been remarkably naive if he thought a former U.S. Army officer could gain a large civilian medical practice in Mobile in 1866.[30]

There were no severe yellow fever epidemics in Mobile in the years im-

29. Nott, *Contributions to Bone and Nerve Surgery* (Philadelphia, 1866), Preface, 49–50, 91–95, and *passim*.

30. Mobile *Register,* December 10, 1865; W. C. Mitchell to Hugh N. Mitchell, January 9, 1867, in William Letcher Mitchell Papers, SHC.

mediately following the war, but there were some cases, particularly among the federal troops occupying the city. Nott's friend Dr. Stanford E. Chaillé of New Orleans commented much later that when Nott was asked by the federal authorities to use his experience in treating these cases, "he did with the same generosity that he showed in caring for his own people." Nott's deep-rooted prejudices against both the blacks and the occupying forces apparently did not interfere with his medical dedication. One of the cases he commented on in his book on surgery was that of a mulatto man he was visiting in consultation with a surgeon of the United States Army.[31]

Nott's work was increased by a smallpox epidemic in the winter of 1865–1866, but the individual case that most absorbed him in the early months of 1866 was that of a Mobile friend, for whom he had been the family physician for some fifteen years. In his published report on this case, Nott once again demonstrated his willingness to admit bafflement as well as an interest in aspects of medicine that were as yet very little understood. The case, Nott argued, might throw light on conditions that perhaps owed their origin and symptoms "to a morbic condition of some portion of the great *sympathetic nerve.*" He was particularly interested in the set of organs he referred to as the "blood glands"—the spleen, the suprarenal bodies, the thyroid gland, and the uterus—which he said were intimately connected to the sympathetic system. He included the uterus in this list because he said that its function was analogous in some respects to the others.[32]

Nott reported on this particular case in detail because he thought it illustrated the difficulties in diagnosing and treating problems involving little-understood organs. His patient had felt vaguely ill for years with floating pains about the abdomen and chest and some oppression of breathing. About three months before his death, he had more severe symptoms—dull, deep-seated distress in the region of the stomach and kidneys and particularly in the area of the pancreas. Nott had treated him with quinine, iron and vegetable tonics, gentian, cinchona, and similar medicines, which had done him no good. He also had tried bromide of

---

31. Nott file, School of Medicine, in University of Pennsylvania Archives; Nott, *Contributions to Bone and Nerve Surgery,* 10.

32. Nott, "Small-Pox Epidemic in Mobile During the Winter of 1865–1866," *Nashville Journal of Medicine and Surgery,* n.s., II (1867), 372–80; Nott, "Case of Disease of Supra-Renal Capsules and Pancreas," *New Orleans Medical and Surgical Journal,* XIX (1866), 318–19.

potassium without effect, had used "blisters" on his abdomen, and finally had given "an occasional mercurial purge and thirty to forty drops of tincture of digitalis three times a day." A week before his death, the patient appeared much improved, and Nott stopped the medication except morphine. During the final illness (some three months), Nott had injected from half a grain to a grain of morphine a night to enable his patient to sleep. Nott had visited the patient daily during this period.

One morning, after eating a mutton chop, tea, and toast, the patient died. Nott conducted a hasty post-mortem, omitting various organs, but discovered that there was no suprarenal body over the right kidney and that the left suprarenal body was greatly atrophied. The pancreas was heavy and dense, and there were various other abnormal signs. Nott drew no conclusions as to the specific nature of the disease that had killed his patient, but he discussed at length both Addison's disease and Graves' disease because he assumed that it was in some way related to them. He decided that actual death had been caused by the stopping of circulation through the pulmonary artery "by a coagulum of blood." Nott's modest conclusion to his report was that he was trying to reveal facts about the diseases of renal capsules that would be of help to pathologists. He also stressed his method—"the *logic of exclusion*"—by which he had systematically excluded healthy organs to determine the true seat of the disease.[33] For much of his medical life Nott was a generalist, treating, observing, and reporting on a variety of obscure conditions that came his way. He always read widely in the medical literature and in his published reports usually cited a variety of authorities on the particular disease or condition he was discussing. But given the eclectic nature of Nott's medical interests and practice, both in internal medicine and surgery, it was impossible for him to keep up with all the developments sweeping through the medical world in the second half of the nineteenth century. In the last years of his life this was to lead him to greater specialization.

Nott's increasing absorption with his medical practice did not change his views of the state of affairs in the South. He now avoided public controversy, but his private letters are filled with his frustrations. When Squier made the mistake of commenting about the tempers flaring in the South, Nott was quick to respond. The South's predicament, he said, could not be adequately described even through Squier's own temper and vocabulary. Southerners, Nott wrote, had believed that the Declaration of

33. Nott, "Case of Disease," 320–33, 325, 333 (quotations).

Independence had given them the right to self-government and secession "& that we had a Constitutional right to niggers." The South had been beaten and had been ready to reconstruct in good faith, but if Squier could come south "& see how the damd Military, the nigger troops, the Freedmen Bureau spit upon us & rub it in, You would not wonder at our blasted tempers." If President Andrew Johnson's policies could be carried out promptly, southerners might be brought back, "but as long as they are placed below the negroes & considered utterly faithless," the flag would be hated. There was no chance of further rebellion, but unless the northerners wanted a union like that of Austria and Venice they should rise up and put down the Radical Republicans. Nott told Squier, as he had Leidy earlier, that the United States government would become a centralized empire; the states were now useless. Although he hoped he was mistaken in his dismal prophesies, he was pessimistic because "the history of Mankind, is the history of Crime and folly."[34]

In reality, the condition of Mobile in the winter of 1865–1866 was not as Nott suggested, for Alabama whites were temporarily beginning to re-impose dominance over the black population. President Johnson's policies had led by December, 1865, to an Alabama state government in which representation was based on the white population, and this new government began to pass black codes to restrict the freedom of the freedmen. White power increased in Alabama in 1866, and it was not until the spring of 1867 and the passage of the first Reconstruction Act that the North temporarily began to enforce black equality in Alabama.[35]

In Mobile the seeming revolution in black-white relations that had come with the arrival of troops in April, 1865, was being sharply modified in the early months of 1866. One Mobile businessman commented in January, 1866, that by the fall it would be possible to tell whether "this free nigger system" was going to be a success or a fiasco. If the latter, they, with the rest, would have "to dig for a living." He commented, however, that most whites were becoming sanguine because blacks were signing work contracts. The mayor saw about fifty Negroes on vagrancy charges every morning, and they were generally sent to the guard house until they made a contract to work for someone. Before noon the guard house was usually empty.[36]

34. Nott to Squier, March 2, 1866, in Squier Papers, LC.
35. Fleming, *Civil War and Reconstruction*, 333–491; Bond, *Negro Educaton*, 63–64.
36. William C. Reynolds to H. L. Reynolds, January 27, 1866, in Henry Lee Reynolds Papers, SHC.

For Nott this partial reestablishment of white authority was not enough, and well before military reconstruction was imposed on the South in 1867 he had decided to leave Mobile. The way of life he had known had disappeared, and he was unwilling to compromise. Early in the summer of 1866, Nott remained on the Gulf while his family went north to Cape May and Niagara Falls. He kept up some of his practice but lived at Point Clear, which had been converted back from military hospital to summer resort. He enjoyed the Gulf breezes and said at the end of July that he had received a parcel of newly imported books, "which I am devouring with delight." By mid-August, however, Nott was concerned for his family. He had heard that there was cholera in Canada, and he had determined to travel by rail via Chicago to Niagara to join them.[37]

Although at this time he expected the medical college to reopen in the fall (it remained closed for another year), he had little optimism about conditions in the South. Over the entire region, he wrote, there is "a most extraordinary apathy." The people "are Conquered, dispirited, degraded & have no country, or patriotism. The feeling of almost every one is to get out of it if they can." This was certainly Nott's view, and on his way back to Mobile he stopped in Baltimore and began to look for a house suitable as a residence and office. He wanted to move after spending a last winter in Mobile. He explained to Leidy that he was reconnoitering in Baltimore with a view to moving: "I have but one Child left—I have some income outside of the Profession—My social relations &c are much broken up by the war & moreover the climate of Baltimore is one where I could set down quietly for the whole year & not be under the necessity of going off in the summer any distance to look for a Change of air." To Squier he revealed his instinctive motivation—"I hope to leave the Negroland to You damd Yankees—It is not now fit for a gentleman to live in."[38]

The excitement of the war was over, nearly all Nott's children were dead, his father-in-law was no longer alive to greet the various members of his family in his summer home at Spring Hill, and thousands of blacks were free in Mobile. Even the prospect of reopening the medical college

37. Nott to Joseph M. Toner, July 29, 1866, in Joseph M. Toner Papers, LC.
38. Nott to Toner, August 15, 1866, *ibid.;* Nott to Ella N. Mackenzie, September 18, 1866, in Ella N. Mackenzie Papers, SHC; Nott to Leidy, September 19, 1866, in Leidy Papers, CPP; Nott to Squier, January 12, 1867 (misdated as 1866 by Nott), in Squier Papers, LC.

did not induce in Nott his customary excitement, for it was proving extremely difficult to assemble a class. Many of the students who should have been there were dead, maimed, or unable to afford a medical education. In Philadelphia in mid-September, Nott told Leidy that he had "got the Collg out of the hand of the negroes only a few weeks ago" and was "trying to rake up the fragments" and reopen it in November. Although he was buying chemicals for the college, he was not optimistic about the prospects of a class for the coming year—"*our* Country is terribly crushed," he said in October.[39] Indeed, the notice was so short and the conditions so depressed and confused that it proved impossible to reopen the college for the 1866–1867 academic year.

The inability of the medical college to reopen helped convince Nott that he must leave the Gulf region, and to add to his frustrations, his financial situation was less comfortable than it had been before the war. He had always made sure that his family lived well, but much of this good living depended on Nott's annual income from his flourishing practice. He was by no means destitute after the war, but in the economic situation of Alabama in the postwar years his income sharply dropped from its prewar highs, and prospects for the future economic prosperity of the region were bleak. One of his correspondents writing from Demopolis, Alabama, in January, 1867, told him that the cotton crop of 1866 was only a quarter of what it had been before the war.[40]

Nott left Mobile for Baltimore in the spring of 1867. From his point of view, he left just in time. By the fall, preparations for Radical Reconstruction were in full swing, and one Mobilian reported to his wife in November that blacks and radical whites were meeting in convention in Montgomery, that juries were now composed of Negroes, that Negro judges were expected soon, and that the planters were in deep economic trouble—in short, "the whole country is ruined, & the people broke, no one has any money."[41] Even without his private obsession with race, Nott would have had ample reason for leaving Mobile.

Before Nott left the city, his male friends gathered at the Battle House to bid him farewell. The dining room was filled with the elite of Mobile, and they sat down to a meal prepared by a French chef and accompanied

39. Nott to Leidy, September 19, October 8, 15, 28, 1866, in Leidy Papers, CPP.
40. J. S. Lyon to Nott, January 8, 1867 (enclosed in Nott to Squier, January 12, 1867), in Squier Papers, LC.
41. William Ketchum to his wife, November 8, 1867, in Creagh Family Papers, SHC.

by a long list of wines. It was a very long evening, there were numerous toasts and responses, and Nott said that confronted by such kindness he was prepared to recant on his oft-expressed belief that human nature was a failure.[42]

Soon after Nott left Mobile, one of his last close family ties with the Gulf was broken. Early in June his brother Adolphus Nott died while on a visit to Montgomery. Adolphus had spent many years as professor of materia medica in the University of Louisiana in New Orleans and had lived in Mobile during the war. Nott had always given Adolphus the close support he typically provided to family members. He had told Squier in 1849 that Adolphus was "greatly my superior in talent." One odd result of Adolphus' death was that it gave Nott the opportunity to read his own obituary, an opportunity that delighted him. A year later, when he attended a meeting of the New York Ethnographical Society, a friend caused a sensation by reading a eulogy to Nott that had appeared in the *Anthropological Review* of London. The editor had confused Adolphus with Josiah. Nott's public letter of explanation to the review was as frank and informal as one of his private letters. He wrote that "were it not for fear of damaging the reputation of the Society, I would gladly hang myself, just at this fortunate juncture, when I have made all the reputation I am capable of, and far more than my vaulting ambition ever aspired to." He sent the editor a copy of his 1866 article on the instincts of races with the comment that all he had prophesied in that article was coming to pass in the South. "The condition of our Southern States," he wrote, "is such that no white man belonging to the soil, who has any self-respect, can live there longer." That is why, he said, he had left the South.[43]

In the last years of his life Nott was to devote practically all his efforts to medicine. He kept in touch with ethnologists, read books and articles in the field, and attended meetings, but once he had left the deep South he no longer felt a compelling obsession to warn of the dangers of trying to raise blacks to the level of whites. He had tried to defend a particular way of life and had lost. He now worked intensely to build up a medical reputation outside of the Gulf states.

42. Newspaper clipping in Nott file, Local History Room, Mobile Public Library.
43. Proceedings of the Montgomery Medical Society, June 6, 1867, regarding the death of Gustavus A. Nott, clipping in the Emma Mettee Scrapbook, Alabama Department of Archives and History; Nott to Squier, February 14, 1849, in Squier Papers, LC; Nott to Kenneth R. Mackenzie, June 12, 1868, in *Anthropological Review* (London), VI (1868), 450–51. The obituary is in *Anthropological Review* (London), VI (1868), lxxix–lxxxiii.

Chapter 14
THE LAST YEARS

At Baltimore, in a state that had not seceded, Nott could still enjoy something of a southern ambience without the sense that he had in Mobile of the world turned upside down. There were blacks in Baltimore, and freedmen, but existing social relationships had not been shattered by the conflict. In nonseceding states there was no enforcing army to transform existing relationships between blacks and whites. Baltimore, however, proved unsatisfactory to Nott. His practice did not flourish as he wanted, and he found that the city lacked the intellectual and cultural stimulation he had hoped for. Also, Nott had escaped one variety of civic tension for another. Baltimore was a tumultuous city in the summer of 1867. Widespread strikes led to violence, the National Guard was called in, and there was fighting in the streets.[1]

After a few months in Baltimore, Nott was restless. He told Leidy that he was comfortably settled in the cleanest city he had ever seen, but he found it "the most unintellectual & unprogressive community I ever saw—no scientific association—no medical society even, no journal, no concert of action." In the time he had been in Baltimore, he said, he had met no one, except two or three professors of medicine, "who seem ever to have read a book of any kind."[2] Nott was ready for good talk, or at least the tightly knit society he had known in Mobile before the war, and he invited Leidy to visit at any time. Baltimore was neither lively enough nor intellectual enough for Nott. Before the war he had constantly complained about Mobile's lack of libraries and books, but the medical com-

1. Baltimore *American and Commercial Advertiser,* July 21, 1867.
2. Nott to Leidy, July 2, 1867, in Leidy Papers, CPP.

munity was close-knit and intellectually active, the intellectual scene was enlivened by prominent visitors, and a lively social life provided a break from Nott's labors. With his practice now much smaller than it had been in Mobile and a lack of social and intellectual stimulus, Nott was bored.

Against this background, Nott for the first time in his life began to develop a medical specialty. He was to maintain a general practice until the end of his life, but in these last years of his career he began to specialize in his research and writing, and to some extent in his practice, in gynecology. In the years before the Civil War, Nott, frustrated at his lack of success in treating a variety of gynecological problems, had avoided such cases and referred them to his colleagues. "The physiology of the uterus was little known," wrote Nott, "its pathology less, and least of all did we understand the diagnosis of its endless maladies."[3]

Nott gained a new interest in gynecology after the Civil War, when, in the course of his normal, extensive medical reading he took up the writings of the famous Dr. J. Marion Sims, late of South Carolina and Alabama and now of New York, and Dr. James Young Simpson of Edinburgh. Nott was impressed by what they had achieved and in his last years in Mobile began to take an interest in gynecological problems: "I come back after reading the works of Simpson and Sims, to uterine surgery and therapeutics, with feelings very different from those which induced me to abandon this practice a few years ago." Throughout his career, Nott had proved willing to test new surgical procedures, but when he had little success, or thought that surgical intervention aggravated rather than helped a condition, he had been quick to reverse his course. What impressed Nott in his post–Civil War reading on gynecological problems was that this department of medicine had now begun "to assume the aspect of a science instead of blind empiricism; many of these diseases, before obscure, are now easily diagnosed and treated, on fixed rational principles."[4]

One is also tempted to believe that in specializing in uterine diseases in his last years, Nott was reacting to the deaths that had surrounded him since the early 1850s: the yellow fever epidemics, the deaths of his young children, the countless deaths in the war. Nott had seen far too many of his family, friends, and colleagues die, and he had watched the slaughter

3. Nott, "Remarks on the Operation of J. Marion Sims for Dysmenorrhoea, depending on Anteflexion of Uterus," *American Journal of the Medical Sciences,* LIV (1867), 98.
4. *Ibid.,* 98–99.

of the South's young men in the Civil War. It was perhaps not solely chance and an eye for a promising new specialty that inspired Nott to develop a gynecological practice in these last years.

Nott was undoubtedly encouraged in his new interest by the role of J. Marion Sims in women's medicine and by the proximity of New York to Baltimore. Sims had a background not unlike Nott's, and they were acquainted. Sims was born in South Carolina in 1813 and in the early 1830s had attended South Carolina College with Nott's brother Rufus, yet another Nott physician. Like Nott, Sims moved to Alabama in the mid-1830s, although he settled not in Mobile but in the small town of Meigs in Montgomery County. Sims eventually moved to Montgomery and there became an extremely successful physician. His national and international fame stemmed from his discovery of a surgical procedure to treat the debilitating condition of vesicovaginal fistula; in this condition, often the result of a difficult birth, urine constantly passed into the vagina, causing inflammation and ulceration. To develop his procedure, Sims had special instruments made—including the well-known Sims speculum—and over several years operated on slave women who were admitted to his infirmary suffering from this previously incurable condition. His final success, achieved by the use of silver wire sutures, was in the thirtieth operation undergone by a particular slave who had been with him for years.[5] Sims had an arrangement with the owners by which he agreed "to perform no experiment or operation . . . to endanger their lives, and will not charge a cent for keeping them," but the owners had to pay their taxes and clothe them. In 1850, the year after he achieved his first successes, Sims bought a slave who presented one of the most difficult cases to treat that he had seen. He was forced to buy, he wrote, because "the owner was unwilling to run any risks about cure," although Sims told him "no cure no pay."[6]

In 1853, when beset by ill health, Sims moved to New York. There he was enthusiastically received by doctors anxious to learn his technique for the treatment of vesicovaginal fistula and anything else he had learned about the treatment of gynecological problems. In these mid-Victorian

5. Sims to Eliza T. Jones, November 3, 1835, in James Marion Sims Paper, SHC. For Sims see Seale Harris, *Woman's Surgeon: The Life Story of J. Marion Sims* (New York, 1950); J. Marion Sims, *The Story of My Life* (1884; rpr. New York, 1968), 226–46; see also Todd Savitt, "The Use of Blacks for Medical Experimentation and Demonstration in the Old South," *Journal of Southern History*, XLVIII (1982), 344–46.

6. Sims, *Story of My Life*, 236; Sims to Dr. H. V. Wooten, January 23, 1850, quoted in Minnie C. Boyd, *Alabama in the Fifties: A Social Study* (1931; rpr. New York, 1966), 194.

years the freedom with which Sims had been able to examine, treat, and operate on slave women patients was impossible for a physician with a practice among the general white population. Soon after arriving in New York, Sims decided to establish a hospital for the treatment of the diseases of women. He gained the cooperation of prominent New York women who incorporated as a board of lady managers for the hospital. The hospital opened in rented quarters in 1855 and in 1857 obtained a charter from the state as the Woman's Hospital of the State of New York. There was a male board of governors, and the board of lady managers served as a board of supervisors with general control over the domestic affairs of the hospital. Sims secured the cooperation of the prominent New York physician Dr. Valentine Mott as a consulting surgeon and as his own assistant at the hospital appointed Dr. Thomas Addis Emmet. By 1858 he had secured from the city a block of land between 49th and 50th streets and Lexington and 4th avenues, which had been the burial ground for the city's paupers. The new hospital on that location was not opened until after the Civil War. It had room for sixty-eight beds, and in the following years more than two hundred patients were usually treated each year.[7]

Nott was well-known to Sims as a general physician and surgeon of great reputation in the Southwest, and beginning in July, 1867, Nott began to make himself heard on gynecological matters. In that month the *American Journal of the Medical Sciences* published Nott's comments on Sims's operation for dysmenorrhea. The article mostly consisted of a case in which Nott had followed Sims's principles but had introduced some modifications of his own. Nott also, however, asserted his new confidence in the possibility of treatment of gynecological problems and his new interest in this area of medicine. He stated that he now felt "competent to diagnose and treat many cases which were formerly beyond my reach." He also, in the usual Nott manner, made it clear that he was not prepared to follow blindly either Dr. Sims, Dr. Simpson, or anyone else. Although he wrote that he was pleased at the new rational approaches, he added that "we have yet much to learn in uterine surgery and therapeutics." All reformers, he wrote, whether in politics, religion, or medicine, were inclined to run to extremes. One writer had gone wild in the use of caustics, another thought caustics of little use, and now Sims and Simp-

7. Harris, *Woman's Surgeon*, 111–86; *First Report of the Woman's Hospital Association* (New York, 1856); *Annual Report of the Governors and the Board of Lady Supervisors of the Woman's Hospital*, 1868–72 (New York, 1868–72).

son advocated the knife. What was probably wanted, wrote Nott, was a middle road.

The woman Nott discussed in his article had been under his care for dysmenorrhea in Mobile during the previous winter. Nott decided that the condition could be relieved by Sims's procedure for excision of the elongated cervix. He performed the operation, using chloroform as an anesthetic. In operating Nott deviated in two ways from the operation as described by Sims, and in his article he explained why. As usual, he explained his errors as a guide for future operations. He had failed to ligate an artery he had cut in operating and as a result had considerable difficulty in stopping the bleeding after the operation. Nott, who operated on his patient at noon, finally left her at 9:00 P.M. after giving her opium and brandy. After examining her the following month Nott decided that she was cured.[8]

For Nott this article was to be the beginning of a series on gynecological problems. In October, 1867, he again reported in the *American Journal of Medical Sciences* on one of the cases he had seen in Mobile during the previous winter, and in Baltimore he threw himself enthusiastically into his new interest; during the winter he delivered a course of lectures on his new specialty. He set about it in typical Nott manner, sending to Paris for *papier mâché* models, asking Leidy to secure appropriate drawings from one of his medical artists, and acquiring all the books he could on the subject. Leidy had some difficulty securing drawings, and Nott told him that it was not necessary. "I find, having a little talent that way, that I can make as good drawings as I require."[9]

Late in October, 1867, Nott visited New York to buy books and to find out all he could about his new specialty. He was immediately as excited by New York as he had been bored by Baltimore. "I have found the visit very interesting & instructive," he told Leidy. "It is an immense and progressive City in every thing & as much in our profession as any thing else." Nott also communicated his excitement at New York and his enthusiasm for his new specialty of gynecology to his friend Dr. Stanford Chaillé in New Orleans. In a letter to Chaillé, intended for publication in the *New Orleans Medical and Surgical Journal*, he could not resist his usual

<hr/>

8. Nott, "Remarks on the Operation of J. Marion Sims," 99–103.

9. Nott, "Case of Extraordinary Hypertrophy of Cervix Uteri," *American Journal of the Medical Sciences*, LIV (1867), 403–405; Nott to Leidy, October 12, 28, 1867, in Leidy Papers, CPP.

didactic approach, suggesting that there were three great epochs in uterine surgery—the first marked by the speculum introduced by Joseph Récamier, the second by the "*Uterine Sound*" of James Simpson, and the third by the speculum, silver wire sutures, uterine sound and redresser, and other improvements of Sims. He gave most credit for striking advances in gynecology to Sims.[10]

Nott wrote about his experiences in New York with all the enthusiasm of a young student. He had spent most of his time with Dr. Thomas Emmet, who had many cases both in the Woman's Hospital and the new public hospital in New York. He was extremely impressed with Emmet's work and by the manner in which Emmet was more cautious in uterine surgery than Sims. Again, as was usual in his medical writings, Nott demonstrated the common sense that was lacking in his writing on race. He said that it was natural that reactions were setting in against some of Sims's confident procedures, in the same way that Sims had reacted against earlier methods. "The fact is," he wrote to Chaillé, "the time during which uterine surgery has had its birth and growth is so short, that our experience has not been sufficiently mature to establish fixed principles. Many of the operations alluded to give *immediate* relief, and even a year or two passes before we discover that new troubles follow the operations, and that some change, from the contraction of cicatrices or other causes, leave the patient in worse condition than before the operation."[11]

Emmet, a Virginian, liked Nott. He gave him much advice, and Nott watched him operate. In the next few years Emmet and Nott were to see a good deal of each other, and Emmet later wrote with warmth of their relationship. Even after the shocks and disappointments of the past few years, Nott could still charm those he liked. "Dr. Nott," Emmet later wrote, "was personally a very attractive man and I became much attached to him. He was a bookworm and with his taste for historical matters, we had much in common, notwithstanding the great disparity in our ages." When they first became well-acquainted, Nott was sixty-three, Emmet thirty-nine. Nott also was helped on his visit to New York by Dr. T. Gaillard Thomas, another South Carolinian connected with the Woman's Hospital. Thomas gave Nott his outline for his own lectures and free use of all his illustrations.[12]

10. Nott to Leidy, November 3, 1867, in Leidy Papers, CPP; Nott, "Female Surgery: Correspondence," *New Orleans Medical and Surgical Journal,* XXI (1868), 82.

11. *Ibid.,* 83–86.

12. *Ibid.,* 86; Thomas Addis Emmet, *Incidents of My Life* (New York, 1911), 199.

After being greeted in New York with warmth and admiration, Nott came back to Baltimore with renewed enthusiasm for life as well as better informed on the gynecological branch of medicine. He now determined that he would leave Baltimore in the spring and practice his profession in New York. In taking this step he would not lack for southern friends and patients, for apart from Sims and Thomas there were many other southerners in New York who had fled from Reconstruction to live in the huge, impersonal northern city. Also, Mobilians and others escaping the summer season were to be found in New York's hotels early every fall.

In May, 1868, Nott moved to New York. Announcing his arrival to Squier, he said that Baltimore was too moral, "& I could find no body to talk to about a book." When in June a meeting was held at the Mott Memorial Library in New York to organize an institute to promote the study of arts and sciences, Nott was there. Diarist George Templeton Strong noted the presence of the "eminent Dr. [Josiah C.] Nott, late of Mobile." The idea of an academy came to nothing, but Nott was to find that his reputation had preceded him.[13]

Nott established his home and practiced medicine in the heart of New York; his first home was on West 22nd Street and his office on West 23d, and this was the area he lived and practiced in during his years in the city. This was still an excellent New York district, but its character was beginning to change. To the south of him still lived the oldest New York aristocracy, reluctant to move, while stretching north, up toward Central Park, the new wealthy were building their great mansions. His own district still had family residences, but it was also becoming the location of a number of large, new hotels as it was gradually transformed into a commercial area of the city. In Nott's years in the city it was still largely residential.[14] Nott found that it was expensive to live in New York and that though his name was well-known to physicians and scientists, it was difficult to establish a successful new practice at the age of sixty-four in a northern, highly competitive city. His success was a tribute to his skill, his energy, and the number of southerners who found their way to New York in these years.

His first year was difficult. Nott had grown used to a flourishing practice and an ample income. Since his departure from Mobile, his practice

13. Nott to Squier, May 28, 1868, in Squier Papers, LC; Allan Nevins and Milton H. Thomas (eds.), *Diary of George Templeton Strong* (4 vols.; New York, 1952), IV, 216.
14. *Trow's New York City Directory,* 1869–72 (New York, 1869–72); Charles Lockwood, *Manhattan Moves Uptown: An Illustrated History* (Boston, 1976), 201–11, 265, 294–99.

had languished, and though he was still comfortably off he felt unable to spend money with his customary ease. He felt a great urgency to become well-established in New York, and when he was not practicing medicine he threw himself into medical writing, which would help build his reputation as a gynecologist. Although his reputation as a physician had been of the highest in the Southwest, he was still best known in New York as an ethnologist. He had enjoyed this fame as a visitor in the 1850s, but now he wanted to attract patients. Nott had little time or inclination for ethnological writing. Now living amid a population that was overwhelmingly white, he no longer felt the need to attack the rationality of those who wished to raise up the blacks to the level of the whites. He was never interested in basic ethnological research in the way that Morton was. If Nott, like so many of his relatives, had been born in Connecticut and had spent his life in New York or Philadelphia, he would probably have devoted himself totally to practicing medicine and writing medical articles.

Nott also discovered in New York that his style of ethnological writing was increasingly out of fashion. The growing scientific acceptance of Darwin's theories of evolution had made Nott's emphasis on permanent, unchangeable racial types obsolete. Darwin's theories threatened religious belief in a far more fundamental way than Nott's. Although Nott had challenged the scientific accuracy of Genesis and had pushed the origin of human beings into a more distant past, he had always conceived of creation in a human shape identical to that of the nineteenth century. He simply argued that there had not been one creation of Adam and Eve less than six thousand years ago but many creations of individuals of a variety of races an indefinite time ago. A colleague of Nott's in New York later said that he "was broad enough to accept to the full all of Darwin's views and conclusions,"[15] but it seems in reality that Nott never really came to terms with Darwin's theories of evolution and natural selection that destroyed his own theories of distinct, permanent types.

In many ways Darwin's *Origin of Species* was too careful and too scientific for Nott. Although he conceived of himself as a physical scientist who often wrote about physical and cranial types, Nott was more a cultural anthropologist when he wrote about race. He liked books such as Gobineau's that ranged generally over the rise and fall of nations and empires and the impact of race on history. A book he enjoyed during his first

15. Dr. William M. Polk, "Josiah C. Nott," *American Journal of Obstetrics*, LXVI (1913), 957.

months in New York, and told Squier to read, was Herbert Spencer's *Illustrations of Human Progress*, which he described as "a book of wonderful thought, diversity of knowledge, & combination of forces in illustrating an argument."[16] Nott liked to bolster his general racial views with scientific arguments, but his racial work was simply impressionism cloaked with supposed scientific proofs.

In New York Nott wanted to escape from what he viewed as the increasing idiocies of American life, and he could best do this by throwing himself into his medical work. He remained convinced that most human beings were irrational. When Squier became involved in a committee that was arranging a public meeting to urge a defense of the Monroe Doctrine and the general interests of the United States in Latin America, he asked Nott to give his support. Nott signed the document and returned it to Squier with the comment that "I beg the association to understand that I am in favour of all wars and perpetual war—Regarding as I do the human Race as a grand humbug & utter failure, I go in for speedy & entire extermination—We have been building churches and school houses for two thousand years, & all to no good." He signed himself as a former member of the Mobile Jockey Club, member of the London and Paris Ethnological Societies, personal friend of Gliddon and Squier, and author of *Types of Mankind*.[17]

Nott's household in his first months in New York consisted of his wife, his son (now in his early twenties), his sister-in-law Margaret Auzé, and her daughter, Adele, who was in her mid-twenties. Margaret Auzé, who had appeared crushed by the death of her husband and son in the 1850s and the tragedies of the Civil War, found New York a congenial town. Dr. Thomas Emmet, who knew both Mrs. Auzé and the famous Mobile hostess, Octavia Le Vert, who also moved to New York after the war, said that Mrs. Auzé probably had "as extensive an acquaintance and as many personal friends as her townswoman." He said that both were remarkable women, "and although they were past middle life they were so bright and attractive in their manners that they would be immediately surrounded by men of all ages at any assemblage, and in greater number than any girl could bring about her."[18]

In their first months in New York the Notts and Mrs. Auzé had to

16. Nott to Squier, September 27, 1868, in Squier Papers, LC.
17. Undated circular with comments by Nott, in *ibid*.
18. Emmet, *Incidents of My Life*, 198–99.

cope with a familiar problem. Adele, Mrs. Auzé's only surviving child, was taken ill. By October Nott was writing, "My niece still hangs on—living on a few spoonfuls of gum wafer daily—& I do not know how it will end." It ended six weeks later, when Adele died.[19] Few physicians in nineteenth-century America could have had more personal experience of their own fallibility than Josiah Nott.

In his first half year in New York Nott did not build as large a practice as he desired. "I have been fighting on here in the profession for 8 months," he told Leidy early in 1869, "& am doing about as well as I expected, with some reason to expect more rapid progress in a few months." His effort to increase his practice was accompanied by a flurry of medical writing and publication, nearly all on gynecological problems and cases. In his first year in New York, Nott published on the method he had used to stop hemorrhage after operating on the cervix; on a modified speculum he had developed for uterine examination; and on an old procedure—extirpation of the two lower bones of the coccyx in a case of coccygodynia—which he had originated and had previously written on in the 1840s.[20]

The second article, on his modified speculum, demonstrated the practical turn of mind that had inspired Nott since he had first written on the care of leeches more than thirty years before. He argued that the speculum that he had had made by a New York instrument maker was particularly useful for a private practitioner, who, in going from house to house to examine his patients, could not command trained assistants, a suitable table, a horizontal light, or other conveniences available in a hospital. It had become almost obligatory for a successful gynecologist to develop his own variant of the speculum—Sims's was the most famous, but Thomas Emmet, T. Gaillard Thomas, and Nathan Bozeman had all written about their own instruments. Because Nott had always enjoyed adapting surgical instruments for his own use, it was comparatively simple for him to join that select group who defended the advantages of their own particular speculum. Nott devoted much of his article to point-

19. Nott to Squier, October 29, 1868, in Squier Papers, LC; Helen Thomas (ed.), *Magnolia Cemetery* (New Orleans, 1974), 63. Adele died on December 13, 1868.
20. Nott to Leidy, January 3, 1869 [mistakenly dated 1868 by Nott], in Leidy Papers, CPP; Nott, "Secondary Hemorrhage, Tetanus, &c, after Incisions of Cervis Uteri," *American Journal of the Medical Sciences*, LVI (1868), 100–102; "On a New Duck-bill Speculum, for Private Practice," *ibid.*, LVI (1868), 420–25; "Case of Coccyodynia—Extirpation of Two Lower Bones of Coccyx," *American Journal of Obstetrics*, I (1868), 243–54.

ing out why his instrument, unlike those of Sims and Emmet, could easily be carried about and used in private houses without assistance. He thought its most important feature was that it did not need a special table, or a special light, or an assistant. In the same article, Nott gave general specifications for a portable canvas cot that he said could be used in an office or home in place of an operating table or expensive chair. Nott's cot was some three and a half feet long, with projecting bars on which a woman could place her feet. When not in use it could be folded up and set aside.[21]

In returning to the operation on the coccyx that Nott had introduced into the literature in the 1840s, he was bringing one of his more successful and original procedures before the New York Obstetrical Society, a body that had been founded in 1863. The society originally consisted of twenty members, who held meetings every two weeks at one of their own homes. Drs. Emmet and Thomas were among the founders (Sims was away in Europe during most of the 1860s). The rules of the society required that a candidate for membership should present, through a member, a specimen of morbid anatomy, with a written history. Nott presented the two terminating bones of an *os coccygis* and an account of how he had removed them from the wife of an Alabama physician who had come to New York to consult Nott soon after his arrival in the city.

It seems likely that Nott's main object in using this case for his entry was to provide himself with the opportunity of pointing out that he had anticipated the famous Professor Simpson of Edinburgh in describing the condition of coccygodynia. In his *Clinical Lectures,* Simpson had said that coccygodynia was a neglected condition, which he believed had not previously been described. Nott was able to point out in this paper for the New York Obstetrical Society, subsequently published in the *American Journal of Obstetrics,* that he had anticipated Simpson's printed lectures by some fifteen years with articles in the *New Orleans Medical Journal.* In this new case Nott described a condition that had arisen as the result of a painful and difficult childbirth. He summarized what had been learned about the condition since he first wrote and noted that Simpson described two possible operations—one, the separation of the coccyx from its muscular and fibrous attachments, and, two, the removal of the whole or a part of the coccyx. Nott had no acquaintance with the first

21. Nott, "On a New Duck-bill Speculum," 420–25.

operation—he had always extirpated the coccyx—but he said that as far as he knew he was the first to perform the specific operation for coccygodynia.[22]

The evidence which showed that Nott had anticipated the great Simpson was well-designed to increase his standing in the New York medical profession, and he was warmly welcomed into the Obstetrical Society. Beginning in the fall of 1870, this southern newcomer became vice-president and then president of the society. Nott was intellectually stimulated by the large number of first-class physicians and the various medical societies available in New York. Eventually he belonged to four of these societies.[23] He also belonged to the New York Ethnological Society but took little part in its proceedings.

By the late summer and early fall of 1869, Nott's practice was beginning to flourish, and his spirits were the best they had been in years. He commented in September that "the Hotels here are overflowing with Southerners & I am overwhelmed with professional and other calls." Two days later, on a Sunday, he begged off from a dinner and meeting with Squier with the excuse that he had patients in all the hotels and that he would be working from noon to nine or ten that night. He did, however, invite Squier to dinner for Tuesday, saying that he would try to make special arrangements about his patients on that evening. A physician friend in Savannah, Georgia, had sent him a box of saltwater terrapins with the suggestion that Nott invite a few of his friends to eat them with him. Nott was often embarrassed that he had to put Squier off regarding meetings. He suggested to Squier that the ethnologists should get rid of him because he was becoming a drone: "I am busy working for bread—can no longer buy new books without stopping to count the cost & have not time to quit my office to go to public libraries." He said that if Astor would support him with $10,000 a year, he would live in the library and devote himself to anthropology, but he did not mean it. Medicine always came first.[24]

22. Nott, "Case of Coccyodynia," 243–54. For the New York Obstetrical Society see *American Journal of Obstetrics*, LXVII (1913), 945–70. Nott's original article on coccygodynia is in *New Orleans Medical and Surgical Journal*, I (1844), 58–60. Simpson's *Clinical Lectures on the Diseases of Women* was published in Philadelphia in 1863.

23. See Nott to Squier, January 30, 1872, in Squier Papers, LC.

24. Nott to Squier, September 12, 1869, *ibid.*; Nott to Richard D. Arnold, September 10, 1869, in Richard D. Arnold Papers, SHC; Nott to Mary Broun, August 28, 1869, in Nott Papers, William Stanley Hoole Special Collections Library, University of Alabama, Tuscaloosa.

Again in November Nott had to miss an evening meeting at Squier's because of professional demands, and once more he suggested to Squier that perhaps he should sever his connection with the Ethnological Society. He did not have time for it, he wrote, and he never had been nor would he be useless in any endeavor he was connected with. His excuse for his erratic attendance was that he had been driven from the South "crippled in fortune" and that he had to work hard at his profession because of the expenses of living in New York.[25] This was only part of the truth, for Nott always found time to write what he wanted to write. He was now living in a mostly white society and no longer felt the compelling need to warn of supposed racial dangers.

As his practice began to prosper in 1869 and 1870, Nott continued to find time to write and publish medical articles, most of them on aspects of uterine medication and surgery. In Mobile in the 1850s he had become inured to long professional hours combined wth the swift writing of his ethnological pieces, and he now used the same technique to publish articles on medicine. Not even a fire in early 1870, which destroyed much of his library and personal papers, stopped the flow of articles from his pen.[26]

His most substantial contributions at this time were three long pieces on intrauterine injections, particularly in the treatment of endometritis (inflammation of the lining of the mucous membrane of the womb). One of the pieces was read, by invitation, before the Medical Society of the County of New York. Nott's general conclusion was that the profession in the city did not agree on how to treat the problems included under the general term "endometritis." He said that he had come to New York well-read in the current literature on uterine diseases and with a respectable amount of experience in treating them, but with much less experience than that of distinguished specialists in large metropolitan areas. Since coming to New York he had visited the appropriate hospitals and dispensaries, talked frequently with specialists, and regularly attended the meetings of the Obstetrical Society. He now felt he could offer his conclusions with some basis of experience.

Once again Nott could not resist including a practical, mechanical suggestion for the improvement of treatment. After making sound sugges-

25. Nott to Squier, November 18, 1869, in Squier Papers, LC.
26. See Nott to Lyman C. Draper, August 11, 1870, in Draper Manuscripts, 13VV47, State Historical Society of Wisconsin, Madison; Nott to Squier, March 4, 1871, in Squier Papers, LC.

tions about improving the general health of the patient and encouraging reasonable exercise, he argued that the disastrous results of some intra-uterine injections arose from using an inadequate instrument and from injecting caustics that were too harsh. As an instrument, Nott recom-mended a uterine catheter he had had constructed by a New York instru-ment maker, and he also pointed out that his own speculum, which had now been slightly improved, could be used to start the procedure without an assistant.

Most of Nott's discussion in these articles concerned the question of what to use and what not to use for intrauterine injections. He attacked the use of harsh solutions, advocated great care in the injection of caus-tics, and stressed the necessity for building up tolerance by the use of gradually stronger solutions. Moderation was essential, and physicians, he argued, should remember the therapeutic laws that governed the treat-ment of other organs. The uterus, he wrote, "has been cut too much, and burnt too much." One of his suggestions was for the daily injection of a solution of carbolic acid and water, alternating with a dilute solution of iodine. Weak solutions of iodine were, he thought, particularly useful for intrauterine medication. He admitted that one of the problems with the cautious course of treatment that he suggested was that it was too time-consuming for a doctor making his rounds in private practice, but he sug-gested that a gynecologist with an extensive practice might make use of a trained female nurse, under supervision, once the treatment had been started. Although Nott made various other suggestions for solutions that could be injected, his major emphasis was on the danger of heroic treat-ments. His conclusion was that intrauterine medication had been em-pirical and unsatisfactory and that experiments were needed to devise more rational procedures. He said that he had made simple experiments with a number of different chemicals to discover their likely effects before injecting them. In passing, Nott mentioned the work of Joseph Lister and others in demonstrating how antiseptics could prevent inflammation and putrefaction. The tone of Nott's articles on intrauterine injections was balanced and sensible; he disagreed with those who would put all their faith in the knife or in caustics.[27]

27. Nott, "The Treatment of Endometritis by Uterine Injections," *American Journal of Obstetrics*, II (1869), 470–504, 494 (quotation); Nott, "Intra-Uterine Medication," *ibid.*, III (1870), 36–63; Nott, "Intra-Uterine Medication," *New York Medical Journal*, XI (1870), 337–53.

Nott's medical work in New York, his papers, and his publications impressed many of the best surgeons and physicians in the city, particularly those specializing in gynecology. He was also helped by his personality. Most of those who met him liked him. Sims regarded him as a friend, Emmet said that he became "much attached to him," and several of the other younger physicians who met him wrote highly of him in later years. Dr. William Polk, who knew him at this time, wrote more than forty years later that Nott "fulfilled as completely as any one he ever met, the place which belongs to the highest type of physician, surgeon and man." [28]

Nott also impressed his colleagues by his frankness and by his obvious desire to advance medical knowledge. In New York, as in Mobile, he had no hesitation in discussing his failures as well as his successes. In early 1870 he published in the *American Journal of Obstetrics* a description of a case of lacerated perineum. He said he was publishing it for two reasons: first, because it had intrinsic interest, physiologically, pathologically, and practically; second, because "I am charged by the patient with ignorance and malpractice." Many would have tried to hide the controversy; Nott had the confidence to air the question before the profession.

The patient was a woman from New Orleans who had been advised to consult Nott by his friend Dr. Stanford Chaillé. Nott first began to treat her in May, 1869. The bluntness of Nott's description of the woman perhaps reflected the trouble he had had with her—"she is of very short stature, and excessively fat" (she weighed 250 pounds). In 1869 she was thirty-seven years old. More than twelve years before, in giving birth, she had suffered a badly lacerated perineum. No operation had ever been performed to mend the laceration. She had not menstruated for eight years, and Nott said that his examination revealed an atrophied uterus. The scar formed over her laceration was extremely sensitive, and she also had severe pain from coccygodynia. Nott decided to operate to remove the scar, but the woman wanted to vacation with her family at Newport before the operation. In the meantime, Nott treated her uterus by the insertion of a sponge tent. Shortly afterward, she bled for several days; Nott assumed it was a hemorrhage. Finally, in October, after she returned from Newport, Nott operated to remove the scar tissue on the perineum. He invited Dr. Sims and Dr. T. Gaillard Thomas, two of New York's finest gynecologists, to assist him. He operated with the patient under local anesthetic—an

28. Sims, *Story of My Life*, 90; Emmet, *Incidents of My Life*, 199; Polk, "Josiah C. Nott," 958.

ether spray. He removed the scar tissue in a few seconds and used four silver sutures to repair the perineum. Sims advanced the opinion that after eight years without menstruation and with an atrophied uterus she would never menstruate again or have a child. The bleeding that had followed Nott's insertion of a sponge earlier in the summer was ignored.

Nott's problems arose because it subsequently became apparent that his patient had been two months pregnant at the time of the operation. The operation itself was a success, but in the middle of December she had a miscarriage. The woman dismissed Nott and replaced him with Dr. T. Gaillard Thomas. She was bitter about Nott operating when she was pregnant and for the way he had treated the miscarriage. Nott concluded his article by arguing that there was no way he could have known or expected her to have become pregnant in Newport and that in any case the operation was necessary and justified. The "patient," he wrote, "has taken upon herself to decide points of practice when none but medical men are competent to judge."[29] By giving a detailed account of his problems with this patient, Nott left it to his colleagues to judge the merits of her complaints.

In the summer of 1870, Nott was given the opportunity to renew his acquaintance with one of his older specialties—the study of yellow fever. He was also obliged to remember the saddest days of his life. In this year Mobile once again suffered a severe yellow fever epidemic. Nott heard a good deal about it, not only by letter from his friends there but also from the Mobilians who lingered in New York until they were sure it was safe to return. Willie Ketchum, who had lunched at Nott's the previous month, wrote to his daughter early in November that there were still about a dozen families from Mobile in the hotel in which he was staying, all of them waiting for a good frost in Mobile before returning home.[30]

Nott's memories of yellow fever were brought back even more sharply by an outbreak of the disease near New York. During August, September, and October there were 159 cases at the military post on Governor's Island, out of a population of 774. Of those who caught the disease, 52 died. Because of his great experience, Nott was called in to the Gover-

29. Nott, "Case of a Lacerated Perinaeum—Hyperasethesia of Cicatrix—Reflex Action on Uterus and Nervous System," *American Journal of Obstetrics*, II (1870), 637–48. The quotations are on pp. 637–38 and 648.

30. Willie Ketchum to Amanda De Ford, October 11, November 5, 1870, in Creagh Family Papers, SHC.

nor's Island outbreak, and he was asked to write a report for the New York City Board of Health. In his report Nott repeated many of the arguments he had developed in Mobile in the 1840s and 1850s. He had nothing new to say; in some respects he seemed further from a solution than he had been twenty years before. He again argued that the most likely cause of the disease was an insect, invisible to the naked eye, that traveled on the ground and could be transported in vessels or baggage. "It is *possible*," he wrote, "that even insects may exist a million times smaller than any microscope has yet reached." He was still convinced that the disease was not contagious, but he stressed that at least one type was portable in baggage. He was also still convinced that emanations from decaying matter could not cause the disease, but he now suggested that miasmas could produce conditions favorable to its development. There was still little that could be done, he argued, to stop a full-scale epidemic. He later commented that had the 1870 epidemic swept the city of New York rather than Governor's Island, it might have caused thirty to forty thousand deaths.[31]

Nott used his report to the Board of Health as the basis of a paper which he gave in the fall of 1871 at the New York Academy of Medicine. The paper was followed by a vigorous discussion, which extended to the next meeting. In this discussion, some still maintained, in contradiction to Nott, that yellow fever was somehow connected to other fevers. Nott, however, was convinced that yellow fever was distinct from the various marsh fevers. He was never to know, however, how the yellow fever that had brought so much tragedy into his life had been carried to Spring Hill.[32]

While occupied in investigating the Governor's Island outbreak, Nott had to dig even further back into his southern memories, for Lyman C. Draper of the State Historical Society of Wisconsin was busily trying to collect information about the Revolution in the backcountry of the South. He started a correspondence with Nott because he had learned that Nott's brother Henry, who had drowned in 1837, had contemplated writing a biography of General Thomas Sumter. Nott was of little help—

31. *First Annual Report of the Board of Health of the City of New York* (New York, 1871), 330–38, 348–98; John Duffy, *A History of Public Health in New York City* (2 vols.; New York, 1968–74), II, 162; Nott, "Natural History of Yellow-Fever," *Medical Record*, VI (1871–72), 452.
32. Nott, "Natural History of Yellow-Fever," 451–56; "Discussion of Yellow Fever," *ibid.*, 519–22.

death and time, he wrote, had severed links and association, and the fire in his New York home had destroyed much of his library and his correspondence with his brother. He did send Draper his candid memories of the first Wade Hampton of South Carolina, who had established the fortunes of a family that Nott had kept in touch with over the years. The Hamptons were friendly with his South Carolina relations and, like Nott, they frequented the Virginia Springs. In the early fall of 1872, when Nott was very ill, he traveled to Baltimore to examine the third Wade Hampton's wife. He diagnosed her problem as nonorganic and decided that she was suffering from "hysteria."[33] Hysteria or not, she died less than two years later.

In the winter of 1870–1871, only eighteen months after Nott had arrived in New York, he had become a respected and successful member of the New York medical profession. He was now vice-president of the New York Obstetrical Society and regularly participated in its meetings, and Dr. Emmet, who had succeeded Sims as surgeon in chief at the Woman's Hospital, invited Nott to become one of the physicians attached to the outpatient department of the hospital. Many years later, Emmet suggested that though Nott knew but little of the practice of gynecology, he felt that his personal reputation would be of advantage to the hospital. Emmet was here confusing Nott's comparative inexperience before 1867 with his far greater expertise in 1870; he also misdated Nott's settling in New York by several years.

What appeared to be the beginning of a distinguished new phase in Nott's career turned out to be an unfortunate experience. Nott quickly became involved in the ongoing struggle between Emmet and the board of lady managers of the hospital. Emmet had always assumed that his selections for appointment were to be approved "without question." The board of lady managers, however, expected to exercise the right of approval or disapproval. The normal procedure was for Emmet to offer a position at the hospital and for the nominee to accept and begin work before the board of lady managers acted on the proposal. Although Emmet assumed that approval should be automatic, the board had often annoyed him by turning back nominations. He said that they did so on the advice of some of their private physicians, but it seems likely that they wanted to assert their own authority.

33. Nott to Lyman C. Draper, August 11, 26, October 28, December 16, 1870, in Draper MSS, 13VV47–51; Wade Hampton III to Dr. D. H. Trezevant, October 2, 1872, in Charles E. Cauthen (ed.), *Family Letters of the Three Wade Hamptons, 1782–1901,* (Columbia, 1953), 144.

When Nott was offered the position by Emmet, he accepted and began work at the hospital. The lady managers were supposed to act on the appointment at their next monthly meeting, but, according to Emmet, because of "uncalled for interference of one or two members of the profession, who happened to be the family physicians of some of the Lady Managers, and who volunteered their criticism on Dr. Nott's fitness for the position," there was a delay of several weeks. Emmet attended a meeting of the lady managers and persuaded them to let Nott continue to work at the hospital, but they would not make it a permanent appointment. Long after Nott's death, Emmet said that during the months Nott was at the Woman's Hospital he was subjected to constant harassment. If he was a few minutes late he would be requested by official communication to be more punctual, and all other "offenses" were treated in a similar manner. He was also informed that his patients were complaining about his rough manner and want of dexterity. These were fabrications, wrote Emmet, "as he held the reputation of being an expert and successful surgeon, and he was in manner one of the gentlest and kindest persons I ever knew." This opinion was confirmed by Dr. William Anderson of Mobile, who said that Nott's manner "was gentle and tender, and his assiduous attention to his patients endeared him to all who put themselves under his medical care." [34]

Although Emmet blamed jealous physicians for Nott's problems at the Woman's Hospital, he gave unwitting evidence in his later account of the affair that his own attitude toward women as managers most likely stirred up much of the trouble. "Women without reasoning power and as partisans," he wrote, "holding the management of the Woman's Hospital at this time, demonstrated that they are not, as a rule, fitted by nature for such a trust." [35] It seems likely that the board of lady managers was determined not to be browbeaten on the question of appointments by the arrogant Emmet. It is also possible that there was some substance in the supposed complaints of lady patients about Nott's manner. In the past twenty years Nott's hospital experience had been mostly in his own infirmary for slaves and in Confederate army hospitals. He was comparatively new to the specialty of gynecology. It would not be surprising if Nott, in his late sixties, had a manner that was more brusque and direct than that of a new breed of post–Civil War New York gynecologists, although

34. Emmet, *Incidents of My Life*, 200; Harris, *Woman's Surgeon*, 267–68, 271, 288; William H. Anderson, *Biographical Sketch of Dr. J. C. Nott* (Mobile, 1877), 5.
35. Emmet, *Incidents of My Life*, 200.

Nott's ability to win private patients, and the comments of his fellow physicians, make it obvious that he could be charming when he wanted to. Be that as it may, Nott did not receive a permanent appointment at the Woman's Hospital and within a few months had returned exclusively to private practice.

Nott had weathered too many personal tragedies to be crushed by his brief experience at the Woman's Hospital, and his pride was assuaged by the prominent role he took as vice-president in the 1870–1871 meetings of the Obstetrical Society. As usual, he was busy tinkering with surgical instruments, trying to effect an improvement in design, and at the November, 1870, meeting of the Obstetrical Society he exhibited a new form of an écraseur. He recommended his modified version for the removal of hemorrhoids. He continued to refine his model and in April, 1872, gave a fuller description in the *American Journal of the Medical Sciences,* in which he included a letter from a southern physician stating that he had used the improved écraseur with success. Nott's article pointed out the weaknesses in Edouard Chassaignac's established écraseur and the advantages of his own. One of the most substantial advantages, he claimed, was that it crushed rather than severed the tissues and reduced hemorrhaging in a variety of operative procedures in which an écraseur was used. Even in these last years Nott was always a general physician and surgeon rather than a gynecologist, and he was always willing to comment on other subjects. In January, 1871, for example, he reported on his success in removing carbuncles from a patient's back by making an incision and stuffing in cotton saturated with pure carbolic acid.[36]

The pattern of Nott's life continued to run reasonably evenly through 1871 and into early 1872. His practice was now a success, and he was still apologizing to Squier for neglecting the Ethnological Society. He told him that he had "quite as much to do as a 'bald headed benevolent' old gentleman can well keep up with." Nott had not lost all his hair, but his white hair was thinning, and in these last years he was a lean, almost cadaverous figure with well-marked cheekbones and a wispy goatee.[37] Nott

36. "Meetings of the New York Obstetrical Society, 1870–1871," *American Journal of Obstetrics,* IV (1871), 325, 547, 717, 724; Nott, "Remarks on the Use of a Rectilinear Écraseur, in the Removal of Hemorrhoids, the Cervix Uteri, Penis, Tongue, Naevi, Folds of the Vagina, &c.," *American Journal of the Medical Sciences,* LXIII (1872), 378–85; Nott, "Carbolic Acid as a Remedy for Carbuncle," *New York Medical Journal,* XIII (1871), 47–49.

37. Nott to Squier, March 4, 1871, in Squier Papers, LC. There are two photographs of Nott in his later years in the Prints and Photographic Division of the Library of Congress.

was proud that as an old, defeated southerner he had been able to make a success of his profession in New York. He told Leidy that he was "making a comfortable support, & altogether getting on about as well as a ruined rebel could expect." He said he liked New York "very much." Although he seldom could find the time to attend the meetings of the Ethnological Society, he continued to read on ethnological matters. He still found it hard to take evolutionary theory seriously. After reading one article, he commented to Squier that "you may be Kin to frogs but I aint."[38]

Nott was extremely busy in the winter of 1871–1872. "The days have been short," he told Squier, "& I have been under whip & spur to keep up." Nott's difficulties were increased by a nagging feeling that he was "out of sorts" and by what appeared to be a continuing "Catarrh." In the middle of May he suddenly experienced hemorrhaging from his throat and lungs; the hemorrhaging recurred three or four times each day for about a week. He had no cough, fever, or pain and was eating and sleeping well, but he was forbidden to talk for fear of bringing on the bleeding. He had clear signs of tuberculosis. He told Squier of the hemorrhaging about ten days after it began, with the good sense and balance that Nott brought to most subjects except race. "At my age such an attack looks unpromising," he told Squier, "& as I have made all out of my life worth having, my mind is very calm as regards myself—I am the centre of a little family circle that would be pained to give me up & my labor is important to them, but telle est la vie."[39]

Nott had seen too many cases to deceive himself with false hopes. More to reassure Squier than to deceive himself, he said that there were "many encouraging points about my case—I may throw the attack off— At all events, it is my duty to do the best I can to that end." Late in May, Nott left for a rest at Washington Hollow in Dutchess County, New York, and after returning to the city for a brief visit early in July went for a holiday on the St. Lawrence. By that time the news had reached Mobile that Nott was very ill. One Mobilian told Squier in August that he had heard that Nott, who was as highly esteemed as any man by the Mobilians, was "very much depressed and is evidently afraid that he will not be able to do much more work."[40]

38. Nott to Leidy, May 1, 1871, in Leidy Papers, CPP; Nott to Squier, November 28, 1871, in Squier Papers, LC.
39. Nott to Squier, January 30, May 26, 1872, in Squier Papers, LC.
40. Nott to Squier, May 26, 1872; Jerome Cochran to Squier, July 7, August 6, 1872, *ibid*.

Depressed or not, the old Mobilian kept a brave front before the world. In October, 1872, when the New York Obstetrical Society met for its fall season, Nott was in the chair as president. In the early fall he was also working hard at his practice, treating the many southerners who were in town. Nott felt a need to leave his family as well provided for as possible. By early October, however, he told Squier that he was "broken down & am going south for the winter." He did not say so, but he knew that he was going home to die. Though much of his library had been burned in 1870, he asked Squier the best manner of disposing of the many books he had left. They would bring only a trifle compared to their cost, he wrote, but "I shall never have any use for them again and the sooner they go the better." Nott loved his books, but he was now winding up his affairs. In December his remaining volumes were auctioned in New York. There was still a useful library of more than six hundred volumes, mainly a combination of ethnological and medical works, particularly on the diseases of women. But there were a few books that had probably survived from earlier days. An 1826 edition of Ovid's *Epistles and Art of Love* might well have been bought when he was a student in Philadelphia.[41]

On hearing of Nott's illness, Squier, the president of the New York Anthropological Institute, had arranged that the position of vice-president of the institute be conferred on him. In the middle of October, Nott formally wrote to Squier to resign from the position. He was now coughing badly, and early in November he had to take to his bed with severe lumbago. While bedridden, he suffered another hemorrhage. He was back on his feet in mid-November and ready to leave for Aiken, South Carolina. "Whether I shall live or get back to N. York in the spring is doubtful," he told Squier. "But I shall take events quietly as they come."[42]

Nott was now very ill, and he did not stay long in Aiken. While he was still able, he traveled on to Mobile. Early in January, he wrote his will, "being of sound mind but in weak health." He left everything to his wife, "feeling entirely confident she will do full justice to our son Josiah Charles Nott, and promote his interests so far as she can consistently with pru-

41. Transactions of the New York Obstetrical Society meeting of October 2, 1872, in *American Journal of Obstetrics*, V (1872), 473; Nott to Squier, October 7, 1872, in Squier Papers, LC; *A Catalogue of the Remaining Portion of the Library Collected by Dr. J. C. Nott, of Mobile, Ala.* [New York, 1872]. There are copies of this catalog in the New York Academy of Medicine and in the Lister Hill Library, School of Medicine, University of Alabama, Birmingham.

42. Nott to Squier, October 18, November 17, 1872, in Squier Papers, LC.

dence." His wife was made the sole executrix. Nott was not a rich man; on his death his estate was estimated at between $30,000 and $40,000. Nott lingered on into March. His friend and colleague Dr. William Anderson said that from the day of Nott's arrival in Mobile to his death there was "one continued ovation for him." Presents arrived every day— the "choicest fruits, the daintiest dishes, the most beautiful flowers, and the rarest game of the season were sent in profusion to him." In Mobile, among his old medical colleagues, he was now known as the "Old Roman." He died on March 31, his sixty-ninth birthday.[43]

The funeral was a great occasion, on which many Mobilians must have cast their thoughts back to the days before the war. His body lay in state at the home of his wife's brother-in-law, N. Harleston Broun, and "vast crowds of people" filled Broun's home and the streets around, "the latter being rendered almost impassable." An Episcopal minister conducted the rites, but this represented not his own but his wife's beliefs. The service was followed by a procession through the streets to the cemetery. The cortege was headed by the Fire Department brass band and a detachment of police, followed by a battalion of volunteers, the pall bearers (who included General Braxton Bragg), the hearse, the family, the physicians of Mobile, the mayor, the aldermen, the common council, the bar association, and citizens and friends. The Mobile Cotton Exchange, the Board of Trade, and many business houses and shops were closed during the funeral. Long before the time of the procession, people gathered in the streets and on balconies along the route.[44] Nott was buried alongside six of his children in the town in which he had spent much of his life.

It was appropriate that Nott should be buried not in New York but in the South, for no man better represented its strengths and weaknesses. Generous, good-humored, dedicated to science, healing, education, and improved medical care, he was also a passionate racist. Though generous and even gentle to those around him, he could in his writings blithely condemn whole races to inevitable destruction. He became a doctor because he wanted to cure and because he wanted scientific, rational answers to human difficulties. He became an ethnologist because he wanted to preserve the way of life he knew and loved in South Carolina and in Mobile. To do so, he had to convince the world that slavery was the best

43. Probate Records, in Mobile County Court House, Mobile; William H. Anderson, *Biographical Sketch of Dr. J. C. Nott,* (Mobile, 1877), 3.
44. Mobile *Register,* April 1, 2, 3, 1873.

possible existence for blacks. He found that this task was not incompatible with his search for scientific truth because the best minds he revered both in the North and in Europe became convinced in the mid-nineteenth century that the white race was inherently superior, the bearer of civilization, and the colored races permanently inferior, incapable of contributing to world progress. Nott believed, with good reason, that his views on race were more in accord with the latest scientific opinion than those of the abolitionists. He took ideas that were current throughout the United States and Europe, added his own conclusions based on a biased observation of the society around him and on the historical record, and in vigorous, often vehement language defended slavery and the existing social structure of the South. He believed that many of his opponents were hindered in their thinking by a false faith in the scientific credibility of the Bible and by the views of organized religion. In spite of his anticlericalism he was deeply admired by the society in which he lived. To a later generation much of Nott's ethnological writing seems to place him among the lunatic fringe of racist writers. In his own time he was never that. He was controversial but he was in the mainstream of American, not just southern, ethnological writing.

EPILOGUE

Sarah Nott and Margaret Auzé returned to New York, lived in hotels, and spent their summers at Narragansett Pier or Saratoga. Sarah died in 1883 and was buried beside her husband in Mobile. Their surviving son, Josiah Charles Nott, died as a comparatively young man in Texas in 1891; he was only forty-five. Margaret Auzé lived on and on. This lively, attractive woman who had grown up in the South Carolina of the 1820s and 1830s, who watched her husband and son die in Mobile in the 1850s and her daughter die young in New York in the late 1860s, survived until the Windsor Hotel on Fifth Avenue burned on March 17, 1899. She died in the fire at the age of eighty-five. Even then, New York had tenuous ties to the Notts and to antebellum Mobile. Zach Deas, Sarah Nott's brother, lived in New York after the war. He died there in 1882. Deas's wife survived in New York until the 1920s, in a world that would have seemed as irrational to Josiah Nott as the one he lived and worked in.[1]

1. Thomas A. Emmet, *Incidents of My Life* (New York, 1911), 199; gravestones, Magnolia Cemetery, Mobile.

NOTE ON PRIMARY SOURCES

Because there is no body of Nott papers, the letters of Josiah C. Nott and materials relating to him have to be sought in a variety of manuscript collections scattered around the country. The most useful collections of Nott letters are in the Samuel G. Morton Papers in the Historical Society of Pennsylvania, Philadelphia; in the Ephraim G. Squier Papers in the Library of Congress, Washington, D.C.; and in the Joseph Leidy Papers in the College of Physicians of Philadelphia and in the Academy of Natural Sciences of Philadelphia. There are also Nott letters in a variety of other collections, including the James M. Gage Papers in the Southern Historical Collection of the University of North Carolina, Chapel Hill; the James Henry Hammond Papers in the South Caroliniana Library, University of South Carolina, Columbia, and in the Library of Congress; and the John R. Bartlett Papers in the John Carter Brown Library, Brown University, Providence, Rhode Island.

For Nott's family background, youth, and early manhood, the collections in the South Caroliniana Library of the University of South Carolina, in the University of South Carolina archives, and in the South Carolina Department of Archives are particularly useful. All of these collections are in Columbia, South Carolina. There is also some material relating to his father in the Historical Society of South Carolina in Charleston. For Nott's student days in Philadelphia, there is material in the University of Pennsylvania archives in Philadelphia, and his later Philadelphia connections can be followed in the Samuel G. Morton Papers and the Joseph Leidy Papers. The Morton Papers in the Historical Society of Pennsylvania are of particular importance for Nott's career as an ethnologist in the 1840s. The collection of Morton Papers in the American Philosophical Society in Philadelphia is of great importance for Morton's early career but is not useful for Nott. The Joseph Leidy Papers in the Academy of Natural Sciences of Philadelphia and in the College of Physicians of Philadelphia are essential for Nott's career in the 1850s. These papers supplement the excellent material on the 1850s in the Nott letters in the Ephraim G. Squier Papers in the Library of Congress. The Squier Papers are also essential for Nott's life and career after the Civil War. There is also information on Nott's scientific circle in the Louis Agassiz Papers in the Houghton Library, Harvard University, Cambridge, Massachusetts.

Nott's life in Mobile for the thirty years after 1836 can be recreated in a number of other archival collections. The land and probate records of the Mobile County Court House, Mobile, Alabama, provide basic material, which can be supplemented by the Mobile City Records and by some of the transcripts in the local history room of the Mobile Public Library. There is also useful material in the Alabama Department of Archives and History in Montgomery and in the William Stanley Hoole Special Collections Library of the University of Alabama, Tuscaloosa. The Sarah Ann and William B. Crawford Papers in the latter archives have some revealing comments on Nott. There are also some items of interest in the Lister Hill Library, University of Alabama Medical School, Birmingham.

For the general history of the society in which Nott moved in Mobile, the archives of the Southern Historical Collection in the University of North Carolina Library, Chapel Hill, are indispensable. Among the collections of particular use are the Levert Family Papers, the Mordecai Family Papers, and the Eliza Carolina Clitherall Diary, but a variety of other collections throw light on Mobile and on Nott's friends and colleagues. The details are given in the footnotes.

Nott's career in the Civil War is difficult to reconstruct because the medical records of the Confederacy were left in great confusion. Of particular value are the scattered Samuel H. Stout Papers. I made use of them in the Robert W. Woodruff Library, Emory University, Atlanta, Georgia; the William R. Perkins Library, Duke University, Durham, North Carolina; and the Confederate Museum in Richmond, Virginia; as well as in the microfilm in the Southern Historical Collection of the University of North Carolina. The letterbook of Dr. Andrew J. Foard in the Virginia State Library, Richmond, is also extremely useful, and there are a few Nott letters in the Braxton Bragg Papers, Western Reserve Historical Society, Cleveland, Ohio. The military service records of Nott and his sons are available in the National Archives, Washington, D.C., and there is considerable information on Alabama regiments in the Alabama Department of Archives and History, Montgomery.

For Nott in the years after the Civil War the material in the Squier Papers is basic, but there is also some information in the Maryland Historical Society, Baltimore, and in the New York Academy of Medicine. Also the collections of the Southern Historical Collection at the University of North Carolina throw light on these years.

The most useful printed materials for a biography of Nott are his own abundant writings in the form of books, pamphlets, and articles in medical and ethnological journals. I also made extensive use of Mobile newspapers, particularly the *Mobile Register*. My debt to secondary works on the South, nineteenth-century medicine, the Civil War, and a variety of other subjects is indicated in the footnotes.

INDEX

Abolitionism, 48, 80, 83, 100, 106, 125, 223, 224, 225, 336
Academy of Natural Sciences, Philadelphia, 102, 105, 203, 213
Adams-Onis Treaty, 58
Agassiz, Louis: and zoological provinces, 90, 104, 117, 234; sketch of, 104; and blacks, 105; and hybridity, 106; and polygenesis, 115, 116, 170; in Mobile, 176, 177; opinion of Nott, 177; in *Types of Mankind*, 181–82; mentioned, 9, 107, 114, 117, 126, 180, 183, 210, 211, 212
Alabama: growth of, 53; slavery in, 57, 125; medical regulation in, 70, 71–72; legislature, 126, 227, 237, 283; Medical Association, 137, 238, 297; secession in, 252, 253
Alabama regiments: 3rd Alabama, 259, 260, 260*n*, 266, 273; 4th Alabama, 261, 264; 5th Alabama, 261; 6th Alabama, 261; 22nd Alabama, 270, 271, 273, 276, 284–85; freedmen in, 291, 297; racial violence, 294; mentioned, 52, 92, 254
Alabama Planter (Mobile), 160, 161, 162, 164, 197
Alison, William, 143
American Association for the Advancement of Science, 114
American Ethnological Society, 111
American Journal of Obstetrics, 323, 327
American Journal of the Medical Sciences, 72, 86, 316, 332
American School of Ethnology, 85, 108
American Whig Review, 113
Ancient Monuments of the Mississippi Valley, 107
Anderson, William H., 2, 51, 130, 132, 133, 238, 245, 331, 335
Andral, Gabriel, 44, 50, 143

Anthropological Review (London), 1, 170, 312
Appomattox, 290
Army of Mississippi, 272
Army of Tennessee, 289
Arnold, Richard D., 82
Auzé, Adele, 321, 322, 322*n*
Auzé, Charles, 131, 164, 178
Auzé, Margaret, 164, 243, 276, 285, 289, 321, 322, 337

Bachman, John: sketch of, 113; and unity of races, 116; and Nott, 118, 121, 172, 199–200, 203; mentioned, 113*n*, 115, 117, 125, 170, 205, 208
Baltimore, 32, 238, 310, 311, 313–14, 317, 319
Bartlett, John R., 111
Bartlett and Welford, publishers, 111
Bassett, John, 50
Beauregard, Pierre G. T., 261, 262, 263, 272, 274
Bernhard, Karl, Duke of Saxe-Weimar-Eisenach, 34
Blacks, racial views of, 18, 38, 83–84, 86, 88, 90, 107, 110, 116, 124, 125, 126, 193, 195, 196, 199, 233, 234, 295, 296, 299–300, 303, 304, 336
Blanding, Abraham, 13
Blockley, 226
Blumenbach, Johann F., 101
Boston, 38, 203
Boston Medical and Surgical Journal, 86
Botanic Medicine, 70, 71, 72. *See also* Thomsonianism
Bozeman, Nathan, 322
Bragg, Braxton, 224, 266, 272, 274, 279, 280, 281–82, 287, 305, 335
Bragg, John, 224, 266
Bremer, Fredrika, 129